P9-BHT-558

THE ILLUSTRATED DICTIONARY OF Constitutional Concepts

THE ILLUSTRATED DICTIONARY OF

Constitutional Concepts

ROBERT L. MADDEX

CONGRESSIONAL QUARTERLY INC.
WASHINGTON, D.C.

Project Director: Diane Maddex
Editor: Gretchen Smith Mui
Editorial Assistant: Kristi Flis
Designer: Robert L. Wiser

Library of Congress Cataloging-in-Publication Data
Maddex, Robert L.
The illustrated dictionary of constitutional concepts / Robert L. Maddex.
p. cm.
Includes bibliographical references and index.
ISBN 1-56802-170-4 (cloth : alk. paper)
1. Political science—Dictionaries. 2. Constitutional history—Dictionaries.
I. Congressional Quarterly, inc. II. Title.
JA61.M28 1996
321.8'03—dc20 96-32484
CIP

Printed in the United States of America

Robert L. Maddex, author of *Constitutions of the World,* is an attorney in Washington, D.C., who specializes in international law. He has served as chief counsel of the Foreign Claims Settlement Commission of the United States and as an adviser on constitutional issues to several nations.

Gisbert H. Flanz is editor of *Constitutions of the Countries of the World,* a series providing translated versions of national constitutions. He is also professor emeritus of political theory and comparative politics at New York University and has taught and lectured widely on law and political science in the United States and abroad.

Contents

Foreword

In recent years there has been a remarkable and encouraging revival of interest in constitutions and constitutionalism. As the worldwide effort toward democratization gains momentum, there is an increasing awareness that well-drafted constitutions not only matter but also provide the indispensable foundation for the process of institution building and for the safeguarding of fundamental rights.

The constitution makers of our time are using new terms that are not always clearly defined and that are difficult to translate because they cannot be found in general dictionaries. There are many good legal dictionaries in several languages. They include some constitutional concepts but, because of the many fields of law and jurisprudence from which the terms have to be drawn, it is impossible to treat them in sufficient detail.

As editor of *Constitutions of the Countries of the World,* which includes the constitutions and fundamental laws of every country of the world, I have been responsible for providing accurate and up-to-date translations from a great variety of languages. Although many governments publish English translations of their constitutions, these vary greatly in quality and accuracy. This applies not only to printed translations but also to electronically transmitted material. The Internet can be very helpful in providing a great amount of information on many constitutions, but scholars and legal practitioners find it necessary to have material checked against official texts. Such critical reviews are often frustrating because we do not have a sufficiently standardized terminology in major languages. It will take time and the coordinated efforts of highly qualified specialists to produce a multilingual dictionary of constitutional concepts and terminology.

I was glad to learn that Robert L. Maddex has been working on an illustrated dictionary of constitutional concepts. Rather than compiling standardized definitions of words and phrases used in national constitutions, Mr. Maddex set out to produce a dictionary of constitutional concepts and key terms that includes their definitions and historical development as well as excerpts showing their use in the context of current world constitutions. Many of us who are working in the field welcome his initiative and the publication of this work.

—*Gisbert H. Flanz*

Preface

Strong representative democracies are essential to world peace and economic growth. Governments based on constitutions and a participatory citizenry promote domestic prosperity and foster international cooperation and development. *The Illustrated Dictionary of Constitutional Concepts* was undertaken as a tool for learning about the language of constitutions—the supreme laws of nation-states—and thus for making us all better citizens of our own countries and the world.

Too often discussions about what a constitution or constitutional provision means founder in the absence of correct definitions for basic concepts and terms. Comparisons between national constitutions may suffer without an understanding of how another country's constitution works and what its language means. Debates over political issues or personalities conducted without an accurate knowledge of the true vocabulary of constitutional dialogue and argument are often counterproductive.

Phrases such as majority rule, freedom of speech, due process, the rule of law, and even basic concepts such as liberty and democracy—all drawn from constitutions—are used repeatedly in everyday exchanges. These and the hundreds of other concepts and terms selected for inclusion here are words that appear in many national constitutions or are reflected in the structure of governments created by constitutions, either written (as in the United States) or unwritten (as in the United Kingdom). In addition to being defined, each term in this dictionary is placed in historical perspective and, where relevant, its etymology is given. Supplementing constitutional words and phrases are biographies of people who have had a significant impact on the constitutions of a number of countries, such as Simón Bolívar in South America, or on a single country, such as David Ben-Gurion in Israel.

The development of modern constitutional concepts owes a great debt to the cultures of ancient Greece and Rome, England (later Great Britain and the United Kingdom), and the United States. For this reason the political organization of these nations and the writings of their key legal and philosophical observers play a prominent role in any discussion of the history of constitutional terms. Constitutional analysis began with the ancient Greeks, particularly with Plato (ca. 427–347 B.C.) and Aristotle (384–322 B.C.). Plato, in *The Republic* and especially in his final work, *The Laws*, provides a comprehensive view of the intellectual desire to create a perfect system of supreme laws for an ordered and just society. In *The Politics*, Aristotle deduces general principles of government in the ancient Greek world from data collected on at least 158 constitutions. After Greece and Rome, notably the period of the Roman republic, constitutional concepts next flowered in England. William Blackstone's *Commentaries on the Laws of England*, produced between 1755 and 1765, provides valuable insights into this phase of political and social development and informed the framers of the Constitution of the United States in 1787. This seminal document is particularly illuminated in *The Federalist* (1788), a series of essays by Alexander Hamilton, John Jay, and James Madison written to support adoption of the Constitution, which since its ratification in 1789 has helped shape many constitutions worldwide. For these reasons, the ideals expressed by prominent analysts such as Plato and Aristotle, Blackstone, and the leaders who drafted the American Constitution recur throughout the book and serve as touchstones for understanding constitutionalism itself.

To illustrate how various concepts and terms are actually used in constitutions, relevant excerpts from current national constitutions and constitutional documents are provided at the end of entries. These excerpts were selected to expand the definitions given, but sometimes an excerpt may contrast with the main definition. On the whole the excerpts show how different nations use similar concepts or words but of course are not exhaustive. Particular attention has been given to demonstrating the similarities within the diverse constitutional materials from the major countries of the world.

In the excerpts, citations of written constitutional documents (most translated into English) reflect the original form of the document headings. Numerals—whether roman or arabic, figures or spelled-out words—are retained as in the originals. In some instances, however, minor spelling, capitalization, punctuation, and grammar of translated documents have been standardized for clarity and the facilitation of comparisons. Space limitations occasionally resulted in the deletion of explanatory material. Therefore, original documents should be consulted for more formal or legal uses.

All the constitutions and excerpts used in *The Illustrated Dictionary of Constitutional Concepts* were selected on the basis of their general aptness to the concept or term defined. In certain instances, a translator's selection of a particular word or phrase may have affected whether an excerpt was considered appropriate in the English-language context of this book. No attempt has been made to weigh factors such as how well these provisions are observed or enforced in a particular nation-state or how well an excerpt was originally written or translated. The impact on world constitutions of the personalities included here is likewise discussed without regard to their positive or negative impact, as it is often possible to learn as much if not more from the failures in constitutional development as from the successes.

The staffs of many embassies were helpful in providing constitutional materials for use in this book. In addition, the following people deserve special appreciation for their assistance: At Archetype Press, Gretchen Smith Mui, editor; Kristi Flis, editorial assistant; and Robert L. Wiser, designer. At Congressional Quarterly Books, David R. Tarr, editor-in-chief; Nancy Lammers, director of editorial design and production; and Jeanne Ferris, former acquisitions editor. Also Gisbert H. Flanz, professor emeritus of political theory and comparative politics, New York University; Jefri Ruchti, Thunderhead Production; and Phuong-Khanh Nguyen, senior foreign law specialist, Library of Congress. And for her devotion to the cause of helping me make constitutional concepts more understandable, my wife, Diane Maddex, president of Archetype Press.

Introduction

The Western world's concept of a constitution that defines and limits political power took root and proliferated in the twentieth century. The process of turning nonconstitutional national governments into constitutional democracies has proceeded steadily—slowly at first but with amazing rapidity in the last two decades. In 1974 only thirty-nine countries had true democratic governments. Today as many as 179 of the world's 192 nations elect their lawmakers. Constitutional concepts have flourished recently in countries as different as Russia, whose huge land mass spans parts of two continents, and the Republic of Palau, a tiny island nation in the Pacific.

The Movement Toward Constitutionalism

The struggle to attain true constitutional democracy has been long and hard in many countries, and for some the effort may not be completely over. Others still have a distance to go to turn fledgling constitutional governments into stable, long-term realities. One fact seems certain, however: national governments by the few and for the few, including single-party systems and personal and military dictatorships, are losing ground to national governments by and for all citizens. Even countries that are not yet democracies—those under the rule of a single party, a single person, or the military—have felt the need to exhibit constitutions to the international community as symbols, albeit hollow ones, of their conformity with the traditions of constitutionalism. The world community as represented by the United Nations, regional associations and alliances, and the international economic and communications networks makes it harder for the few remaining nondemocratic nations to deny to their citizens the political freedoms and rights enjoyed by so many others.

National constitutions represent the highest form of human aspiration. They are attempts, although imperfect, at ordering human society on the grand scale of the nation-state. Nothing comparable exists on the global scale. The United Nations is not a world government, and the historic religious texts containing directions for ordering one's life are acknowledged to be of divine, not human, inspiration.

Today all nation-states have a constitution, at least in the general sense of the term, and most, like the United States, have written constitutions. Of the major countries of the world only the United Kingdom, New Zealand, and Israel have unwritten constitutions—consisting of a number of key documents and laws passed by a legislature with relatively supreme government powers. A written constitution is not necessarily better than an unwritten one, and having a written constitution does not always mean that the government is a democratic one. Every country's constitution and constitutional development is unique.

A constitution is in one sense a description of how a nation's government works. Aristotle viewed constitutions in this way, and in the fourth century B.C. he and his colleagues collected 158 constitutions, including the constitution of Athens. Since Aristotle, many laws and documents, such as Magna Carta in 1215 in England, have significantly influenced the development of constitutions throughout the world. The first true written constitution is that of the United States, which took effect in 1789. Most current constitutions can trace their basic form of government to the parliamentary system that developed in what is now the United Kingdom or to the presidential system created by the U.S. Constitution, with its federalism and stricter separation of powers. Some national governments blend elements of both.

The Evolution of Constitutional Concepts

The history of most constitutional concepts and terms is extensive. Key words that find their way into national constitutions are generally those that have been used in a precise way and accepted for many centuries. They may have had one meaning in ancient Greece or Rome, but they have been honed by philosophers, judges, scholars, and political leaders until today they have a rich history and a clear, sharp meaning.

Both the analytical work of Aristotle and the earlier contributions of Plato, who approached the subject through deductive reasoning, have been the springboards for serious political scientists and philosophers ever since.

Ancient Greece. Athens became a democracy, albeit a direct rather than a representative one, in 508 B.C. This form of government, however, was seldom without its critics. Alcibiades, a general and politician in the fifth century B.C., called it an "acknowledged folly," and in the following century Plato complained that democracy granted equality to "the equal and unequal alike." Nevertheless, Athenian democracy worked efficiently when compared with the administration of many contemporaneous political entities and states.

About forty times each year the people of Athens met in a regular sovereign assembly, which any male citizen eighteen years of age could attend. Athens in the fourth century B.C., during the time of Plato and Aristotle, had a population of between 20,000 and 40,000 adult males. Their assembly nominated and chose government officials, who were magistrates, treasurers, military leaders, and the like. Most of these officials were chosen by lot, rather than by vote, and were paid a modest salary for performing their duties. The term for such offices was one year, so a majority of citizens could expect to get some government experience during their lifetime. Generals, however, were elected, usually one from each of the twelve Athenian tribes.

Candidates for both government and military positions would often be wealthy citizens. In fact, political leadership consistently came from the wealthy and aristocratic classes; there were no political parties as we know them today. The richer and poorer classes were split, observed Aristotle, particularly when it came to waging war. Poorer citizens, having less to lose and more to gain from a favorable military campaign, tended to support going to war in the hope of acquiring some of the spoils.

A council of five hundred persons was chosen by lot annually. The council, which met daily, made decisions that could not be handled by the government officials and also established the agenda for the citizen assembly meetings. To prevent members from becoming entrenched, no one could serve on the council more than twice. As a result, however, little expertise was developed.

Athenian democracy tolerated freedom of speech, even criticism of the government, up to a point, and condoned political equality among free male citizens only. As in any society, social position and economic wealth made some citizens more equal than others. Although Demosthenes, who lived from approximately 385 to 322 B.C., defended Athens's broad-based democracy, both Plato and Aristotle criticized it. The works of these two Greeks nevertheless provide the best insight into early constitutional concepts and terms.

Ancient Rome. The laws and constitution of ancient Rome, particularly in its early days as a republic, from 509 to 27 B.C., have contributed significantly to the evolution of modern constitutional definitions. Not surprisingly, most of the key words used today in constitutional documents have Latin roots. In addition to being the language of early Rome and the Roman Empire, Latin continued for many centuries as the common language of scholarship in Europe.

Rome's constitutional history can be divided into four parts: the monarchy, the early republic, the late republic, and the empire. The early and late republic periods especially affected the development of constitutional concepts and terms.

Until 509 B.C. Rome was ruled by a king along with the Senate, consisting of one hundred leading upper-class citizens (the patricians), and the Assembly (the *comitia curiata)*, also consisting of patrician citizens. It is believed that the king had both government and religious functions. The Senate's role was to advise the king, who appointed its members, while the Assembly voted on laws proposed by the king and on important issues such as war and peace. The lower class (the plebeians) could not participate in government or intermarry with the patricians.

When Rome became a republic in 509 B.C., the Senate, which was expanded to three hundred members, took control of the state, designating some of its own to handle specific government functions. Two assemblies, the *comitia centuriata* and the *comitia tributa*, replaced the *comitia curiata.* Membership was still restricted to the patricians. Slowly and after many confrontations, the plebeians gained admittance to the power structure.

In 471 B.C. the plebeians were allowed to have their own assembly, called the *concilium plebis.* This assembly's decisions, called *plebiscita*, applied only to the plebeians, however. A law passed in 367 B.C. required that one of the two highest government officials, called consuls, be a plebeian. Full participation in politics, as in Athens, was still limited to free male citizens, but freed slaves *(libertini)* were accorded some rights. The *concilium plebis* and the *comitia tributa* merged gradually.

Voting in all the assemblies took place in two stages. In the *comitia centuriata* the members were divided into "centuries," a term derived from the military unit of one hundred foot soldiers. In the early days of the republic the *comitia centuriata* had 197 centuries. The other upper-class assembly was based on a unit called a *tribus* (tribe), as was the lower-class assembly. There were four urban tribes and twenty-one rural tribes. In each assembly votes were first cast within the individual groups and then by all the groups together. These assemblies selected the major government administrators or magistrates, such as consuls, censors, praetors, quaestors, and aediles, but their decisions had to be ratified by the Senate.

As in the city-states of ancient Greece, the actual constitutional law of the Roman republic was largely based on tradition and convention; however, two constitutional law provisions have been found in fragments of a 450 B.C. codification of early Roman law, the Law of the Twelve Tables. Roman law was divided into criminal law and civil law. The *jus civile*, the oldest type of law, applied to the settlement of disputes between Roman citizens. Gradually, as Rome expanded and engaged in trade with other peoples, a *jus gentium* (law covering transactions with foreigners) developed. Like the distinction between common law and equity in England later on, the *jus gentium* was less harsh and more flexible than the older type of law.

The Roman Empire dates from 27 B.C., when Octavian, later Augustus Caesar, relinquished his dictatorship and "restored" the republic. In A.D. 212 the emperor Antonine, known as Caracalla, granted citizenship to almost all free inhabitants of the empire. This *constitutio Antoniniani* also extended the jurisdiction of Roman law.

The Roman Empire retained its influence in the western part of Europe until about A.D. 476–79. Thereafter the economic and political structures of medieval Europe were molded by feudalism and the Christian church, and church scholars such as St. Augustine and St. Thomas Aquinas wrestled with the problems of the government of humans under the governance of God.

From Magna Carta to the U.S. Constitution. In A.D. 930 Iceland undertook an early limited experiment in parliamentary government, centered on its Althing (parliament), but not until the Renaissance in Europe, beginning in Italy in the fourteenth century, did major new developments occur in modern constitutionalism. Roman law had already been rediscovered in the eleventh century in the universities of northern Italy and in France, and during the Renaissance the works of the ancient Greeks and Romans and Roman laws were reintegrated into the theory of politics and government

The concepts of limited and accountable executive power and representational democracy, however, first took firm hold in England in the late seventeenth century. Roman law, which had influenced the canon law of the church, also influenced the English common law and the country's constitutional development. In 1215 Magna Carta (the Great Charter) gave English nobles some assurances of protection against the arbitrary powers of the king.

Roughly from Magna Carta to the Glorious Revolution of 1688–89, England developed a form of government that became known as a limited or constitutional monarchy. No single document describes the parliamentary government of that time or of the United Kingdom today. In addition to Magna Carta, the present-day constitution of the United Kingdom can be found in a number of important statutes passed by Parliament and assented to by monarchs, in the common law (law of precedent established independently by the English courts), and in a number of national traditions. The parliamentary form of government that evolved there has greatly influenced many national constitutions, most notably those of countries that were once British dominions or colonies.

The limited British monarchy—composed of a hereditary head of state, representatives to a constitutionally supreme legislature elected by the people, and a head of government selected by the legislature—are ably described by the eighteenth-century commentator William Blackstone, along with the protections of rights rooted in the English common law. Blackstone's *Commentaries on the Laws of England* (1755–65) have been justly praised as "an incomparable work, and the most beautiful outline that has ever been exhibited by any human science" (Sir William Jones). In addition to illuminating the constitutional law of England in the eighteenth century, Blackstone's writings greatly influenced the constitutional development in thirteen rebellious British colonies in America.

The next great leap forward in constitutionalism came in the form of the 1789 U.S. Constitution. The first written constitution, this document remains in effect without change except for twenty-seven formal amendments and some added informal traditions, such as the role of political parties. Because of its significance in the development of modern world constitutions, it, like the constitution of the United Kingdom, has been a model for numerous constitutional concepts and terms.

In the study of world constitutions the U.S. Constitution is additionally important because of the contemporaneous work *The Federalist* (1788). This collection of essays on the Constitution originally appeared as newspaper articles written to promote the revolutionary charter's adoption by the American people. Using pseudonyms, the authors—Alexander Hamilton, John Jay, and James Madison, the latter known as the "Father of the U.S. Constitution"—bridged the gap from the ancient world and the development of constitutionalism in Great Britain to the dawn of a new era in a new world.

The British prime minister William Gladstone in 1887 called the U.S. Constitution "the most wonderful work ever struck off at a given time by the brain and purpose of man." It endeavors to set in motion, like the harmonious spheres of the solar system under the mathematically precise control of Sir Isaac Newton's laws of gravity, a mechanically balanced system of supreme governance. Not a system arrived at after centuries of patchwork measures or one relying on divine providence to make the rulers responsive to the needs of the ruled, it is clearly a daring blueprint by people taking full responsibility for ordering their own society. In contrast to the British parliamentary monarchy, the U.S. Constitution prescribes a classless political community with a head of state and government elected periodically by the people, together with coequal legislative and judicial branches of government.

Constitutionalism for the New Millennium

If the twentieth-century trend toward constitutionalism continues, the complete triumph of constitutional democracy for all nation-states will occur in the twenty-first century. To be sure, many obstacles are yet to be overcome: poverty, ignorance, racial and religious hatred, and economic and social inequality, as well as the ever-present threat of demagogues who can destroy the foundations of constitutionalism for their personal aggrandizement.

Knowledge, dedication to the principles of constitutional democracy, and participation in the political process are strategies that citizens must use to protect and extend the concept of government of the people, for the people, and by the people. As citizens better understand the constitutional concepts and terms from which their own and other constitutions are constructed, they will be better able to meet the challenge of making democracy work everywhere.

ΑΡΙΣΤ
Mongeot Sculp.

Abdul Rahman Putra Al-Haj

By creating a strong, economically aggressive nation-state out of territory ruled by sovereign potentates and inhabited by people with major ethnic, cultural, and linguistic differences, Tunku (Prince) Abdul Rahman Putra Al-Haj (1893–1990) played a key role in the development of modern Malaysia and its unique constitution.

Abdul Rahman Putra was born on February 8, 1893, in Alor Star (also spelled Setar), the capital of Kedah, a state that would become a part of the Malaysian federation. Called Putra by his father and Awang (tanned) by his brother and sisters, he attended a local Malay elementary school and an English school before traveling to Bangkok and then to England in 1920, where he eventually obtained his law degree.

While in England during the 1920s, Abdul Rahman formed the Malay Society of Great Britain and served as its secretary. When he returned home, he took a job in the Kedah civil service. Later he held positions in civil defense and education in the Kedah government before becoming a prosecutor in the attorney general's office in Kuala Lumpur.

In 1951 Abdul Rahman became president of the United Malays National Organization (UMNO), a political party. In 1952 the party's slogan was changed from "Long Live Malay" to "Independence" from British influence. Having criticized the five Malay states (Kedah, Perlis, Kelantan, Trengganu, and Jahore) for joining with several nearby British colonial states to create the Malayan Union, which became the Federation of Malaya in 1948, Abdul Rahman allied the UMNO with other ethnic groups, primarily the Chinese and Indians, to form a strong political coalition called the Alliance Party. In 1955 the party won fifty-one of the fifty-two contested seats in the federation legislative council, and Abdul Rahman became the chief minister of the Malayan government.

The following year, the Federation of Malaya held a constitutional conference in London. Abdul Rahman, having politically united the Malays, Chinese, and Indians, now played a key role in the formation of the new constitution. First, he ensured the dominance of Malayan interests and special rights for the Malayan people, which are clearly embodied in the document. Second, he secured the positions of the rulers of the Malayan states by establishing a council of rulers, each of whom would serve as monarch on the basis of rotation. Third, he established Islam as the state religion. The new constitution was promulgated on August 31, 1957, which is still celebrated as Merdeka (Independence) Day, and Abdul Rahman became the newly independent nation's first prime minister.

In late 1963, while still serving as prime minister, Abdul Rahman became embroiled in a constitutional controversy when he was named as a defendant in a suit

Aristotle's works in the fourth century B.C. initiated the field of study known as political science. He analyzed the political theories and constitutions of the ancient Greek world in *The Politics*.

Abdul Rahman's diplomatic skills united the peoples of Malaysia and brought about its 1957 constitution, which provides for a unique council of rulers.

brought by the Malay state of Kelantan. On September 16, 1963, the federation had changed its name to Malaysia, and Singapore, North Borneo (now called Sabah), and the Borneo state of Sarawak had became members. The sultan of Kelantan claimed that such drastic changes required consultation with the rulers of the Malay states and that he had not been consulted. However, the court found that the language of the 1957 constitution did not require consultation with a ruler as a prerequisite for an amendment.

Abdul Rahman, who served as prime minister at the same time as the monarch of the same name (they were not related), gave up his position in the government in 1970 and retired from politics altogether in 1971. Afterward he wrote a newspaper column entitled "Looking Back" and a number of books on politics in Malaysia. He died on December 6, 1990, in Kuala Lumpur.

Absolute Majority

One of the cornerstones of constitutionalism is majority rule, but constitutions often specify different types of majorities as they define how votes are to be taken and counted for various decisions: passage of ordinary laws by the legislature; repassage after a veto; special legislation or acts such as declarations of war or articles of impeachment; election of members to the legislature, the executive branch, and in some cases the judiciary; amendments to the constitution; and referendums. Many constitutions state that a legislative action or the election of a government official must be based on more than a simple majority vote.

If an absolute majority is required by a legislature for votes on a single issue, the winning side must receive a minimum of one-half the votes plus one vote of all members who are entitled to vote. A simple majority in such a case would be one-half the votes plus one vote of all those members who are present and voting.

Parliamentary procedures derived from the British Parliament require that a rule may be amended at a regular business meeting by a majority of the entire membership or, if the proposed amendment has been submitted in writing at a previous meeting, by two-thirds of the members present and voting.

In an election between two or more candidates, an absolute majority of votes includes at least one-half the votes plus one vote of all those voting. If there are more than two candidates and none receives an absolute majority, then a runoff election is usually held between the two candidates with the most votes. Many countries, however, elect officials by requiring a plurality of the votes cast, so that regardless of how many candidates are running, the one who garners the most votes, even if less than an absolute majority, wins.

A supermajority is generally any majority greater than a simple majority, such as a two-thirds majority.

Constitution of Algeria (1976), Title II, The Organization of the Powers, Chapter 1, The Executive Power, Article 68: "The president of the republic is elected by universal, direct, and secret suffrage. Election is achieved by an absolute majority of recorded votes. . . ."

Constitution of Finland, Constitution Act (1919), IV, Government and Administration, Section 23b (added in 1991):

"If one of the candidates receives more than half of the votes cast in the election, he shall be elected president of the republic."

Constitution of France (1958), Title V, On Relations between Parliament and the Government, Article 46: "Nevertheless [referring to passage or amendment of organic laws], lacking an agreement between the two assemblies [the upper and lower chambers of the parliament], the text may be adopted by the national assembly on final reading only by an absolute majority of its members."

Louis XIV, who ruled France from 1643 to 1715, was the paradigm of the absolute monarch during an age of absolutism. He is reported to have declared, "I am the state."

Absolutism

As the unrestrained exercise of government powers, absolutism is the opposite of constitutionalism. In such a system of government, power is vested in some person or persons and is unchecked and uncontrolled by any law, institution, constitutional device, or coordinate body.

The development of nation-states in Europe in the seventeenth and eighteenth centuries occurred during the reigns of absolute monarchs. The twentieth century has witnessed the continuation of absolutism in the form of fascist and communist governments and totalitarian dictatorships based on unchecked personal command of military power by so-called strongmen. The merging of military, political, and religious forces has brought about virtual absolutism in a number of nation-states today, continuing the struggle between the forces of absolutism and constitutional democracy within and among nation-states.

Saudi Arabia, Statement by King Faud, March 28, 1992: "The democratic system that is predominant in the world is not a suitable system for the peoples of our region. The system of free elections are not within the Islamic system . . . [and are] not suitable to our country, the Kingdom of Saudi Arabia—a country that is unique in that it represents the Muslim world in supervising the holy shrines. . . . In my view, the Western democracies may be suitable in their own countries but they do not suit other countries."

Constitution of North Korea (1972), Chapter I, Politics, Article 10: "The Democratic People's Republic of Korea exercises the dictatorship of the proletariat. . . . "

Accountability

The principle that public officials are responsible and liable under law for their public actions is a basic concept underlying democratic government. In an absolute monarchy, such as Saudi Arabia today, government officials are accountable only to the monarch, who is accountable only to God. Although the precise term *accountability* is not always used in constitutions, it is implied in the very nature of regular elections, checks and balances, interpellation, and impeachment.

The Roman statesman and orator Marcus Tullius Cicero observed in the first century B.C. that elected Roman consuls could not become tyrants because their tenures were annual and accountable. The periodic election process makes elected officials accountable to the voters. Appointed officials, in turn, are accountable to elected officials and through the courts.

A primary example of political accountability is interpellation, the procedure by which members of a parliament may question a cabinet minister or even the prime minister about his or her official conduct. If ministers receive a vote of no confidence as a result of such questioning, they may be dismissed or forced to resign.

Most constitutional monarchies exempt the monarch from being held accountable for his or her actions, but any official act of the monarch must be countersigned by an appropriate minister, who must take responsibility for it. Presidents, unlike monarchs, may be held accountable for their official acts by the legislative and judicial branches, as well as by the voters. Some constitutions also expressly provide for financial accountability with respect to the expenditure of public funds.

Julius Caesar, the Roman general, statesman, and writer, also held the position of consul, an official accountable for his acts.

The media play a significant although unofficial role in scrutinizing public officials by publicizing their misconduct, and the political opposition often performs a similar function. Federalism, with its various levels of government, may enhance accountability by requiring officials elected in political subdivisions to answer for certain acts not only to the national government but also to their own constituencies.

Constitution of Spain (1978), Title II, Concerning the Crown, Article 56: "The person of the king is inviolable and not subject to liability. His acts shall always be countersigned in the manner established in Article 64. Without such countersignature they shall lack validity, except as provided for in Article 65, 2 [with respect to personal household staff]."

Constitution of South Africa (1994), Chapter 12, Finance, Section 193(1): "The auditor-general shall audit and report on all the accounts and financial statements of all the accounting officers at the national and provincial level of government, other than that of the office of the auditor-general, and of all other persons in the national and provincial public services entrusted with public assets, trust property, and other assets." [A new constitution was adopted in 1996.]

Accused, Rights of the

Guarantees of the rights of persons accused of crimes have a long history and are often expressly included in constitutions. Greek citizens during the time of Demosthenes in the fourth century B.C. who believed that they had been unjustly fined by a magistrate could appeal their cases as debtors of the state or in a hearing into the proper conduct of the magistrate; juries were used in trials. In thirteenth-century England, Magna Carta (1215) provided that no official could place a person on trial based on his own statement alone; credible witnesses to the truth of a person's admissions had to be found. Many constitutional rights of the accused that are recognized

An accused prisoner in the dock of a Canadian court is considered innocent until proven guilty by the government.

today evolved during the development of the English constitution and are reflected in the national constitutions of former British colonies.

Protections against miscarriages of justice by government officials who apprehend, prosecute, and judge individuals for violations of the law include prohibiting self-incrimination, requiring a speedy trial, and allowing the accused to confront witnesses for the prosecution. More generally these rights of persons accused of a crime are known as guarantees of personal liberty, although they also protect against the unjust taking of property.

Even if a right of the accused is not explicitly stated in a written constitution, such as the presumption of innocence in the United States, it may be enforced by the courts as the law of the land. Conversely, in some countries where the rights of the accused are clearly expressed in the constitution, they may not be vigorously enforced by the courts.

Constitution of Panama (1972), Title III, Individual Rights and Social Rights and Duties, Chapter 1, Fundamental Guarantees, Article 23: "Persons accused of committing a crime have the right to be presumed innocent until proven guilty, at a public trial, under due process of law. Whoever is arrested shall have the right, from that moment, to legal counsel in all police and judiciary proceedings."

Constitution of Canada, Constitution Act (1982), Charter of Rights and Freedoms, Section 7: "Everyone has the right to life, liberty, and security of the person and the right not to be deprived thereof except in accordance with the principle of fundamental justice."

Constitution of Bulgaria (1991), Chapter 2, Fundamental Rights and Obligation of Citizens, Article 31, Section (4): "The rights of the accused may not be restricted beyond what is necessary for the administration of justice."

Act

A law enacted by a legislature is called an act. An act may also be called a statute, although in France, for example, *statuts* refer to the constitutions of legal entities other than persons, such as organizations. Acts include both public and private laws and are generally identified by a title and number, which may include the year of enactment or the designation of the legislative session during which they were enacted.

In the United States, once a bill has been passed by one house of Congress, it is known as an act, but generally an act refers only to a proposed law that has been approved by both houses of a bicameral legislature. An act of parliament, however, is generally a bill that has been passed by both houses and has been approved by the monarch or president. In Norway, a country whose parliament is elected as a single body and then divides itself into two chambers, an act of parliament is called a *lov*, whereas the law in general is called *retten.*

Some acts may have constitutional status. For example, in constitutional monarchies a special form called an act of succession sets forth the procedure for selecting a monarch. Other special acts of constitutional status deal with the procedures of parliaments, such as Sweden's Riksdag Act.

An act of state refers to a sovereign's action or decision that may not be questioned in court.

Constitution of Zambia (1991), Part V, The Legislature, Section 78(9): "All laws made by parliament shall be styled 'Acts,' and the words of enactment shall be 'Enacted by the Parliament of Zambia.' "

Constitution of Portugal (1976), Part III, Organization of Political Power, Section III, Assembly of the Republic, Chapter II, Powers, Article 169, Form of the Acts: "1. The acts provided for in article 164(a) [constitutional revision] shall take the form of constitutional laws. 2. The acts provided for in article 167(a)–(e) [election, referendum, organizational, and emergency laws] shall take the form of organic laws. 3. The acts provided for in article 164(b)–(i) and (m) [other political and legislative powers of the assembly] shall take the form of laws. . . . "

Constitution of Sweden, The Instrument of Government (1974), Chapter 4, The Business of the Government, Article 10: "Additional provisions concerning the business of the Riksdag are laid down in the Riksdag Act."

Act of Succession. *See* Succession

Adjournment

When a legislative session is suspended until another time or another place, it is in adjournment. The term also refers to the period of time of the suspension. Dissolving and proroguing a legislative body are similar acts generally taken by a monarch or president with respect to a session of a parliament. In the lower house of the British Parliament, however, a motion may be made by a member of the government at the end of a sitting "that the House do now adjourn," which allows some members to discuss matters in a short debate. A motion to adjourn may also be used procedurally to attempt to delay or prevent action on a matter.

Unlike a recess, which suspends action only for a short time, adjournment, if made in the form of an unqualified motion, terminates proceedings. The U.S. Constitution provides that Congress may adjourn from day to day, but one house may not adjourn for more than three days without the consent of the other. Final adjournments of sessions are *sine die* (without a day).

Constitution of the United States of America (1789), Article II, Section 3: " . . . he [the president of the United States] may, on extraordinary Occasions, convene both Houses, or either of them, and in Case of Disagreement between them, with Respect to the Time of Adjournment, he may adjourn them to such Time as he shall think proper. . . . "

Constitution of Egypt (1972), Part V, System of Government, Chapter II, The Legislature, Article 136: "The president of the republic shall not dissolve the people's assembly unless it is necessary and after a referendum of the people. The president of the republic shall issue a decision terminating the sessions of the assembly and conducting a referendum within thirty days. If the total majority of the voters approve the dissolution of the assembly, the president of the republic shall issue the decision of dissolution."

Constitution of Singapore (1959), Part VI, The Legislature, Article 65: "(1) The president may, at any time, by proclamation in the Gazette, prorogue parliament. . . . (3) The president may, at any time, by proclamation in the Gazette, dissolve parliament if he is advised by the prime minister so to do, but he shall not be obliged to act in this respect in accordance with the advice of the prime minister unless he is satisfied that in tendering that advice, the prime minister commands the confidence of a majority of the members of parliament."

Administration

In public law, government administration—from the Latin *minister* (servant) and *administratio* (aid, management, or arrangement)—is the practical management and direction of the executive department or the operations and machinery of the various government bodies under the sovereign. The term also designates the whole body of public functionaries. In politics it refers to the policies and the top level of the executive branch of government put in place by an incumbent president; for example, the

"Lincoln administration" describes the policies and political appointees of the U.S. president Abraham Lincoln.

In constitutions, the word *administrative* generally refers to the government's executive rather than legislative or judicial functions. Administrative law deals with the actions and policies of government agencies and the activities of executive branch officials.

Constitution of China (People's Republic of China) (1982), Chapter Three, Structure of the State, Section III, The State Council, Article 85: "The state council, that is, the central people's government, of the People's Republic of China is the executive body of the highest organ of state power; it is the highest organ of state administration."

Constitution of Germany (1949), VIII, The Execution of Federal Statutes and the Federal Administration, Article 87b (added in 1956): "(1) The Federal Armed Forces Administration shall be conducted as a direct federal administration with its own administrative substructure. Its function shall be to administer personnel matters and directly to meet the material requirements of the armed forces."

Admission of New States

The constitutions of many federal, rather than unitary, governments contain provisions for the addition of new semisovereign political subdivisions, or states. Often new states are created out of territory over which a country already exercises some form of sovereignty, as in the case of the states of Alaska and Hawaii in the United States; these territories were admitted into the Union on an equal

Pending the U.S. Senate's approval of Hawaii's request to be admitted as the forty-ninth state, delegates to a 1950 convention drafted a state constitution. Alaska was admitted before Hawaii, however, and became the forty-ninth state.

The United Nations, a voluntary affiliation of nation-states created at the end of World War II, is headquartered in New York City. The predecessor League of Nations, established in 1920 and dissolved in 1946, met in Geneva.

footing with the existing states. A new state (known variously as a province or, in Switzerland, a canton) may also be created from an existing state or states or from new territory. Some constitutions make exceptions for special treatment of selected states, as in the case of Sabah and Sarawak in the Malaysian federation.

Unitary nation-states may acquire new territory by conquest, annexation, or treaty, but the sovereignty of the acquired territory is generally merged completely into the sovereignty of the acquiring country. In some cases the acquired territory may be treated as a separate kingdom, territory, dominion, or colony.

Constitution of India (1949), Part I, The Union and Its Territory: "2. Admission or establishment of new states.—Parliament may by law admit into the union, or establish, new states on such terms and conditions as it thinks fit. 3. Formation of new states and alteration of areas, boundaries, or names of existing states.—Parliament may by law—(a) form a new state by separation of territory from any state, or by uniting two or more states, or by uniting any territory to a part of any state; (b) increase the area of any state; (c) diminish the area of any state; (d) alter the boundaries of any state; (e) alter the name of any state. . . . "

Constitution of Brazil (1988), Title III, The Organization of the State, Chapter 1, The Political and Administrative Organization, Article 18: "2—The federal territories are a part of the union and their establishment, transformation into states, or reintegration into the state of origin shall be regulated by supplementary law. 3—The states may merge into each other, subdivide, or dismember to be annexed to others or to form new states or federal territories, subject to the approval of the population directly concerned, by means of a plebiscite, and of the national congress, by means of a supplementary law."

Constitution of Austria (1920), Chapter I, General Provisions, Article 3: "(1) The federal territory comprises the territories of the federal *Länder* [states]. A change in the federal territory, which is at the same time a change in the *Land* [state] territory, just as the change of a *Land* boundary within federal territory, can—apart from peace treaties—ensue only from corresponding constitutional laws of the Bund [the federation] and the *Land* whose territory undergoes change."

Advice and Consent. *See* Confirmation

Affiliated States

The concept of affiliated or associated states implies a voluntary union of individual nations in a community for economic, political, or other purposes. The relationship is neither total independence of each state nor total submergence in the sovereignty of the whole, as in a federated nation-state. The states of a federative country, such as Brazil, or of a country with a federal system, such as the United States, are considered indissoluble; the constituent states are not affiliated or associated states.

The British Commonwealth of Nations, with forty-nine members ranging from Canada to Brunei, is an example of affiliated states, as is the community of nations described in the French constitution, Title 12, On the Community, Articles 77 through 87. Another example is the European Union of sovereign nation-states, whose membership includes fifteen Western European countries representing 370 million people in 1995.

Constitution of France (1958), Title XIII, On Agreements of Association, Article 88: "The republic [of France] or the community may make agreements with states that wish to associate themselves with the community in order to develop their own civilizations."

Constitution of Germany (1949), Preamble (amended in 1990): "Animated by the resolve to serve world peace as an equal part in a united Europe [the European Union], the German people have adopted, by virtue of their constituent power, this basic law."

Constitution of Portugal (1976), Fundamental Principles, Article 7 (added in 1992): "6. Subject to reciprocity and the principle of subsidiarity, Portugal may, with a view to building up economic and social cohesion, enter agreements on the joint exercise of the powers necessary to build the European union."

Agenda

In parliamentary procedures, members follow a prepared list of items in the order in which they have been proposed for consideration. This agenda is sometimes called the order of business or order of the day. Some legislatures use an agenda that is prepared before every meeting day during a legislative session. The chairman or speaker is responsible for preparing and disseminating the order of the day to all members before the beginning of each day's meeting. After the session has begun, members may vote to rearrange the items on the agenda.

In the U.S. Congress, the leadership of the majority party in each house places in order on a calendar the bills to be considered during the two-year session of each legislative body; the calendar is used throughout the whole session. Placement on a legislative calendar or an agenda may be critical to the fate of legislative proposals.

Constitution of Finland, Procedure of Parliament (1927), Plenary Sittings, Section 32: "The agenda of a plenary sitting, containing a list of the matters to be considered in the sitting and of the documents pertaining to them, shall, where possible, be posted on the parliamentary bulletin boards well in advance of the plenary sitting."

Constitution of Monaco (1962), Title 7, The National Council, Article 62: "The national council draws up its agenda. It is communicated to the minister of state at least three days in advance."

Aggression. *See* Defense; Invasion

Agreement. *See* Contract; Treaty

Alberdi, Juan Bautista

Argentina's constitution of 1853, which is still in effect today, was significantly influenced by the constitutionalist Juan Bautista Alberdi (1810–84).

Alberdi was born in 1810 in San Miguel de Tucumán, in what is today Argentina. Orphaned as a young boy, he was educated in Buenos Aires and chose a legal career. In addition to studying law and writing on legal subjects, he contributed to a musical journal and wrote a booklet on piano instruction.

A member of the intellectual literary salon of Marcos Sastre, which included the poet Estaban Echeverria and the educator Domingo Sarmiento, Alberdi and others incurred the displeasure of the dictator Manuel de Rosas and fled the country in 1838. In exile with an influential group of expatriates in Uruguay, he continued to study law, taking time also to travel to Chile and Europe.

After Rosas was overthrown in 1852, Alberdi wrote *Bases and Starting Points for the Political Organization of the Argentine Republic.* In this work he outlined proposals, derived from the ideas of Jean-Jacques Rousseau, Echeverria, and the U.S. Constitution, for building a federal democratic republic in Argentina. He also urged the new government to solicit foreign capital and encourage immigration, using the slogan "*Gobernar es poblar*" ("To govern is to populate").

An 1852 constitutional convention held in Santa Fe adopted Alberdi's design for a federal government as the basis for a new constitution. The role his vision played at the convention was critical, especially after the loss of the delegates' only copy of *The Federalist* (1788), with its essays by Alexander Hamilton, James Madison, and John Jay arguing for adoption of the U.S. Constitution (1789). The delegates' attention shifted to Alberdi's *Bases*, and he quickly sent them another copy, along with a guide for the drafting committee. The guide contained Alberdi's concepts for the convention's procedures: it should have full powers to completely carry out its task, harmonize the federal and unitary principles that had divided the country in the past, and jettison any notions that did not foster the economic, intellectual, and moral progress of the nation. In this last regard he offered as an example the 1849 state constitution of California.

After the Argentine constitution was adopted, Alberdi was sent on diplomatic missions to Paris, Madrid, Washington, D.C., and London, but he fell out of favor with the Argentine government because of his opposition to the 1864–70 war with Paraguay. He returned to Argentina to serve a term as a legislator but left again for Europe before completing it. Alberdi died on June 18, 1884, in Paris.

Drawing on the ideas of Jean-Jacques Rousseau and the U.S. Constitution, Juan Bautista Alberdi's design for a federal government in Argentina was accepted in 1853.

Alien

Constitutions may expressly limit or extend the rights, privileges, and duties of its citizens to alien inhabitants of its territory—any persons who are not subjects, citizens, or nationals. In *The Politics*, Aristotle contrasts a citizen of a state with a resident alien, who may not sue or be sued except under a treaty. Long treated as outlaws, aliens were extended legal rights under the Roman law of *jus gentium* (law of nations). The Alien and Sedition Laws (1798) in the United States segregated aliens as a separate class and were clearly unconstitutional, although the Supreme Court never ruled on the question; under this law aliens were prosecuted for criticizing President John Adams.

Aliens include foreign government officials, such as ambassadors, as well as tourists, residents who may become citizens by naturalization, and, during times of war, enemies in a territory. Each nation-state may regulate and expel aliens in accordance with its own laws and international standards of human conduct.

Constitution of Colombia, Title III, Concerning the Population and the Territory, Chapter 3, Concerning Aliens, Article 100: "Aliens in Colombia will enjoy the same civil rights as Colombians."

Constitution of Argentina (1853), First Part, Declarations, Rights, and Guarantees, Article 20: "Foreigners enjoy in the territory of the nation all the civil rights of a citizen. . . ."

Constitution of Greece (1975), Part Two, Individual and Social Rights, Article 4: "1. All Greeks are equal before the law. . . . 4. Only Greek citizens shall be eligible for public service, except as otherwise provided by special laws."

Ambassador

An ambassador is an official messenger between sovereign nation-states and other entities or a minister of high rank sent by one sovereign nation-state on a mission to another. Ambassadors head foreign diplomatic missions in embassies headquartered in the capitals of the host countries. The name comes from the French word *ambassadeur*, while *embassy* is derived from the French word *ambassade*.

In *The Laws*, a work prescribing a constitution and laws for a new colony, Plato discusses how offenses of ambassadors and other members of diplomatic missions are to be dealt with. Today, however, ambassadors are regarded as personal representatives of the heads of state who sent them and as such are accorded special honors and privileges, including diplomatic immunity from prosecution. Offenses by ambassadors are punishable either by recall of the offending diplomat by his or her own nation or by expulsion by the host state, which makes him or her *persona non grata*.

Historically, a distinction was made between an ambassador ordinary, who was sent to head a nation's permanent mission, and an ambassador extraordinary, who was dispatched to conduct special business. That distinction no longer exists. Today, in addition to ambassadors who head missions, governments may appoint ambassadors at large (those not accredited to a particular foreign government), special ambassadors plenipotentiary (those with full powers to act on behalf of the sending government), and ambassadors to international and regional organizations.

In presidential systems of government, ambassadors and other high-ranking representatives to foreign governments are appointed by the president, although confirmation by the legislature may be required. The president also accepts the credentials of ambassadors from foreign countries. Generally in parliamentary systems the monarch or other head of state formally accredits and receives ambassadors, although the prime minister directs relations with foreign countries.

Constitution of France (1958), Title II, President of the Republic, Article 13: "Councilors of state, the grand chancellor of the legion of honor, ambassadors and envoys extraordinary, master councilors of the audit office, prefects, representatives of the government in the overseas territories, general officers . . . and directors of central administrations shall be appointed in meetings of the council of ministers [cabinet]."

Constitution of Kuwait (1962), Part IV, Powers, Chapter II, The Head of State, Article 74: "The amir shall appoint and dismiss civil and military officials and diplomatic representatives to foreign countries in accordance with the law. He shall also accept the credentials of the representatives of foreign countries."

As a matter of protocol ambassadors from a foreign country must present themselves for approval by the head of the host nation. U.S. President Rutherford B. Hayes received the first Chinese minister to the United States at the White House in 1878.

Constitution of the United States of America (1789), Article II, Section 2: "He [the president] shall have Power, by and with the Advice and Consent of the Senate, to make Treaties . . . and he shall nominate, and by and with the Advice and Consent of the Senate, shall appoint Ambassadors, other public Ministers and Consuls. . . ."

Amendment

Changes in constitutions and legislative measures are called amendments. Unwritten constitutions may be changed by an act passed by a majority vote of the legislature or by custom and tradition, as in the United Kingdom. Written constitutions may be changed in a number of ways.

Depending on the difficulty of the amendment process, constitutions are classified as either flexible or rigid. Flexible constitutions, generally unwritten, are usually found only in countries with unitary systems of government, while federal nation-states have more rigid documents to protect the powers of the semisovereign political subdivisions. Making the amendment process more arduous also provides the public an opportunity to express its views, thus ensuring serious deliberation of proposed constitutional changes, and it also protects the rights of linguistic, religious, and cultural minorities.

Some rigid constitutions require only a supermajority vote by the legislature for passage of an amendment, while others require approval by the voters in a referendum. Another procedure is a general election that is held before final approval may be given to an amendment. Although proposed amendments are generally introduced in legislatures, the Swiss constitution permits voters to initiate as well as ratify amendments. The U.S.

Constitution (1789) provides alternative procedures for amendment. James Madison, in essay 39 of *The Federalist* (1788), explains that the methods of amendment are neither wholly national—requiring the approval only of the citizens at large—nor wholly federal—requiring the approval only of the states—but a combination of both.

Constitutional amendments may take various forms. The 1979 Zimbabwean constitution, for example, is amended by acts that simply refer to the article and sections to be amended and set forth the amendment. Amendments to the U.S. Constitution stand alone, relying on interpretation to redact the original document. The Cuban constitution and others are simply reprinted in the amended form.

Some constitutions provide for major revision as well as amendment. Other nation-states, such as Canada, build in increasing levels of difficulty for passage of amendments that involve important powers or provisions.

Constitution of the Czech Republic (1993), Chapter One, Basic Provisions, Article 9: "(1) The constitution may be amended or altered solely by constitutional laws. (2) Any change of fundamental attributes of the democratic law-observing state is inadmissible. (3) Legal norms cannot be interpreted as warranting the removal or threatening of the foundations of the democratic state."

Constitution of Malaysia (1963), Part XII, General and Miscellaneous, Article 159, Amendment of the Constitution: "(1) Subject to the following provisions of this article and to article 161E [constitutional safeguards for the states of Sabah and Sarawak] the provisions of this constitution may be amended by federal law. . . . (3) A bill for making any amendment to the constitution . . . [other than certain exceptions] . . . (4) . . . shall not be passed in either house of parliament unless it is supported on second and third readings by the votes of not less than two-thirds of the total members of that house."

Amirate. *See* Monarchy

Amnesty. *See* Pardon

Amparo

The constitutions of a number of Latin American countries guarantee citizens protection from infringements of civil rights by the government. This concept of *amparo,* which takes the form of a summary judicial proceeding, was developed in Mexico. In Spanish-American law, *amparo* was a document issued to protect rights in land.

According to the 1917 Mexican constitution, a trial under the principle of *amparo* is always held if requested by an injured party, and a deficiency in a complaint filed by the injured party can be corrected in *amparo* trials by the federal courts in accordance with "reglamentary law." A writ of *amparo* may be brought in judicial, administrative, and labor matters but generally only where ordinary remedies are not available or where irreparable damage may occur out of court. The Mexican constitution provides that the supreme court on its own motion "may take cognizance of direct *amparos* by reason of special circumstances that merit such acceptance."

Constitution of Nicaragua (1987), Title IV, Rights, Duties, and Guarantees of the Nicaraguan People, Chapter 1, Article 45: "Persons whose constitutional rights have been violated or are in danger of violation shall have recourse to habeas corpus or protection *(mandamus),* according to the case and in accord with the law of *amparo.*"

Constitution of Honduras (1982), Title V, Branches of the Government, Chapter XII, The Judicial Branch, Article 319: "The supreme court of justice shall have the following powers and duties: . . . 8. To hear cases of protection against authority *(amparo).* . . ."

Appointment

The discretionary power to select or nominate persons for appointment to government positions is delimited in all constitutions, written and unwritten. Although the term applies generally even to the routine hiring of government employees at all levels, in accordance with the doctrine of separation of powers the process for appointment to important positions is often shared between the executive and legislative branches of government. As a rule, presidents nominate and the legislature or a subdivision of it confirms appointments. Persons confirmed receive a formal document of appointment, which is the legal basis for their authority to act in an official capacity.

The appointment power stems historically from the right of the absolute monarch to name whomever he or she pleased to provide advice and carry out instructions. This authority gives the head of government, whether a president or prime minister, the opportunity to put loyal persons in key government positions to ensure implementation of policies. The formal appointment power of heads of state such as monarchs, governors-general, and some presidents in parliamentary systems is purely ceremonial; the discretionary power resides in the head of government (the prime minister) and in other parliamentary leaders.

Constitution of Chile (1980), Chapter IV, Government, President of the Republic, Article 32: "The special powers vested in the president of the republic are the following: . . . 9. To appoint and remove at will the ministers of state, undersecretaries, intendants, governors, and mayors appointed by him; 10. To appoint ambassadors and diplomatic ministers and representatives to international organizations. Both these officers and those specified in number 9 above shall be of the exclusive confidence of the president of the republic and shall remain in their positions as long as they continue being reliable to him. . . . "

Constitution of Zambia (1991), Part IV, The Executive, Section 44(4): "When any appointment to an office to be made by the president is expressed by any provision to this constitution to be subject to ratification by the national assembly—(a) The [assembly] shall not unreasonably refuse or delay such ratification, but the question whether the [assembly] has so acted unreasonably shall not be enquired into by any court. . . ."

Constitution of Australia (1901), Chapter II, The Executive Government, Article 64: "The governor-general may appoint officers to administer such departments of state of the Commonwealth as the governor-general may establish. . . . After the first general election no minister of state shall hold office for a longer period than three months unless he is or becomes a senator or member of the house of representatives."

Apportionment

The division of national territory into constituencies and the allotment of seats in legislative bodies are known as apportionment. This allocation is also used, as in the U.S. Constitution (1789), as a basis for taxation. In essay 54 of *The Federalist* (1788), James Madison points out that giving the states representation and also taxing them on the basis of population balances out the tendencies to maximize and minimize population.

How the territory of a constituency or an electoral district is determined can have a large impact on the number of legislators from the same party. "Rotten-boroughs" in England and gerrymandered districts in the United States (after Vice President Elbridge Gerry, 1813–14) are examples of creative constituency making—

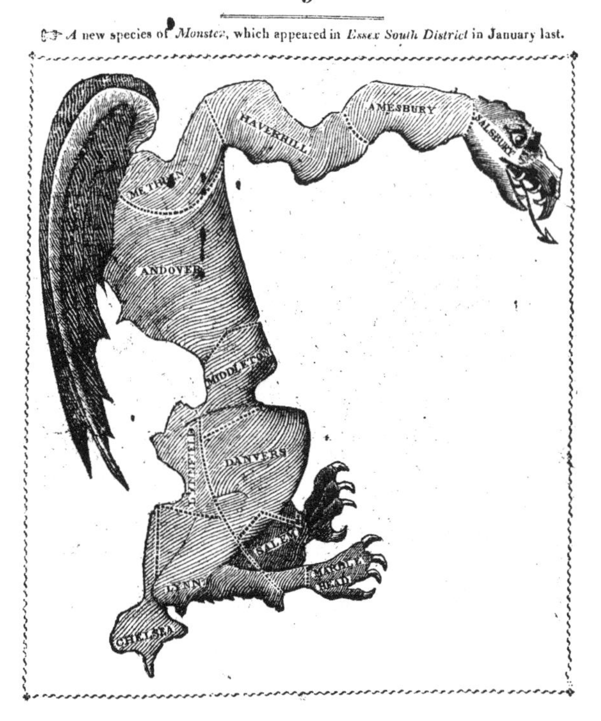

The gerrymander, derived from the name of the nineteenth-century U.S. politician Elbridge Gerry and the word *salamander,* represents the irregular shape of an electoral district created to ensure an electoral majority.

electoral districts purposefully drawn to ensure the election of candidates from a particular party. In 1647 the Levellers, an English direct-democracy movement, proposed that the standard for apportionment be indifferent—that is, not manipulated to obtain a particular result but created solely according to the number of inhabitants.

Where electoral districts are apportioned on the basis of population, reapportionment or redistricting generally occurs after a census provides information on population shifts. In the United States, for example, some states regularly gain seats in the House of Representatives, while others lose seats every ten years after a census.

Simple numerical apportionment is not, however, the only method of determining constituencies. The desire to ensure minority representation may play a part in allotting legislative seats through proportional representation or special measures. Pakistan, Bangladesh, and other countries, for example, reserve seats in their national legislatures for women and other minorities.

Constitution of the United States of America (1789), Amendment XIV (1868), Section 2: "Representatives shall be apportioned among the several States according to their respective numbers, counting the whole number of persons in each State, excluding Indians not taxed. . . ."

Constitution of Austria (1920), Chapter II, Federal Legislation, A, The Nationalrat, Article 26(2): "The federal territory will be divided into self-contained constituencies whose boundaries may not overlap *Länder* [state] boundaries. The number of deputies [members of the Nationalrat] shall be divided among the qualified voters of a constituency (electoral body) in proportion to . . . the number of federal nationals who in the last census had their domicile in the constituencies. A division of the electorate into other electoral bodies is not admissible."

Appropriations. *See* Budget

Aquinas, Thomas. *See* St. Thomas Aquinas

Corazon Cojuangco Aquino's dedication to democratic principles led to the adoption of the 1987 constitution of the Philippines and a new government representing the people.

Aquino, Corazon Cojuangco

The widow of a presidential candidate, Corazon Cojuangco Aquino (b. 1933) became president of the Philippines herself, kept her promise to reinstitute constitutional democracy, and spearheaded passage of the 1987 constitution.

Born on January 25, 1933, in the Tarlac province into the rich and politically powerful Cojuangco family of Chinese mestizo ancestry, Corazon Aquino had a privileged upbringing. She was educated at Ravenhill Academy in Philadelphia and the Notre Dame Convent School and Mount St. Vincent, both in New York. After studying mathematics and French she returned to the Philippines to pursue an education in the law. In 1954 she married Benigno Aquino Jr., a member of another prominent Tarlac family whose career in politics led him to become a mayor, a governor, and a senator in the Philippine legislature.

To stop Benigno Aquino's probable election to the presidency of the Philippines, in 1972 the incumbent president, Ferdinand Marcos, declared a state of martial law and had Aquino arrested and jailed for seven years. Marcos allowed him to live in exile in the United States, but seconds after his return to the Philippines in August 1983 Aquino was gunned down. Later, the ailing Marcos called for a "snap" election in February 1986. Corazon Aquino commanded widespread public support although she had no political experience. But with the aid of Cardinal Jaime Sin, she ran for president with a veteran politician, Salvador H. Laurel, who lacked public support, as her vice presidential candidate. Aquino's goals were clear. "I propose to dismantle the dictatorial edifice Mr. Marcos has built," she told the voters. "In its place I propose to build for the people a genuine democracy." Although Marcos was constitutionally declared the winner of the election, the discovery of widespread voting fraud resulted in popular outrage, supported by the Catholic Church and the military, which forced Marcos into exile in Hawaii.

After being sworn in on February 25, 1986, President Aquino named a cabinet the next day that included human rights activists. A month after taking office, Aquino dissolved the legislature and suspended the 1973 constitution then in effect, establishing a "revolutionary" government under a "freedom" constitution to deal with the immediate problems of the Marcos legacy. True to her principles of constitutionalism and democracy, however, she soon set in motion the process for creating a new democratic constitution for approval by a national plebiscite to be held sixteen months later.

On May 25, 1986, President Aquino personally appointed forty-four of the fifty members of the constitutional drafting committee. The committee's members, which included many respected and prominent citizens, were barred from running for office for one year after ratification of the new constitution. Like previous constitutional drafters, the members were wealthy and well educated. They included many lawyers and two former supreme court justices, as well as a nun, a priest, and a bishop. Five seats were reserved for Marcos supporters. Although Aquino undoubtedly had a general influence on the committee's direction—based on her political reform program to reduce the concentration of power in the executive's hands by using effective checks and balances—she is reported to have intervened directly in the proceedings only once to permit the president under the constitution to declare nuclear weapons on U.S. military bases in the country to be "in the national interest." She also influenced the speed of the drafting process, asking that it be completed in ninety days.

The constitutional proposal establishing a presidential rather than a parliamentary system favored by Marcos was presented to her a month late, although the constitutional committee was nearly unanimous in its endorsement of the document. One of the world's longest constitutions, it divides power among the traditional legislative, executive, and judicial branches of government. It also creates commissions on elections, audit, human rights, and good government. On June 30, 1992, Fidel V. Ramos, a candidate endorsed by Aquino, succeeded peacefully to the presidency of the Philippines.

Aristotle

Although not all his written works have survived, Aristotle (384–322 B.C.) made monumental contributions to understanding and classifying governments as constitutional systems.

Born in the Ionian city of Stagira, Greece, in 384 B.C., Aristotle was the son of Nicomachus, court physician to the king of Macedonia, Amyntas II. After his father's death he was sent to Athens, where he began studying at Plato's Academy probably around 367 B.C., remaining there until after Plato's death in 347 B.C.

Aristotle then traveled for twelve years, establishing academies at Assus and Mytilene. For three years he lived at Pella, the capital city of Macedonia, north of Greece, where he tutored King Philip's young son, the future Alexander the Great. At the age of fifty he returned to Athens and established the Lyceum, which in time would rival Plato's Academy. For the next twelve years he used the Lyceum as a center for compiling information on all aspects of scientific inquiry, from plants to governments.

For Aristotle governments and constitutions were essentially identical concepts. Among his significant written works on the subject, he completed a reference on 158 constitutions of city-states, such as Athens and other regional political entities, and a series on constitutional law. His most influential works with respect to the development of political science and constitutionalism are the *Nicomachean Ethics* and *The Politics.* In the former work Aristotle, like Plato before him, attempts to answer the questions of what makes a good citizen and what is justice. In *The Politics* he deals with principles and forms of government, such as democracy, aristocracy, monarchy, and tyranny.

Aristotle's concepts of political science and constitutional government had a profound effect on many great thinkers. In the thirteenth century St. Thomas Aquinas relied on Aristotle's writings as the basis for his own development of constitutional principles. Aristotle's notion of humans as political animals marked the beginning of political science as a discipline. His description of democracy at work in Athens—with its decline in citizen involvement, necessitating increased government compensation to ensure quorums at meetings so that measures could be ratified—foreshadowed the problem of low voter turnout in modern democracies.

Aristotle's characterization of democracy as the selfish rule by the numerous poor and of aristocracy as rule by the best may seem elitist and antidemocratic. He was viewing Athens, as Plato had, in the wake of its loss to Sparta in the Peloponnesian War (431–404 B.C.) and during the decline of the city-states, which led to his loss of faith in democracy. After the death of Alexander the Great in 323 B.C., sentiment in Athens turned against Macedonia, and Aristotle was forced to return there. He settled in Chalcis, where he died a year later.

Armed Forces

Armies have been necessary for the protection of political entities since the dawn of civilization. To a great extent, however, unbridled military force, particularly in peacetime, poses an internal threat to civilian constitutional government, and during the past two hundred years a number of countries have alternated frequently between military dictatorship and constitutional government.

The armed forces parade in review before Kremlin leaders in Moscow three years before the breakup of the Soviet Union in 1991. Under constitutional governments the military is subordinate to elected civilian officials.

In *The Laws,* Plato has his constitution maker warn that military service is a subject that requires a great deal of advice and a large number of regulations. To show that the power to raise armies can be lodged nowhere else except in the legislature, Alexander Hamilton, in essay 26 of *The Federalist* (1788), quotes from the English Bill of Rights (1688): " . . . the raising and keeping of a standing army within the Kingdom in time of peace, *unless with the consent of Parliament,* was against the law" [Hamilton's emphasis].

Many constitutions include specific provisions to control and limit the use of armed forces and to minimize their influence on the political process. The elected president of a country is often designated the commander in chief of the armed forces. In constitutional monarchies, although the monarch may be formally designated the commander in chief, the armed forces are in fact under the direction of the legislature through the prime minister. Some constitutions, however, are merely paper facades for the exercise of political power by military regimes and dictatorial leaders.

Constitution of Finland, Constitution Act (1919), VII, The Armed Forces, Section 75: "Every Finnish citizen shall be under an obligation to participate or assist in the defense of the country in the manner prescribed by act of parliament. . . . "

Constitution of Honduras (1982), Title V, Branches of the Government, Chapter VI, The Executive Branch, Article 240: "The following may not be elected president of the republic: . . . 2. Commanders and general officers of the armed forces; 3. Senior officers of the armed forces and the police or state security forces; 4. Service men on active duty and members of any other army body. . . . 5. The spouse and the relatives of military commanders serving as members of the high council of the armed forces, within the fourth degree of relationship by blood or the fourth degree of relationship by marriage. . . . "

Constitution of Germany (1949), VIII, The Execution of Federal Statutes and the Federal Administration, Article 87a (added in 1956): "(3) While a state of defense or a state of tension exists, the Armed Forces shall have the power to protect civilian property and discharge functions of traffic control insofar as this is necessary for the performance of their defense mission. . . . "

Arrest

William Blackstone, the eighteenth-century commentator on English law, detailed four types of arrest: by warrant issued by a court; by legal officers without a warrant but with probable suspicion; by a private person without a warrant but with probable suspicion; and by "hue and cry" raised when a felony has been committed.

In constitutions as well as in the law, *arrest* generally refers to the apprehension and detention of a person suspected of a criminal offense. Such references occur particularly in guarantees protecting the individual against arbitrary or illegal acts committed by government authorities and in provisions granting certain government officials immunity from arrest or detention although suspected of certain offenses. The Bill of Rights (1791) of the U.S. Constitution guarantees a speedy trial after arrest and prohibits excessive bail for persons detained on criminal charges; and Article 1, Section 6, of the Constitution provides that members of Congress cannot be arrested during their attendance at legislative sessions.

Constitution of Romania (1991), Title II, Fundamental Rights, Freedoms, and Duties, Chapter II, Fundamental Rights and Freedoms, Article 23(4): "Arrest shall be made under a warrant issued by a magistrate for a maximum period of thirty days. The person arrested may lodge a complaint to the court about the legality of the warrant, and its judge is bound to make a pronouncement by a motivated decision. The period of arrest may be extended only by a decision of the court."

Constitution of Lebanon (1926), Part II, Public Powers, Chapter III, Provisions Relating to the Chamber, Article 40: "During the session no member . . . may be prosecuted or arrested for a criminal offense without the authorization of the chamber, unless he is caught in the act."

Article

An article is a distinct portion of a written constitutional document. The term—from the Latin *articulus* (joint or movement)—literally means a connection between two parts of a body. Not all constitutional documents,

The arrest of suspects was the first step in prosecuting a 1954 shooting in the U.S. House of Representatives that wounded five members of Congress. Arrest provisions in constitutions extend varied protection to alleged criminals.

however, are divided into separate articles, and the basis for division into articles may vary. In some constitutions, especially those that are passed as legislation, the major designation for individual parts of the document is section, from the Latin *seco* (to cut or separate).

In constitutions using articles, subdivisions are often called sections, which in turn may be divided into subsections, clauses, or paragraphs. The U.S. Constitution (1789), following the preamble, is divided into seven major articles. Article 1 contains provisions relating the legislative functions, and Articles 2 and 3 describe the executive and judicial functions respectively. The remaining four articles deal with subjects including the rights of citizens and the states, amendment procedures, debts, the supremacy of the Constitution, and a prohibition against religious tests for government office.

An article is also a charge on a list of formal allegations of causes for impeachment, similar to an indictment in a criminal proceeding.

Constitution of Venezuela (1961), Chapter 3, The States, Article 17: "The following are within the competence of each state: . . . 3. The administration of its property and expenditure of the constitutional allotment and other revenues pertaining to it, subject to the provisions of Articles 229 and 235 of this constitution. . . ."

Constitution of Zimbabwe (1979), Act to Amend the Constitution of Zimbabwe . . . (1989), Section 21: "Section 60 of the constitution is amended in Subsection (2) by the deletion of 'eighty' and the substitution of 'one hundred and twenty.' "

Hafiz al-Assad has been the only president of Syria under the 1973 constitution, which he personally crafted.

Assad, Hafiz al-

Syria's 1973 constitution, promulgated by Hafiz al-Assad (b. 1930), clearly falls short of being a blueprint for a Western form of democracy but has helped stabilize a formerly volatile country in a volatile part of the world.

Born in Qurdaha, Syria, in 1930, Assad was one of nine children of a poor farmer who was a member of a small minority clan, the Alawis. He was educated first in the rural mountain village where he was born, but his family later moved to the Syrian coast. Soft-spoken and intensely private, as a teenager Assad joined the socialist-nationalist Arab Ba'ath (Renaissance) Party.

Choosing a military career, he was admitted to the Homs Military Academy in 1952 and studied military science in the Soviet Union in 1957. After the union of Egypt and Syria, Assad founded a secret society with two other Alawis who were also serving at military outposts in Egypt. The society members vowed to reform the Ba'ath Party that had promoted the union. A skilled military pilot, Assad was promoted to general in 1964 and became the commander in chief of the air force the following year. After the overthrow of the ruling Ba'ath Party faction in 1966, he became defense minister. Assad's 1969 attempt to take over the government himself was unsuccessful, but in 1970 he became the prime minister and then in 1971 the president of the Republic of Syria, as well as the head of the regional command of the Ba'ath Party.

On February 22, 1971, President Assad presented a mandate to the Syrian legislature, called the People's Assembly. He charged the assembly with passing legislation and drafting a permanent constitution that would consolidate the principles of the revolution, show the way for building Syrian society, and vest power in the law. The document was to be the first Arab constitution to make socialist-nationalist thought its guiding principle and to "consolidate adherence of the Arab socialist Ba'ath party to the masses of the Syrian people. . . . "

The legislature approved the draft constitution on January 31, 1973, after twenty-three days of "serious debate." The document was then approved by more than ninety-seven percent of the nearly eighty-nine percent of all eligible voters who voted in a national referendum and became effective the next day, March 14, 1973, by presidential decree. In the parliamentary elections that followed, Assad's Ba'ath Party won 122 of the 186 seats in the legislature.

The constitution, which makes the Ba'ath Party the nation's leading party, requires that the president be a Muslim and designates Islamic doctrine and jurisprudence as the main sources of legislation. Assad has been reelected to the seven-year-term presidency ever since this constitution went into effect.

Assemble. *See* Convene

Assembly

Aristotle describes an assembly in *The Politics* as a group of citizens meeting together to legislate, consult the constitution, and hear edicts of the magistrates. In his eighteenth-century commentaries on English law, William

Blackstone characterized an unlawful assembly as three or more persons coming together to do an unlawful act.

Today a lawful assembly consists of two or more persons meeting in public or private for any purpose, as long as they do not commit a breach of the peace or another offense. The U.S. Constitution's Bill of Rights (1791) prohibits Congress from making any law limiting "the right of the people peaceably to assemble" and to petition the government for redress of grievances.

National legislatures may style themselves as assemblies. On August 26, 1789, the National Constituent Assembly of French revolutionaries issued the Declaration of the Rights of Man and of the Citizen. France's parliament is now called the National Assembly, while Algeria's is the National People's Assembly.

Constitution of Germany (1949), I, Basic Rights, Article 8, Freedom of Assembly: "(1) All Germans shall have the right to assemble peaceably and unarmed without prior notification or permission. (2) With regard to open-air meetings, this right may be restricted by or pursuant to a statute."

A 1935 disarmament demonstration in London takes advantage of the right of peaceful assembly, which is enshrined as a fundamental freedom in many constitutions.

Constitution of Kuwait (1962), Part IV, Powers, Article 51: "Legislative power shall be vested in the amir and the National Assembly in accordance with the constitution."

Constitution of Egypt (1971), Part Seven, New Rulings, Chapter I, The Shoura Assembly, Article 194: "The Shoura Assembly [advisory council] is concerned with the study and proposal of what it deems necessary to preserve the principles of the July 23, 1952, revolution and the May 15, 1971, revolution, to consolidate national unity . . . , to protect the alliance of working forces of the people . . . , and to entrench the democratic socialist system and widen its scope."

Assent. *See* Consent

Assessor. *See* Lay Judge

Associated States. *See* Affiliated States

Association

When people join together to live, work, play, achieve mutual goals, or just enjoy one another's company, they form associations. The fact that humans create wider associations—*societas* or *consortio* in Latin; *associatio* in Middle Latin—beyond families and, in particular, establish political associations creates the need for constitutions.

At least since the time of Plato's *Republic* in the fourth century B.C., cynics such as Thrasymachos have argued that the unjust person always has the advantage over the just person in human associations or society. They have viewed the ordering of human affairs to create justice for all as an illusion perpetrated by the strong against the weak for their own advantage. After the Renaissance natural law scholars, however, developed a theory of association to account for the nature of prevalent human relationships, especially the family and the state. The seventeenth-century English philosopher Thomas Hobbes concluded that the state and all other associations were alike in that they were based on either a monarchical or a republican constitution. As a monarchist, he reasoned that associations should have no division of functions or power.

An association, unlike an assembly, is generally based on shared values or interests and continues for a long time. People associate with each other for some mutual advantage, whereas they may assemble to confront each other or another association. Political parties are associations, for example, while legislatures are assemblies where associations of people may cooperate on or compete over issues. Freedom of association generally refers to the right to form alliances such as unions or political organizations; freedom to assemble is the right to come together in a body to criticize the government or demonstrate in support of grievances against it.

"The Americans of all ages, all conditions and all dispositions constantly form associations," observed Alexis de Tocqueville in 1835. "Wherever at the head of some new undertaking you see the government of France or a man of rank in England, in the United States you will be sure to find an association."

Constitution of Canada, Constitution Act (1982), Part I, Charter of Rights and Freedoms, Fundamental Freedoms: "2. Everyone has the following fundamental freedoms: (a) freedom of conscience and religion; (b) freedom of thought, belief, opinion, and expression . . . (c) freedom of peaceful assembly; and (d) freedom of association."

Constitution of Romania (1991), Title II, Fundamental Rights, Freedoms, and Duties, Chapter II, Fundamental Rights and Freedoms, Article 37: "(1) Citizens may freely associate into political parties, trade unions, and other forms of association. (2) Any political parties or organizations which, by their aims or activity, militate against political pluralism, the principles of a state governed by the rule of law, or against the sovereignty, integrity, or independence of Romania shall be unconstitutional."

Attainder, Bill of

To further punish convicted persons who displeased the English monarch, attainder was used between the fifteenth and nineteenth centuries to extinguish the civil rights of subjects found guilty of a felony or treason. For those facing a judgment of death or outlawry, a bill of attainder could be introduced in the British Parliament to require forfeiture of their real property to the state and to debar them from inheriting, holding, or transferring land to anyone by descent. The bill, or legislation, was usually instituted in the upper house, the House of Lords. It could take effect without a trial, although sometimes the accused was allowed to be represented by counsel. For an heir to recover the rights of peerage, the bill had to be reversed by a later act of Parliament. Bills of attainder were abolished in 1938.

The U.S. Constitution (1789) expressly prohibits bills of attainder and attainder of treason that would cause any "corruption of the blood," or extension of the penalty to heirs of the person against whom a bill of attainder might be directed, or forfeiture except during the lifetime of the person attainted. In other constitutions a bill of attainder is prohibited in different ways—for example, by guaranteeing anyone accused of a crime the right to a trial in a court of law, a judgment in accordance with due process of law, and a strict separation of powers.

Attainder is distinguished from a writ of attaint, which was once a proceeding to determine if a jury had given a false verdict.

Constitution of the United States of America (1789), Article I: "Section 9. . . . No Bill of Attainder or ex post facto Law shall be passed. . . . Section 10. . . . No State shall . . . pass any bill of Attainder. . . ."

Constitution of Argentina (1853), First Part, Declarations, Rights, and Guarantees, Article 18: "No inhabitant of the nation may be punished without previous trial, based on an earlier law than the date of the offense, nor tried by special commissions, nor removed from the judges designated by law before the date of the offense."

Attorney General

The designation of attorney general began in England during the reign of Edward IV (1461–70, 1471–83), when the title referred to the king's attorney to distinguish him from attorneys appointed to act only in special matters. Today the title is often given to a nation-state's highest legal officer, whose appointment, qualifications, and duties may be spelled out in the constitution. Attorneys general act under a general commission or power of attorney to represent their principal or client in all legal matters, unlike an attorney special or an attorney particular.

In English law the attorney general is the chief legal officer of the realm who prosecutes for the Crown or the state in criminal matters and has responsibilities for matters relating to the state's revenue. In the United States the attorney general is head of the Department of Justice and a member of the president's cabinet, a position similar to that of a minister of justice in some other countries. The attorney general advises the president and other government agencies on legal matters, directs the work of the federal prosecutors, and supervises the U.S. marshals and the federal penal institutions.

Constitution of Zambia (1991), Part IV, The Executive, Section 54: "(1) There shall be an attorney general of the republic who shall, subject to ratification by the national assembly, be appointed by the president and shall be the principal legal adviser to the government. (2) A person shall not be qualified to be appointed to the office of attorney general unless he is qualified for appointment as judge of the high court."

Constitution of Panama (1972), Title VII, The Administration of Justice, Chapter 2, The Public Ministry, Article 219: "The special functions of the attorney general of the republic are: 1. To arraign before the supreme court of justice those officials whose trials correspond to that body; [and] 2. To see to it that the other officers of the public ministry faithfully discharge their duties and to take appropriate action to hold them responsible for offenses or crimes committed by them."

Audit

The concept of an independent or separate office to conduct a systematic examination, or audit, of public accounts is an old one. Aristotle, in *The Politics*, refers to officers who audit offices that handle public money as scrutineers, auditors, accountants, and controllers. Impartial financial auditing is one aspect of the constitutional concept of accountability for conducting the affairs of the public. A financial audit is basically the technical function of an accountant; however, the extent to which an audit uncovers bad judgment or malpractice can have legal and political consequences.

In the United States the auditor is called the comptroller general and is appointed by the president and approved by the Senate. Although neither an audit nor the position of auditor is mentioned in the U.S. Constitution, the constitutions of many U.S. states and many nation-states provide for audits and auditors.

Constitution of Kenya (1963), Chapter VII, Finance, Section 105: "(1) There shall be a controller and auditor-general whose office shall be an office in the public service. (2)(a) It shall be the duty of the controller and the auditor-general to satisfy himself that any proposed withdrawal from the consolidated fund is authorized by law, and if so satisfied, to approve such withdrawal; (b) to satisfy himself that all moneys that have been appropriated by parliament and disbursed have been applied to the purposes to which they were so appropriated, and that the expenditure conforms to the authority that governs it. . . . "

Constitution of the Netherlands (1987), Chapter Four, Council of State, General Chamber of Audit, and Permanent Advisory Bodies, Article 76: "The General Chamber of Audit (Algemene Rekenkamer) shall be responsible for examining the states' revenues and expenditures."

Congress OF THE United States,

begun and held at the City of New-York, on
Wednesday, the fourth of March, one thousand seven hundred and eighty nine.

THE Conventions of a number of the States having, at the time of their adopting the Constitution, expressed a desire, in order to prevent misconstruction or abuse of its powers, that further declaratory and restrictive clauses should be added: And as extending the ground of public confidence in the Government, will best ensure the beneficent ends of its institution.

RESOLVED, by the Senate and House of Representatives of the United States of America in Congress assembled, two thirds of both Houses concurring, That the following Articles be proposed to the Legislatures of the several States, as Amendments to the Constitution of the United States; all, or any of which articles, when ratified by three fourths of the said Legislatures, to be valid to all intents and purposes, as part of the said Constitution; viz.

ARTICLES in addition to, and Amendment of the Constitution of the United States of America, proposed by Congress, and ratified by the Legislatures of the several States, pursuant to the fifth Article of the original Constitution.

Article the first.... After the first enumeration required by the first Article of the Constitution, there shall be one Representative for every thirty thousand, until the number shall amount to one hundred, after which, the proportion shall be so regulated by Congress, that there shall be not less than one hundred Representatives, nor less than one Representative for every forty thousand persons, until the number of Representatives shall amount to two hundred, after which the proportion shall be so regulated by Congress, that there shall not be less than two hundred Representatives, nor more than one Representative for every fifty thousand persons.

Article the second.... No law, varying the compensation for the services of the Senators and Representatives, shall take effect, until an election of Representatives shall have intervened.

Article the third.... Congress shall make no law respecting an establishment of religion, or prohibiting the free exercise thereof; or abridging the freedom of speech, or of the press; or the right of the people peaceably to assemble, and to petition the Government for a redress of grievances.

Article the fourth.... A well regulated Militia, being necessary to the security of a free State, the right of the people to keep and bear Arms, shall not be infringed.

Article the fifth.... No Soldier shall, in time of peace be quartered in any house, without the consent of the owner, nor in time of war, but in a manner to be prescribed by law.

Article the sixth.... The right of the people to be secure in their persons, houses, papers, and effects, against unreasonable searches and seizures, shall not be violated, and no Warrants shall issue, but upon probable cause, supported by oath or affirmation, and particularly describing the place to be searched, and the persons or things to be seized.

Article the seventh.... No person shall be held to answer for a capital, or otherwise infamous crime, unless on a presentment or indictment of a grand jury, except in cases arising in the land or naval forces, or in the Militia, when in actual service in time of War or public danger; nor shall any person be subject for the same offence to be twice put in jeopardy of life or limb; nor shall be compelled in any criminal case, to be a witness against himself, nor be deprived of life, liberty, or property, without due process of law; nor shall private property be taken for public use without just compensation.

Article the eighth.... In all criminal prosecutions, the accused shall enjoy the right to a speedy and public trial by an impartial jury of the State and district wherein the crime shall have been committed, which district shall have been previously ascertained by law, and to be informed of the nature and cause of the accusation; to be confronted with the witnesses against him; to have compulsory process for obtaining witnesses in his favor, and to have the assistance of counsel for his defence.

Article the ninth.... In suits at common law, where the value in controversy shall exceed twenty dollars, the right of trial by jury shall be preserved, and no fact, tried by a jury, shall be otherwise re-examined in any Court of the United States, than according to the rules of the common law.

Article the tenth.... Excessive bail shall not be required, nor excessive fines imposed, nor cruel and unusual punishments inflicted.

Article the eleventh.... The enumeration in the Constitution, of certain rights, shall not be construed to deny or disparage others retained by the people.

Article the twelfth.... The powers not delegated to the United States by the Constitution, nor prohibited by it to the States, are reserved to the States respectively, or to the people.

Frederick Augustus Muhlenberg Speaker of the House of Representatives.

ATTEST,

John Adams, Vice-President of the United States, and President of the Senate.

John Beckley, Clerk of the House of Representatives.

Sam. A. Otis Secretary of the Senate.

B

Ballot

In some constitutions balloting includes any act of voting, whether for government officials or for legislative proposals. A ballot—from the Italian *ballota* (a round bullet or ball used to choose or draw lots)—is a ticket or piece of paper used to vote in secret. England's Ballot Act of 1872 instituted voting by secret ballot in parliamentary elections. Since 1888 all U.S. states have used the Australian secret ballot—a ballot prepared, distributed, and counted by government officials at public expense—so called because election reform instituting the secret ballot was first successful in the British colony of South Australia. Today all democratic governments use the secret ballot in general elections. Voting machines are a form of mechanical balloting.

Constitution of the United States of America (1789), Amendment XII (1804): "The Electors shall meet in their respective states and vote by ballot for President and Vice-President . . . they shall name in their ballots the person voted for as President, and in distinct ballots the person voted for as Vice-President. . . ."

Constitution of France (1958), Title II, The President of the Republic, Article 7: "The president of the republic shall be elected by an absolute majority of the votes cast. If this is not obtained on the first ballot, there shall be a second ballot on the second Sunday following. Only the two candidates who have received the greatest number of votes on the first ballot shall present themselves. . . ."

Bankruptcy

Originally a bankrupt was a trader who had defrauded creditors; today the term refers to an individual or business whose debts exceed assets and the ability to make timely payments on the debt. Bankruptcy laws provide these individuals and businesses a discharge by a court from such debts; nonexempt assets of the bankrupt are used to pay creditors in the order of priority determined by law. The bankruptcy laws, therefore, allow individuals and businesses to make a fresh start.

In the United Kingdom a person who has legally been adjudged a bankrupt, however, is disqualified from being elected to or holding a seat in Parliament. The constitutions of other countries also disqualify persons who are bankrupt or insolvent from holding certain offices.

According to James Madison in essay 42 of *The Federalist* (1788), a compilation of essays urging the adoption of the U.S. Constitution, "The power of establishing uniform laws of bankruptcy is so intimately connected with the regulation of commerce, and will prevent so many frauds

The U.S. Bill of Rights (1791), consisting of the first ten amendments to the Constitution, guarantees individual liberties such as freedom of speech, religion, assembly, and the press and the right to be secure against unreasonable searches and seizures.

where the parties or their property may lie or be removed into different states, that the expediency of it seems not likely to be drawn into question." Some constitutions of other federal nation-states specifically refer to bankruptcy laws as an area of authority for the national government.

Constitution of Bangladesh (1972), Part V, The Legislature, Chapter 1, Parliament, Article 66: "(1) A person shall, subject to the provisions of clause (2), be qualified for election as, and to be, a member of parliament if he is a citizen of Bangladesh and has attained the age of twenty-five years. (2) A person shall be disqualified for election as, or for being, a member of parliament who (a) is declared by a competent court to be of unsound mind; (b) is an undischarged insolvent [bankrupt]. . . ."

Constitution of Switzerland (1874), Chapter I, General Provisions, Article 64: "1. The confederation is entitled to legislate . . . on suits for debts and bankruptcy. . . ."

Basic Law

A nation-state's constitution and constitutional laws are its basic laws—the laws from which all other laws are derived and which determine the legality of other laws and actions. A basic law is thus a fundamental and supreme law that prescribes how a nation is to be governed. It is a supreme organic law.

Germany's constitution is an example of a written constitution that is called a basic law *(Grundgesetz für die Bundesrepublik Deutschland).* As indicated in the preamble, this phrase was carefully chosen in 1949 to indicate that the Federal Republic of Germany (West Germany) considered the constitution to be provisional or preliminary, in view of the post–World War II division of Germany into eastern and western sections and the anticipated reunification, which occurred in 1990. The document, therefore, was aimed at "preserving the national and political unity of the constituent *Länder,* or states" and "giving a new order to political life for a transitional period." After the unification treaty of August 31, 1990, which reunited the former German Democratic Republic (East Germany) and West Germany, the provisional nature of this constitution ceased.

Israel's unwritten constitution contains legislative enactments of constitutional status called basic laws. Certain decrees by the ruling monarch of the preconstitutional nation-state of Saudi Arabia are also called basic laws or a basic system of rules.

Constitution of Germany (1949), Basic Law for the Federal Republic of Germany of May 23, 1949, Preamble (amended in 1990): "The Germans in [all] the *Länder* . . . have achieved the unity and freedom of Germany in free self-determination. This Basic Law is thus valid for the entire German people."

Basic Law of Government of Saudi Arabia (1992), Article 83: "This law may be amended only in the same manner in which it has been approved [by royal decree of the king]."

Der Parlamentarische Rat hat das vorstehende Grundgesetz für die Bundesrepublik Deutschland in öffentlicher Sitzung am 8. Mai des Jahres Eintausendneunhundertneunundvierzig mit dreiundfünfzig gegen zwölf Stimmen beschlossen. Zu Urkunde dessen haben sämtliche Mitglieder des Parlamentarischen Rates die vorliegende Urschrift des Grundgesetzes eigenhändig unterzeichnet.

BONN AM RHEIN, den 23. Mai des Jahres Eintausendneunhundertneunundvierzig.

Konrad Adenauer

PRÄSIDENT DES PARLAMENTARISCHEN RATES

Adolph Schönfelder

I. VIZEPRÄSIDENT DES PARLAMENTARISCHEN RATES

Hermann Schäfer

II. VIZEPRÄSIDENT DES PARLAMENTARISCHEN RATES

The 1949 German constitution is known as *Grundgesetz* (basic law) and was signed by Konrad Adenauer, who served as chancellor (prime minister) from 1949 to 1963.

Ben-Gurion, David

David Ben-Gurion (1886–1973) set Israel on the path to a traditional unwritten constitution, which is unusual considering the modern age in which he lived.

Ben-Gurion was born David Yosef Gruen in Plonsk, about forty miles from Warsaw, Poland, in 1886. He was only eleven years old when he became a follower of Theodor Herzl and Zionism, the movement for a Jewish homeland in Palestine. As a student in Warsaw in 1905, he was an active member of Poalei Zion (Workers of Zion), an organization that synthesized Zionism and Russian socialism. In 1906, together with other "pioneers," he went to Palestine, a territory in the Middle East later placed under a British mandate by the League of Nations.

There Ben-Gurion founded the first united Labor Zionist Party in 1919, and in 1920 he established the General Federation of Laborers in the Land of Israel (Histadrut). This latter group formed a tightly controlled autonomous Jewish economy within Palestine. As secretary general of Histadrut, Ben-Gurion oversaw the economic and military development in the Yishuv, the Jewish community in Palestine.

The issue of Israel's autonomy was superseded by the events of World War II. Action by the General Assembly of the United Nations, backed by both the United States and the Soviet Union but opposed by the League of Arab States, set the stage for a declaration of independence on May 14, 1948, that proclaimed the establishment of the sovereign state of Israel and the termination of the British mandate.

The declaration called for an elected constituent assembly to draft a constitution for the new nation-state; however, the assembly opted to set aside work on such a document and reconstitute itself into a legislative assembly, the Knesset. Ben-Gurion, who became the first prime minister of Israel in 1948, led the opposition to a written constitution. In a classic speech he successfully urged that basic laws for governing the country be enacted in piecemeal fashion. He declared that a written constitution was needed only to weld together a federation or establish a republic; because Israel was not a federation and had always been republican, no written constitution was necessary.

An unwritten constitution was adopted for other reasons as well. The religious and secular factions clashed over separation of religion from the state, a situation that a written constitution would undoubtedly have exacerbated. Some members of the assembly believed that there should be input from the many immigrants who would be coming to Israel. Others believed that a constitution should evolve over time, as in the United Kingdom. When the constituent assembly transformed itself into a legislative body, its constitutional authority to enact supreme laws continued because any basic or constitutional law could be enacted or amended by an absolute majority of the members of the Israeli parliament.

Ben-Gurion died in Tel Aviv on December 1, 1973, having left his indelible mark on Israel's constitutional process.

David Ben-Gurion (shown with Richard M. Nixon) successfully fought for an unwritten constitution for Israel consisting of basic laws passed by the parliament over many years.

Bicameral Legislature

Both Aristotle and the second-century Greek historian Polybius argued that the best governments consist of a mix of democracy and oligarchy, a goal served by bicameral legislatures. The eighteenth-century English jurist and philosopher Jeremy Bentham is credited with first applying the term *bicameral*—from the Latin *camera* (a vault or chamber)—to a legislature consisting of two houses or chambers.

In 1787 the United States became the first nation to design a national legislature with two distinct and separate legislative chambers—the Senate and House of Representatives—both of which had to agree on the same legislation before it could be enacted into law. Members of the lower House of Representatives are elected directly on the basis of population every two years, which reflects the framers' desire for a popular representative democracy. Membership in the Senate, including two senators elected from each state for six-year terms, was designed to provide some form of parity to the semisovereign constituent states, a compromise necessitated by the federal nature of the United States. The Senate was also to provide a more stable legislative body that could act as a check on the popular, but perhaps rash, legislative passions of the more representative lower house.

A majority of the legislatures of the world's major countries are bicameral. The British Parliament has evolved over the centuries so that it is now bicameral in name only, its lower House of Commons serving as the supreme legislative body. Denmark and New Zealand have changed from bicameral to unicameral parliaments, and Iceland and Norway have semibicameral legislatures, meaning that the legislature is elected together as one body and then divides itself into upper and lower chambers.

Constitution of Japan (1889, significantly revised in 1947), Chapter IV, The Diet, Article 42: "The Diet shall consist of two houses, namely the house of representatives and the house of councillors."

Constitution of Russia (1993), Part One Chapter 5, The Federal Assembly, Article 95: "1. The federal assembly shall consist of two houses—a federal council and a state Duma."

Bill

The primary constitutional meaning of the word *bill* is a draft of an act that has been introduced into a legislature but not yet enacted into law. Proposed legislation is often captioned "A bill for an act. . . . "

Most bills are public bills—they affect the general public—but some legislatures, including the U.S. Congress, permit private bills, which affect only certain persons or entities. Constitutions often provide special procedures for bills that involve public funds, called money bills, and for bills for laws that supplement or amend the constitution. They also often set forth procedures for introducing a bill and turning a bill into an act or a law.

I

102D CONGRESS
1ST SESSION

H. R. 1688

Entitled the "Omnibus Insular Areas Act of 1991".

IN THE HOUSE OF REPRESENTATIVES

APRIL 10, 1991

Mr. DE LUGO (for himself, Mr. FUSTER, Mr. FALEOMAVAEGA, Mr. LAGOMARSINO, Mr. BLAZ, Mr. UDALL, Mr. MILLER of California, Mr. MURPHY, Mr. VENTO, Mr. LEHMAN of California, Mr. RICHARDSON, Mr. DARDEN, Mr. OWENS of Utah, Mr. LEWIS of Georgia, Mr. DEFAZIO, Mr. JONTZ, Mr. YOUNG of Alaska, and Mr. GALLEGLY) introduced the following bill; which was referred to the Committee on Interior and Insular Affairs

A BILL

Entitled the "Omnibus Insular Areas Act of 1991".

1 *Be it enacted by the Senate and House of Representa-*
2 *tives of the United States of America in Congress assembled,*
3 That this Act may be cited as the "Omnibus Insular Areas
4 Act of 1991".
5 **TITLE I—INSULAR AREAS DISASTER**
6 **SURVIVAL AND RECOVERY ACT OF 1991**
7 **SECTION 101. SHORT TITLE.**
8 This title may be cited as "The Insular Areas Disas-
9 ter Survival and Recovery Act of 1991".

A bill is the official form in which draft legislation is introduced for consideration by a legislature.

Other constitutional meanings for the term *bill* include a list of individual rights or guarantees, such as a bill of rights; extrajudicial punishments, such as a bill of attainder or a bill of pains and penalties; government bills sponsored usually by the executive branch; and proposed legislation that would affect the general public introduced in parliaments by members rather than by the government.

In English law a criminal indictment is also called a bill.

Constitution of Mexico (1917), Title II, Chapter II, Section II, Introduction and Enactment of Laws, Article 71: "The bills submitted by the president of the republic, by the legislatures of the states, or by deputations thereof shall consequently be referred to committee. Those which are introduced by deputies or senators shall be subject to the procedures prescribed in Rules of Debate."

Constitution of Nepal (1990), Part 9, Legislative Procedure, Article 71(3): "Except for the money bills, if his majesty is of the opinion that any bill needs further deliberation, he may send it back with his message to the house of origin within one month from the date of submission."

Constitution of Portugal (1976), Part III, Organization of Political Power, Section III, Assembly of the Republic, Chapter II, Powers, Article 171, Discussion and Voting: "1. Discussion of bills shall include two readings."

Bill of Attainder. *See* Attainder, Bill of

Bill of Rights

The best-known bill of rights is the first ten amendments to the U.S. Constitution, ratified in 1791, which include the fundamental rights of individuals guaranteed by the nation. Other early declarations setting forth natural rights of citizens to be guaranteed or protected by the state include the 1776 constitution of the British colony of Virginia and France's 1789 Declaration of the Rights of Man and of the Citizen.

A bill of rights enacted by England's Convention Parliament in 1689 was based on the Declaration of Right of 1688, which William of Orange accepted in return for the English Crown. It was a declaratory document and did not introduce new rights and freedoms for individuals. Like the Petition of Right of 1627, it protected the rights of English subjects from infringement only by the monarch, not by other government bodies such as Parliament.

The 1791 U.S. Bill of Rights, however, was unique for its time in that it provided guarantees for both individual citizens and the constituent states of the federal United States against infringement by any institution or agency of the national government.

Some countries, including the United Kingdom and Australia, have considered adopting a bill of rights similar to that of the United States, as Canada did in 1982, but have not yet done so. Merely listing rights in a constitutional document, however, is no guarantee that they will be vigorously protected by the government.

Constitution of Russia (1993), Part One, Chapter 2, Human and Civil Rights and Freedoms, Article 17: "1. Within the Russian Federation human rights and civil rights shall be recognized and guaranteed under universally acknowledged principles and rules of international law in accordance with this constitution. 2. Basic human rights and freedoms are inalienable and belong to each person from birth. 3. The exercise of human and civil rights and freedoms may not infringe on the rights and freedoms of other persons."

Constitution of China (People's Republic of China) (1982), Chapter Two, The Fundamental Rights and Duties of Citizens, Article 35: "Citizens of the People's Republic of China enjoy freedom of speech, of the press, of assembly, of association, of procession, and of demonstration."

Bodin, Jean

The works of the sixteenth-century Frenchman Jean Bodin (1530–96) bridged the gap between the Renaissance Italian political theorist Niccolò Machiavelli and the seventeenth-century English philosopher Thomas Hobbes and have greatly influenced the development of the modern nation-state.

Bodin was born in 1530 in France, probably in Anjou,

into a Catholic family. At an early age he began his studies with the Carmelite friars of Angers at their school in Paris. Later he studied in Toulouse, a town influenced by the Renaissance, and became a member of the law faculty there. Strife between Catholics and the Protestant Huguenots led him to ally himself with the Catholic Politiques, who argued for toleration to maintain the integrity of the French state. Bodin became their best-known theorist, advocating a strong government to protect citizens and property in his major work, *The Six Books of the Republic* (1576). In it he posited that "all the force of civil laws and custom lies in the power of the sovereign prince."

A writer on law and politics as well as history and religion, Bodin became known internationally. He was befriended by Henry III of France, who reigned from 1574 to 1581, and he represented the French government on trips to England and Belgium.

In the spirit of the Renaissance, Bodin expounded a theory of absolute sovereignty based on Roman law and the French monarchy. He defined sovereignty as "the absolute and perpetual power of a republic, that is to say the active form and personification of the great body of a modern state." A state, according to Bodin, could be a monarchy if sovereign power resided in one person, an aristocracy if power resided in a minority, and a democracy if power resided in a majority.

Although a proponent of a strong monarchical government, Bodin espoused constitutional limitations on the monarch's power. A member of the French bourgeoisie and the third estate of the Estates-Général, the preparliamentary French assembly of the clergy, nobles, and middle class, he declared that the monarch had to be legitimate (acquiring the throne by royal descent or lawful conquest), obey the laws of God and nature, and honor contracts with his subjects and other rulers. Furthermore, the monarch could not raise taxes without the consent of the Estates-Général or change the fundamental laws of the realm regarding royal succession and the public domain. Bodin believed in the rule of law as it was derived from constitutional, natural, and divine law, contending that even the monarch could not take private property without due process of law.

Bodin's works were neglected after the mid-seventeenth century, but his contributions to political thought and early constitutionalism were restored in 1853 through Henri Baudrillart's book *Jean Bodin and His Times.*

Jean Bodin's theory of absolute sovereignty influenced the development of the modern nation-state.

The democratic constitutions of many South American countries resulted from the courage and vision of Simón Bolívar.

Bolívar Palacios, Simón

More than any other individual, Simón Bolívar Palacios (1783–1830), known as "The Liberator," fought for freedom and constitutionalism in nineteenth-century South America.

Born in Caracas in 1783 into the Venezuelan Creole aristocracy, Bolívar was orphaned at the age of nine, but he inherited one of the largest fortunes in Spanish colonial America. While enjoying the privileges of his class, he used his vast fortune and even greater leadership qualities to liberate much of South America from Spain.

An admirer of Napoleon, Bolívar studied military strategy, a crucial skill in Venezuela following the French emperor's overthrow of the Spanish monarchy in 1810. Sent to England by Venezuelan revolutionaries to bring back General Francisco de Miranda, a Venezuelan leader on a mission to get support for the revolutionary cause, Bolívar returned only to inexplicably hand him over to the Spanish forces in his native country. Venezuela declared its independence on July 5, 1811, and a short-lived republic was established under the country's first constitution.

Bolívar, now the leader of the revolution, launched a successful "war to the death" and in 1814 was given full dictatorial powers by the Venezuelan popular assembly. He was made president in 1819 under a new constitution. Unlike George Washington in the earlier American Revolution to the north, however, Bolívar had personal ideas regarding how constitutions should be written and made his influence felt as he went about liberating Spanish colonies and forging new nations—Venezuela, Colombia, Ecuador, Peru, and Bolivia. He also tried to unite these countries in a grand federation.

Bolívar's efforts at creating constitutions, most notably the 1819 Colombian constitution and the 1825 Bolivian constitution, failed. A student of Montesquieu and Jean-Jacques Rousseau, he also admired the British monarchy and wanted to unite the stability of a hereditary monarch with the ideals of a republic. He claimed to seek not the best government but the one most likely to succeed. Recognizing the need to educate the masses in democracy and civic participation, he proposed for Colombia a chamber of censors to watch over the nation's youth and mete out punishment for violations of the constitution and public decency; his proposal was rejected.

Bolívar died on December 17, 1830. His legacy is acknowledged in the preamble of Venezuela's 1961 constitution: "The Congress of the Republic of Venezuela . . . with the aim of . . . preserving and increasing the moral and historical patrimony of the nation, forged by the people in their struggles for freedom and justice, and by the thoughts and deeds of the great servants of their country, whose highest expression is Simón Bolívar, The Liberator, decrees the following constitution."

Borrowing Power

In *The Politics,* Aristotle describes a state where revenues are mismanaged: there is no money in the treasury to prosecute great wars, and the citizens are unwilling to pay taxes. A likely solution to such a state's financial problems would be to borrow money, either from its own citizens or from sources outside the state.

Many constitutions today specifically grant to the national government, usually the legislative branch, the

Thomas Nast's 1876 cartoon depicts the American eagle trying to establish its good credit with the British lion.

power to borrow money or assume liabilities on behalf of the national government; some place restrictions on the procedures for such borrowing, however. Borrowing power implies that the resources of the particular nation-state are available to guarantee or, if necessary, pay off the indebtedness to be incurred. Often, however, countries borrow too heavily and are not able to pay their debts.

The U.S. Constitution in Article 1, Section 8, gives Congress the exclusive and unrestricted power to borrow money on the credit of the United States. Today the country is a debtor nation not only externally, having for many years purchased more goods and services from other countries than it has sold to them, but also internally, annually amassing huge budget deficits and piling up an enormous national debt. As long as a government is perceived as being able to manage its debts and make payments when due, however, excessive borrowing will not generally have a severe effect on its operations.

Constitution of Liberia (1986), Chapter V, The Legislature, Article 36: "The Legislature shall have power: . . . (d) to lay and collect taxes, imposts, excise, and other revenues, to borrow money. . . . (iii) no loans shall be raised by the government on behalf of the republic or guarantees given for any institution or authority otherwise than by or under the authority of legislative enactment. . . ."

Constitution of Israel, Basic Law: The State Economy (1975), Section 2: "Transactions in state property and the acquisition of rights and assumption of liabilities on behalf of the state shall be effected by a person empowered in that behalf by or under law."

Boundaries. *See* Admission of New States

Bribery

For Plato the only penalty for a public official found guilty of taking a bribe was death, and Aristotle criticized the Lacedaemonian (Spartan) constitution for requiring that certain officials be chosen from the whole population, stating in *The Politics* that some of them might be poor and therefore open to taking bribes. William Blackstone, the eighteenth-century English commentator on the common law, agreed that bribery is an offense against public justice; he commended Plato for his stand against it and took the Romans to task for allowing magistrates to receive small presents.

In criminal law, bribery applies to both the person giving and the public official receiving a gift that is intended to influence the official's behavior contrary to his or her duty. Elected officials, judges, other public officers, and even voters may be found guilty of bribery. Article 1, Section 4, of the U.S. Constitution (1789) expressly includes bribery along with treason, high crimes, and misdemeanors as grounds for impeachment and removal from office on conviction.

Constitution of Liberia (1986), Chapter VI, The Executive, Article 65: "The president and vice-president may be removed from office by impeachment for treason, bribery, and other felonies, violation of the constitution, or gross misconduct."

Constitution of Uganda, Simplified Draft (1992), Chapter 15, Inspectorate of Government (Government Overseer), Section 2: "The function of the inspectorate of government shall be set out by parliament and shall include the following: . . . to fight corruption and abuse of public office. . . ."

Budget

Derived from the French word *bougette,* a diminutive of *bouge* (a leather bag or wallet), a budget is a revenue and spending plan. Many constitutions establish procedures for the development, approval, and execution of a national budget—usually submitted on behalf of the executive branch to the legislature for its approval—as well as for accounting for expenditures in accordance with the approved budget.

Although the term *budget* does not occur in the U.S. Constitution (1789), the Budget and Accounting Act of 1921 makes the president responsible for formulating the national budget and submitting it to Congress as a request for the appropriation of funds to be expended. In the United Kingdom the estimate of national revenues and expenditures is given annually to Parliament by the chancellor of the exchequer.

Reacting to allegations of bribery and corruption in the Italian government, taxpayers demonstrating in 1993 use an effigy of a political leader to dramatize their point that such practices weaken the foundations of representative democracy.

The legislature, which according to many constitutions has the formal authority to tax the citizens and appropriate public funds, may generally change a budget that has been submitted. The typical legislative cycle begins with the submission of a budget and extends through approval of appropriations by the legislature, obligation of funds, expenditure, and finally accounting for the expenditures.

Budget or money bills are often treated differently from other legislative measures. In Finland, for example, the parliament's determination on the state budget is made in only one reading and is therefore not considered a law in the same sense as other enacted laws, whereas budget appropriation acts in countries such as the United States are considered the same as enacted laws.

Constitution of Peru (1993), Section III, Chapter IV, Concerning the Tax and Budget System, Article 78: "The president will send the proposed budget to congress by 30 August of each year. On that same date he will also send the debt and financial balancing bills. The proposed budget must be effectively balanced."

Constitution of Jordan (1952), Chapter Seven, Financial Matters, Article 112: "(i) The draft law covering the general budget shall be submitted to the national assembly for consideration in accordance with the provisions of the constitution at least one month before the beginning of the financial year. (ii) Voting with respect to the budget shall take place on each chapter separately."

C

Cabinet

The cabinet under a parliamentary government, sometimes known as the council of ministers, differs in many important respects from the cabinet under a nonparliamentary system, and some hybrid forms exist.

The parliamentary cabinet evolved in England from the monarch's privy council, which often met in the monarch's cabinet, or private room. After the restoration of the British monarchy in 1688, the monarch's most trusted advisers from the privy council would meet as a committee to make decisions before the full council met. During the reign of Queen Anne (1702–14), this smaller decision-making body became the true executive power of government, while the privy council continued in name only.

In a parliamentary system of government, such as in the United Kingdom, the cabinet is synonymous with the government itself, meaning the executive officials or ministers chosen by the current ruling majority in the lower house of the parliament. This type of cabinet consists of the prime minister as the presiding officer and the heads of the functional ministries—for example, the foreign secretary, home secretary, and chancellor of the exchequer. These ministers are selected by the prime minister with the approval of the majority in the parliament and formally accepted by the monarch or a surrogate, such as a governor-general in certain former dominions of the United Kingdom or a president in parliamentary republics.

In a true presidential system of government, such as in the United States, as opposed to a presidential-style parliamentary system, such as in France, the cabinet consists of the executive heads of departments, which are similar to ministries, and other top officials selected by the president. They may have to be approved by the legislature or one of its subdivisions. These cabinet members are primarily advisers to the president who also execute his or her policies and programs in accordance with the law.

In both systems, however, selection of cabinet members often involves overriding political considerations. But generally only in parliamentary systems, where the cabinet is really a committee of the current majority party or parties in the popularly elected house of the parliament, do cabinet members have their own constituencies and participate with the prime minister in setting government policy. In this regard the members of a parliamentary cabinet are far more powerful individually and collectively than cabinet members in a presidential system.

Because the United Kingdom has an unwritten constitution and a parliament with supreme constitutional power, the guidelines for the powers and functions of its cabinet, as well as the cabinets of some of its former dominions, such as Canada and New Zealand, are not legally defined or enforceable but are a matter of custom and tradition. The U.S. Constitution (1789), although a single written document, does not mention a cabinet

English common law—law resulting from the decisions of judges—was systematized by William Blackstone in his *Commentaries on the Laws of England* (1755–65), which influenced the constitutions of many countries, particularly the United States.

Cabinet members Henry Kissinger, secretary of state, and James Schlesinger, secretary of defense, flank U.S. President Gerald Ford in 1975. Unlike many prime ministers, the U.S. president does not need the cabinet's approval for his actions and policies.

either; it provides only that the president may require the advice of such heads of departments as Congress creates.

Constitution of Israel, Basic Law: The Government (1968): "4. The government [cabinet] is responsible to the Knesset [parliament]. 5.(a) The government consists of the prime minister and other ministers. . . . "

Constitution of Honduras (1982), Title V, Branches of the Government, Chapter VI, The Executive Branch, Article 245: "The president of the republic shall be responsible for the general administration of the state; his powers and duties are as follows: . . . (5) To freely appoint and dismiss secretaries and deputy secretaries of the cabinet and other officials and employees whose appointment is not assigned to other authorities. . . . "

Constitution of Kenya (1963), Chapter II, The Executive, Part 2, Ministers and Cabinet, Section 16: "(1) There shall be such offices of ministers of the government [cabinet] of Kenya as may be established by parliament or, subject to any provisions made by parliament, by the president. (2) The president shall appoint the ministers from among the members of the national assembly. . . . "

Calendar. *See* Agenda

Capital City

A capital city—from the Latin *caput* (head)—is the seat of the government, housing the head of the executive branch and also generally the legislature and the highest level of the judiciary. Its location and nature are dealt with in a number of constitutions.

The offices of the highest officials of all three branches of government are usually located in the capital, although in South Africa, Switzerland, and some other countries these officials are dispersed among several cities.

Capital cities such as Ottawa, Canada, generally house the principal offices of the national government's executive, legislative, and judicial branches. Many world-famous cities such as Jerusalem, Rome, Paris, and Tokyo are national capitals.

Constitution of Belgium (1831), Heading VI, General Clauses, Article 126: "The city of Brussels is the capital of Belgium and the seat of the government."

Constitution of Hungary (1949, significantly revised in 1989), Chapter XIV, Capital City and National Symbols of the Republic of Hungary, Article 74: "The capital city of Hungary shall be Budapest."

Capital Punishment. *See* Death Penalty

Capitalism

Modern capitalism began in the thirteenth-century Italian states with international traders and financiers who pursued profit for the sake of accumulating wealth. Derived from the French word *capital* (principal and reimbursement of principal, as well as stock, as in capital stock ownership), the word *capitalism* generally does not appear in constitutions. However, the right of individuals to own private property or engage in private enterprise—principles that form the foundations of capitalism—are often expressly stated.

As the basis of the private-enterprise economic system, capitalism has indirectly influenced many current national constitutions. Through its constitution Singapore, for example, has created a well-ordered political system in which private capitalists can feel at home. Chile, after many years of economic hardship and an attempt at a Marxist regime, turned for inspiration to the constitutions of Singapore and Switzerland, which emphasize order and as little interference as possible with the fruits of labor and business.

Communism, the opposite of capitalism, emphasizes state ownership of property used to produce goods and services in a society and state management of the economy rather than a free-market economy. In recent years a number of Eastern European countries that were dominated by the Communist Party have converted to a multiparty political system and a more capitalistic economic system. All national economies are to some extent mixed economies—that is, they contain some elements of a state-managed economy and some elements of a free-market economy.

Constitution of Chile (1980), Chapter III, Constitutional Rights and Obligations, Article 19: "The constitution guarantees to all persons: . . . 21. The right to develop any economic activity which is not contrary to morals, public order, or national security, abiding by legal norms which regulate it. . . . "

Constitution of Mozambique (1990), Part I, Basic Principles, Chapter IV, Economic and Social Organization, Article 41: "The economic order of the Republic of Mozambique shall be based on the value of labor, on market forces, on the initiatives of economic agents, on the participation of all types of ownership, and on the role of the state in regulating and promoting economic and social growth and development in order to satisfy the basic needs of the people and to promote social well-being."

Cassation, Court of

The right to appeal a decision by an inferior court or magistrate has existed since at least the time of Solon, the Athenian lawgiver of the sixth century B.C. In many constitutions the highest court of appeal is called the supreme court. In France and countries whose legal systems have been significantly influenced by France, however, the highest court of appeal is called the court of cassation *(cour de cassation).*

Derived from the Latin word *cassation* and the French word *casser* (to quash, annul, or set aside a verdict or will), cassation is the power to reverse the force and validity of a court judgment.

Constitution of Haiti (1987), Title V, Chapter IV, The Judiciary, Article 173: "The judicial power shall be vested in the supreme court *(cour de cassation)*. . . . "

Constitution of Lebanon (1926), Chapter IV, The Executive Power, Article 60: "The function of the public prosecutor at the high court shall be exercised by a judge appointed annually by the supreme court *(cour de cassation)* at a general meeting."

Castro, Fidel Ruiz

Since 1959 Fidel Ruiz Castro (b. 1926) has dominated the political processes in Cuba, including the writing and interpretation of the country's constitution.

The son of an immigrant father from Galacia, Spain, Castro was born on his family's sugar plantation in Oriente province on August 13, 1926, and was educated at Jesuit schools in Oriente and Havana. One of his teachers observed that he liked to win in sports, regardless of his efforts, and that he seemed alienated from Cuban society.

Since leading Cuba's communist revolution in 1959, Fidel Castro has ruled first as prime minister and then as president.

After entering the University of Havana law school in 1945, Castro joined a group of political activists called the Unión Insurreccional Revolucionaria. Although ambitious, forceful, and a good speaker, he was defeated at student elections. Suspected of murdering a rival student leader, he was never charged with the crime. In 1947 he left the university to acquire hands-on experience in revolutionary tactics in Colombia. He returned to school and was graduated in 1950.

After leaving the practice of law for politics, Castro was arrested and jailed for leading an attack on a military barracks in Santiago de Cuba on July 26, 1953. Fulgencio Batista, a military strongman in Cuba before retiring to Florida, had recently returned to dictatorial power, and Castro's attack on the barracks was a protest against him. An amnesty in 1955 freed Fidel and his brother Raul, but they returned in 1956 to wage a guerrilla war that ended with Batista's overthrow on January 1, 1959.

The first Castro government was established pursuant to a fundamental law of the republic, a de facto constitution promulgated on February 7, 1959. It was not until October 22, 1974, that the leaders of the Cuban Communist Party and the executive committee of the government's council of ministers, both groups headed by Castro, took steps to create a constitution by setting up a constitutional drafting committee. The Communist Party leadership under Castro's direction supplied the committee with the basic outline for the document, and at the first Cuban Communist Party congress, on April 10, 1975, a central preparatory commission that included Raul and Fidel, the latter as presiding officer, was established to aid in the drafting process.

The constitution that emerged was approved by nearly ninety-eight percent of the voters in 1976 and went into effect on February 24 of that year. As might be expected, the document proclaims Cuba to be a socialist state and identifies the Communist Party as the "highest leading force of society and the state." The supreme organ of state power is a National Assembly of People's Power, which elects from among its members a council of state, whose president is the head of state and government. Fidel Castro has held this position continuously since its inception.

At the fourth Cuban Communist Party congress, in 1991, would-be reformers, including Raul Castro, were to propose changes to the constitution that would take away from the president the day-to-day management of the government while leaving his overall power intact. According to inside sources, Fidel would brook no diminution of his powers and quashed the plan.

Castro's despotism has isolated the Cuban people and driven the country's economy to the brink of disaster. The few cosmetic changes made to the 1976 document, which he finally approved in 1992, do nothing to establish a true constitutional democracy in Cuba.

Censorship. *See* Press; Speech

Censure

In ancient Rome the censor's mark by a person's name on the census list to indicate disreputable conduct would result in great social disgrace. Today an action taken by a legislature against one of its members or a member of the government for improper or disorderly behavior is known as censure—from the Latin and French words *censure* (censorship or reproof). The action can take the form of a vote of censure and can lead to a reprimand or expulsion of the guilty member.

In Article 1, Section 5, of the U.S. Constitution (1789), each house of Congress is authorized to punish its own members for disorderly behavior and, by a two-thirds vote, to expel a member.

In ecclesiastical law, censure is the spiritual punishment of a baptized member, resulting in withdrawal of the church's privileges or expulsion from the church community.

Constitution of Cambodia (1993), Chapter 7, National Assembly, Article 98: "The national assembly can dismiss a member of the cabinet or government from his/her position by the adoption of a motion of censure of two-thirds of all the members. A motion of censure shall be proposed to the national assembly by thirty members of the national assembly in order for the full assembly to decide."

Constitution of Panama (1972), Title V, The Legislative Branch of Government, Chapter 1, The Legislative Assembly, Article 155: "Administrative functions of the legislative assembly are the following: . . . To give votes of censure against ministers of state when they, in the opinion of the legislative assembly, are responsible for threatening or illegal acts, or for grave errors that are considered detrimental to the interests of the state. In order that the vote of censure may be in order, it must be proposed in writing six days before its debate, by no less than half the legislators and approved by the vote of two-thirds of the assembly."

Census

For taxation purposes Rome registered its citizens and their property in a process called a census. In English law the revenue of the Crown was historically known as the *census regalis.* A census now refers to an official counting of the people in a nation or political subdivision and may also include information on wealth, occupation, age, and education, among other items.

The constitutions of many countries require a regular census of the population as the basis for apportioning representation in the national legislature.

The requirement in constitutions for a regular census is based mainly on the need to apportion seats in one house or, more rarely, both houses of the legislature. A census has been taken every ten years since 1790 in the United States, since 1791 in France, and since 1801 in Britain.

Another use for census information is to apportion grants by the national government to states or political subdivisions, allocations that are often made on the basis of relative population. A regular census also aids in distribution of the tax burden.

Constitution of Liberia (1986), Chapter V, The Legislature, Article 41: "The legislature shall cause a census of the republic to be undertaken every ten years."

Constitution of Austria (1920), Chapter II, Federal Legislation, Article 26(2): "The number of deputies [in the Nationalrat, the lower house of the legislature] shall be divided among qualified voters of a constituency (electoral body) in proportion to the number of nationals in the constituencies, that is, the number of federal nationals who in accordance with the result of the last census had their domiciles in the constituencies. . . ."

Chamber. *See* House

Chancellor

In Latin a *cancellarius* was a court usher stationed *ad cancellos* (at the grating that separated the judges from the public). The term *chancellor* is now used in educational, clerical, and legal contexts to denote a high official.

In England the king's chancellor developed into the lord chancellor or lord high chancellor, the highest officer of the Crown and an important member of the cabinet. The United Kingdom's highest ranking judicial officer, he or she outranks all other nobility except for "princes of the blood" and the archbishop of Canterbury. In addition to presiding at debates in the House of Lords, the lord chancellor is the keeper of the Great Seal,

As chancellor of Prussia in the late nineteenth century, Otto von Bismarck chose "iron and blood" rather than constitutional processes to settle disputes.

is called "The Keeper of the King or Queen's Conscience," and is the guardian of all "infants, lunatics, and idiots." The highest financial officer under the prime minister in the United Kingdom is the chancellor of the exchequer.

Chancellor is also the title given to the chief minister in some European countries. In Germany it was awarded to the president of the federal council, which oversaw the imperial administration. France abolished this title after the French Revolution of 1789, but Austria and Germany have retained it to denote the prime minister or head of government; their head of state is called the president.

Constitution of Germany (1949), VI, The Federal Government: "Article 62. The federal government shall consist of the federal chancellor *(Bundeskanzler)* and the federal ministers. Article 63. (1) The federal chancellor shall be elected, without debate, by the Bundestag [lower house of parliament] upon the proposal of the president."

Constitution of Austria (1920), Chapter III, Federal Execution, A, Administration, 2, The Federal Government, Article 69: "(1) The federal chancellor, the vice chancellor, and the other federal ministers are entrusted with the highest administrative business of the *Bund* [federation] in so far as this is not assigned to the federal president. They constitute as a body the federal government under the chairmanship of the federal chancellor."

Checks and Balances

Although Aristotle found the strength of a democracy in its mixture of social and economic classes, Polybius, a Greek historian of the second century B.C., saw the force of the Roman "mixed" constitution (as he called it) in its blend of monarchy, aristocracy, and democracy, which acted as checks and balances that kept the system from going too far in one direction. The authors of the U.S. Constitution (1789) knew of Polybius, and Alexander Hamilton writes in essay 9 of *The Federalist* (1788): "The efficacy of various principles is now well understood, which were either not known, or imperfectly known to the ancients. The regular distribution of power into distinct departments; the introduction of legislative balances and checks. . . . "

Checks and balances is an inelegant name for the principle of constitutional government that calls for the separation of the executive, legislative, and judicial functions into coequal branches. To balance and check the excessive use of power by any other branch, each branch has powers to negate the actions of the others. Such checks and balances may also be found within a branch of government itself. Examples of checks and balances in the U.S. Constitution include the executive veto power over legislation, the confirmation of executive appointments by the Senate, and the power of the judiciary to declare enacted laws unconstitutional and void.

Constitution of Liberia (1986), Chapter I, Structure of the State, Article 3: "Consistent with the principles of checks and balances, no person holding office in one of these branches [legislative, executive, and judicial] shall hold office in or exercise any of the powers assigned to either of the other two branches. . . ."

Constitution of South Korea (1948), Chapter IV, The Executive, Part 1, The President, Article 82: "The acts of the president under law shall be executed in writing, and such documents shall be countersigned by the prime minister and the members of the state council concerned. The same shall apply to military affairs."

Constitution of Mexico (1917), Title III, Chapter IV, Judicial Power, Article 96: "Appointments of the justices of the supreme court shall be made by the president of the republic and submitted to the approval of the chamber of senators."

Chiang Kai-shek

Chiang Kai-shek (1887–1975) planted the seeds of constitutional democracy developed by Sun Yat-sen in Taiwan; however, the people of mainland China have yet to taste the fruits of a true constitutional democracy.

Chiang was born on October 30, 1887, the son of a salt merchant, in the Chinese province of Chekiang. Although at first he did not qualify for military training in Tokyo, he was able to study at the Paoting Military Academy in China. He continued his education at the Shikon Gakko Military Academy in Tokyo, where he joined the revolutionary party of the Chinese leader Sun Yat-sen.

When rebellion against the Chinese imperial government began in Wuhan on October 10, 1911, Chiang returned to fight with the successful revolutionaries. After participating in an aborted second revolution, he went back to Japan before undertaking missions to China for Sun. In 1923 Chiang became Sun's chief of staff, and in May 1924 he was made the commandant of the Whampoa Military Academy in China.

After Sun's death in 1925, Chiang vied to be his successor, reaffirming Sun's three principles of government: nationalism, democracy, and the well-being of the people. After being ousted from Sun's political party, the Kuomintang, by the leftists and communists, Chiang set up his own government in Nanking in 1927. Increased Japanese aggression thwarted his and his rivals' goal of

In the mid-twentieth century Chiang Kai-shek and his nationalist Chinese followers brought to Formosa, now Taiwan, the precepts of Sun Yat-sen's constitutional democracy.

heading a unified China. He was able, however, to persuade the committee working on a new constitutional government to adopt Sun's five-fold concept of the distribution of powers in the government, which would consist of five *yuans* (councils or branches), one each for executive, legislative, judicial, examination (civil service), and control (audit).

After the war the effort to create a constitution for China continued. With a 1936 draft document as a starting point, a conference held in 1946 began making changes to Sun's original plan for a government structure to make it more like a Western parliamentary system. Chiang was elected president under the new constitution in 1948, but again events precluded its full implementation. The Chinese communists, led by Mao Zedong, drove Chiang's nationalist government into exile on the island of Formosa, now called Taiwan, where the new constitution finally could be fully implemented.

Once on Taiwan, however, Chiang ruled virtually as a dictator under continuing martial law provisions. After his death on April 15, 1975, Taiwan, by a slow and steady process, moved out from under his shadow into the light of a true democratic government, with honestly contested elections. On July 15, 1987, martial law was finally terminated on Taiwan.

Chief. *See* Traditional Leader

Chief Executive

A chief executive is synonymous with a president under a constitution similar to the U.S. Constitution (1789), and in the United States this term is often used when referring to the president. The word *chief* is derived from the Middle English *chief* or *chef* and from the Old French and Latin Vulgar *capsum*, which in turn comes from the Latin *caput* (head).

A president is called the chief executive only when he or she is head of both state and government. In a parliamentary system, because the head of state (the monarch or president) shares the duties of a chief executive, even if only in a formal way, with the head of government (the prime minister), there is no true single chief executive.

Constitution of Venezuela (1961), Title VI, The National Executive Power, Chapter I, The President of the Republic, Article 181: "The executive power is exercised by the president of the republic and any other officials determined by this constitution and the laws. The president of the republic is the chief of state and of the national executive."

Constitution of the Philippines (1987), Article VII, Executive Department, Section 17: "The president shall have control of all the executive departments, bureaus, and offices. . . ."

Chief Justice

The Areopagos, the ancient Greek judicial council charged with guarding the laws, punishing offenders, and handling many important matters of state, was often presided over by the *basileis*, a principal magistrate concerned with religious matters. Almost all courts and court systems now have presiding judges who are also their chief administrative officials. The position may have varying degrees of responsibility and may carry other titles: chief judge, president, or first president of the court.

Since 1880 the presiding judge in the British king or queen's bench division of the High Court of Justice has been called the lord chief justice. He or she serves as the president of the High Court in the absence of the lord high chancellor and is an ex officio judge of the Court of Appeals.

The chief justice of the United States, in addition to having an equal vote with the other justices in deciding cases, is responsible for the administrative functioning of the Supreme Court, including assigning to other justices opinions to be written and handling personnel and budget matters. The position is a prestigious one, as the

Warren E. Burger, appointed by President Nixon, served as chief justice of the United States from 1969 to 1986.

chief justice is the head of one of the three coequal branches of the U.S. government. The Constitution (1789) requires the chief justice to preside over an impeachment trial of a president in the Senate, the only time the position of chief justice is mentioned in that document. Other constitutions, however, specifically create this position in the national judicial system.

Constitution of Australia (1901), Chapter III, The Judicature, Section 71: "The high court shall consist of a chief justice, and so many other justices, not less than two, as the parliament prescribes."

Constitution of Algeria (1976), Title II, The Organization of the Powers, Chapter III, The Judicial Power, Article 146: "It [the high council of the judiciary] monitors respect for the provisions of the statutes of the judiciary and the control of the discipline of the judges, under the chairmanship of the first president of the supreme court."

Constitution of India (1950), Part V, The Union, Chapter IV, The Union Judiciary, Article 124, Establishment and Constitution of Supreme Court: "(2) Every judge of the supreme court shall be appointed by the president . . . after consultation with such of the judges of the supreme court and [others] . . . : Provided that in the case of the appointment of a judge other than the chief justice, the chief justice of India shall be consulted. . . . "

Children

In *The Laws,* Plato prescribes walking for pregnant women to ensure development of healthy children. Aristotle continues the theme of child development in *The Politics*, saying that all the "motions"—that is, activities or exercises—to which a child can be subjected are useful. John Stuart Mill, in *On Liberty* (1859), restricts the doctrine of personal freedom to human beings over the age of maturity, excluding children because they are still being cared for by others.

Constitutions may contain provisions relating to young children, generally regarding their education or protection or restrictions on child labor. Children are also referred to in the context of the family and motherhood as well as nationality. Older constitutions tend not to include specific references to children, although new ones often do. The 1995 Ethiopian constitution contains five numbered paragraphs in Article 36 concerning the rights of children.

Constitution of Denmark (1953), Part VIII, Article 76: "All children of school age shall be entitled to free instruction in the elementary schools. Parents or guardians who themselves arrange for their children or wards receiving instruction equal to the general elementary school standard shall not be obliged to have their children or wards taught in an elementary school."

Constitution of Greece (1975), Part Two, Individual and Social Rights, Article 21: "2. Families with many children, disabled war and peace-time veterans, war victims,

Young children such as these Colombian brick haulers sometimes work long hours at hazardous tasks in spite of express constitutional prohibitions against child labor.

widows, and orphans, as well as persons suffering from incurable bodily or mental ailments are entitled to the special care of the state."

Constitution of Mozambique (1990), Part I, Basic Principles, Chapter II, Nationality, Article 18: "Mozambicans are the children of a Mozambican mother or father working for the Mozambican state outside the country, even if born abroad."

Citizen

Derived from the Middle English *citesien,* the word *citizen* can mean an inhabitant of a city or town possessing civic rights and privileges. In *The Politics,* Aristotle defines a citizen as one who shares in governing and being governed. In ancient Rome only a man could be a *civis* (citizen), and he had to be a member of a *familia* (family). Citizens had a status greater than freed slaves, while slaves themselves were considered property or things, rather than people. In the United States it was not until 1868, with the Fourteenth Amendment to the Constitution (1789), that all freed slaves became U.S. citizens.

Under constitutions citizens as individuals enjoy certain rights and franchises, while these same citizens as subjects are bound to obey the law. The citizens of the United Kingdom, for example, are subjects of the government, just as the ancestors of some were once subjects of English monarchs. Constitutions may make a distinction between the rights and duties of inhabitants and those of citizens, the latter generally having the right to vote and be elected to office.

Constitution of Italy (1948), Fundamental Principles, 3: "All citizens have the same social dignity and are equal before the law, without discrimination of sex, race, language, religion, political opinions, personal or social conditions."

Constitution of Canada, Constitution Act (1982), Part I, Canadian Charter of Rights and Freedoms: "Fundamental Freedoms, 2. Everyone has the following fundamental freedoms: . . . [list of freedoms]. Democratic Rights, 3. Every citizen of Canada has the right to vote in an election of members of the House of Commons or of a legislative assembly and to be qualified for membership therein."

Citizenship

In ancient Athens citizenship was not extended to resident aliens, women, or slaves. In ancient Rome *civitas* (citizenship) was somewhat expanded; at least under private law, a distinction developed between citizens who were free born and citizens who were freedmen. Freedmen suffered a number of disabilities under the law. Some rights of citizenship could be lost as a result of disreputable conduct.

Although often used as synonyms, citizenship and nationality are not identical terms. For example, only persons can be said to have citizenship; corporations and other legal entities can have the nationality of a country, but they are never citizens. Citizens are considered nationals of a particular nation-state, but certain classes of people have been defined as nationals, not citizens, and have only some of the rights and duties of citizens. Native Americans before 1924 and Filipinos before the independence of the Philippines in 1946 were nationals, not citizens of the United States.

In some countries citizenship is established by the place of a person's birth *(jus soli* citizenship); in other countries it flows from the citizenship of the parents *(jus sanguinis* citizenship). People born in a *jus soli* country of parents who are citizens of a *jus sanguinis* country may possess dual citizenship. Citizenship can also be lost or taken away by a nation. And, under certain conditions, such as refugees fleeing an oppressive state regime, some persons may, in fact, be stateless, or without citizenship, until they are able to acquire it by naturalization in a new country.

Today citizenship is the legal link between an individual and the political community of a nation-state. A number of modern constitutions define citizenship and its rights and obligations, and some prescribe how citizenship may be acquired or lost. In addition to entitling a person to certain rights, such as voting, it imposes certain obligations, such as serving in the military and paying taxes. A passport is evidence of citizenship when traveling abroad and entitles a citizen to certain services from his or her country's consular and diplomatic missions in a foreign country.

Constitution of Malaysia (1963), Part III, Citizenship, Chapter 3, Supplemental, Article 29, Commonwealth Citizenship: "(1) In accordance with the position of the Federation [of

Demonstrators march in 1963 to support the enactment of legislation guaranteeing enforcement of civil rights for all U.S. citizens. A Civil Rights Act was passed by Congress and signed into law by President Lyndon B. Johnson in 1964.

Malaysia] within the Commonwealth [British Commonwealth of Nations], every person who is a citizen of the Federation enjoys by virtue of that citizenship the status of a Commonwealth citizen in common with the citizens of other Commonwealth countries. . . ."

Constitution of Italy (1948), Part One, The Duties and Rights of the Citizen, Title I, Civil Relations, Article 22: "Nobody can be deprived of his capacity to contract, of his citizenship, or name because of political reasons."

Civil Liberties.

See Bill of Rights; Civil Rights

Civil Rights

In ancient Greece and Rome the rights of the individual were not as important as the rights of society and the state. Citizens there—a limited class, to be sure—had the right to participate in running the government, own property (including slaves), and travel and sometimes to obtain justice in private disputes and criminal prosecutions. For most of the world, however, the rights of individuals—apart from class, status, or force of arms—were unheard of. In feudal Europe the lords and nobles and the clergy had some rights, but the vast majority of vassals and serfs had only whatever rights were meted out to them by those higher up the pyramid of authority.

Civil rights is a relatively new concept, one based on a government's positive acts. Such rights flow from the equality of all citizens and include being able to fully participate in the democratic process—for example, by voting and standing for election. Civil rights differ from civil liberties, which are guarantees against government infringement of basic natural human rights as often expressed in a constitution's bill of rights.

International agreements, statutes, and constitutions all may protect people from arbitrary or discriminatory treatment by the government or other individuals. Together with political rights, equal rights, and rights of the accused, civil rights are catalogued in the Universal Declaration of Human Rights adopted by the United Nations on December 10, 1948. To erase the effects of slavery after the Civil War (1861–65), the Thirteenth and Fourteenth Amendments were added to the U.S. Constitution in 1865 and 1868, respectively. Some constitutions use the broad term *civil rights (Bürgerrechte* in German) to include general rights and freedoms.

Constitution of Belgium (1831), Heading III, Concerning the Authorities, Chapter III, Concerning the Judiciary Power, Article 92: "Contestations arising out of civil rights come under the exclusive jurisdiction of the law courts."

Constitution of Liberia (1986), Chapter III, Fundamental Rights, Article 14: "No religious denomination or sect shall have any exclusive privilege or preference over any other, but all shall be treated alike; and no religious test shall be required for any civil or military office or for the exercise of any civil right."

Civil Service

The name *civil service* was first applied to servants bound by agreement to work for the British East India Company who were not part of the army or navy services. An 1845 handbook on India mentioned hundreds of highly educated members of the civil service who assisted the British government of India.

Civil, derived from the Latin *civilis* (of the citizen or civic), refers to the general commonwealth of citizens. A government's civil, or public, functions usually include all those except the military.

Today most countries have a professional, merit-based civil service that administers government policy, laws, and regulations under the political leadership of elected and appointed officials. The British civil service is a career service whose heads of government divisions continue in office regardless of which party is in power or which parliamentary minister is in charge.

The U.S. Constitution (1789) provides that the president, the vice president, and all other civil officers of the United States can be removed only by impeachment for treason, bribery, and other high crimes and misdemeanors. More recent constitutions deal at some length with the operations of a civil service system, often a significant percentage of the national work force.

Constitution of the Philippines (1987), Article IX, Constitutional Commissions, B, The Civil Service Commission, Section 1(1): "The civil service shall be administered by the civil service commission composed of a chairman and two commissioners who shall be natural born citizens of the Philippines and, at the time of their appointment, at least thirty-five years of age, with proven capacity for public administration and must not have been candidates for any elective position in the elections immediately preceding their appointments."

Constitution of Taiwan (Republic of China) (1947), Amendment (1992), Article 14: "The examination *yuan* [branch of government] shall be the highest examination body of the state and shall be responsible for the following matters. . . . 1. All examination-related matters; 2. All matters relating to qualification screening, security of tenure, pecuniary aid in the case of death and retirement of civil servants; and 3. All matters relating to the employment, discharge, performance evaluation, scale of salaries, promotion, transfer, commendation, and award for civil servants."

Cloture

Most constitutions do not provide detailed instructions on parliamentary procedures to be followed by the legislature, allowing each house to determine its own rules; notable exceptions are Finland and Sweden. To close debate, general parliamentary rules usually require more than a majority vote so that free and complete discussion of issues will be encouraged. Cloture, also closure—a parliamentary device for stopping debate—was introduced in the British Parliament in 1882.

The U.S. Senate, however, observes a controversial rule regarding cloture that requires the approval of sixty of the one hundred members to close debate. This rule has helped sustain a number of filibusters, the continuous monopoly of the floor by one member in an effort to get those in the majority to change or withdraw a proposal.

Constitution of Finland, Parliament Act (1928), Chapter 5, Consideration of Matters in Plenary Sittings and in the Grand Committee, Section 77: "No matter under debate may be presented for decision before parliament, on the proposal of the speaker, has formally concluded the debate."

Constitution of Sweden, Riksdag Act (1974), Chapter 2, Meetings of the Legislature, Article 14, Supplementary Provision 2.14.1: "A member who wishes to speak in debate in the chamber should, if possible, notify the secretariat of the chamber not later than the day prior to the meeting at which the debate will begin. Such notice shall indicate how long the intervention is expected to last. A speech by a member who has failed to give advance notice may not exceed six minutes unless the speaker [of the Riksdag] considers that grounds exist for allowing an extension. The provisions . . . [above] shall not apply when a question is answered."

Coinage

"For [day-to-day commercial dealings], we agree, they must possess coinage, legal tender among themselves, but valueless to the rest of mankind," says Plato in *The Laws*. In constitutions coinage—originally, the action of striking coins—means the right to coin or make money and is often cited as one of the attributes of sovereignty. Many constitutions, especially those of federations, specifically authorize the national government to coin money and issue paper currency.

In England the authority to coin money was never permitted to even the greatest nobles. And Alexander Hamilton, in essay 30 of *The Federalist* (1788), notes: "A complete power, therefore, to procure a regular and adequate supply of revenue, as far as the resources of the community will permit, may be regarded as an indispensable ingredient in every constitution."

The Honduran currency is named for Lempira, the leader of an indigenous peoples' revolt against Spanish colonialists in 1537.

Constitution of Switzerland (1874), Chapter I, General Provisions, Article 38: "1. The confederation is entitled to exercise all rights pertaining to the state monopoly of coinage. 2. It alone has the right to coin money."

Constitution of Argentina (1853), Second Part, Authorities of the Nation, Title I, Federal Government, First Section, The Legislative Power, Chapter IV, Powers of Congress, Article 67: "The congress shall have power: . . . 10. To coin money, to regulate its value and that of foreign moneys, and to adopt a uniform system of weights and measures for the whole nation."

Coke, Edward

The early views of Sir Edward Coke (1552–1634) on judicial review influenced the English constitution and others that have followed, although his support for judicial independence against a king lost him his job.

Born at Mileham, in Norfolk, in 1552, Coke was educated at Norwich School and Trinity College, Cambridge University. At eighteen years of age he left Cambridge to study law and was called to the bar sooner than the average student. He quickly made a name for himself in the field of law. In 1592 he was appointed solicitor general to the queen, in 1593 he became the speaker of the House of Commons, and a year later he was appointed to the position of attorney general. He was chief justice of the common pleas court from 1606 to 1613, when he was removed to the king's bench.

Early in his career, Coke was a strong supporter of the royal prerogative, but under the Stuart monarchs he began a campaign against what he saw as the dangerous absolutism of the church and state. He asserted that the monarch had no authority to decide a law case by himself or herself, that a person could not be forced to incriminate himself or herself, and that acts of Parliament contrary to "common right and reason" could be overturned by judges. Although he later changed his mind on the latter point, his remarks influenced the development of judicial review in the United States nearly two centuries later.

By asserting the independence of the English judiciary in 1616, even against the monarch, Sir Edward Coke championed the constitutional concept of the separation of powers.

In 1616, when judges were asked by the king if they would obey King James I and stay a case in order to give the Crown an extrajudicial opinion, all of them agreed except Coke, who said that if such a case arose he would do "what was fit for a judge to do." A few months later, Francis Bacon, his long-time rival, persuaded the king to remove him from office.

In the 1620s Coke again became a dominant member of Parliament and contributed significantly to the passage of the Petition of Right in 1628, a key element of the constitution of England and the United Kingdom today. His legal writings included *The Reports* and *The Institutes of the Laws of England,* the first part of which was published in 1628.

Collective Security

Collective security arrangements—the pledging of mutual assistance in the case of external and internal aggression—are made to thwart the possibility of war by sovereign nation-states and rebellion by a nation's semisovereign political subdivisions. The ancient Greek city-states formed leagues for collective security against the Persians, and bilateral and multilateral treaties for mutual assistance in time of war have been a part of international relations ever since. Constitutions may provide for collective security at the intranational and international levels. Because collective security involves questions of sovereignty, it may be specifically authorized or defined in constitutional documents.

Constitution of Germany (1949), II, The Federation and the States *(Länder)*, Article 24, Entry into a Collective Security System: "(2) For the maintenance of peace, the federation may enter a system of mutual collective security; in doing so it shall consent to such limitations upon its rights of sovereignty as will bring about and secure peaceful and lasting order in Europe and among the nations of the world."

U.S. General Dwight D. Eisenhower (center) often attended meetings of the North Atlantic Treaty Organization (NATO), which was established in 1949 for the collective security of its member countries, including France and the United Kingdom.

Constitution of Switzerland (1874), Chapter I, General Provisions, Article 15: "In the event of a canton [semi-sovereign constituent state of the Swiss Confederation] being suddenly threatened from without, its government shall seek assistance of other cantons while simultaneously informing the federal authority, this being done without prejudice as to the measures that authority may decide. The cantons called upon are bound to give their assistance. The confederation shall bear the costs."

Collegial Body

Some constitutions create special government bodies that are not strictly hierarchical—that is, the members participate on an equal footing, similar to a college, where colleagues historically were associated for a particular function. Legislatures are often more like collegial bodies, where the members may be elected from roughly equal constituencies and the rules apply equally to all members.

The executive and judicial branches of national governments are generally more hierarchical, with some exceptions. For example, in Switzerland instead of a single head of state, a collegial body called the federal council performs the duties of a head of state, selecting two of its members to be president and vice president once every year during the four-year tenure of the council.

Constitution of Switzerland (1874), Chapter II, Federal Authorities, II, Federal Council: "Article 95. The supreme executive and governing authority of the confederation is a federal council composed of seven members. . . . Article 98. The chairman of the federal council shall be the president of the confederation; he and the vice presi-

As the nation's commander in chief, President Getulio Vargas of Brazil was saluted by soldiers during a World War II inspection tour. Brazil is one of many democracies that place the control of the military in the hands of elected civilian leaders.

dent shall be chosen by the federal assembly [bicameral legislature] from among the members of the council for a term for one year."

Constitution of Cuba (1976), Chapter XIII, The Courts and the Attorney General, Article 124: "All courts function in a collegial form."

Commander in Chief

Constitutions invariably provide for a supreme commander of the armed forces of a nation-state, called the commander in chief. The term apparently derives from the French *commender* (to give in trust or in charge), which has evolved to mean one who gives orders or commands. Some constitutions authorize commanders in chief for specific areas of military activity who are subordinate to the national commander in chief.

Monarchs have historically been the commanders in chief of their armies and, like Ramses II, who ruled Egypt from 1292 to 1225 B.C., have often personally led their troops into battle. By statute during the reign of Charles II of England (1660–85), "the sole supreme government and command of all the militia within his majesty's realms and dominions, and all forces by sea and land and all forts and places of strength, EVER WAS AND IS the undoubted right of . . . [the] kings and queens of England. . . ."

The term *commander in chief* implies supreme control of military operations during a war, including military strategy and political and international aspects. In presidential systems of government, like that of the United States, the president is specified as the commander in chief. In parliamentary systems the monarch or other head of state may be granted the title, although generally the prime minister is the de facto commander in chief.

In nearly all the British colonies, the governor, who was generally a civilian, was the commander in chief of the armed forces in that territory. At the time the U.S. Constitution was adopted in 1789, the president was to be the commander in chief, but this power was checked by the role of Congress in declaring war and raising and regulating the armed forces. After several military actions abroad by U.S. presidents without a formal declaration of war, the U.S. War Powers Act in 1973 pronounced the intent of Congress to participate with the president in making decisions to use American armed forces overseas.

Constitution of Canada, Constitution Act (1867), Title III, Executive Power, Section 15: "The commander-in-chief of the land and naval militia, and of all naval and military forces, of and in Canada, is hereby declared to continue and be vested in the queen [of England]."

Constitution of Germany (1948): "VI, The Federal Government, Article 65a [added in 1956 and amended in 1968]. Power of command in respect of the armed forces shall be vested in the federal minister of defense. . . . Section Xa, State of Defense, Article 115b [added in 1968]. Upon the promulgation of a state of defense, the power of command over the armed forces shall pass to the federal chancellor [prime minister]."

Constitution of Iran (1979), Chapter VII, The Leader or Leadership Council, Article 110: "Following are the duties and powers of the leadership: . . . f. the supreme commanders of the armed forces."

Commerce

Commerce, trade, and commercial affairs—the exchange of goods, products, and property of any kind—have long been the object of laws. Plato devotes an entire section of *The Laws* to commercial law aimed at circumscribing commerce. Aristotle contended that in the best governed state, whose men are absolutely just " . . . and not merely relatively to . . . the constitution, the citizens must not lead the life of artisans or tradesmen. . . . " The Latin word for commerce or trade, *commercium*, also referred to the legal capacity to take part in the *jus civile*, the restrictive law available only to Roman citizens and not to foreign traders. William Blackstone, the eighteenth-century commentator on the laws of England, makes offenses against public trade one of the five major categories of crimes and misdemeanors "that more especially affect the commonwealth."

The interaction between buyers and sellers takes place today in a global marketplace, but commerce has its roots in local markets like this one in Cuba.

According to James Madison in his essay 42 of *The Federalist* (1788), the framers of the U.S. Constitution (1789) perceived the lack of power to regulate commerce between the states as a major defect in the Articles of Confederation (1781); he noted that the Constitution's "commerce clause" was an effective instrument for extending national power over the states. The Swiss constitution goes into great detail to define specific areas of commercial activity over which the federal government has authority.

Constitution of Australia (1901), Part V, Powers of Parliament, Section 51: "The parliament shall, subject to this constitution, have power to make laws for the peace, order, and good government of the commonwealth with respect to: (i) Trade and commerce with other countries, and among the states. . . . "

Constitution of Portugal (1989), Part II, Economic Organization, Section III, Agricultural, Commercial, and Industrial Policies, Article 102, Objectives of Commercial Policies: "The objectives of commercial policy shall be as follows: a. beneficial competition among those in trade; b. rationalization of the distribution chains; c. fight against speculative activities and restrictive trade practices; d. developing and diversifying the external economic relations; e. protecting the consumers."

Commission

William Blackstone, the commentator on English law, remarked that the justices or commissioners at the assizes (court sessions) sat in five authorities, or commissions. From the Latin *committo* (to bring together or entrust), the term *commission* in constitutions generally refers to a relatively small body of people charged with carrying out some limited but ongoing activity, such as a civil service or judicial commission. In some constitutions it may be used interchangeably with *committee*—for example, a legislative commission.

A commission may also be a government board or authority created ad hoc to handle a specific investigation or function, such as a royal commission of inquiry. In addition, it may refer to the government authority usually exercised by the chief executive in granting appointments or promotions—for example, commissions—to military officers.

Constitution of Mexico (1917), Title III, Chapter II, The Legislative Branch, Article 76, V: "The appointment of a governor shall be made by the senate from a list of three proposed by the president of the republic, with the approval of two-thirds of the members present, and during adjournments, by the permanent commission [elsewhere in the Mexican constitution called the permanent committee, which is made up of twenty-nine members of the congress], according to the same rules."

Constitution of the Philippines (1987), Article IX, Constitutional Commissions, A, Common Provisions, Section 1: "The constitutional commissions, which shall be independent, are the civil service commission, the commission on elections, and the commission on audit."

Committee

In Roman law a *comitia* was an assembly of citizens; the *comitia centuriata* was a large legislative assembly of all citizens, including both patricians and plebeians. The English word *committee,* however, derives from the French *comité* and means one or a group to whom persons or matters are committed, such as a trustee. Committees are standard parliamentary institutions for carrying out certain functions entrusted to them by the whole organization.

As used in constitutions, committees generally are groups of members of a legislature assigned matters involving the budget, oversight of government operations, nominations for government positions, and so forth. In parliaments as well as congresses, such committees have a responsibility to collect information, debate and deliberate, and make a report and recommendation to the entire legislature on matters committed to them.

There are many types of legislative committees. A committee of the whole is used when a matter is considered by all the members of a body sitting as a single committee, during which the rules of debate may be relaxed. A standing committee remains in existence continuously throughout a session, generally being assigned matters related to government functions such as defense, the economy, and foreign affairs. Ad hoc committees are temporary committees assigned specific, short-term matters for action. Joint committees, such as conference committees to resolve differences in a bill passed by the two houses of a bicameral legislature, are made up of some members from both houses. There are even committees on committees, which consist of members of the majority party who make the committee assignments for members of the legislature.

Constitution of Belgium (1831), Heading III, Concerning the Authorities, Chapter I, Concerning the Houses of Parliament, Article 37: "At each session, each house nominates its president, its vice presidents, and makes up its steering committee."

Constitution of Sweden, Instrument of Government of Sweden (1974), Chapter 8, Laws and Other Regulations, Article 15: "Not less than nine months shall furthermore elapse between the time when the matter [a fundamental law] was first submitted to the chamber of the Riksdag [the legislature] and the time of the election, unless the constitutional committee of the Riksdag grants an exemption from this provision by means of a decision taken not later than the committee stage. . . . "

Common law

Common law *(jus commune* in Latin) was originally the general law of the church in Europe, distinct from local law and customs. Beginning in the twelfth century juristic theory and a body of laws made by judges began to develop in England and became known as the common law. The French term *droit commun* and the German word *Gemeinrecht* both refer to law common to an entire geographic area as opposed to a smaller locality.

Unlike Roman law or law codes, the common law of England consists of principles governing and securing rights and property derived solely from usages and customs said to be of immemorial antiquity and from the judgments of courts confirming them. In England the common law is distinguished from equity law, which allows more flexibility in remedies, and statutory law, which is enacted by Parliament. Because it relies on precedent to determine legal rights and duties, the common law is the basis for judicial power.

England's common law has been exported to many former colonies of Great Britain and other English-speaking countries and has vastly influenced constitutions, although the term itself does not generally appear in them. In the United Kingdom, which has no single, all-encompassing constitutional document, the common law serves as the basis for certain constitutional powers and rights.

Constitution of the United Kingdom, Halsbury's Laws of England (4th ed., 1974), Volume 8, Constitutional Law, Paragraph 806, Sources of Powers and Duties: "The specific legal sources of governmental powers and duties [in England and the United Kingdom] are the specific sources of law, that is to say: (1) the common law, equity, admiralty law and ecclesiastical law, all of which are largely embodied in judicial decisions; (2) that part of the common law which relates exclusively to the sovereign, and is called the royal prerogative. . . . "

Constitution of the United States of America (1789), Amendment VII (1791): "In Suits at common law, where the value in controversy shall exceed twenty dollars, the right of trial by jury shall be preserved, and no fact tried by a jury, shall be otherwise re-examined in any Court of the United States, than according to the rules of the common law."

Commonwealth

The Middle English term *commen wealthe* was used as early as the fifteenth century to mean the public welfare or general good. Commenting on England's laws in the eighteenth century, William Blackstone used it to mean the public polity of the kingdom.

Today the word *commonwealth* in constitutions refers to the general social condition of a country. In a few states of the United States it is used in place of *state*—for example, the Commonwealth of Virginia, rather than the State of Virginia.

The term also connotes an association of the United Kingdom and a number of its former colonies that are now independent and sovereign countries. Many of these colonies, however, have removed all references to the British Commonwealth from their constitutional language. Australia, however, officially calls itself the Commonwealth of Australia.

Constitution of Australia (1901), Preamble: "Whereas the people of New South Wales, Victoria, South Australia, Queensland, and Tasmania, humbly relying on the blessings of almighty God, have agreed to unite in one indissoluble federal commonwealth under the crown of the United Kingdom of Great Britain and Ireland, and under the constitution hereby established. . . . "

Constitution of the United Kingdom, Halsbury's Laws of England (4th ed., 1974), Volume 8, Constitutional Law, Paragraph 819, Principal Conventions: "Certain conventions regulate the relations between members of the commonwealth."

Communications

Along with transportation, the recent rapid advances in communications technology are changing nation-states from scattered pockets of citizens into a unified and linked community of individuals who can be aware almost instantaneously of their government's policy changes and actions. Television and computer networks now make possible communications at the speed of light between governments and individuals nearly anywhere in the world.

Communications as used in constitutions may refer to internal government communications, such as that between the chief executive and the legislature; communications between the government and its citizens; communications between private individuals; and mass communications, which can disseminate large amounts of information rapidly and greatly influence public opinion.

Constitution of Sweden, Freedom of the Press Act (1992), Chapter 1, On the Freedom of the Press, Article 1: "In accordance with the principles set forth in the preceding paragraph of this article concerning freedom of the press for all, and in order to insure the free interchange of opinion and enlightenment of the public, every Swedish subject shall be entitled, subject to the provisions set forth in the present act for the protection of individual rights and public security, to publish his thoughts and opinions in print, to publish official documents, and to make statements and communicate information on any subject whatsoever."

Constitution of Iran (1979), Chapter XII, Radio and Television, Article 175: "The freedom of expression and dissemination of thoughts in the radio and television of the Islamic Republic of Iran must be guaranteed in keeping with the Islamic criteria and the best interests of the country."

The importance of communications, represented in this 1920s allegorical painting, has led to some constitutional provisions protecting individual privacy in communications and controlling the mass media.

The nineteenth-century writings of Karl Marx, *Das Kapital* and the *Communist Manifesto,* coauthored with Friedrich Engels, led to revolutions and communist-style governments and constitutions in many countries.

Communism

"But indeed, there is always a difficulty in men living together and having all human relations in common, but especially in their having common property," observed Aristotle in *The Politics.* In the Middle Ages it was believed that the earliest societies held property in common, but John Locke later argued that private property must have always existed as the product of an individual's labor and that therefore it was a natural right, along with liberty.

The English word *communism* is related to the Latin *communio* (partnership) and *communis* (common) and is derived from the French *commun* (common, universal, and joint possession). In the political parlance of the twentieth century, communism refers specifically to the doctrine or movement based on the works of Karl Marx, the nineteenth-century German political philosopher and socialist, and first developed in practice by the Russian leader Vladimir Lenin. Communism seeks to overthrow capitalism through a revolution of the proletariat, the working class.

A number of constitutions in this century have been based on the concept of a communist state, with only one ideological party—the Communist Party—monopolizing all social, economic, and political decision making. The communist constitution that has had the greatest impact on constitutional development, albeit to a large extent as a sham formality, was the 1936 "Stalin" constitution of the Soviet Union. Today a few countries, such as China (People's Republic of China), Cuba, North Korea, and Vietnam, have retained communist-style constitutions, although even some of these are slowly evolving away from the pure communistic concept of the economic and political organization of the nation-state.

Constitution of North Korea (1972), Chapter I, Politics, Article 4: "The Democratic People's Republic of Korea is guided in its activity by the *chuch'e* [self-reliance] idea of the Workers' Party of Korea [a communist party], which is a creative application of Marxism-Leninism to our country's reality."

Constitution of Vietnam (1992), Chapter I, The Socialist Republic of Vietnam—Its Political System, Article 4: "The Communist Party of Vietnam, the vanguard unit of the Vietnamese working class and the faithful representative of the interests of the working class, of the laboring people, and of the entire nation, pursues Marxism-Leninism and Ho Chi Minh thought and is the leading force of the state and society. All party organizations operate within the framework of the constitution and the law."

Compensation

In constitutions compensation means both to indemnify losses and to pay a salary or remuneration for services rendered. The first definition has a long history and can be traced to the law code of the Babylonian king Hammurabi, who lived in the twentieth century B.C. or earlier, and the biblical reference to "an eye for an eye." The term now refers to money damages paid to citizens whose property is taken by the state for public use under the theory of eminent domain. This practice is generally not observed in countries dominated by the Communist Party, where to a large extent all property is considered to be owned by the state.

Under the Fifth Amendment (1791) to the U.S. Constitution, privately owned property may not be taken by the government for public use without the payment of just compensation. Many countries that condone or foster capitalism provide similar assurances in their constitutional documents.

Constitutions also contain language relating to the compensation or salaries of elected and appointed officials. In particular, to promote judicial independence, salaries for judges generally may not be reduced during their tenure.

Constitution of South Korea (1948), Chapter II, Rights and Duties of Citizens, Article 23(3): "Expropriation, use, or restriction of private property from public necessity and compensation therefor shall be governed by law. However, in such a case, just compensation shall be paid."

Constitution of Mexico (1917), Title III, Chapter IV, Judicial Power, Article 94: "The remuneration received by the ministers of the supreme court, the circuit magistrates, and the district judges for their services may not be reduced during their term in office."

Comptroller. *See* Audit

Confederation

In essay 9 of *The Federalist* (1788), Alexander Hamilton notes that Montesquieu, the eighteenth-century French philosopher, had called the ancient Lycian confederacy of twenty-three cities in Asia Minor the model of an excellent confederate republic. In making decisions for the confederacy, the larger cities had three votes, the medium-sized cities two, and the smallest cities one.

From 1781 to 1788 the United States was governed nationally, albeit loosely, by the Articles of Confederation (1781). In 1861, when some of the Southern states seceded, they called themselves the Confederate States of America, or the Confederacy, while the remaining northern states were called the Union. In Europe a confederation of German states existed under the Austrian emperor from 1815 to 1866.

In international law a confederacy is an agreement between two or more states to further their mutual welfare. A confederacy or confederation generally differs from a federation or federal republic in that the member states of a confederacy are joined together only for common action in relation to external matters. The internal affairs of each state are relatively free from control; the central government can pass a law applicable to the states only if they agree to it. The sole constitution of a major country that uses the term *confederation* to describe the relationship between the constituent states, called cantons, is that of Switzerland, whose confederation consists of twenty-three cantons and three half cantons.

CONSTITUTION

OF THE

CONFEDERATE STATES OF AMERICA.

We, the people of the Confederate States, each state acting in its sovereign and independent character, in order to form a permanent federal government, establish justice, insure domestic tranquility and secure the blessings of liberty to ourselves and our posterity—invoking the favor and guidance of Almighty God—do ordain and establish this constitution for the Confederate States of America.

ARTICLE I.

SECTION 1.

All legislative powers herein delegated shall be vested in a Congress of the Confederate States, which shall consist of a Senate and House of Representatives.

SECTION 2.

1. The House of Representatives shall be composed of members chosen every second year by the people of the several states; and the electors in each state shall be citizens of the Confederate States, and have the qualifications requisite for electors of the most numerous branch of the state legislature; but no person of foreign birth, not a citizen of the Confederate States, shall be allowed to vote for any officer, civil or political, state or federal.

2. No person shall be a Representative who shall not have attained the age of twenty-five years, and be a citizen of the Confederate States, and who shall not, when elected, be an inhabitant of that state in which he shall be chosen.

The Confederate States of America, which lasted from 1861 to 1865, had its own constitution, under which the constituent states retained significant powers.

Constitution of Switzerland (1874), Chapter I, General Provisions, Article 2: "The aim of the [Swiss] confederation is to preserve the outward independence of the fatherland, to maintain internal peace and order, to protect the freedom and the rights of the confederates and to promote their common prosperity."

Confirmation

The procedure by which one branch of government approves the appointment of officials to another branch is known as the confirmation process. In a true parliamentary system political appointments, such as ministers, deputy ministers, and secretaries, but not career civil servants are selected by the leadership of the majority party or parties in the legislature; the appointees are supervised by the prime minister and parliament. In such systems appointments to the judicial branch are similarly made by the parliamentary majority government.

Ruth Bader Ginsburg faces the media at the confirmation hearing on her nomination to the U.S. Supreme Court in 1993.

In presidential systems the principles of a stricter separation of powers and checks and balances often require that the president's appointment of individuals to important positions in the executive and judicial branches be confirmed by the legislature. Under the U.S. Constitution (1789) the Senate, the upper house of Congress, must give its "advice and consent" for the confirmation of specified appointments by the president to the executive and judicial branches. However, the Twenty-fifth Amendment (1967) permits the president to fill a vacancy in the vice presidency on confirmation by a majority vote of both houses of Congress.

Constitution of Haiti (1987), Title V, Chapter III, The Executive Branch, Section B, Duties of the President of the Republic, Article 141: "With the approval of the senate, the president appoints, by a decree issued in the council of ministers, the commander-in-chief of the armed forces, the commander-in-chief of the police, ambassadors and consul generals."

Constitution of the Philippines (1987), Article VII, Executive Branch, Section 16: "The president shall nominate and, with the consent of the commission on appointments [consisting of the president of the senate as ex officio chairman and twelve members from each house of the congress], appoint the heads of executive departments, ambassadors, other public ministers and consuls, or officers of the armed forces from the rank of colonel or naval captain, and other officers whose appointments are vested in him in this constitution."

Constitution of Brazil (1988), Title IV, Chapter II, Executive Power, Article 84: "The president of the republic shall have the exclusive power to: . . . xiv—appoint, after approval by the senate, the justices of the supreme federal court and those of the superior courts, the governors of the territories, the attorney-general of the republic, the president and directors of the central bank, and other civil servants, when established by law. . . ."

The ornate setting of the Mexican congress, photographed in 1910, reflects a high regard for representative government.

Congress

In international law a congress—from the Latin *congressus* (meeting or combat)—refers to a formal assembly of representatives from various sovereignties meeting for a common purpose. This term is also used in many constitutions, particularly those in Latin America, Brazil, and countries influenced by the U.S. constitutional model of government, to denote their countries' national legislatures.

In principle a congress differs from a parliament or an assembly. A law-making body, a congress is one of several coequal branches of a government that has a president as both the head of state and government. Variations have resulted in hybrid forms of government. In Peru, for example, the congress is a unicameral legislature, and the prime minister and cabinet must approve any act of the president, as in a presidential-style parliamentary system.

The Continental Congress, which convened in 1774, was the first national legislative assembly in the British colonies in North America; all the colonies except Georgia were represented. The delegates were chosen by different methods, and the congress's powers were undefined, but it initiated and successfully prosecuted the Revolutionary War for independence from Great Britain. The term *congress* was carried over to the legislature under the Articles of Confederation (1781) and the subsequent Constitution, which became effective in 1789.

Constitution of Ecuador (1979), Second Part, Title I, The Legislative Function, Section I, The National Congress, Article 56: "The legislative function is exercised by the national congress, located in Quito, composed of twelve congressmen elected by national vote; two congressmen elected by each province, except those with less than one hundred thousand inhabitants, which elect one; and, in addition, one congressman elected for each three thousand inhabitants or fraction thereof over two hundred thousand."

Constitution of the Philippines (1987), Article VI, Legislative Department, Section 1: "The legislative power shall be vested in the congress of the Philippines, which shall consist of a senate and a house of representatives, except to the extent reserved to the people by the provision on initiative and referendum."

Conscience

Now synonymous with the faculty of knowing right from wrong, conscience—from the Latin *conscientia* (joint knowledge or moral sense)—implies an inward knowledge, consciousness, and internal convictions and was used in this sense as early as the thirteenth century in England. "Thus conscience does make cowards of us all," suggests William Shakespeare in his *Tragedy of Hamlet, Prince of Denmark* (1602). In this century Sigmund Freud postulated that the conscience, which he defined as the superego, redirects the aggression of the ego, or self, which is aimed at others, back on the ego, and the resulting tension is what we know as a sense of guilt.

In a number of modern constitutions the term *conscience*

is used with respect to guarantees of rights and freedoms, which include the freedom of conscience or the freedom to make moral judgments on one's own, except of course where an action is proscribed by law. For officials such as judges it is also used in the sense of a moral guide.

Constitution of Nicaragua (1987), Title VI, Rights, Duties, and Guarantees of the Nicaraguan People, Chapter I, Article 29: "All persons have the right to freedom of conscience, thought, and religion, including the right not to profess a religion. No one shall be the object of coercive measures which diminish these rights, or be obligated to declare his or her creed, ideology, or beliefs."

Constitution of Syria (1973), Part Two, Powers of the State, Chapter 3, Judicial Power, (1) Judges of the Bench and the Prosecution, Article 133: "1—Judges are independent. They are subject to no authority other than the law in the discharge of their functions. 2—The honor, conscience, and impartiality of judges shall be a guarantee of the rights and freedoms of individuals."

Consent

Consent—agreement, assent, or acquiescence—is important in the context of constitutions in at least three significant senses.

First, although seldom articulated in these same words, the principle of the consent of the governed underlies most modern constitutions. Like popular sovereignty or the will of the people, it replaces such archaic foundations of government as the legal or historical legitimacy of monarchs and the divine right of kings. The U.S. Declaration of Independence (1776) proclaims that "Governments are instituted among Men, deriving their just powers from

Juan Carlos I de Borbòn y Borbòn became king of Spain in 1975 on the death of the dictator General Francisco Franco, but on December 27, 1978, he consented to the establishment of a limited monarchy by signing the new national constitution.

the consent of the governed." Or, as Alexander Hamilton suggests in essay 22 of *The Federalist* (1788), "The fabric of the American empire ought to rest on the solid basis of *the consent of the people*" [Hamilton's emphasis].

Second, in most constitutional democracies the consent, assent, or signature of the sovereign or other head of state is required to validate laws passed by the legislature. In constitutional monarchies the king or queen's consent, or that of his or her representative, such as a governor-general, is purely a formality. Nevertheless, laws passed by a parliament are generally not valid unless they are consented to by the monarch or by the president in a presidential-style parliamentary government, where the monarch has essentially been replaced by a president.

Third, one branch of government, generally the legislative branch, must consent to certain actions of the head of state. An example is the U.S. constitutional requirement that the upper house of Congress, the Senate, give its "advice and consent" to specified high-level appointments made by the president.

Constitution of Liberia, Chapter I, Structure of the State, Article 1: "All free governments are instituted by [the people's] authority and for their benefit, and they have the right to alter and reform the same when their safety and happiness so require."

Constitution of the United Kingdom, Halsbury's Laws of England (4th ed., 1974), Volume 8, Constitutional Law, Paragraph 819, Principal Conventions: "The sovereign must assent to any bill that has passed both houses of Parliament (or the House of Commons alone under of the Parliament Acts [of] 1911 and 1949)."

Constituency.

See Constituent; Electoral District

Constituent

A constituent—from the French *constituant* (one who confers a power of attorney or one of a group authorized to draft a constitution)—is a person who gives authority to another to act for him or her. In constitutional governments a constituent may be a voter in an electoral district or a constituency (called a riding in Canada) or a member of a body that is authorized or commissioned to draft a constitution.

The mandate to draft a constitution or constitutional amendment is called constituent power. Under the U.S. Constitution (1789), Congress has constituent power or authority to propose constitutional amendments by a two-thirds vote of both houses, or it may call a national convention if petitioned to do so by at least two-thirds of the state legislatures.

Constitution of Ghana (1992), Chapter Seven, Representation of the People, Article 47(1): "Ghana shall be divided into as many constituencies for the purpose of election of members of parliament as the electoral commission may prescribe, and each constituency shall be represented by one member of parliament."

Constitution of Colombia (1991), Title XIII, Concerning Constitutional Amendment, Article 374: "The political constitution of Colombia may be amended by congress, a constituent assembly, or by the people through a referendum."

Constitution

To find what form of government is "the best of all for those who are able to realize their ideal life," Aristotle, in *The Politics*, classifies and compares constitutions of communities in his own and earlier times. He equates a constitution with how a government actually operates. For him the state or political society comes before the individual, and the best government is the one in which everyone can act best and live happily. Plato, on the other hand, sees the constitutions of states as a system for creating and maintaining good and just citizens.

The English word *constitution* (the action of making or establishing) is derived from the Latin *constitutio* (an arrangement or establishment). In Roman law a constitution was an enactment by the emperor, the supreme authority. Today a national constitution is in most cases considered the supreme law of the land. In countries in which the political processes are dominated by a religion or single ideological party, however, a constitutional document may be subordinate to the written rules or pronouncements of leaders of the religion or party.

An allegory on the creation of the first French constitution in 1791 depicts Jean-Jacques Rousseau, Benjamin Franklin, Montesquieu, Voltaire, Cicero, and Demosthenes, among others. At center is Honoré Mirabeau, leader of the French assembly.

A national constitution, whether written or unwritten, is an organic, fundamental, basic, and supreme law. At the least it establishes a political regime with procedures for acquiring, wielding, and transferring political power through government officials and institutions. It may also create rights and duties for the state and for citizens under its jurisdiction.

Unwritten constitutions, like those of the United Kingdom, New Zealand, and Israel, begin with some historical act or document that is accorded constitutional status and proceed to evolve in a piecemeal fashion over time. Written constitutions, like those of the United States and Sweden, are the product of a conscious effort by some citizens with political authority to create a whole system of nation-state government based on one or a few core constitutional documents. Both written and unwritten constitutions are supplemented to varying degrees by unwritten conventions and traditions, which, although generally not enforceable in a court of law, are nonetheless scrupulously observed by those who hold political power.

Constitutions are an expression of the political processes and power structures in nation-states and are blueprints for governance, even if in practice they are not always followed to the letter of the law. They are simply a set of rules for controlling the use of political power and decision making in which a majority of a country's citizens acquiesce. Of course, a minority of dissatisfied citizens, if they have the means, may be capable of revolting against an existing constitutional order.

Constitution of Italy (1948), Fundamental Principles, Article 1: "The sovereignty belongs to the people who exercise it in accordance with the procedures and within the limits laid down by the constitution."

Constitution of South Africa (1994), Preamble: " . . . and whereas it is necessary for such purposes that provision should be made for the promotion of national unity and the restructuring and continued governance of South Africa while an elected constitutional assembly draws up a final constitution. . . [adopted in 1996]."

Constitution of Libya, Declaration on the Establishment of the Authority of the People (1979), Article 2: "The holy [Qur'an] is the constitution of the Socialist People's Libyan Arab Jamahiriya ["state of the masses"]."

Constitutional. *See* Unconstitutional

Constitutional Act. *See* Constitutional Law

Constitutional Committee

Many constitutions authorize regular courts, a constitutional council or court, or other forums to provide judicial or constitutional review—the review of the constitutionality of laws passed by the legislature and acts of officials. Some constitutions establish a constitutional committee within the legislature for this purpose.

Constitutional committees may review proposals to amend the constitution and create laws that may have a substantial impact on the constitution. Although a constitutional committee is technically like other standing committees of a legislature, the members have a special duty to ensure that changes in the constitution are handled in a procedurally correct manner and that the constitution is being enforced properly by the government.

Constitution of Finland, Parliament Act (1928), Chapter 4, Preparation of Matters, Section 46: "The committee for constitutional law shall prepare the matters sent to it relating to the enactment, amendment, expounding or repeal of a constitutional act or to legislation that is in close substantive connection with a constitutional act. The committee shall also examine the proposals sent to it relating to the enactment of the procedures of parliament, the election rules of parliament, and the regulations for the parliamentary ombudsman."

Constitution of Sweden, Instrument of Government (1975), Chapter 12, Parliamentary Control, Article 1: "The committee on the constitution shall examine ministers' performance of their duties and the handling of government business. The committee is entitled for this purpose to have access to the records of the decisions made in cabinet matters and to all documents pertaining to such matters."

Constitutional Convention

One way to draft, amend, or revise a constitution is to hold a constitutional convention of delegates selected by the people at large or from constituent federal states. In countries such as the United Kingdom, where Parliament is the supreme constitutional authority, the legislature can make changes in the constitution simply by enacting laws. But in many countries, especially federal nation-states, the national legislature may not be supreme, and other amendment or revision methods that ensure the legitimacy of changes are accordingly provided for in the written constitution.

The U.S. Constitution was drafted at a constitutional convention called in 1787 by Congress under the Articles of Confederation (1781). The convention went beyond the scope of its original mandate to revise the Articles of Confederation and wrote a completely new document—a reason that this method of amending a constitution is generally avoided. One means of making amendments provided for in the U.S. Constitution is for a constitutional convention to be called on the request of two-thirds of the constituent states; however, this alternative has never been used.

Although some constitutions expressly provide for a constitutional convention or similar body, it is generally believed that the concept of popular sovereignty endows the people with the right to establish such a body whenever they become sufficiently disenchanted with the government. The 1979 constitution of the Federated States of Micronesia provides for the people to call a constitutional convention by referendum every ten years. After the first ten years the Micronesian voters approved the calling of a convention.

Another definition of a constitutional convention is a custom, usage, or tradition that has become an unwritten element of a nation's constitution—for example, the role of the prime minister in the United Kingdom and of political parties in the United States.

Constitution of Argentina (1853), First Part, Declarations, Rights, and Guarantees, Article 30: "The constitution may be amended entirely or in any of its parts. The necessity of amendment must be declared by the congress by a vote of two-thirds of the members; but it shall not be effected except by a convention called for the purpose."

Constitution of South Africa (1994), Chapter 5, The Adoption of the New Constitution, Constitution-making Body, Section 68: "(1) The national assembly and the senate, sitting jointly for the purposes of this chapter, shall be the constitutional assembly. (2) The constitutional assembly shall draft and adopt a new constitutional text in accordance with this chapter [adopted in 1996]."

Constitutional Council

A constitutional council, unlike a constitutional court, generally reviews laws for conformity with the constitution before they are promulgated, rather than after. France's 1958 constitution instituted this device to provide for the review of proposed laws but only at the request of

A painting in the Norwegian Storting (parliament) depicts Christian Magnus Falsen, the "Father of the Norwegian Constitution," presenting to the constitutional convention at Eidsvoll the draft that evolved into the version adopted in 1814.

the executive or the legislature and only to determine if the laws conform to the constitutional division of power. The French council, like others, is also given responsibilities with respect to elections and referendums.

The French people's inherent distrust of judges has made them wary of providing the judiciary the power of judicial review, as in the United States, or of constitutional review, as in Germany. In 1971, however, a French constitutional council assumed the power to review laws before they become effective for conformity with general constitutional principles, including unwritten fundamental principles of the French republican tradition. A few other countries have incorporated a constitutional council into their constitutions for various purposes.

Constitution of Mozambique (1990), Part III, Organs of State, Chapter VIII, Constitutional Council, Article 181: "1. The constitutional council shall have power to: a) adjudicate the constitutionality and legality of legislative and regulatory acts of state organs; b) settle conflicts of jurisdiction between organs of sovereign authority; c) pronounce on the legality of referendums; 2. In the specific areas of election, the constitutional council shall have power to: a) supervise the electoral process. . . . "

Constitution of Algeria (1976), Title III, Concerning the Control and the Consultative Institutions, Chapter I, Control, Article 153: "A constitutional council is established [and] entrusted to watch over the respect for the constitution. The constitutional council watches, among other matters, over the regularity of referendum operations, the election of the president of the republic and legislative elections. It announces the results of its operations."

Constitutional Court

A constitutional court or tribunal is a special body, either within or outside the judicial system of a nation-state, that exercises various degrees of review over the constitutionality of laws and actions of government officials. The first constitution to provide for a constitutional court was Austria's in 1920, a provision due largely to Hans Kelsen's efforts.

Strictly speaking, judicial review of the type practiced in the United States means that the regular courts of the judicial system exercise the function of reviewing the constitutionality of laws and official actions in the normal course of deciding cases. Constitutional review, however, is the review of laws and in some cases actions by officials for conformity with the constitution by a body that is not a part of the regular judicial system.

An authority authorized to conduct constitutional review may be called a constitutional court or tribunal or a constitutional council, the latter being a feature of France's 1958 constitution. A constitutional court implies that the review takes place after a law has been enacted or the action of an official has occurred, while a constitutional council implies that the review occurs before a law has been enacted or promulgated or an official action has taken place. In Poland constitutional review is entrusted to a constitutional tribunal whose decisions may be overruled by a supermajority vote of the lower house of the parliament.

The U.S. Supreme Court does not provide opinions on the law except in the context of rendering decisions on actual cases. The courts in other countries, including constitutional courts, however, may be required to render advisory opinions on matters at the request of the executive or legislative branches.

Constitution of Thailand (1991), Chapter X, The Constitutional Tribunal, Article 205: "After a bill has been approved by the national assembly and before the prime minister presents it to the king for signature . . . : (1) if the senators or the members of the house of representatives or members of both houses of not less than one-fifth of the total number of existing members of both houses are of the opinion that the provision of the said bill is contrary to or inconsistent with the constitution or illegally issues under the provisions of the constitution, they shall submit their opinions to the president of the national assembly, the president of the senate, the president of the house of representatives, as the case may be, and the president of the house that receives the said opinion shall then refer it to the constitutional tribunal for decision and inform the prime minister of it. . . . "

Constitution of Poland, Constitutional Provisions Continued in Force Pursuant to Article 77 of the Constitution Act (1992), Chapter 4, The Constitutional Tribunal, the Tribunal of State, the Supreme Chamber of Control, and the

Judges on Germany's federal constitutional court exercise constitutional review over existing laws and official actions.

Commissioner for Citizens' Rights, Article 33a: "1. The constitutional tribunal shall adjudicate upon the conformity to the constitution of laws and other normative acts enacted by main and central state organs, and shall formulate universally binding interpretations of the laws. 2. Judgments of the constitutional tribunal on the nonconformity of laws to the constitution are subject to the examination by the Sejm [lower house of the legislature]."

Constitutional Law

Constitutional law is the branch of a nation's public law that governs the general framework of the organization and distribution of political and government powers and activities. It thus reflects the fundamental principles that regulate the relationship between the governed and those who govern them. Constitutional law encompasses the establishment of a constitution and the interpretation and validity of enactments by the legislature, tested against the constitution as the fundamental law.

A constitution itself, at least the parts that are enforceable by a court of law, consists of constitutional or supreme laws, compared to other laws of the nation-state, which are by definition subordinate to the supreme laws embodied in a constitution. A constitutional law is one that conforms to the constitution and is, therefore, valid and not unconstitutional. Amendments to constitutions are also the subject of constitutional law. In some constitutions a constitutional amendment passed by the legislature is called a constitutional act.

In a monarchy the act of succession is of constitutional status and therefore relevant to constitutional law study. Ordinary laws that relate to a constitution are sometimes called constitutional laws.

Constitution of Italy (1948), Part Two, The System of the Republic, Title I, The Parliament, Section II, The Formation of Laws, Article 71: "The initiative of laws belongs to the government, to any member of the chamber, and to bodies and agencies which are entitled to do so by a constitutional law."

Constitution of Finland, Constitution Act (1919), III, Legislation, Section 20: "It shall be stated in the preamble of each act of parliament that the act has been enacted according to a decision of parliament and, when an act has been enacted pursuant to the procedure in force for the enactment of constitutional acts, it shall also be stated that this procedure has been complied with."

Constitutional Review

To determine if legislation is unconstitutional, a body outside a nation-state's regular judicial system may be authorized to review it. This procedure may occur before or after a law is promulgated; in either case an unconstitutional law will not be effective. Constitutional review may also extend to the unconstitutional actions of government officials.

The process is accomplished by special constitutional courts, tribunals, or other bodies such as constitutional councils. Many of these extrajudicial or nonjudicial bodies have certain limitations on the type of laws that can be challenged, the manner in which challenges to the constitutionality of a law can be made, and the effect of a successful challenge.

Constitutional review, like judicial review, is technically precluded in countries such as the United Kingdom because the supremacy of the legislature means that it can change the constitution by a majority vote of its members. Only when a treaty, such as one adopting an international or regional standard of human rights, is held to supersede parliamentary legislation—as in Belgium, for example—can acts of a supreme parliament be declared void by a court for not conforming to the terms of the treaty.

Although judicial review and constitutional review are similar processes, judicial review of the type practiced in the United States or in countries that strictly follow the U.S. model takes place in the normal course of case adjudication by regular rather than special courts.

Constitution of Hungary (1949, significantly revised in 1989), Chapter IV, Constitutional Court, Article 32/A: "(1) The constitutional court shall review the constitutionality of laws and statutes and shall perform the tasks assigned to it by law. (2) In the case of determining unconstitutionality, the constitutional court shall annul the laws and other statutes."

Constitution of Greece (1975), Part Three, Organization and Functions of the State, Section V, The Judicial Power, Chapter Two, Organization and Jurisdiction of the Courts, Article 100: "1. A special highest court shall be established the jurisdiction of which shall comprise: . . . e) settlement of contestations on whether a law enacted by parliament is fundamentally unconstitutional, or on the interpretation of provisions of such law when conflicting judgments have been pronounced by the council of state [administrative review body], the supreme court, or the court of auditors."

Constitutional Tribunal.

See Constitutional Court

Constitutionalism

Aristotle concluded that constitutional governments—ones other than tyrannies—try to combine oligarchy (rule by the few) with democracy (rule by the many); he also claimed that democracy is safer because there is strength in greater numbers and because people who are equal are contented. Plato was suspicious of democracy and believed that the best government is one that operates according to philosophical principles.

Constitutionalism may be said to merge the notions of these ancient Greeks: popular democracy combined with majority rule checked by philosophically developed principles, such as individual and minority rights, separation of powers, and the rule of law, which are now the legal norms of most modern constitutions. The word *constitutionalism* is not often found in constitutions, although its principles are obvious in constitutional documents from Magna Carta (1215) to Ethiopia's 1995 constitution.

Constitutionalism today refers both to a constitutional system of government with limited or checked powers as well as to the adherence to principles embodied by constitutions. A nation-state may have a written constitution that purports to limit the powers of government, thereby meeting the first definition of constitutionalism, but it may be flawed or those exercising power may simply fail to adhere to the principles espoused in the document, thereby not meeting the second definition.

Over the centuries many people have contributed to concepts of constitutionalism. Historians such as the Greek Polybius, who described constitutionalism in Rome around 200 B.C. as resting on strength and stability, have catalogued constitutional forms tried throughout the world. Both St. Augustine in the fourth century and St. Thomas Aquinas in the thirteenth century advanced the cause of constitutionalism in their philosophical works by separating the spiritual and temporal worlds. During the period in which absolute monarchies dominated Europe, natural law theorists argued for and against limitations on sovereignty, finally admitting by the eighteenth century the possibility of individual rights and popular sovereignty.

A landmark in the development of constitutionalism was the drafting and adoption of the U.S. Constitution (1789). The framers of that seminal document drew heavily on the histories of earlier constitutions. James Madison, in essay 63 of *The Federalist* (1788), cites Polybius's comments on the senate of Carthage in discussing the institution of the U.S. Senate. The U.S. Constitution has become a guide for many nation-states' subsequent experiments in constitutionalism.

Today most modern national governments are based on the principles of constitutionalism, which is rooted in the sovereignty of the people to create their own constitution, giving powers and duties to specified authorities, establishing checks and balances and separations of power within the system of government, and holding everyone to account before the law. Governments today may not seem structurally different from absolute monarchies, but most people now have the right to participate in the selection of those who will represent them and will make, enforce, and interpret their laws.

Constitution of Portugal (1976), Fundamental Principles, Article 3, Sovereignty and Legality: "1. Sovereignty, one and indivisible, rests with the people, who shall exercise it in accordance with the forms laid down in the constitution. 2. The state shall be subject to the constitution and based on democratic legality. 3. The validity of the laws and other acts of the state, the autonomous regions, or local authorities shall depend on their being in accordance with the constitution."

Constitution of Greece (1975), Part One, Fundamental Provisions, Section I, The Forms of Government, Article 1(3): "All powers derive from the people and exist for the nation; they shall be exercised as specified by the constitution."

Contract

The concept of an enforceable agreement between parties—a contract, from the Latin *contractus*—is an old one. The Germanic god Wotan was supposed to have ruled by contract with the other gods, and the biblical God of the Israelites is recorded as having entered into a covenant, a form of contract, with Abraham. In *The Laws,* Plato prescribes an action in a tribal court for an unfulfilled agreement, and Aristotle, in *The Politics,* discusses the consequences for contracts when a state changes from one form of constitution to another.

The law of contracts is a broad area of legal study, like torts or criminal law. Contract law differs generally from criminal law in that it prescribes rules to be complied with to obtain legal sanctions for basically private relationships, while criminal law deals with proscribed behavior for which the state can mete out punishment. In some countries contracts must be witnessed and recorded by a government official or notary to be valid.

The contractual theory of constitutions posits a consensual relationship between the governed and those who govern them. Natural law theorists grappled for centuries with the concept of a social contract—the general view that society is the result of a calculated act of reason by individuals. A form of tacit consent, therefore, is necessary for all social organization, including political organization. Jean-Jacques Rousseau argued in the eighteenth century that the only form of social contract is a political one.

Modern constitutions are generally expressed in contractual terms—that is, certain obligations and duties are required of the citizen and the state. Of course, the state would seem to have the advantage when it comes to enforcing the obligations of citizens.

Some constitutions also deal specifically with certain types of contractual relationships in such areas as labor and property rights.

Constitution of Argentina (1853), First Part, Declarations, Rights, and Guarantees, Article 15: "Any contract for the purchase or sale of persons is a crime for which those committing it, and the notary or official authorizing it, shall be responsible."

Constitution of the United States of America (1789), Article I, Section 10: "No State shall . . . pass any . . . Law impairing the Obligation of contracts. . . . "

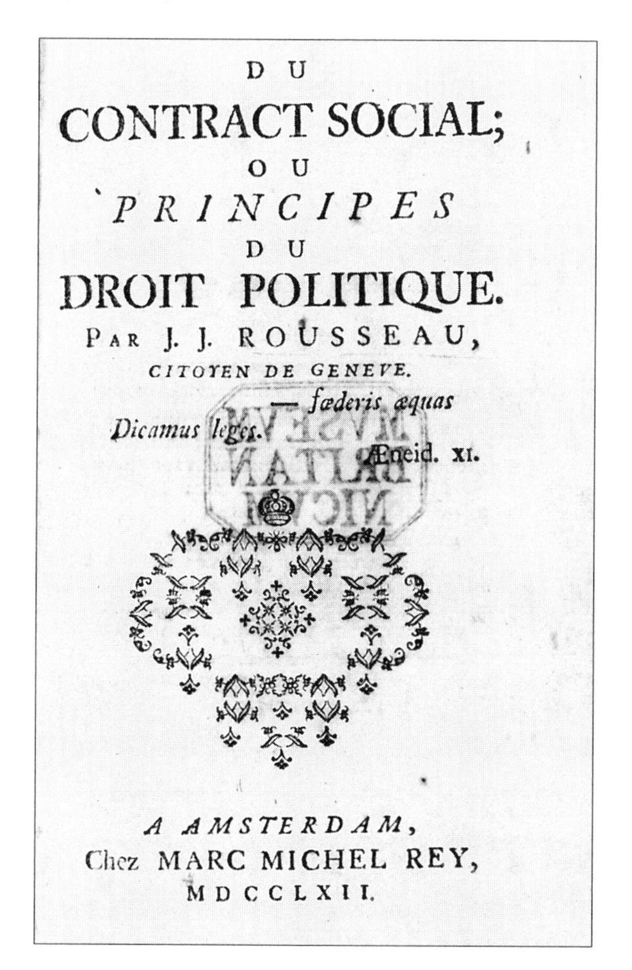

DU
CONTRACT SOCIAL;
OU
PRINCIPES
DU
DROIT POLITIQUE.
PAR J. J. ROUSSEAU,
CITOYEN DE GENEVE.
— *fœderis æquas*
Dicamus leges.
Æneid. XI.

A AMSTERDAM,
Chez MARC MICHEL REY,
MDCCLXII.

The *Social Contract* (1762), by Jean-Jacques Rousseau, provided a theoretical basis for instituting government on the consent of the governed.

Controller. *See* Audit

Convene

A collective body assembles or convenes—from the Latin *convenio* (assemble, agree with, or meet)—for a united purpose. The term is more prevalent in Scotland, where its use was recorded as early as the fifteenth century, and in the United States, although in England it was used also from the fifteenth century on to denote a person being summoned before a tribunal. In Anglo-American civil law *convene* means to bring a legal action.

According to parliamentary procedures, when an ad hoc body is assembled one member must move that the body come to order and that a chairman be designated. In a similar manner the first meetings of legislatures must be assembled, convoked, or convened. However, the constitution or the rules of the legislatures themselves generally set forth procedures on when and where to convene and how to begin conducting business. Sometimes the president or monarch must summon the legislature to convene, at least ceremonially. The dates on which legislatures are to convene may be set forth in a constitution.

Constitution of the United States of America (1789), Amendment XX (1933): "The Congress shall assemble at least once in every year, and such meeting shall begin at noon on the 3rd day of January, unless they shall by law appoint a different day."

Constitution of Slovakia (1993), Chapter Six, Executive Power, Section One, The President of the Slovak Republic, Article 2: "The president . . . c) convenes the constituent session of the national council [parliament] of the Slovak Republic. . . . "

Constitution of Thailand (1991), Chapter VI, The National Assembly, Part 4, Provisions Applicable to Both Houses, Article 128: "The king convokes the national assembly. He opens and prorogues its sessions. The king may be present to perform the opening ceremony of the first annual ordinary session . . . or may command the heir to the throne who is *sui juris* or any other person to perform the ceremony as his representative."

Convention

In Roman law a convention was an agreement, and in English law it is an extraordinary assembly of the House of Lords and House of Commons, with or without the approval of the monarch. Both these meanings have evolved into modern-day constitutional terms.

The rules by which a national government operates, whether or not it has a written constitution, usually include some conventions—generally accepted agreements, customs, and traditions that supplement or even contradict the express provisions of a written constitutional document. In the United States the two major political parties have a nonlegal agreement on how to organize Congress after elections, and in England there is a political agreement that the monarch can act only on the direction, or "advice," of the prime minister, who is selected by the House of Commons. These agreements or conventions are not expressed in any documents of constitutional stature. They are rules of constitutional behavior that are binding on politicians and government officials but that may not necessarily be enforced by the courts, even though they may recognize the existence of the conventions.

A constitutional convention may also be a special gathering of delegates meeting either pursuant to constitutional authority or extraconstitutionally to deliberate on changes to, revision of, or replacement of an existing constitution, or to write a constitution for the first time. The French assembly elected in 1792—which proclaimed the republic, executed the king, and established committees to rule France until it dissolved itself in 1795—called itself a convention.

Constitution of Canada, Excerpt from the Decision of the Supreme Court of Canada, Reference Re Amendment of the Constitution (1981): "Conventions by their nature develop in a political field and it will be for the political actors, not this court, to determine the degree of provincial consent [for amendment] required."

Constitution of the United Kingdom, Halsbury's Laws of England (4th ed., 1974), Volume 8, Constitutional Law, Paragraph 819, Principal Conventions: "The paramount convention is that the sovereign must act on the advice tendered to her by her ministers, in particular the prime minister."

Convoke. *See* Convene

Copyright

A copyright—a legally sanctioned right to intellectual property granted to a creator of certain works or artistic productions for a limited period of time—gives the grantee the sole and exclusive privilege of reproducing copies of his or her work and publishing and selling them. Some constitutions, especially those of federal nation-states, expressly give to the national government

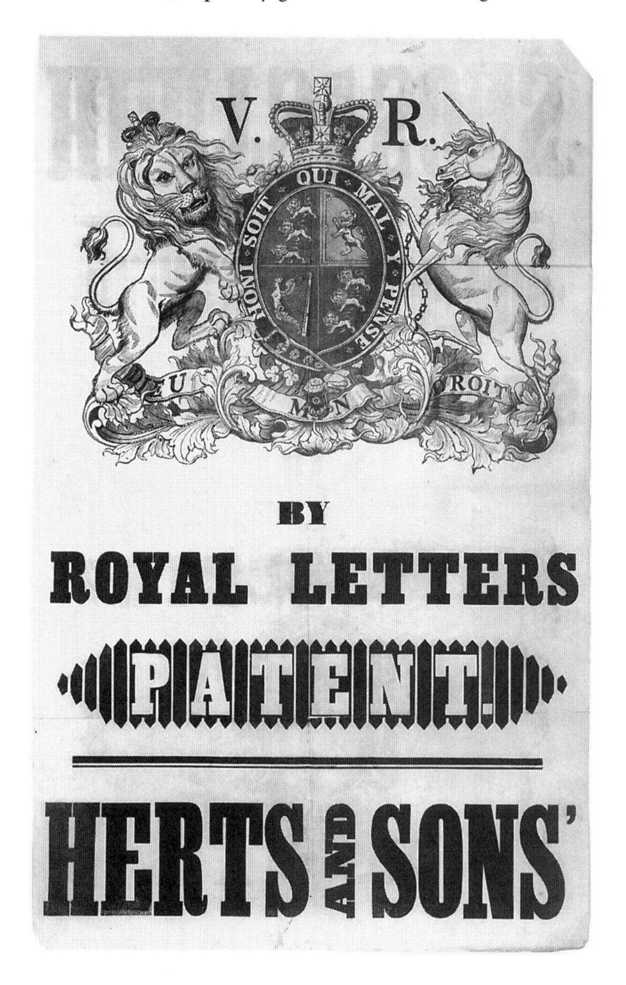

Similar to copyright protections, British letters of patent grant an exclusive right to make and sell a new invention.

the jurisdiction or authority to grant copyrights as well as patents for inventions.

Article 1, Section 8, of the U.S. Constitution (1789) grants to Congress the power to promote the progress of science and useful arts by securing for limited times to authors and inventors the exclusive right to their respective writings and works. James Madison comments on this grant of power in essay 43 of *The Federalist* (1788), saying that in Great Britain the copyright of authors was recognized under common law and that the states of the United States could not make effectual provision for either copyright or patents.

Constitution of Germany (1949), VII, Legislative Powers of the Federation, Article 73, Exclusive Legislative Power, Catalogue: "The federation shall have exclusive power to legislate in the following matters: . . . 9. industrial property rights, copyrights, and publishing law. . . . "

Constitution of Ethiopia (1995), Chapter Five, The Structure and Division of Powers of the Federal Democratic Republic of Ethiopia, Article 51, Powers of the Federal State: "It shall patent inventions and protect copyrights."

Corruption. *See* Bribery

Council of Ministers. *See* Cabinet

Council of State

To protect the morals and aims of the state, Plato in *The Laws* creates a nocturnal council, so called because it was to meet before dawn. The term *council* is derived from the Latin *consilium* (deliberate, plan, and advise).

In England the council of state evolved from the Great Council, or Witenagemote, the assembly of the Witan, the wise men who advised the Anglo-Saxon kings. In France the *conseil d'état* (council of state) began as an advisory body to the king, but today it is France's highest administrative court and also acts as an advisory body on the conformity of proposed laws with existing law. In what is now Belgium, a council of state to oversee the administrative courts was set up during the French period from 1795 to 1814; it was abolished and then reinstated in 1946. Like the French council, however, it is not mentioned in the written constitution.

Not to be confused with a council of ministers (cabinet), a council of state may act as the highest administrative court in a nation-state or as an advisory body for the executive branch.

Constitution of Portugal (1976), Part III, Organization of Political Power, Section II, President of the Republic, Chapter III, Council of State, Article 144: "The council of state is the advisory body of the president of the republic."

Constitution of Greece (1975), Part Three, Organization and Functions of the State, Section V, The Judicial Power, Chapter Two, Organization and Jurisdiction of the Courts, Article 95: "The jurisdiction of the council of state pertains mainly to: a) The annulment upon petition of executive acts of administrative authorities for excess of power or violation of the law. b) The petition to cassate final judgments of administrative courts for excess of power or violation of law. c) The trial of substantive administrative disputes submitted thereto as provided by the constitution and laws. d) The elaboration of all decrees of a regulative nature."

Countersignature

The seemingly innocent formality of a countersignature—a second signature that confirms or attests to the authenticity of a first signature—is the linchpin of constitutional monarchies and many presidential-style parliamentary democracies. In the constitutions of such countries—for example, the unwritten constitution of the United Kingdom and the written constitution of Germany—a law or other government act signed only by the head of state is invalid. To be valid, it must be countersigned by the appropriate minister or other acceptable official. An act to increase the size of the army, therefore, would have to be signed by the head of state and the minister for defense to be a valid law.

The countersigning minister is then responsible for his or her acts, as well as the acts of the head of state, to the parliament or at least to the chamber of parliament

The failed revolt of the Irish nationalist and rebel Robert Emmet ended up in court in 1803, followed by his execution.

responsible for forming a government after elections. The fact that the heads of state in true parliamentary systems of government, both monarchs and presidents, are not held accountable for their acts is acceptable in a democracy only as long as some elected official or a delegate is held accountable by virtue of his or her countersignature.

Constitution of the Netherlands (1814), Chapter Two, Government, Section I, The King, Article 47: "All acts of parliament and royal decrees shall be signed by the king and by one or more ministers or secretaries of state."

Constitution of Romania (1991), Title III, Public Authorities, Chapter III, The Government, Article 107: "(4) Decisions and orders adopted by the government shall be signed by the prime minister, countersigned by the ministers who are bound to act to carry them into execution, and shall be published in the official gazette of Romania. Absence of publicity entails non-existence of a decision or order. Decisions of a military character shall be conveyed only to the institutions concerned."

Court

"Of course, any state without duly established courts simply ceases to *be* a state," Plato avers in *The Laws.* In *The Politics,* Aristotle identifies eight types of courts, one of which handles treason against the constitution. The Latin word for a law court was *judicium,* and the English word *court* is derived from Middle English and Old French. In English law a court was originally the palace of the monarch or the mansion of the feudal lord. The term evolved to refer to the advisers and administrators who carried out judicial functions in the name of the sovereign or lord.

In constitutional terms a court is an organ of the judicial branch of government that applies laws to cases or controversies over which it has jurisdiction and carries out other specified judicial functions. Some courts are authorized by constitutions to give advisory opinions, review election results, and try impeachments of high government officials. The term *court* is also used in common parlance to refer to a judge or judges sitting as a court and to the place where court is held, the courthouse.

Constitutions often establish various types and levels of courts, tribunals, and councils, which are given some judicial functions. Constitutions also generally contain provisions regarding both the makeup and administration of courts of law, as well as the jurisdiction of each court. Sometimes courts are granted jurisdiction over religious matters or persons of a certain religious faith.

Constitution of Ethiopia (1995), Chapter IX, Structure and Powers of the Courts, Article 79, Judicial Powers: "Both at federal and state levels judicial powers are vested in the courts."

Constitution of Panama (1972), Title VII, The Administration of Justice, Chapter 1, The Judicial Branch of Government, Article 206: "In the courts of appeals and lower courts established by law, justices shall be appointed by the supreme court of justice and judges shall be appointed by their immediate superiors. Subordinate personnel shall be appointed by the respective tribunal or judge."

Crime

A crime—from the Latin *crimen*—is an action or omission that is deemed to be an offense against the state and thus is punishable by the state according to law. William Blackstone, the eighteenth-century commentator on the laws of England, defined a crime or misdemeanor as an act committed or omitted in violation of a public law either forbidding it or commanding it. In common usage, he suggested, crimes such as felonies are generally considered more serious than misdemeanors. Crimes are public wrongs, in contrast to civil injuries, which are private wrongs.

Modern constitutions generally contain provisions regarding crimes and criminal law such as the rights of those accused of a crime, procedural safeguards for criminal trials, immunity of officials such as legislators from arrest for certain crimes, court jurisdiction for criminal cases, and the types of crime that constitute impeachable offenses.

Constitution of Ghana (1992), Chapter Five, Fundamental Human Rights and Freedoms, Article 19: "A person charged with a criminal offense shall be given a fair hearing within a reasonable time by a court."

Constitution of China (People's Republic of China) (1982), Chapter Three, Structure of the State, Section VII, The People's Courts and the People's Procuratorates, Article 135: "The people's courts, people's procuratorates, and public security organs shall, in handling criminal cases, divide their functions, each taking responsibility for its own work, and they shall coordinate their efforts and check each other to ensure correct and effective enforcement."

Crown. *See* Monarchy

Cruel and Unusual Punishment. *See* Punishment

Culture

A people's civilization, customs, and artistic achievements, especially at a particular stage in their development, have come to be seen as their culture (from the Latin *cultus*). This is generally the sense of the word as used in constitutions, particularly those of countries with distinct and entrenched ethnic groups who wish to remain to some degree unassimilated into the mainstream of the dominant culture or political system.

A number of constitutions expressly identify cultural groups and indigenous populations within their territorial jurisdictions and make special provision to protect or advance them or guarantee their equal or proportionally equal treatment vis-à-vis other cultural groups. The 1919 Finnish constitution guarantees that the cultural and economic needs of the Swedish-speaking population will be given equal treatment by the state, and the 1947 Taiwanese constitution pledges the state to foster, among other things, the culture of "various racial groups in the frontier regions" of the country.

Constitution of Belgium (1831), Heading III, Concerning the Authorities, Chapter I, Concerning the Houses of Parliament, Section III, Concerning the Community Councils, Article 59b: "2. The community council, each in its own sphere [Flemish and French], shall regulate by decree: 1. cultural matters. . . . "

Constitution of Nicaragua (1987), Title IX, Political Administrative Division, Chapter II, Communities of the Atlantic Coast, Article 180: "The communities of the Atlantic coast have the right to live and develop themselves under the forms of social organization that correspond to their historical and cultural traditions. . . . Furthermore, it [the state] guarantees the preservation of their cultures and languages, religion and customs."

Currency

Aristotle explains in *The Politics* that as the people of one country became dependent on imports from another country, money necessarily came into use. Although the term *currency* technically embraces both coins and paper money, including bank notes, it is colloquially used to

Historic examples of of French currency include *assignats,* bank notes that were used during the French Revolution of 1789.

refer only to paper money. In 1755 the English lexicographer Samuel Johnson defined currency specifically as "the papers stamped in the English colonies by authority and passing for money."

Many constitutions, especially those of federal nation-states, expressly grant the national government the authority to issue and regulate currency. Article 1, Section 10, of the U.S. Constitution (1789) expressly forbids the states to "emit" bills of credit. A series of court cases was necessary before the Supreme Court declared that Congress could issue notes as legal tender, a medium of exchange that must be accepted in full payment for a debt. To reach this conclusion, however, the Court had to create a new category of federal powers, which it called resulting powers.

Constitution of Brazil (1988), Title IV, The Organization of the Powers, Chapter I, The Legislative Power, Section II, Powers of the National Congress, Article 48: "The national congress shall have the power with the sanction of the president of the republic . . . to provide for all the matters within the competence of the union and especially on: . . . XIV—currency, currency issuance limits, and amount of the federal indebtedness. . . . "

Constitution of Kuwait (1962), Part IV, Powers, Chapter IV, The Executive Power, Section II, Financial Affairs, Article 154: "Law shall regulate currency and banking and determine standards, weights, and measures."

Custom

Eagerness to abandon old laws for new ones reduces the effectiveness of laws, Aristotle observes in *The Politics,* concluding that the law cannot command obedience except out of custom. The Romans recognized customary laws, but such laws could not override reasonableness or statutory laws. The word *custom* derives from the Italian *custome* (dress, manners, or usage) and the French *coutume* (custom, habit, or practice).

Like tradition and to a lesser degree convention, custom is a practice of the people that by common adoption or acquiescence and long, unvarying habit acquires the force of law. Many elements of constitutions, especially unwritten ones, stem from custom and tradition. In some instances these elements may be enforceable by law; in cases where they are considered political accommodations rather than legal rights, however, they may not.

In the United States the Supreme Court has rejected jurisdiction in cases it considers fundamentally political questions. Similarly, the strictly customary or conventional elements of Canada's constitution have been found by its supreme court to be outside its jurisdiction. When a custom is enshrined in a written constitution, it becomes law. A number of former British colonies have turned British constitutional customs into supreme written laws.

The two-party system in the United States is an example of a constitutional element that had its basis originally in the British colonists' familiarity with the two-party system—one party in power (the majority party) and the other party (the minority party, considered the loyal opposition) out of power. The role of political parties, however, is not addressed in the written U.S. Constitution (1789).

Custom, which rests on tacit consent, is also one of three bases of international law identified by the seventeenth-century Dutch jurist and statesman Hugo Grotius; the others are voluntary law, which rests on presumed consent, and conventional law, which rests on express consent.

Customs, in the plural form, refers to tariffs, taxes, or duties on exports and imports, as well as to the culture and traditions of ethnic and aboriginal groups that may be accorded special rights and protections in constitutions.

Constitution of Canada, Constitution Act (1982), Part I, Canadian Charter of Rights and Freedoms, Section 6(3): "The rights specified in subsection (2) are subject to (a) any laws or practices [*usages* in the French version] of general application in force in a province other than those that discriminate among persons primarily on the basis of province of present or previous residence. . . . "

Constitution of Spain (1978), Title VIII, Concerning Territorial Organization of the State, Chapter III, Concerning the Self-Governing Communities, Article 149: "1. The state holds exclusive jurisdiction over the following matters: . . . 10) Customs and tariff regulations. . . ."

D

de Gaulle, Charles-André-Joseph-Marie

Charles de Gaulle (1890–1970) succeeded to a great extent in remaking France's constitution in his own image and restoring the position of head of state to a preeminent status, reminiscent of that of monarchs during the *Ancien Régime,* the period before the French Revolution.

De Gaulle was born in Lille, France, on November 23, 1890. His father, who came from a long line of French patriots, was an embittered veteran of the Franco-Prussian War of 1870 and raised his sons to avenge France's defeat in that war. Young Charles enjoyed reading the histories and other works written by his paternal grandparents and his uncle, for whom he was named.

In 1909 de Gaulle entered the elite military academy of Saint-Cyr. After distinguishing himself—he almost died of wounds—in World War I, he enrolled in the army general-staff school. His criticism of French tactics fell on deaf ears, but the Germans later found his proposals useful in the development of the *Blitzkrieg* (lightning war) against France and other countries in World War II. When France fell to the Nazis in 1940, de Gaulle, then a brigadier general, refused to surrender. He fled to England and directed the resistance force from there.

As interim president of France after the war, de Gaulle became disgusted with French politicians and the 1946 constitution adopted for the Fourth Republic. On June 16, 1946, he gave a speech in Bayeux outlining his vision for a new constitution, which he held ready until the 1946 document failed to provide the decisive leadership the nation needed during its 1954 crisis in Algeria, which had been annexed by France in 1842. Revolting against the French colonial rule, a national liberation front erupted into guerrilla warfare. The French army fighting in Algeria was discouraged by the irresolute 1946 constitutional system, a feeling that intensified after French forces were defeated on November 7, 1954, at Dien Bien Phu in Vietnam, a French colony in Indochina acquired in stages between 1867 and 1883.

On June 1, 1958, de Gaulle, who had been named prime minister, asked for and received a vote of confidence to change the constitution and present it for referendum. The principles of his new constitution included universal suffrage as the basis for executive and legislative powers, effective separation of executive and legislative authority, a government responsible to the parliament, judicial independence, and a procedure for institutionalizing the relationship of the French republic with the peoples of other countries, such as Algeria.

De Gaulle claimed that the text of the 1958 constitution, although drafted by others, "emerged under my guidance." Later he noted that he had originally not specified that the president be directly elected but that he intended " . . . at the outset to assume the functions of the head of state." He envisioned the power and authority of a head of state elected for seven years as a counterbalance to the possible excesses of the parliament. He

Charles de Gaulle's vision of a French constitution with a strong president was approved by the people of France in 1958.

also recognized the need to enhance the separation of powers by forbidding simultaneous membership in both the parliament and the government (France's council of ministers, or cabinet), a basic change from the traditional parliamentary system of government.

De Gaulle served as president of the Fifth Republic from 1959 to 1969. He died on November 9, 1970, at Colombey-les-Deux-Eglises.

de Valera, Eamon

Seldom has a single personality had such a great influence on the constitutional development of a modern nation over such a long period of time as Eamon de Valera (1882–1975) had on the constitution of his adopted country, Ireland.

De Valera, the son of a Spanish father and a mother from Knockmore, Bruree, County Limerick, was born in New York City on October 14, 1882. His father died when he was two years old, and his mother then sent him to live in Ireland. Raised by his maternal grandmother, de Valera attended the national school at Bruree and later credited a parish priest for his fierce Irish patriotism. When he was older he walked seven miles a day each way to attend the Christian Brothers school at Charlesville. At sixteen he received a scholarship to college, eventually won more scholarships, and obtained an appointment as a professor of mathematics. He was also a fine rugby player and had a deep appreciation for the Irish language.

Eamon de Valera, although born in the United States, helped Ireland gain independence from Great Britain and drafted Ireland's 1937 constitution.

In 1913 de Valera became active in the Irish nationalist movement for separation from Great Britain and was sworn into the Irish Republican Brotherhood, whose constitution declared that its supreme council was the sole government of the Irish republic, with the right to make treaties and declare war, and its president the president of the republic. Although not among the seven who signed the 1916 Irish Declaration of the Republic, which became the equivalent of Magna Carta for Irish republicans, he was nevertheless arrested that year for his role in the 1916 rebellion known as the Easter Rising. The sentence of death against him, however, was never carried out, and he became the elected leader of the inmates at Dartmoor Prison in England.

After his release from prison in 1917, de Valera won a parliamentary by-election as a republican constitutionalist against the Irish party nominee and was later elected president of the "new" Sinn Fein, a political and cultural society founded in 1905 to promote Irish independence from Britain. In 1919 he visited the United States to obtain support for an independent Irish republic. When he returned, the British in Ireland were being subjected to guerrilla tactics. After a truce on July 11, 1920, the Irish parliament, the Dáil, accepted a treaty with Britain in 1922, although over de Valera's objections. Civil war broke out that same year, and de Valera was again arrested. Once released, he continued to work tirelessly for the independence movement, founding a republican newspaper, *The Irish Press*, in 1931. His efforts culminated in 1937 in a new constitution for his Irish republic, which he wrote, and the Anglo-Irish Agreement of 1938, which completed Britain's relinquishment of sovereignty over all but Northern Ireland.

Using democratic and parliamentary means, de Valera had dismantled the 1922 treaty with Britain that he had opposed and the 1922 constitution that reflected it. Singlehandedly he drafted the 1937 constitution, under which he served as prime minister until 1948, again from 1951 to 1954, and again from 1957 to 1959. He was elected president of Ireland in 1956 and 1966; he retired from

"Madame Guillotine," a swiftly descending sharp blade that decapitated its victims, was a popular way to administer the death penalty during France's Reign of Terror (1793–94) that followed the 1789 revolution.

office in 1973, having served in that capacity for fourteen years. Described as the "constitutional Houdini of his era," de Valera in one sense merely rebottled the old wine of the 1922 constitution to reflect his republican views, even though the 1937 document falls short of declaring Ireland a republic.

De Valera's constitution, like the U.S. document, contains provisions for judicial review and a statement of fundamental rights, although personally he was less than enthusiastic about a bill of rights, calling it "headlines for the legislature." Reflecting both the breadth and depth of his political powers and personal understanding of the Irish people, the document is divided into three basic categories: the nature of the state and government, the details of the operation of the government, and fundamental rights. De Valera believed that the constitution should be adopted by the people—which it was, by referendum on July 1, 1937 (the effective date of operation was December 29, 1937)—and that after a transitional period it should be amended only by referendum.

De Valera's last attempt at constitutional reform, which would have changed the proportional voting system to a direct one, however, was rejected in a referendum. After a long and illustrious career he died at the age of ninety-two on August 29, 1975.

Death Penalty

The debate over whether the state should impose the death penalty on conviction for certain crimes has gone on for centuries. In *The Laws,* Plato devotes a section to capital offenses—crimes that call for the death penalty—

and includes among them robbery from temples, political subversion, and treason. Jean-Jacques Rousseau, the eighteenth-century French philosopher and writer, argued that even capital punishment has its basis in consent, because if a person is willing to have others—for example, soldiers—risk their lives for him or her, he or she must risk losing his or her own life for the sake of others. However, William Blackstone, the eighteenth-century commentator on English laws, quoted the French philosopher Montesquieu to the effect that a law that punishes too severely risks failure of execution by those who are charged with imposing it.

In 1972 the U.S. Supreme Court declared the death penalty to be cruel and unusual punishment and therefore in violation of the Eighth Amendment (1791) to the Constitution. In 1976 the Court reversed itself, ruling that the death penalty in some cases was not cruel and unusual punishment and upholding a two-step procedure that required a second trial after a conviction to determine the propriety of imposing the death penalty.

Many modern constitutions contain specific language limiting or prohibiting the death penalty. South Africa's new multiracial constitutional court abolished the death penalty in June 1995, ruling unanimously that it was unconstitutional.

Constitution of Brazil (1988), Title II, Fundamental Rights, Chapter I, Individual and Collective Rights and Duties, Article 5, 47: " . . . there shall be no punishment: a) of death, save in case of declared war. . . . "

Constitution of Mozambique (1990), Part II, Fundamental Rights, Duties, and Freedoms, Chapter I, General Principles, Article 70: "2. In the Republic of Mozambique there shall be no death penalty."

Debate

The formal discussion of some question of public interest in an assembly or a legislature—debate—is a major parliamentary device for ensuring responsible and democratic government. For his nocturnal council, the protective state body proposed in *The Laws,* Plato envisioned that elder members would debate policy with their younger associates to gain their assistance and advice.

In legislative bodies when the votes are already assured for passage of a particular measure under discussion, debate is often seen as a mere formality. Nevertheless, the requirement for debate provides a forum for minority response and a record of dissent in the event that a measure proves ill advised after enactment. And it is politically advantageous for majority members to be on record in support of a well-conceived measure. Debate procedures in modern legislatures are generally subject to precise formal rules to ensure an opportunity for members to express themselves in a fair and orderly fashion.

A filibuster is an attempt by members in the minority opposing a measure to use the rules of debate to maintain the floor and continue to talk on any subject until the majority side tires and changes or withdraws its proposal. The "gag rule," like cloture, is a special parliamentary procedure for limiting or cutting off debate.

Constitution of Mozambique (1990), Part III, Organs of State, Chapter III, Assembly of the Republic, Article 140: "The assembly of the republic may only enter into debate when more than one half of its members are present."

Constitution of Finland, Parliament Act (1928), Chapter 5, Consideration of Matters in Plenary Sittings and in the Grand Committee, Section 55: "The speaker shall issue the summons to plenary sittings, present the matters and preside over the debates therein. . . . The speaker shall not participate in a debate or a vote."

Debt.

See Borrowing Power; Obligation

Declaration of Independence

A declaration is a proclamation or a public statement generally in writing. Southern Rhodesia, now Zimbabwe, issued a Universal Declaration of Independence in 1962, and in 1948 Israel proclaimed a Declaration of the Establishment of the State of Israel, which is referred to as its declaration of independence.

The best-known declaration of independence is the July 4, 1776, document, written primarily by Thomas Jefferson, that proclaimed on behalf of the people of the

A rendering by Howard Bodie shows two members of the U.S. Senate, Jacob Javits and Leverett Saltonstall, listening to Richard B. Russell filibuster against the Civil Rights Act in 1964. Senator Russell was considered a master of the art of the filibuster.

American colonies their independence from Great Britain and announced that henceforth they were to be considered a sovereign and independent country. The declaration, which drew on the principle of natural rights espoused by John Locke, included a list of grievances against the British Crown and defended individual rights and the right of self-government. The words of the document have inspired the peoples of other countries ever since.

Declarations of independence as a rule are not constitutional documents, especially in countries with written constitutions. The Israeli declaration, however, is considered to have quasi-constitutional status because it confirms the creation of the nation-state of Israel, the rule of law, and the rights of individuals.

Declaration of Independence of the United States of America (1776): "We hold these truths to be self-evident, that all men are created equal, that they are endowed by their Creator with certain inalienable rights, that among these are life, liberty, and the pursuit of happiness."

Declaration of the Establishment of the State of Israel (1948): "We extend our hand to all neighboring states and their peoples in an offer of peace and good neighborliness, and appeal to them to establish bonds of

The signing of Venezuela's declaration of independence from Spain and France on July 5, 1811, was the colony's first step toward becoming a nation. Venezuela adopted its first constitution the same year.

cooperation and mutual help with the sovereign Jewish people settled in its own land. The State of Israel is prepared to do its share in a common effort for the advancement of the entire Middle East."

Declaration of the Rights of Man and of the Citizen

The 1789 Declaration of the Rights of Man and of the Citizen, a primarily political document, was adopted in popular assemblies in France during the French Revolution. It was a triumph of libertarianism over egalitarianism, detailing the expectations of ordinary French citizens to be treated with equal justice before the law and with equal respect in the course of their daily lives. Even after the forces of legitimacy restored the French monarchy in 1814, Louis XVIII acknowledged the Rights of Man.

Since 1789 the Rights of Man, like the U.S. Declaration of Independence, has become a symbol of the struggle for individual freedom, equality, and justice against absolutism and government oppression. France's 1958 constitution incorporates by reference the Rights of Man, and the constitutions of other countries on which France and the French Revolution have had an impact also refer to it and its principles.

Constitution of France (1958), Preamble: "The French people hereby solemnly proclaims its attachment to the Rights of Man and the principles of national sovereignty as defined by the declaration of 1789, reaffirmed and complemented by the preamble of the constitution of 1946."

Constitution of Algeria (1976), Title I, General Principles, Chapter 4, Concerning the Rights and Liberties, Article 31: "The fundamental liberties and the Rights of Man and of the Citizen are guaranteed. They constitute the common patrimony of all Algerians *(Algeriens et Algeriennes)* who have the task of transmitting it from generation to generation in its integrity and inviolability."

Declaration of War. *See* War

Decree

In ancient Rome a *decretum* was a pronouncement by a Roman emperor deciding an appeal from a civil suit, while a *decreto* (decree) under Spanish colonial law was an order of a superior tribunal issued in the name of and under the authority of the sovereign. In English law a decree is a judgment of an equity or admiralty court answering the judgment of a common law court.

In constitutions, however, the term *decree* is more closely related to the French law concept of *decret*—an act of the legislature or sovereign that has the force of law. A decree, sometimes called a decree law or law decree, generally refers to an order by an officer in the executive branch, usually the president, that may or may not have to be authorized by the legislature but that has the force of enacted law.

Constitution of France (1958), Title V, On Relations Between Parliament and the Government, Article 37: "Those legislative texts which may be passed after the present constitution has become operative shall be modified by decree, only if the constitutional council has stated that they have a regulatory character. . . . "

Constitution of Peru (1993), Section IV, Concerning the Structure of Government, Chapter II, Concerning the Legislative Function, Article 104: "Congress may delegate to the executive branch the power to legislate by means of legislative orders on the specific subject and for the term established by the authoritative law. . . . In terms of their promulgation, publication, enforcement, and effects, legislative decrees are subject to the same standards as the law."

Decree law. *See* Decree

Defense

In *The Laws,* Plato commits the protection of the city to the generals, other officers, the leaders of tribes, and members of the executive organs. He suggests that, as far as practicable, nothing should be left unguarded. Ancient Rome had its military leaders, some of whom went on to become emperors, and its legions, whose lines of defense extended as far from Rome as Hadrian's Wall in the British Isles. The history of Europe from feudal times into the twentieth century, like the world at large, is fraught with the ebb and flow of aggression and the

After World War II radar installations became the first line of defense against attack by nuclear missiles.

defense of territory. During the cold war, which followed World War II, some nations based their defense on nuclear weapons whose capabilities were characterized as MAD (Mutually Assured Destruction).

Clearly, defense against internal and external aggression—or, less euphemistically, war—is an important element in the design and implementation of constitutions. Internal aggression is the subject of provisions on police power, emergency power, martial law, and internal security in general. External aggression is the subject of provisions on raising, maintaining, and directing the armed forces of the state. A department or ministry of defense is invariably specified in sections of modern constitutions that detail the various government departments or ministries.

Constitution of Nicaragua (1987), Title V, National Defense, Chapter I, Article 92: "It is the duty of Nicaraguans to struggle for the defense of life, homeland, justice, and peace for the full development of the nation."

Constitution of Iraq (1970), Chapter IV, Institutions of the Iraqi Republic, Section III, President of the Republic, Article 57: "The president of the republic exercises the following competences: (a) Preserving the independence of the country, its territorial integrity, safeguarding its internal and external security, and protecting the rights and liberties of all citizens."

Delegate

In Roman law the substitution of a debtor to pay the creditor of another debtor was an example of *delegatio debitoris.* In English common law a delegate is one who is given authority to act for another.

As used in constitutions a delegate is a person sent to represent others—for example, to a convention or legislature. In the United States delegates may be members of a convention, such as a political or constitutional convention, or representatives sent to the House of Representatives from U.S. territories or possessions as allowed for by the rules of that body, or the members of a few of the lower houses of the legislatures of constituent states of the United States.

To delegate may also refer to a transfer of power, generally temporarily, to one person to act on another's behalf or on behalf of an entire government body, such as the legislature.

Constitution of Indonesia (1945), Chapter II, The Majelis Permusyawaratan Rakyat, Article 2(1): "The Majelis Permusyawaratan Rakyat [a largely ceremonial body that meets at least once every five years to elect the president and vice president and "determine the constitution and the guidelines of the policy of the state"] shall consist of the members of the Dewan Perwakilan Rakyat [legislature] augmented by the delegates from the regional territories and groups as provided for by statutory regulations."

Constitution of Hungary (1949, significantly revised in 1989), Chapter II, National Assembly, Article 21(2): "The national assembly shall form standing committees from among its members and may delegate a committee for the investigation of any matter."

Deliberation

One of the three elements that Aristotle claims may be found in any constitution is deliberation, which he says has authority over war and peace, alliances, law making and punishments, the election of magistrates, and the audit of accounts.

In modern constitutions the legislature is generally considered the deliberative body, although members of a council of ministers or judges on a court may also deliberate—weigh or consider carefully matters for the purpose of making a decision. Deliberating, debating, and voting on proposed legislation, resolutions, and motions are the major activities of the members of legislatures.

Constitution of Ghana (1993), Chapter Ten, The Legislature, Article 106(5): "Where a bill has been deliberated upon by the appropriate committee, it shall be reported to parliament."

Constitution of Haiti (1987), Title V, Chapter II, The Legislative Branch, Section D, Exercise of Legislative Power, Article 111-4: "If a disagreement occurs with regard to any other law, a decision will be postponed until the following session. If, at that session . . . no agreement is reached . . . a parliamentary committee [is] to decide on the final text that will be submitted to the two (2) assemblies. . . . If these additional deliberations produce no result, the bill or proposed law will be withdrawn."

Democracy

For ancient Greeks a pure democracy was more akin to anarchy or licentiousness than the government of free and equal citizens enshrined in most constitutions today. Plato, in *The Laws,* equates good government with the correct combination of monarchy and democracy, but he warns against "a freedom from inhibitions that has gone too far." In *The Politics,* Aristotle calls democracy a perversion of constitutional government. The Roman republic at first was an aristocracy, and the lower class, known as plebeians, had to fight, often militarily, to gain any voice in the government. As an empire, Rome became an authoritarian and totalitarian state.

The modern concept of democracy, derived from the Greek *demokratia* (rule by the people), grew out of the development of natural law principles and the eighteenth-century Enlightenment movement in Europe. Paralleling the rise of nationalism and the nation-state, popular, representative democracy, as distinguished from the direct democracies of the early Greek city-states, developed in Europe—gradually in England, more abruptly in France. The precept of the divine right of kings and the interlocking relationship between the state and religion slowly gave way to the idea of popular sovereignty, the basis of representative democracy, and greater tolerance for religious sects, which freed governments to become secular or at least more ecumenical. The philosophical groundwork was laid by John Locke and Jean-Jacques Rousseau, among others, who discovered a natural law and natural order that dictated the creation of governments by a rational society of free people—a contractual society in which the people are sovereign and the rulers are responsible to them for the conduct of government affairs.

The key revolutions in the evolution of representative democracy were England's Glorious Revolution of 1688–89, which restored the monarchy on Parliament's terms; the American Revolution of 1775–83; and the French Revolution of 1789. These historic occurrences established the power of the commoners—the people—to abolish and limit governments.

Democracy today, as reflected in the government structures created by national constitutions, requires decision making based on majority rule, with protection for minority rights and individual freedoms and guarantees to ensure state protection of life, liberty, and property, as well as access to the country's political processes. Above all, democracy requires strict adherence to the rule of law to ensure rational government. Key concepts that undergird democracy are individualism, liberty, equality, and fraternity.

The democratic character of the governments established by modern constitutions is inherent in the language used and the institutions created, not the mere recitation of the words *democratic* or *democracy,* as evidenced particularly in so-called democratic constitutions of countries dominated by the Communist Party.

Constitution of Russia (1993), Preamble: "Renewing the sovereign statehood of Russia and acknowledging the immutability of its democratic foundations. . . . "

Constitution of Greece (1975), Part Three, Organization and Functions of the State, Section I, Structure of the State, Article 29: "1. Greek citizens possessing the right to vote may freely found and join political parties, the organization of which must serve the free functioning of democratic government."

Constitution of North Korea (1972), Chapter I, Politics, Article 10: "The Democratic People's Republic of Korea exercises the dictatorship of the proletariat. . . . "

Department

In constitutions a department—from the French *département* (an area of assignment or responsibility)—is generally a division of administrative responsibility headed by a secretary, just as ministries are headed by ministers. In some hybrid forms, however, ministers head departments and ministries have secretaries.

The French Département de l'intérieur, for example, is similar to the British Home Office and the U.S. Department of the Interior. In France departments are

The headquarters of the U.S. Department of Defense is located just south of Washington, D.C., in the Pentagon, one of the largest office buildings in the world. The other U.S. departments are also located in the nation's capital and its suburbs.

also districts into which the country is divided for administrative purposes.

Constitution of the United States of America (1789), Article II, Section 2: "The President . . . may require the Opinion, in writing, of the Principal Officer [the secretary] in each of the executive Departments. . . . "

Constitution of Argentina (1853), Second Part, Authorities of the Nation, Title I, Federal Government, Second Section, The Executive Power, Chapter IV, Ministers of the Executive Branch, Article 90: " . . . the ministers of the cabinet shall submit a detailed report on the state of the nation in connection with the business of their respective departments."

Deputy

The three estates represented in the Estates-Général between 1302 and 1789, during the French monarchy, were the clergy, the nobles, and the deputies *(députés)* for the cities and towns. The latter group is similar to the

The Chamber of Deputies in Paris is the historic meeting place for the elected representatives of the French people.

commons in England from which the designation of the House of Commons for the lower chamber of the British Parliament is derived.

Deputies are delegates elected to represent a constituency or a member of a legislative assembly. The English word *deputy* generally refers to one who acts for another. But a special application of the term means one who is deputed to exercise authority on behalf of the sovereign. In constitutions based on popular sovereignty, elected representatives of the people come within the ambit of this definition. In constitutions the term *deputy* generally refers to an elected member of the legislature and specifically to a member of the more popularly elected lower chamber or house. France's constitution states that the parliament is to consist of a national assembly and a senate and that the "deputies to the national assembly shall be elected by direct suffrage." But in some constitutions the term may be used in the second sense—for example, deputy minister or deputy secretary.

Constitution of Argentina (1853), Second Part, Authorities of the Nation, Title I, Federal Government, First Section, The Legislative Power, Article 36: "A congress consisting of two chambers, one of deputies of the nation and the other of senators of the provinces and of the capital, shall be vested with the legislative power of the nation."

Constitution of China (People's Republic of China) (1982), Chapter Three, Structure of the State, Section V, The Local People's Congresses and the Local People's Governments at Different Levels, Article 101: "At their respective levels, the local people's congresses elect and have the power to recall governors and deputy governors, or mayors and deputy mayors, or heads and deputy heads of counties, townships, and towns."

Dignity

The phrase *human dignity* may be used in constitutions to reinforce the value of each citizen of the nation-state and his or her consequent right to be treated honorably and fairly by the state and its officials, not inhumanely or with contempt. When the concept is mentioned, it often occurs in a constitution's preamble, opening provisions, or section on individual rights and freedoms.

Through its posters, the United Nations promotes the concept of human dignity, along with individual freedom and rights, as the basis for harmonious relationships.

In English law dignity—from the Latin *dignitas* (worthiness, rank, or authority)—refers to an honor such as a title, status, or distinction of honor, and dignities are a type of incorporeal property right that may be inherited.

Constitution of Cuba (1976), Preamble: "We declare our will that the laws of the republic be guided by the following strong desire of José Martí, at last achieved: I want the fundamental law of our republic to be the tribute of Cubans to the full dignity of man. . . . "

Constitution of Bangladesh (1972), Part II, Fundamental Principles of State Policy, Article 11: "The republic shall be a democracy in which fundamental human rights and freedoms and respect for the dignity and worth of the human person shall be guaranteed. . . . "

In ancient Athens the public gathered at the arch at the *agora* (marketplace) to implement the Greeks' direct, rather than representative, form of democracy.

Direct Democracy

Direct democracy, the system practiced in ancient Greece and Rome and in some cantons of Switzerland, stands in contrast to the currently prevailing form of representative democracy. Jean-Jacques Rousseau, the eighteenth-century French philosopher, criticized the democracy of England, saying that the English people were free only during parliamentary elections—after the elections they could not control the members of Parliament.

Although the notion that all citizens of a nation-state could participate directly in government by voting on all decisions affecting them seems totally impractical, some devices introduced into constitutions have elements of direct democracy. These include procedures for popular referendums, initiatives, and recall of officials. With today's technological advances in communications, it may be possible in the near future to reinstate true direct democracy in some form. While this would obviously increase the opportunity for all citizens to participate directly in government decision making, there is no evidence that their decisions will be better than those made by elected representatives.

Constitution of Switzerland (1874), Chapter III, Revision of the Federal Constitution, Article 120: "2—The popular initiative consists of a request, presented by a hundred thousand Swiss citizens entitled to vote, aiming at the introduction, setting aside, or modification of specified articles of the federal constitution."

Constitution of Libya, Declaration of the Establishment of the Authority of the People (1979), Preamble: "Believing in the establishment of the direct democratic system heralded by the great first of September revolution and regarding it as the absolute and decisive solution to the problem of democracy. . . . "

Directive. *See* Regulation

Dirigiste Constitution

The 1988 Brazilian constitution and the 1976 Portuguese constitution, on which it is based, are called *dirigiste* constitutions because they do more than just organize political power: they contain detailed directions for shaping, or reshaping, society and set out goals to be achieved and programs to be implemented. The neo-Marxist Portuguese term *Constitutiçã-Dirigente* (dirigiste constitution) was coined by Joaquim Gomes Canotilho, a professor at the University of Coimbra, in his work *Constituoção do Legislador* (1982). It is derived from the Latin word *dirigo* (to put in a straight line), and its French correlatives are *diriger* (to direct, manage or govern, or control) and *dirigisme* (planning).

A *dirigiste* constitution contains both procedural laws, which allow the existing political and economic forces in society to express themselves, and substantive laws, which prescribe what those changes should be and how to make them. This constitutional form is distinctly unlike the 1936 "Stalin" constitution of the Soviet Union, described as a balance-sheet constitution because it contained only a summation of the political state before the time of adoption. A *dirigiste* constitution details specific guidelines for accomplishing future political and social change. Under it, not only can enacted laws be held unconstitutional by oversight authorities such as constitutional courts, but even a legislature's failure to implement constitutional provisions can be found to be in violation of the constitution.

Constitution of Brazil (1988), Title I, Fundamental Principles, Article 3: "The fundamental objectives of the Federative Republic of Brazil are: I—to build a free, just, and solidary society; II—to guarantee national development; III—to eradicate poverty and substandard living conditions and to reduce social and regional inequalities; IV—to promote the well-being of all, without prejudice as to origin, race, sex, color, age, and any other forms of discrimination."

Constitution of Portugal (1976), Part IV, Safeguards and Revision of the Constitution, Section I, Supervision of the Constitutionality, Article 283, Unconstitutionality by Omission: "1. At the request of the president of the republic, the ombudsman, or, on the grounds that the rights of the autonomous regions have been violated, the presidents of the regional assemblies, the constitutional court shall judge and verify failure to comply with the constitution by omission on the part of legislative acts necessary to implement the provisions of the constitution."

Disability

Many constitutions provide for the assumption of the functions of the chief executive in the event that he or she becomes unable to carry out the functions of the office. Some constitutions also define or construct a procedure for determining what constitutes a disability, inability, or incapacity severe enough to warrant a transfer of executive power to another person or institution until a new chief executive can be chosen. Nicaragua's 1987 constitution, however, addresses the problem of the temporary or permanent absence of the chief executive, rather than partial, temporary, total, or permanent disability.

Generally, if the position of vice president exists, he or she assumes the powers and duties of the president in case of serious temporary or permanent disability. Article 2, Section 1, of the U.S. Constitution (1789) provides for the inability of the president or both the president and the vice president to carry out the duties of their offices. The Twenty-fifth Amendment (1967) specified that the vice president becomes president on the removal, death, or resignation of the president, but it did not change the provisions for disability.

Although crippled by polio, Franklin D. Roosevelt (shown with his wife, Eleanor) never let his disability interfere with his constitutional duties as president of the United States.

Constitution of Russia (1993), Part One, Chapter 4, The President of the Russian Federation, Article 92: "(2) The president of the Russian Federation shall discontinue the execution of the office before its expiration in the cases of resignation, continued inability to discharge the powers and the duties of the office for reasons of health, or removal from office by impeachment. (3) In the case of the inability of the president of the Russian Federation to execute presidential powers and duties, they shall devolve to the chairman [prime minister] of the government of the Russian Federation."

Constitution of Ireland (1937), The President, Article 12.2.1: "The president shall hold office for seven years from the date upon which he enters upon the office, unless before the expiration of that period he dies, or resigns, or is removed from office, or becomes permanently incapacitated, such incapacity being established to the satisfaction of the supreme court consisting of not less than five judges."

Dismissal

Absolute monarchs have held the power to appoint ministers who would give advice and run aspects of the government and to discharge or remove them at will. Used in constitutions, especially of constitutional monarchies and other parliamentary systems, the term *dismissal* indicates an action terminating the appointment of a person to a position in the government. In some instances, however, appointed officials may be dismissed only at the end of a specified term of office or for cause.

In parliamentary systems ministers or department heads may be terminated by a vote of no confidence by the parliament, or the entire government—the prime minister and the cabinet—may be dismissed by a vote of no confidence.

Less frequently, the term may also be used in the judicial sense of disposing of a case or suit with or without a hearing on its merits.

Constitution of the Netherlands (1814), Chapter 2, Government, Section 1, The King, Article 43: "The prime minister and the other ministers shall be appointed and dismissed by royal decree." [This is a formality only; by convention the appointment and dismissal actions must conform to the will of the majority in the parliament.]

Constitution of Indonesia (1945), Chapter V, The Ministers of State, Article 17: "(1) The president shall be assisted by the ministers of state. (2) These ministers shall be appointed and dismissed by the president. (3) These ministers shall head the government departments."

Disqualification. *See* Qualification

Dissolution. *See* Adjournment

Domicile. *See* Inhabitant

Dominion

In classical Roman law the word *dominium* referred to ownership, which was essentially perpetual and not subject to division into a bundle of rights as in English law. In English law the term *dominion* also means ownership or a right to property in the broadest sense. Historically, the word referred to the land and domain of a feudal lord.

Constitutionally speaking, dominion is the power to govern and has been used generally to refer to certain British possessions. In the 1931 Statute of Westminster, the British dominions included the Dominion of Canada, the Commonwealth of Australia, the Dominion of New Zealand, the Union of South Africa, the Irish Free State, and Newfoundland. The 1947 Indian Independence Act created the independent dominions of India and Pakistan. Today the term refers to the independent nation-state of Canada, which, however, still recognizes the monarch of England as its formal head of state.

Constitution of the United Kingdom, Bill of Rights (1688), Acceptance of the Crown . . . : "Upon which their said majestyes did accept the crown and royal dignitie of the kingdoms of England, France, and Ireland, and the

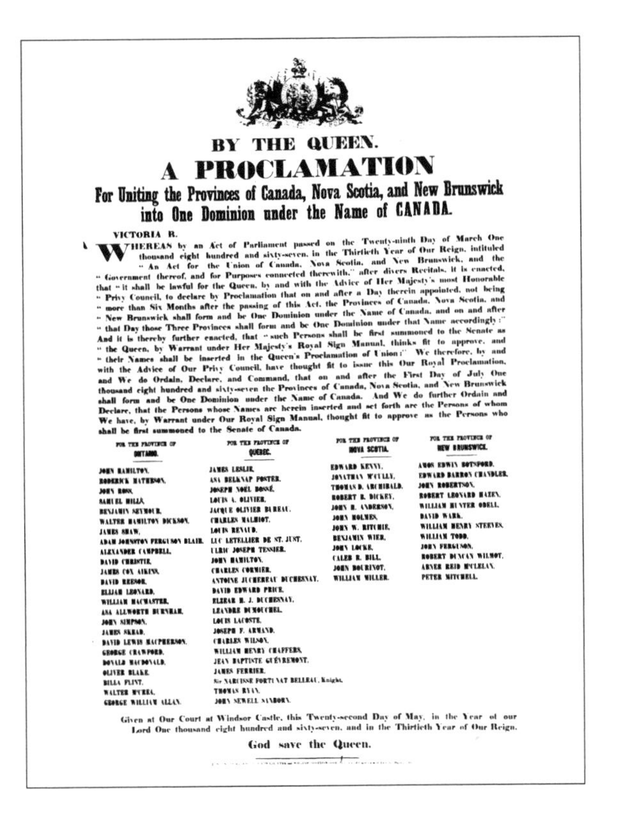

BY THE QUEEN.

A PROCLAMATION

For Uniting the Provinces of Canada, Nova Scotia, and New Brunswick into One Dominion under the Name of CANADA.

VICTORIA R.

WHEREAS by an Act of Parliament passed on the Twenty-ninth Day of March One thousand eight hundred and sixty-seven, in the Thirtieth Year of Our Reign, intituled "An Act for the Union of Canada, Nova Scotia, and New Brunswick, and the "Government thereof, and for Purposes connected therewith," after divers Recitals, it is enacted, that "it shall be lawful for the Queen, by and with the Advice of Her Majesty's most Honorable "Privy Council, to declare by Proclamation that on and after a Day therein appointed, not being "more than Six Months after the passing of this Act, the Provinces of Canada, Nova Scotia, and "New Brunswick shall form and be One Dominion under the Name of Canada, and on and after "that Day those Three Provinces shall form and be One Dominion under that Name accordingly:" And it is thereby further enacted, that "such Persons shall be first summoned to the Senate as "the Queen, by Warrant under Her Majesty's Royal Sign Manual, thinks fit to approve, and "their Names shall be inserted in the Queen's Proclamation of Union:" We therefore, by and with the Advice of Our Privy Council, have thought fit to issue this Our Royal Proclamation, and We do Ordain, Declare, and Command, that on and after the First Day of July One thousand eight hundred and sixty-seven the Provinces of Canada, Nova Scotia, and New Brunswick shall form and be One Dominion under the Name of Canada. And We do further Ordain and Declare, that the Persons whose Names are herein inserted and set forth are the Persons of whom We have, by Warrant under Our Royal Sign Manual, thought fit to approve as the Persons who shall be first summoned to the Senate of Canada.

FOR THE PROVINCE OF ONTARIO.

JOHN HAMILTON.
RODERICK MATHESON.
JOHN ROSS.
SAMUEL MILLS.
BENJAMIN SEYMOUR.
WALTER HAMILTON DICKSON.
JAMES SHAW.
ADAM JOHNSTON FERGUSON BLAIR.
ALEXANDER CAMPBELL.
DAVID CHRISTIE.
JAMES COX AIKINS.
DAVID REESOR.
ELIJAH LEONARD.
WILLIAM MACMASTER.
ASA ALLWORTH BURNHAM.
JOHN SIMPSON.
JAMES SKEAD.
DAVID LEWIS MACPHERSON.
GEORGE CRAWFORD.
DONALD MACDONALD.
OLIVER BLAKE.
BILLA FLINT.
WALTER M'CREA.
GEORGE WILLIAM ALLAN.

FOR THE PROVINCE OF QUEBEC.

JAMES LESLIE.
ASA BELKNAP FOSTER.
JOSEPH NOËL BOSSÉ.
LOUIS A. OLIVIER.
JACQUE OLIVIER BUREAU.
CHARLES MALHIOT.
LOUIS RENAUD.
LUC LETELLIER DE ST. JUST.
ULRIC JOSEPH TESSIER.
JOHN HAMILTON.
CHARLES CORMIER.
ANTOINE JUCHEREAU DUCHESNAY.
DAVID EDWARD PRICE.
ELZEAR H. J. DUCHESNAY.
LEANDRE DUMOUCHEL.
LOUIS LACOSTE.
JOSEPH F. ARMAND.
CHARLES WILSON.
WILLIAM HENRY CHAFFERS.
JEAN BAPTISTE GUÉVREMONT.
JAMES FERRIER.
Sir NARCISSE FORTUNAT BELLEAU, Knight.
THOMAS RYAN.
JOHN SEWELL SANBORN.

FOR THE PROVINCE OF NOVA SCOTIA.

EDWARD KENNY.
JONATHAN M'CULLY.
THOMAS D. ARCHIBALD.
ROBERT B. DICKEY.
JOHN H. ANDERSON.
JOHN HOLMES.
JOHN W. RITCHIE.
BENJAMIN WIER.
JOHN LOCKE.
CALEB R. BILL.
JOHN BOURINOT.
WILLIAM MILLER.

FOR THE PROVINCE OF NEW BRUNSWICK.

AMOS EDWIN BOTSFORD.
EDWARD BARRON CHANDLER.
JOHN ROBERTSON.
ROBERT LEONARD HAZEN.
WILLIAM HUNTER ODELL.
DAVID WARK.
WILLIAM HENRY STEEVES.
WILLIAM TODD.
JOHN FERGUSON.
ROBERT DUNCAN WILMOT.
ABNER REID M'CLELAN.
PETER MITCHELL.

Given at Our Court at Windsor Castle, this Twenty-second Day of May, in the Year of our Lord One thousand eight hundred and sixty-seven, and in the Thirtieth Year of Our Reign.

God save the Queen.

The royal proclamation of Queen Victoria promulgating the 1867 constitution of Canada refers to the country as "One Dominion under the Name of Canada."

dominions thereunto belonging according to the resolution and desire of said lords and commons contained in the said declaration."

Constitution of Canada, Constitution Act (1867), Preamble: "Whereas the provinces of Canada, Nova Scotia, and New Brunswick have expressed their desire to be federally united into one dominion under the crown of the United Kingdom of Great Britain and Ireland, with a constitution similar in principle to that of the United Kingdom. . . . "

Due Process of Law

Due process of law encompasses law in its regular course—legislation, actions by government officials, and legal proceedings that conform to the standards of the constitution and principles and rules of established courts and jurisprudence. It is a protection against arbitrary or unreasonable loss of life, liberty, or property.

Substantive due process of law has been used by the U.S. courts to invalidate legislation and acts of the executive branch that the courts deem arbitrary or unreasonable or that go beyond the scope of constitutional government. Procedural due process of law was defined by Daniel Webster, the nineteenth-century U.S. statesman and orator, as procedure that hears before it condemns, proceeds upon inquiry, and renders judgment only after trial.

The Fifth Amendment (1791) and the Fourteenth Amendment (1868) to the U.S. Constitution forbid the national and state governments, respectively, from denying anyone life, liberty, or property without due process of law.

Constitution of Canada, Constitution Act (1982), Part I, Canadian Charter of Rights and Freedoms, Legal Rights, Article 7: "Everyone has the right to life, liberty, and security of person and the right not to be deprived thereof except in accordance with principles of fundamental justice."

Constitution of Japan (1947), Chapter III, Rights and Duties of the People, Article 31: "No person shall be deprived of life or liberty, nor shall any other criminal penalty be imposed, except according to procedure established by law."

Durham, Earl of

The Durham Report of 1839, submitted to the British government by John George Lambton (1792–1840), First Earl of Durham, served as the blueprint for Canada's 1867 constitution, which still guides the country today.

John Lambton, the son of a large landowner in Durham County, England, was born on April 12, 1792, in London. At the age of twenty-one he became a member of Parliament. In 1828 he was raised to the peerage as Baron Durham and was made an earl in 1833. His second marriage made him the son-in-law of Earl Grey, the Whig Party prime minister from 1830, when Durham entered his cabinet as lord privy seal, to 1832.

Lord Durham helped draft a British parliamentary

reform bill that was finally enacted in its third version in 1832. After resigning the position of lord privy seal, he was made ambassador to Russia in 1835. In 1838 he was appointed governor and lord high commissioner of Canada.

In 1777 the British Parliament had guaranteed that there would be no direct taxation of the Canadian colonies without the consent of the local legislative assemblies, and under a constitution act of 1791 the mostly French-speaking province of Lower Canada, in what is now Quebec, had been given its own legislative assembly. As soon as Durham arrived in Quebec in May 1838, however, he realized that the British North American colonies were in virtual anarchy. He also recognized the threat of possible annexation by the United States.

When the British government disavowed as "too liberal" the steps Durham took to ameliorate the situation in Canada, he resigned. On January 31, 1839, he filed his report on measures to be taken to restore order and solidify Canadian support for Britain. Written by Durham's chief secretary in Canada, Charles Butler, the report became the basis for Canada's constitution as enacted by the British Parliament in 1867.

The 1839 report of John George Lambton, the First Earl of Durham of Great Britain, on the political status of Canada led to Canada's 1867 constitution.

In the report Durham advocated several measures: the union of Lower Canada with Upper Canada, or Ontario Province; a large degree of self-government to preserve Canadian loyalty to Britain and to thwart the possibility of annexation by the United States; in accordance with the theory of imperial government, a cabinet of colonists whose recommendations on internal affairs would be carried out at the direction of a governor-general acting as the British monarch's representative, with foreign policy and international trade being directed from London; and measures to force the French-speaking Canadians to be assimilated into the Anglo-Canadian culture.

John Lambton died on July 28, 1840, at Cowes on the Isle of Wight. A year later the union of the two Canadas was proclaimed by Great Britain, but it merely perpetuated the minority status of the French colonists. Only on July 1, 1867, twenty-six years later, were many recommendations in the Durham Report implemented in a constitution for Canada, similar in principle to that of the United Kingdom.

Duties

Jeremy Bentham and John Stuart Mill, eighteenth- and nineteenth-century British philosophers, respectively, were concerned with the nature of a citizen's duties. In his work *On Liberty* (1859), Mill characterizes the concept of duty based on the sixteenth-century religious leader John Calvin's vision as "whatever is not a duty, is a sin." Bentham, however, found that a citizen has a duty to obey the law if it is good or if there are sanctions for disobeying it.

Duties appear in three different constitutional contexts: (1) Almost all written constitutions provide a list of powers and duties of the chief executive and on occasion other high officials of the government; (2) a number of constitutions include citizens' duties along with their rights; and (3) some constitutions, such as the U.S. Constitution

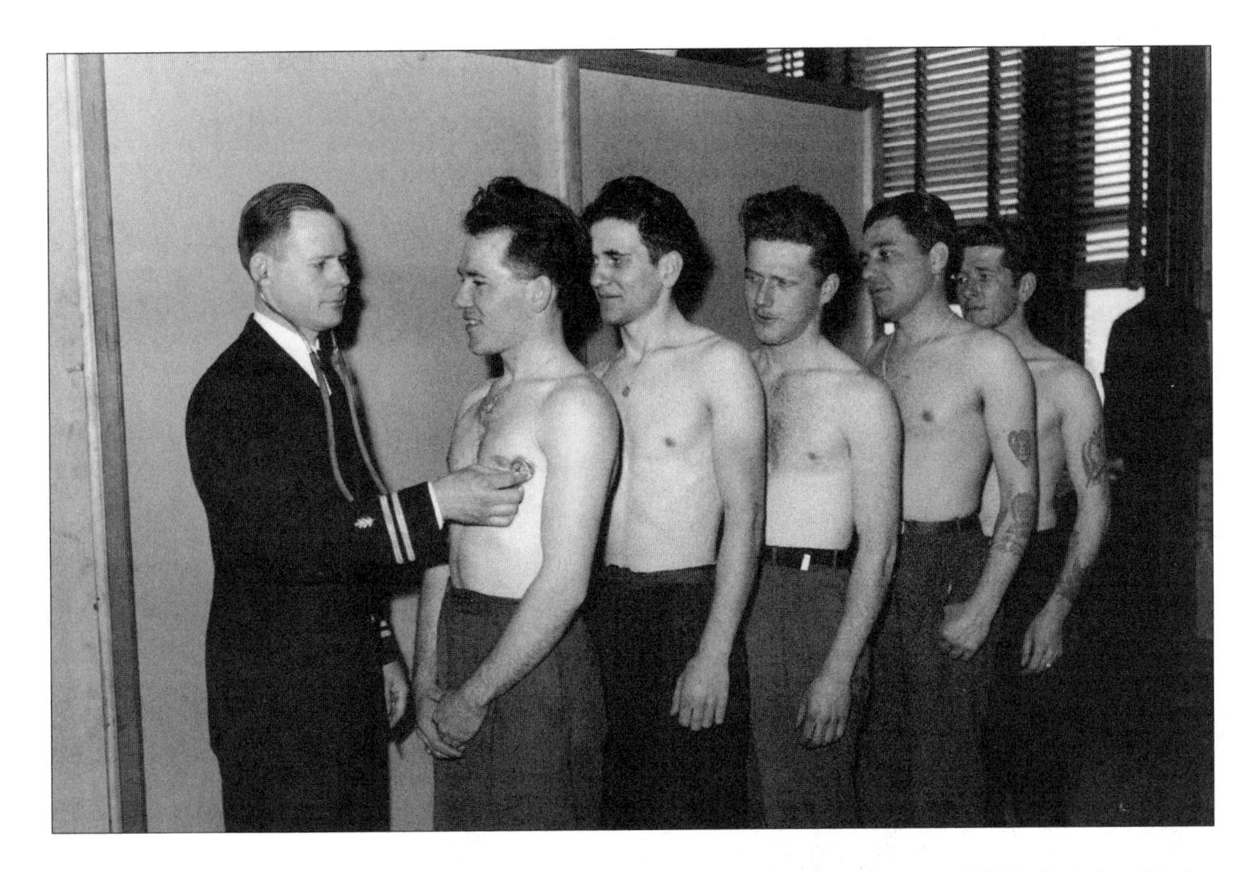

Doing their duty, the five Sullivan brothers enlisted together in the U.S. armed forces during World War II. Assigned to the same ship in the Pacific, they were all killed during a Japanese attack. A battleship was later named for them.

(1789), refer to duties, meaning taxes on imports or tariffs. Executive duties are generally stated in the section on the president or other chief executive. It is sometimes not clear, despite the use of the words *shall* and *may*, which duties are mandatory and which are discretionary. Similarly, the duties of citizens may be legal duties or moral duties, and the distinction is not always clear.

Constitution of South Korea (1948), Chapter IV, The Executive, Part 1, The President, Article 66: "(2) The president shall have the responsibility and duty to safeguard the independence, territorial integrity, and continuity of the state and the constitution. (3) The president shall have the duty to pursue sincerely the peaceful unification of the homeland."

Constitution of Peru (1993), Section I, Concerning the Individual and Society, Chapter III, Concerning Political Rights and Duties, Article 38: "All Peruvians have a duty to honor Peru and to protect its national interests, as well as to respect, obey, and defend the constitution and the nation's code of laws."

Constitution of Iraq (1970), Chapter III, Fundamental Rights and Duties, Article 32(b): "Work is an honor and a sacred duty for every able citizen. . . . "

PUNCH CANDIDATE for

E

Economy

In a section of *The Laws* devoted to agriculture, economics, and trade, Plato proposes limiting retail trade to alien residents, whose resulting moral decay from making a profit would not overly damage the state. Government economic policies now can promote or retard national growth, so many constitutions deal extensively with the nation's economy and economic development.

Economy—from the Greek *oikonomia* (one who manages a household), which evolved into the Latin *oeconomy*—generally means the national system of producing goods and services, exporting and importing, transacting business, and all other elements that make up the country's gross national or domestic product and its international balance of payments. Because a nation needs revenue to carry out government activities, its national wealth as produced by its economy is crucial as a basis for taxation, a major source of revenue.

Political economy is the management of a country's resources to maximize prosperity as well as the theory of using laws to regulate the production and distribution of wealth. The "economic" theory of constitutional interpretation, at least with respect to the U.S. Constitution (1789), is based on the notion that the framers were all relatively wealthy men who created a document to further their own best interests. To a large extent, judicial interpretations of constitutions can be analyzed on the basis of competing economic interests.

Constitution of North Korea (1972), Chapter II, Economy, Article 18: "In the Democratic People's Republic of Korea the means of production are owned by the state and cooperative organizations."

Constitution of South Korea (1948), Chapter IX, The Economy, Article 119: "(1) The economic order of the Republic of Korea shall be based on a respect for the freedom and creative initiative of enterprises and individuals in economic affairs. (2) The state may regulate and coordinate economic affairs in order to maintain the balanced growth and stability of the national economy to ensure proper distribution of income, to prevent the domination of the market and the abuse of economic power and to democratize the economy through harmony among the economic agents."

Education

Thomas Jefferson believed that free public education is the key to an informed electorate in a democratic system of government. In contrast to totalitarian and autocratic governments, democratic nations emphasize education to enforce social goals and normative behavior rather

A British artist's illustration of an election day in England shows two political activists attempting to influence a voter.

than the use of physical coercion or force. In a democratic society education, discourse, and even propaganda are preferable tools for resolving conflicts. Education is also important in the development of the work force necessary to the economy of a modern nation-state.

The constitutions of many countries, from China to Ghana and Iceland, contain specific provisions on education, although the United States and the United Kingdom do not address the topic. Typical provisions promote education in general, extend educational benefits such as free education to school-aged children, and, as in Sweden, give a general grant of power to the government to regulate education and vocational training along with health, safety, and traffic.

Constitution of Belgium (1834), Heading II, Concerning the Belgians and Rights, Article 17: "Education is free; any preventive measure is forbidden; the punishment of misdemeanors is regulated by law. Public education provided at the expense of the state is also regulated by law."

Constitution of Panama (1972), Title III, Individual and Social Rights and Duties, Chapter 5, Education, Article 89: "It is recognized that the purpose of Panamanian education is to encourage in the student the formation of a national conscience based on knowledge of the history and problems of the country."

Election

An elaborate system for electing guardians of the laws is described by Plato in *The Laws,* beginning with military veterans who write on tablets the name of a candidate, the name of their own father's tribe and *deme* (a subdivision of the tribe), and their own name and then place these tablets on the altar of the most venerated temple in the state. In *The Politics,* Aristotle also discusses methods of selecting officials, including voting and random selection (by lot).

In modern constitutions an election—from the Latin *electus* (choice)—sometimes called voting or polling, is the process of choosing one or more persons from a larger number to act in some official capacity, such as representing the people or carrying out government functions on their behalf. Election of individuals as representatives, along with majority rule and separation of powers, is a major component of the constitutional democratic process.

In a sense democratic election is the means by which the will of the people is translated into action in the three basic branches of government—the executive, legislative, and judicial. Sovereignty, which in earlier times resided in an absolute monarch, is now expressed through elections that invest those elected with the authority to perform government functions and that preserve the ability of the electorate (those who vote) to withdraw that authority and confer it on others.

Constitutions generally prescribe recurrent elections for the offices of president and vice president and members of the legislature, especially the lower houses of bicameral legislatures, but rarely for judges. In some constitutions, such as those of Malaysia and Cambodia, even monarchs may be chosen by a restricted election process. After a general election members of a legislature may be required to hold elections to determine legislative officers, such as a speaker.

Political parties often play a large role in organizing and supervising elections in democracies. Even the constitutions of countries in which the government is dominated by a single party, such as the Communist Party, prescribe elections, although the actual selection process may be done behind the scenes.

Constitution of Syria (1973), Part Two, Powers of the State, Chapter I, Legislative Power, Article 58(1): "Elections shall take place within 90 days following the expiry of the mandate of the people's council [legislature]."

Constitution of New Zealand, New Zealand Electoral Act (1956), Part II, House of Representatives, 14, Election of the Speaker: "The house of representatives shall, immediately on its first meeting after the general election of its members, and immediately on its first meeting after a vacancy occurs in the office of the speaker (whether by death, resignation, or otherwise), choose one of its members as its speaker. . . ."

Constitution of Taiwan (1947), Amendments (1992), Article 12: "Effective from the 1996 election for the ninth-term president and vice president, the president and the vice president shall be elected by the entire electorate for the free area of the Republic of China."

Elector. *See* Electoral College

Electoral College

A body invested with certain powers may be known as a college. The sacred college includes Catholic cardinals who vote for a new pope, while an electoral college is a group of delegates or electors who indirectly elect a head of state.

In the United States the electoral college, consisting of 538 members, elects the president every four years on the basis of the popular vote in the electors' respective states. Each state is entitled to as many electors as its total number of representatives in both houses of Congress; the capital district, pursuant to the Twenty-third Amendment (1961), has three electors. The electors are nominated by the political parties whose candidates are running for president and vice president, and their votes go to the party whose candidates receive a plurality of the votes in that jurisdiction. The electors are pledged to vote for their party's candidates and generally do, even though the Constitution gives them discretion. A majority of 270 electors is required for election.

In the first African Gold Coast Colony elections in 1951, a farmer was nominated and elected unopposed to the electoral college. Some constitutions require that the president be elected by an electoral college rather than directly by the people.

In the few other countries that have adopted the electoral college method of selecting the head of state, as opposed to direct election, the electors are chosen by a different method than in the United States. In Malaysia, a constitutional monarchy, the monarch and deputy monarch are elected from among and by a conference of rulers. In Turkey, as in some other countries, the head of state (the president) is elected by the national legislature by a two-thirds majority vote of the members.

In Ireland and the United Kingdom an elector is any person entitled to vote for a member of its parliament.

Constitution of the United States of America (1789), Article II, Section 1: "[The president] shall . . . together with the Vice President, chosen for the same term, be elected, as follows: Each State shall appoint, in such Manner as the Legislature thereof may direct, a Number of Electors, equal to the whole Number of Senators and Representatives to which the State may be entitled in the Congress: but no Senator or Representative, or Person holding an Office of Trust or Profit under the United States, shall be appointed an Elector."

Constitution of India (1950), Part V, The Union, Chapter I, The Executive, Article 54: "Election of President.—The president shall be elected by members of an electoral college consisting of—(a) the elected members of both houses of parliament; and (b) the elected members of the legislative assemblies of the states."

Electoral District

An electoral district, like a constituency, is a group of voters within a specified geographic area of a nation-state who may vote for a representative or representatives to the national legislature from that district. In the United States an electoral district is called a congressional district; depending on the size of its population, a small state may have one such district encompassing the territory of the entire state, while a larger one will have a number of separate districts.

The United Kingdom uses the term *constituency* rather than *electoral district.* Before April 1, 1974, the county of Yorkshire was divided into three administrative districts called ridings, and in Canada administrative or electoral districts are also called ridings.

Constitutions that provide for some representation in the national legislature based on population or separate constituencies, as opposed to at-large representation, generally include guidelines as to how electoral districts are to be constituted. Sometimes multiple legislative seats may be assigned to single districts, and sometimes existing political subdivisions such as states or provinces may be defined as an electoral district or its equivalent.

Constitution of Finland, Parliament Act (1928), Chapter 1, General Provisions, Section 4: "The representatives shall be elected by a direct and proportional ballot, for which purposes the country shall be divided into no fewer than twelve and no more than eighteen electoral districts."

Constitution of Ecuador (1979), Second Part, Title I, The Legislative Function, Section I, The National Congress, Article 56: "The legislative function is exercised by the national congress, located in Quito, composed of twelve congressmen elected by national vote [at large]; two congressmen elected by each province, except those with less than one hundred thousand inhabitants which elect one; and, in addition, one congressman elected for each three hundred thousand inhabitants or fraction thereof over two hundred thousand."

Electorate. *See* Vote

Eligibility

Constitutions often define the qualifications a person must have to serve in an office or a position, such as important elective and appointive government positions, including president and vice president. Eligibility often depends on a person's status as a citizen, age, and place of residence. If not otherwise specified, eligibility is determined at the time that office is taken, not at the time of election.

The U.S. Constitution (1789) defines eligibility for the president and vice president, the electors of the president and vice president, and the members of the Senate and House of Representatives. In constitutional monarchies documents of constitutional stature, sometimes called acts of succession, often spell out in detail the eligibility of the person who should succeed to the throne.

Constitution of Germany (1949), III, The Federal Parliament (Bundestag), Article 38, Elections (2): "Anyone who has attained the age of eighteen shall be entitled to vote; anyone who has attained majority shall be eligible for election."

Constitution of Iceland (1944), Chapter Three, Article 34: "Any citizen of unblemished character who has the right to vote in elections to the Althing [legislature] is eligible to stand for election to it. Judges who do not hold administrative office, however, are not eligible."

Constitution of Germany (1949), VIII, The Execution of Federal Statutes and the Federal Administration, Article 91, Internal Emergency: "(1) In order to avert any imminent danger to the existence or the free democratic basic order of the federation or a *Land* [state], a *Land* may request the services of the police forces of other *Länder*, or of the forces and facilities of other administrative authorities and of the federal border guard."

Constitution of Taiwan (1947), Chapter IV, The President, Article 43: "In the case of a natural calamity, an epidemic, or a national financial or economic crisis that calls for emergency measures, the president, during the recess of the legislative *yuan* [body], may, by resolution of the executive *yuan* council, and in accordance with the law on emergency orders, issue emergency orders as may be necessary to cope with the situation."

Emergency Powers

As a political term *emergency*—from the Latin *emergo* (to come out)—describes a condition, similar to a state of war, in which some ordinary processes of government may be altered or suspended to deal with an unforeseen occurrence or threat.

The U.S. Constitution (1789) does not expressly grant the president emergency powers in a time of crisis except for the authority to convene Congress on extraordinary occasions. However, the president has some inherent powers with respect to foreign affairs, for example, and may be given powers by Congress. The U.S. Congress itself has specific powers under the Constitution to call out the militia to execute the laws of the country and to suppress insurrection and repel invasion. In times of emergency the president has been given the power to declare parts of the country disaster areas, thus entitling them to special relief and assistance.

Many more recent constitutions, however, do provide expressly for emergency situations, in many cases giving the president special authority and allowing the suspension of certain individual rights and guarantees until the emergency has abated. They may also provide for the imposition of martial law in emergencies; in this case law enforcement is handled by the military rather than by domestic law officers.

Emigration. *See* Immigration

Emperor

Roman generals victorious in the field were often acclaimed *imperator* by their troops. Later the title, from which the English word *emperor* is derived, was bestowed on Julius and then Augustus Caesar by the Roman Senate in recognition of their status as commander in chief of the Roman armies. Thereafter every Roman ruler except Tiberius and Claudius adopted the title.

After the fall of the Roman Empire in the West, many rulers in Europe took the title of Holy Roman Emperor. In 1804 Napoleon crowned himself emperor of France. The title of emperor of China has been given to some Asian rulers.

The word *emperor* and its feminine form, *empress*, have come to refer to a sovereign who rules more than one kingdom or territory. In the nineteenth century Victoria was queen of England but empress of India. Today Japan is the only major country to still refer to the ceremonial head of state or monarch as emperor.

Constitution of Japan (1889, significantly revised in 1947), Chapter I, The Emperor, Article 1: "The emperor

Before his death at the hands of the Spanish conquistadors in 1521, the emperor Montezuma ruled a large empire centered in what is now Mexico.

shall be the symbol of the state and of the unity of the people, deriving his position from the will of the people with whom resides sovereign power."

Empress. *See* Emperor

Enforcement of the Laws. *See* Execution of the Laws

Enquête. *See* Interpellation

Entitlement

The English poet Geoffrey Chaucer used the word *entitled* in the late fourteenth century, and its usage in that country as a right to possession dates from the fifteenth century. The English words *entitle* and *intitule* (to furnish with a heading) are derived from the Latin *in* and *titulus* (title or honor).

In constitutions entitlements encompass the granting of titles as well as benefits and rights. Article 1, Section 9, of the U.S. Constitution (1789) expressly prohibits the granting of titles of nobility from a foreign government or their acceptance by officeholders without the consent of Congress. Article 1, Section 10, prohibits any of the states of the United States from granting titles of nobility.

In the broadest sense an entitlement is any right that a constitution bestows on citizens or inhabitants. The German constitution provides protections and privileges—entitlements—for deputies to the lower house of the legislature. U.S. entitlement programs include Social Security and other benefits granted by the government to citizens. In Canada, however, an entitlement is more narrowly defined as a pension payable for disability.

Constitution of Thailand (1991), Chapter II, The King, Section 9: "The king has the prerogative power to create titles and confer decorations."

Constitution of Denmark (1953), Part VIII, 75(2): "Any person unable to support himself or his dependents shall, where no other person is responsible for his or their maintenance, be entitled to receive public assistance, provided that he shall comply with the obligations imposed by statute in such respect."

Entrenched Provision

An entrenched provision of a constitution is a statement or clause used to safeguard a position or right. Constitutional clauses, provisions, and concepts that may be amended or repealed only by relatively more stringent procedures are also known as entrenched provisions—from the Latin *trunco* (to cut off).

Entrenched provisions are similar to unamendable provisions in that the framers of a particular constitutional document believed that some aspects of a constitution are more important in maintaining the integrity of the democratic system or more in need of protection from hasty or ill-advised amendments. As a result, for entrenched provisions the normal amendment process is rejected and a more restrictive procedure is prescribed.

Constitution of South Africa (1994), Chapter 3, Fundamental Rights, Limitation: 33(1): "The rights entrenched in the chapter may be limited by law of general application, provided that such limitation—(a) shall be permissible only to the extent that it is—(i) reasonable; and (ii) justifiable in an open and democratic society based on freedom and equity. . . ."

Constitution of Chile (1980), Chapter XIV, Amendment to the Constitution, Article 118: "In order to be approved, the amendment proposals concerning chapters I, VII, X, and XI of this constitution shall meet the requirements stated in the paragraph above [approval of the president and both chambers of the legislature by a vote of two-thirds of the members in office in each chamber]. However, the proposals shall not be promulgated, and will be kept until the following joint renewal of the chambers, and in the first session held by these chambers they shall submit the text already approved to debate and voting. . . ."

Environment

Before the Industrial Revolution, which began in England in the late 1700s, the general environmental conditions under which people lived were controlled or protected by ad hoc legislation or by private legal actions for damages or restraining orders. Corrective government action at the national level did not keep pace with

Degradation and pollution of the land, water, and atmosphere have led to the inclusion of environmental protection and improvement provisions in some recent constitutions.

increased environmental pollution and degradation from large-scale industrial activities. Only recently has the environment become the subject of constitutional provisions.

Both nation-states and regional and global organizations have begun to come to terms with the need for environmental protection. Some countries now have constitutional provisions that acknowledge citizens' rights to a healthy environment and that promote corrective action by the government.

Constitution of the Netherlands (1814), Chapter I, Fundamental Rights, Article 21: "It shall be the concern of the authorities to keep the country habitable and to protect and improve the environment."

Constitution of Brazil (1988), Title VIII, The Social Order, Chapter VI, Environment, Article 225: "All have the right to an ecologically balanced environment, which is an asset of common use and essential to a healthy quality of life, and both the government and the community shall have the duty to defend and preserve it for present and future generations."

Envoy. *See* Ambassador

Equal Protection of the Law

Equal protection of the law, like due process of law, is a traditional form of constitutional guarantee of fair treatment for all citizens, regardless of sex, race, national origin, religion, or political views. It is grounded in the principle of natural law—that everyone is created equal and that if citizens constitute the ultimate sovereign authority of a nation-state, its government should treat those citizens alike. Many constitutions contain a provision declaring that all citizens or inhabitants are entitled to equal protection of the laws.

The U.S. Supreme Court has held that "the equal protection of the laws" required by the Fourteenth Amendment to the U.S. Constitution, ratified in 1868, does not necessarily mean identical treatment. People may be classified for different treatment as long as the classification is reasonable and bears some relationship to the ends to be obtained. Classification for purposes of taxation on the basis of ability to pay is acceptable, for example, although classification for purposes of taxation by race is not.

The term *equal rights* usually refers specifically to the rights of women vis-à-vis men.

Constitution of Thailand (1992), Chapter III, Rights and Liberties of the Thai People, Section 25: "All persons are equal before the law and shall enjoy equal protection under the law."

Constitution of Uganda, Simplified Draft (1992), Chapter 5, Fundamental Human Rights and Freedoms, Individual Rights 1: "Every person in Uganda is entitled to enjoy equal protection of the law. In particular, men and women must be equal under the law in all aspects of life."

Before the Little Rock, Arkansas, schools were integrated in the 1950s, National Guardsmen were used to bar black students from attending, denying them equal protection of the law.

On Women's Equality Day in 1977 marchers in Washington, D.C., show support for passage of the Equal Rights Amendment.

Equal Rights

Some recent constitutions include equal rights provisions—language that attempts to equalize traditional societal disparities between men and women. Going beyond equal protection clauses, such passages guarantee equal treatment specifically for women on the same basis as men in a nation-state's social, economic, and political activities.

An Equal Rights Amendment to the U.S. Constitution (1789) failed to achieve ratification in the 1970s by three-fourths of the states within the time period set by Congress. Originally Congress allowed seven years, from 1972 to 1979, but extended the period to June 1982. Opponents of the amendment argued that equal rights protection for women in the United States could be ensured without a constitutional amendment.

Constitution of Russia (1993), Part One, Chapter 2, Human and Civil Rights and Freedoms, Article 19: "3. Men and women shall have equal rights and freedoms and equal opportunities to exercise them."

Constitution of Mozambique (1990), Part II, Fundamental Rights, Duties, and Freedoms, Chapter I, General Principles, Article 67: "Men and women shall be equal before the law in all spheres of political, economic, social and cultural affairs."

Constitution of Bulgaria (1991), Chapter 2, Fundamental Rights and Obligations of Citizens, Article 46(2): "Spouses enjoy equal rights and obligations within marriage and the family."

Ex Officio

In a legal context the Latin term *ex officio* (out of or according to office or duty) means that solely by virtue of holding one office a person is able to exercise other functions not specifically conferred on him or her. A judge, for example, has ex officio powers of a conservator of the peace simply by reason of being a judge. William Blackstone, the eighteenth-century commentator on the laws of England, distinguished between a criminal information filed in the monarch's court by the attorney general ex officio, whose presence indicates that this matter directly affects the Crown, and a criminal information filed by the attorney general, in which the Crown is only a nominal prosecutor on behalf of the state or public.

Some constitutions establish rights and duties of certain officials to be performed ex officio. In these cases the holder of a position ex officio may not have all the rights and duties of a person who holds such a position directly. In constitutions the term may also refer to the acts of government officials taken on their own authority and initiative, rather than at the request of another party.

Constitution of Kenya (1963), Chapter III, Parliament, Part 1, Composition of Parliament, Article 37(4): "The speaker shall be an ex officio member of the national assembly, whether or not he is elected from among the members of the assembly."

Constitution of Spain (1978), Title VI, Concerning the Judicial Power, Article 124.1: "The office of the public prosecutor, without prejudice to the functions entrusted to other bodies, has as its mission that of promoting the working of justice in the defense of the rule of law, of citizens' rights, and of the public interest as safeguarded by the law, whether ex officio or at the request of interested parties. . . ."

Ex Post Facto Law

The Latin term *ex post facto* (made after the fact) refers generally to laws promulgated as punishment for acts that were not punishable at the time they were committed. Forbidden in a number of constitutions, such laws may create new categories of offenses, increase the punishment for existing offenses, or reduce the standard of proof for such offenses. A law that reduces punishment or raises the standard of proof is not considered an ex post facto law.

The framers of the U.S. Constitution (1789) had an aversion to ex post facto laws. Alexander Hamilton, in essay 78 of *The Federalist* (1788), specifies: "By a limited constitution, I understand one which contains specified exceptions to legislative authority; such, for instance, as that it shall pass no bills of attainder, no ex post facto laws, and the like." In 1810 in *Fletcher v. Peck*, U.S. Chief Justice John Marshall reasoned that any legislative change in a law, in contractual matters as well as in criminal law, that has an adverse impact on people could be considered an ex post facto law.

Constitution of Slovakia (1993), Section Seven, The Right to Judicial and Other Legal Protection, Article 50(6): "The criminal nature of an act is considered, and penalties are imposed, according to the law valid at the time when the act was committed. A subsequent law shall be applied if it is more favorable to the offender."

Constitution of Mexico (1917), Title I, Chapter I, Individual Guarantees, Article 14: "No law shall be given retroactive effect to the detriment of any person whatsoever."

Execution of the Laws

The U.S. Constitution (1789), Article 2, Section 3, charges the president to "take Care that the Laws be faithfully executed. . . ." The execution powers of government are those that carry out, execute, or enforce the laws. In law the word—from the French *exécuter* (to carry out)—means to enforce a sentence of a court, including a sentence of death, as well as to sign, seal, and deliver a deed or will; to obey commands (such as executing a writ issued by a court); and to perform a contract.

Based on the principle of the separation of government powers espoused by Montesquieu in the eighteenth century, many constitutions vest in separate institutions the three processes of making laws, interpreting laws, and executing or carrying out laws. Execution of the laws in a parliamentary system of government lies primarily with the head of government (the prime minister) and the departments or ministries of government. Civil servants and law enforcement officials in the departments or ministries, in addition to the politically elected ministers, see that the laws and decisions of the courts are carried out. Some countries have attorneys general, prosecutors general, or procurators general who specifically supervise the execution of the laws by bringing to trial for punishment those who break the law.

In countries such as the United States, which has a strict separation of powers, the president, as head of the executive branch of government, is responsible for executing the national laws. State laws are enforced under the direction of the governors of each state, and municipalities have executive personnel and law enforcement authorities under the overall supervision of mayors.

Constitutions may also refer to execution powers of law

enforcement authorities or acts such as signing a document or carrying out a sentence of capital punishment.

Constitution of the Philippines (1987), Article VII, Executive Department, Section 17: "The president shall have control of all the executive departments, bureaus, and offices. He shall ensure that the laws are faithfully executed."

Constitution of Ghana (1992), Chapter Eight, The Executive, The President, Article 63(9): "An instrument which—(a) is executed under the hand of the chairman of the electoral commission and under the seal of the commission; and (b) states that the person named in the instrument was declared elected as the president of Ghana at the election of the president, shall be *prima facie* evidence that the person named was so elected."

Women were involved in executing the laws by serving as police officers in Muncie, Indiana, as early as 1914.

Executive Branch

The first person in modern history to identify the English monarchy's three major branches of government—executive, legislative, and judicial—was Montesquieu, although Aristotle had noted such divisions in connection with the constitution of the Athenian democracy. The executive branch of government is charged with the execution or enforcement of the laws as enacted by the legislature and as interpreted by the courts.

In the United Kingdom, the prime minister, a member of Parliament who can command a majority vote in the House of Commons, is head of the executive branch, although the monarch, as the formal head of state, theoretically must assent to all executive actions. In fact, the monarch has no power to act other than as directed by the prime minister. The executive branch consists of the prime minister's office and the departments and ministries of the government.

In presidential-style parliamentary governments, a president takes the place of a monarch, but he or she will generally have some exclusive executive powers. In some nominally parliamentary systems, such as those created by the constitutions of France and Russia, the president is vested with significant executive powers.

In the United States and other countries with similar nonparliamentary constitutions, the president, who is both head of state and government, is the exclusive head of the executive branch.

Constitution of Nepal (1990), Part 7, Executive, Article 35, Executive Power: "(1) The executive power of the kingdom of Nepal shall, under this constitution and other laws, be vested in his majesty and the council of ministers. (2) The powers of his majesty, except those to be exercised exclusively by him or at his discretion or on the recommendation of any institution or official as clearly specified, shall be exercised under this constitution by him with the advice and consent of the council of ministers. Such advice and consent shall be submitted through the prime minister."

Constitution of Honduras (1982), Chapter VI, The Executive Branch, Article 235: "The president of the republic shall exercise the executive power on behalf and for the benefit of the people."

Expenditure

The action of laying out or expending money is one of the five major phases of using public funds to carry out a public activity. The first phase is a budget request by the government. The second is authorization, in which the legislature passes an act to approve a government activity requiring an expenditure of public funds. In the third phase, appropriation, a specific amount as proposed in a budget is approved by the legislature for a particular activity. The fourth phase is expenditure, in which the money is drawn from the funds authorized, usually the general fund of the treasury. The final phase occurs when the expenditure of funds is audited to ensure that it was duly authorized and spent as intended under the law. Often the second and third phases occur at the same time.

Constitution of Zambia (1991), Part VII, Finance, Section 103(2): "When the estimates of expenditure have been approved by the national assembly, the [categories] of the estimates together with the amount approved in respect of each shall be included in a bill to be known as an appropriation bill. . . . "

Constitution of South Korea (1948), Chapter IV, Part 2, The Executive Branch, Section 4, The Board of Audit and Inspection, Article 99: "The board of audit and inspection shall inspect the closing accounts of revenue and expenditures each year, and report the results to the president and the national assembly in the following year."

Expression. *See* Speech

External Affairs

In *The Laws,* Plato suggests limiting foreign travel to only those persons more than forty years of age. To make a good impression on other states, moreover, he proposes that the state should send as its representatives to interstate religious ceremonies and games only its finest, noblest citizens.

Relations with other nations—external affairs—have traditionally been considered functions primarily of the executive branch of government. Historically, only the sovereigns of nation-states could speak to other sovereigns, although of course such conversations could take place through emissaries or representatives. Unauthorized citizens of a country have no standing to conduct foreign relations with another country. Most constitutions require or permit external affairs to be handled by the chief executive, with or without the involvement of the cabinet or the legislature, through a department or ministry of state in the executive branch.

Under the U.S. Constitution (1789) the president, who has the authority to make treaties and appoint ambassadors with the advice and consent of the Senate, plays the major role in conducting foreign affairs and developing foreign policy. As John Jay, author of the 1777 New York state constitution, notes in essay 64 of *The Federalist* (1788), the manner by which the president and the Senate are chosen ensures that they will "best understand our national interests whether considered in relation to the several states or to foreign nations."

Constitution of Slovakia (1993), Chapter Six, Executive Power, Section One, The President of the Slovak Republic, Article 102: "The president a) represents the Slovak Republic in external affairs, negotiates and ratifies international treaties. He or she may delegate to the government [cabinet] of the Slovak Republic or, with the consent of the government, to its individual members, the negotiating of those international treaties which do not require the approval of the national council [legislature] of the Slovak Republic; b) receives and accredits ambassadors. . . . "

Constitution of Jordan (1952), Chapter Four, The Executive Power, Part 1, The King and His Prerogatives, Article 33: "(i) The king declares war, concludes peace, and ratifies treaties and agreements. (ii) Treaties and agreements which involve financial commitments to the treasury or affect the public or private rights of Jordanians shall not be valid unless approved by the national assembly. In no circumstances shall any secret terms contained in any treaty or agreement be contrary to their overt terms."

Exterritoriality. *See* Extraterritoriality

Diner d'un ministre Européen avec le grand vezir depicts an official state dinner given by a high official of the Ottoman Empire. Historically, external affairs have been conducted on an informal as well as a formal basis.

Extradition

The Latin words *ex* (out of), *trado* (to hand over), and *traditio* (to surrender) form the basis of the English word *extradition*, which means the surrender by one nation-state of a person accused or convicted of an offense outside its territory to the nation-state in whose jurisdiction the offense was committed. Extradition requires a request or demand by the latter country, which will deal with the offender according to its own laws after he or she is surrendered.

A nation-state's laws have no extraterritorial effect in another nation-state, and no principle of international law requires extradition. However, a person accused of a crime in another country may be surrendered as a courtesy or pursuant to an extradition treaty between two countries. Political offenses, however, may be exempted from the normal criminal extradition process.

The U.S. Constitution (1789), recognizing the semi-sovereign nature of the constituent states, expressly requires one state to surrender to another, on demand by the executive authority of such state, a person who is charged with treason, felony, or another crime but who has fled from justice.

Constitution of Panama (1972), Title III, Individual and Social Rights and Duties, Chapter 1, Fundamental Guarantees, Article 24: "The state may not extradite its nationals, nor may it extradite aliens, for political offenses."

Constitution of Jordan (1952), Chapter Two, Rights and Duties of Jordanians, Article 21: "(i) Political refugees shall not be extradited on account of their political beliefs or for their defense of liberty. (ii) Extradition of ordinary criminals shall be regulated by international agreements and laws."

Extraordinary Session

The sessions of legislatures, councils, and other government bodies are often set at regular intervals and for a prescribed maximum or minimum length of time. Realizing that emergencies and exigencies may require action when a government body is out of session, however, the framers of most constitutions have provided for a means of calling extraordinary sessions. Others have dealt with this problem by creating special committees of the legislatures to handle matters when they are not in regular session.

Article 2, Section 3, of the U.S. Constitution (1789) provides that the president may convene both houses or either house of Congress on "extraordinary Occasions." Alexander Hamilton, in essay 77 of *The Federalist* (1788), tells us that the only concern about this power related to the president's being able to convene only one house of the legislature without the other, which therefore might have some political implications. Hamilton points out, however, that the Senate has a special role in the confirmation of treaties, which would make it improper and unnecessary also to convene the House of Representatives under certain circumstances.

Constitution of Ecuador (1979), Second Part, Title I, Legislative Function, Section 1, The National Congress, Article 64: "The congress may meet in extraordinary session by convocation of its chairman, the president of the republic, or two-thirds of its members, to deal solely with the matters for which the session is called."

Constitution of Monaco (1962), Title IX, The Commune, Article 82: "Extraordinary sessions [of the communal council of Monaco's single commune] may be held at the request or with the authorization of the minister of state for specific purposes."

Extraterritoriality

The laws of a nation-state generally cannot reach beyond its own borders, but through treaties with other nations and under certain conditions recognized by international law, a country's laws may have extraterritorial effect. International mandates or trusteeships with respect to colonies have allowed many nation-states to exercise extraterritorial jurisdiction over possessions and foreign dependencies. Some constitutions deal specifically with extraterritoriality. Problems can arise, however, in enforcing extraterritorial laws, because technically under international law a nation-state may not impose its laws beyond its own territorial jurisdiction.

The Irish constitution of 1937, under The Nation, Article

1, states: "The national territory consists of the whole island of Ireland, its islands, and the territorial seas." Because this includes the United Kingdom's territory of Northern Ireland, the provision represents an effort by Ireland to give its national laws extraterritorial effect.

Extraterritoriality differs from exterritoriality, which refers to the privileges of ambassadors and certain other members of diplomatic missions not to be treated as subject to the laws of the host nation.

Constitution of Australia (1901), Chapter I, The Parliament, Part V, Powers of Parliament, Section 51: "The parliament shall, subject to this constitution, have power to make laws for the peace, order, and good government of the commonwealth with respect to:—. . . (x) Fisheries in Australian waters beyond territorial limits. . . . "

Constitution of Malaysia (1963), Ninth Schedule (Article 74, Subject Matter of Federal and State Laws, 77, Residual Power of Legislation), Legislative Lists, List I, Federal List: "1. External affairs including—. . . (g) Foreign and extraterritorial jurisdiction. . . . "

Constitution of Taiwan (1947), Chapter III, The National Assembly, Article 26: "The national assembly shall be composed of the following delegates: . . . 2. Delegates to represent Mongolia. . . . 3. The number of delegates to be elected from Tibet shall be prescribed by law. . . . "

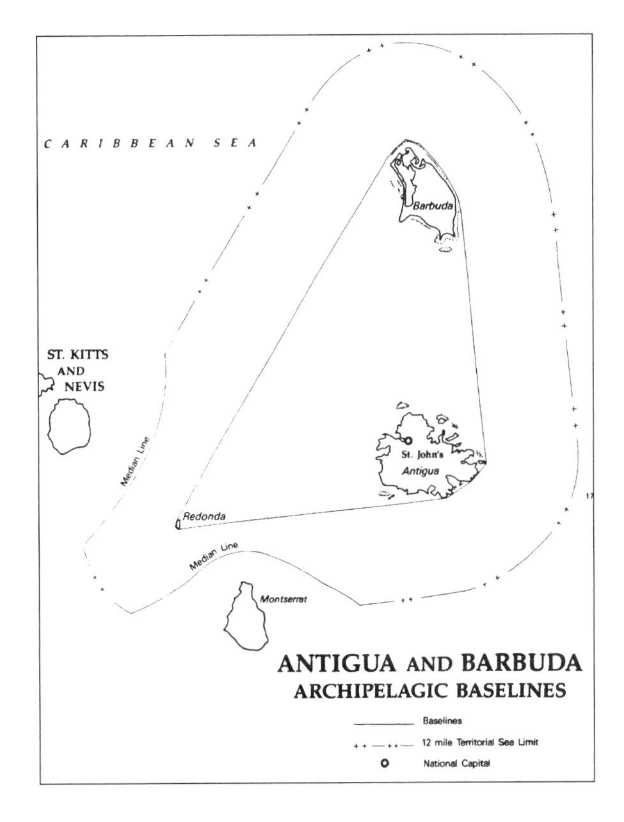

To determine a country's territorial and extraterritorial jurisdiction, detailed measurements and complex calculations are often required to find internationally acceptable boundaries.

F

Falsen, Christian Magnus

Christian Magnus Falsen (1782–1830) is known as the "Father of the Norwegian Constitution," the second oldest written constitution still in effect.

Falsen was born in Norway in 1782 into a family of officials of Danish descent. His grandfather and father were physiocrats, who believed that government should interfere as little as possible in the workings of the natural laws of economics. A champion of farmers on the west coast, the elder Falsen wrote that it was "the poor farmer, who, in fact, should be the strength of the country. . . . "

In the spring of 1813 Sweden officially claimed Norway, and under the Treaty of Kiel, signed on January 14, 1814, the union of Norway with Denmark was dissolved. The Norwegians were outraged, not particularly at being separated from Denmark but at being treated as if they had no sovereign rights or say in the matter. Prince Christian Frederik, the heir apparent to the Danish throne who was then governor of Norway, supported a movement for a national constitutional assembly, which met in a mansion at Eidsvoll, some forty miles from Oslo.

Led by Christian Magnus Falsen, a judge of commanding personality and political savvy, the great majority of the assembly wanted to establish unconditional independence for Norway. Falsen took the initiative in shaping the new constitution, although the assembly reviewed many drafts.

In its deliberations the assembly considered the ideas of Montesquieu and Jean-Jacques Rousseau, as well as

Although he guided the drafting of the 1814 Norwegian constitution, Christian Magnus Falsen lost his faith in democratic government by the common people.

Ancient Assyrian slaves and criminals were forced by the government to labor on construction projects such as this mound on which a royal palace was built.

the constitutions of England, France (1791), Spain (1812), Sweden (1809), and the United States (1789). Falsen, who had named two of his sons Washington and Franklin in honor of the American patriots, became the president of the assembly's committee on the constitution. His preliminary draft, which closely resembled the French constitution, was used as the basis for discussions about the articles of the Norwegian constitution. Despite his admiration for the United States, Falsen favored a powerful monarchy, a position that later earned him the epithet "defender of royal power." The resulting document, which was much shorter than Falsen's draft and a composite of various ideas, was adopted and became law on May 17, 1814.

Falsen later grew disillusioned with the common people. In the early 1820s, believing the constitution flawed, he proposed an amendment to strengthen the role of the upper classes in the Storting, the Norwegian parliament. Because of this proposal he was persecuted mercilessly by the opposition press. He died in 1830.

Family

The Latin words *familia* (family or household), *gens* (clan), and *domus* (house or home) all connote aspects of a family, from nuclear to extended. Exactly what constitutes a family—and what role it plays in a nation-state—are questions that have long been debated. Plato devotes an entire section in *The Laws* to "Marriage and Related Topics" and "Family Law." In *The Politics,* Aristotle concludes that the theory of the family is a part of the overall theory of the state, which he suggests is composed of households or families consisting of master and slave, husband and wife, and father and children.

Some European political theorists after 1500 considered the family and the state to be the only associations that possessed a basis in natural law. The German law professor Otto Von Gierke, in notes for his work on natural law, *The German Law of Associations* (1868–1913), comments that while Jean Bodin defined the state as a family, Bodin rejected Aristotle's inclusion of the theory of the family as a part of political science. Bodin, however, did recognize the family as a fundamental element in the state.

Anglo-American law has expanded Aristotle's definition of family to encompass a collective body of people who live in one house or within the same curtilage (a fenced-in yard surrounding a house), including domestic servants, lodgers, and guests. National statistical data, including the census, are now often based on the concept of households, or a family living together.

Although some constitutions make no reference to the family, many constitutions do include specific provisions for it. The 1992 Vietnamese constitution, for example, undertakes in Article 64 to protect marriage and families, and in Article 39 of the 1978 Spanish constitution public authorities guarantee the social, economic, and legal protection of the family.

Constitution of Italy (1948), Part One, The Duties and Rights of the Citizens, Title I, Civil Relations, Article 29: "The republic acknowledges the rights of the family as a natural society founded on marriage. Marriage is based on the moral and juridical equality of the spouses, within limits provided for by law for ensuring the unity of the family."

Constitution of Egypt (1971), Part Two, Basic Constituents of the Society, Chapter I, Social and Moral Constituents, Article 9: "The family is the basis of the society founded on religion, morality, and patriotism. The state is keen to preserve the genuine character of the Egyptian family—with what it embodies of values and traditions—while affirming and developing this character in the relations within the Egyptian society."

Federal Capital District

Nation-states that comprise constituent semisovereign states or provinces often set aside some territory that is not under the control of any one state or province to be the seat of government. Such a federal capital district houses all the principal offices of the major branches of government. In some federal nations—Switzerland and South Africa, for example—branches may be located in different cities.

James Madison in essay 43 of *The Federalist* (1788) warns that without power to create a federal district, " . . . not only the public authority might be insulted and its proceedings interrupted, but dependence of the members of the general government on the state [in which the seat of

Federal capital districts such as Brasilia in Brazil, created in 1960, are often located in territory owned and administered by the national government, not any of the constituent states.

the federal government was located] . . . might bring on the national councils an imputation of awe or influence equally dishonorable to the government. . . . "

Constitution of the United States of America (1789), Article I, Section 8: "The Congress shall have Power . . . To exercise exclusive Legislation in all Cases whatsoever, over such District (not exceeding ten Miles square), as may, by Cession of particular States, and the Acceptance of Congress, become the Seat of the Government of the United States. . . . "

Constitution of Australia (1901), Chapter II, Miscellaneous, Section 125: "The seat of Government of the Commonwealth shall be determined by the Parliament, and shall be within territory which shall have been granted to or acquired by the Commonwealth and shall be vested in and belong to the Commonwealth, and shall be in the state of New South Wales, and be distant not less than one hundred miles from Sydney."

Constitution of Brazil (1988), Title III, The Organization of the State, Chapter V, The Federal District and the Territories, Section I, The Federal District, Article 32, Paragraph 4: A federal law shall provide for the use by the government of the federal district of the civil and military police and the military fire brigade."

Federal District. *See* Federal Capital District

Federalism

Federalism is the principle of political organization under which a nation-state includes both a central (national or federal) government and semisovereign state or provincial governments. The English word *federal* is derived from the Latin *foederatus* (allied), whose root word is *foedus* (treaty).

A federal nation-state differs from a unitary nation-state, which has only one government and whose lower-level authorities are all subdivisions of the national government without any autonomous powers or residual sovereignty of their own. Constituent federal states are also unlike autonomous regions in a unitary state—for example, the self-governing communities and enclaves under the 1978 Spanish constitution—in that all the federated states are considered at least theoretically equal, whereas autonomous regions are often treated distinctly.

There are exceptions to this rule. In the quasi-federal system of Canada, the province of Quebec is guaranteed a certain number of seats in Parliament. In the United States, because membership in the House of Representatives is based on population, states with larger populations have disproportionate power in that body. Belgium is a unique example of a nation-state that once had a unitary system of government but has since evolved into a primarily federal system because of linguistic and cultural differences.

Constitution of Ethiopia (1995), Chapter One, General Provisions, Article 2, Ethiopian Territorial Jurisdiction: "The territorial jurisdiction of Ethiopia extends to all boundaries, including the boundaries of all members of the federation, as defined by international agreements."

Constitution of Argentina (1853), First Part, Declarations, Rights, and Guarantees, Article 1: "The Argentine nation adopts for its government the federal, republican, representative form, as established by the present constitution."

Federation

A federation—similar to a league, compact, or covenant—is a group of political entities associated or allied for some common cause or purpose. Federations are not recent phenomena. The Dorian League, an alliance of three Greek states to fight a common enemy, the Assyrians, is mentioned by Plato in *The Laws*.

Federations appear in constitutions as a political union of formerly separate states, provinces, or colonies, each of which retains some unfettered control over its internal affairs. Unlike states or provinces of a federal nation-state, the members of a true federation or federative union do not permanently relinquish a portion of their sovereignty.

Today, however, the terms *federation* and *federative* in national constitutions may also refer to a federal relationship in which semisovereign states or provinces are united under a central, federal government.

Constitution of Nigeria (1989), Chapter I, General Provisions, Part I, Federal Republic of Nigeria, Article 2: "(2)Nigeria shall be a federation consisting of states and a federal capital territory."

Constitution of Brazil (1988), Title 1, Fundamental Principles, Article 1: "The Federative Republic of Brazil, formed by the indissoluble union of the states and municipalities and of the federal district, is a legal democratic state. . . . "

Federative. *See* Federation

Filibuster. *See* Cloture; Debate

Flag. *See* Symbol

Flagrante Delicto. *See* Offense

Forced Labor

Many great historic feats of construction, such as the Pyramids of Egypt and the Great Wall of China, undoubtedly were achieved with forced labor. Under such involuntary servitude, even people who have committed no crimes are compelled against their will to work for the government.

Like slavery, forced labor is specifically prohibited in some constitutions. Nations with a history of conscripting citizens for work may emphasize in their constitutions that the practice is now prohibited.

Not considered forced labor are military duty and work for a private party, whether or not any payment is made for such services.

Constitution of Uganda, Simplified Draft (1992), Chapter 5, Fundamental Human Rights and Freedoms, Individual Rights, 7: "A person shall not be forced to work except as allowed by law."

Constitution of Honduras (1982), Title III, Declarations, Rights, and Guarantees, Chapter II, Individual Rights, Article 70: "No personal service may be exacted, nor must it be rendered gratuitously, except by virtue of the law or by a sentence based on the law."

Foreign Policy.

See External Affairs; International Relations

Foreign Relations.

See External Affairs; International Relations

Forms of Government. *See* Government

Fraternity

In Old English law a fraternity referred to people who were united not by a financial investment, as in a corporation, but by a "mystery" or business whose laws and regulations could not bind outsiders. In constitutions the term *fraternity*—from the Latin *fraternitas* (brotherhood)—is one of the three qualities, along with liberty and equality, said to be required for justice.

"Liberté! Égalité! Fraternité!" was the rallying cry of the French Revolution of 1789, one intended to convey a feeling of solidarity, mutual trust and aid, and support for common needs. In the preamble to its 1958 constitution, France offered the nation's overseas territories "new institutions based on the common ideal of liberty, equality, and fraternity. . . ." Article 2 of the same document proclaims the motto of the republic: "Freedom, Equality, Fraternity."

The motto "Liberté, Égalité, Fraternité" is inscribed on both sides of the doorway of this government building in Paris.

Constitution of Haiti (1987), Title I, The Republic of Haiti, Its Emblem and Its Symbols, Chapter I, The Republic of Haiti, Article 4: "The national motto is: liberty, equality, fraternity."

Constitution of Liberia (1986), Preamble: "Being solemnly resolved to live in harmony, to practice fraternal love, tolerance, and understanding as a people, fully mindful of our obligation to promote African unity, international peace, and cooperation. . . ."

Freedom. *See* Liberty

Full Faith and Credit

To require that one jurisdiction accept without inquiry the laws, records, and judicial decisions of another, many constitutions of federal nation-states use the term *full faith and credit.* It gives these enactments a conclusive, obligatory effect and thereby allows individuals in one jurisdiction to rely on them, obviating the need for extensive proceedings to prove them again to the satisfaction of officials in another jurisdiction.

Some federal constitutions include the specific phrase *full faith and credit* or its equivalent to ensure that citizens will be treated equally throughout the country with respect to the official acts of any one constituent state. The U.S. "full-faith" provision applies only to civil matters, not to criminal cases, but it ensures that contracts, deeds, and other property rights, as well as judicial decisions, will be honored and enforced in all the constituent states.

Constitution of the United States of America (1789), Article IV, Section 1: "Full Faith and Credit shall be given in each State to the public Acts, Records, and judicial Proceedings of every other State. And the Congress may by general Laws prescribe the Manner in which such Acts, Records and Proceedings shall be proved, and the Effect thereof."

Constitution of Argentina (1853), First Part, Declarations, Rights, and Guarantees, Article 7: "The public acts and judicial proceedings of one province enjoy full faith in the others; and congress may, by general laws, determine what shall be the probative form of these acts and proceedings, and the legal effects which they shall produce."

Constitution of Australia (1901), Part V, Powers of the Parliament, Article 51: "The Parliament shall, subject to this constitution, have power to make laws for the peace, order, and good government of the commonwealth with respect to:— . . . (xxv) The recognition throughout the commonwealth of the laws, the public acts and records, and the judicial proceedings of the states. . . . "

Fundamental Justice. *See* Fundamental Law

Fundamental Law

Constitutions are considered a nation-state's fundamental law or laws and contain supreme or basic laws—that is, laws grounded in what Hans Kelsen of Austria has referred to as legal norms. Germany's 1949 constitution is called the Basic Law, and in Israel, a country with an unwritten constitution, laws of constitutional stature are called basic laws.

In legal theory, however, fundamental laws are those that may be invoked by the people to limit the exercise of absolute authority by rulers. Natural law theorists came to realize that if all laws emanate from the absolute ruler or monarch, he or she must therefore be above the law itself, but if divine or natural laws form the basis of human society and human laws, then these fundamental laws can be used as a referent to check a ruler's improper actions.

Fundamental justice, as used in constitutions, refers to principles of justice and fairness generally accepted throughout the civilized world.

Constitution of Turkey (1982), Part I, General Principles, XI, Supremacy and Binding Force of the Constitution, Article 11: "The provisions of the constitution are fundamental rules binding upon legislative, executive, and judicial organs, and administrative authorities and other agencies and individuals."

Constitution of Canada, Constitution Act (1982), Part I, Canadian Charter of Rights and Freedoms, Section 7: "Everyone has the right to life, liberty, and security of the person and the right not to be deprived thereof except in accordance with the fundamental principles of justice."

Fundamental Rights

A right, in the abstract, is the power to demand and receive justice from the social organization of which one is a member. Rights may accrue from the good will or acquiescence of others, from position or status, from laws, and from generally accepted beliefs or principles. Fundamental rights are basic rights that accrue by virtue of being a human in a society of other humans. They are rights that others may not give or take away, unless there is some other right to do so; for example, if a law gives a person the right to compensation as redress for a trespass by another, then the right to keep one's own property may be forfeited by trespassing.

Some natural law theorists have reasoned that in the idealized process by which an individual surrenders the rights inherent in living a solitary existence for the social benefits of living among others, some natural or fundamental rights are retained and that it is the duty of human society to maintain them. These fundamental rights to be protected from others and from the state are referred to in documents such as the U.S. Declaration of Independence (1776) and the French Declaration of the Rights of Man and of the Citizen (1789). From John Locke and the theory of economic liberty—the right to work and retain the property created by one's work—to the concept of the sovereignty of the individual that evolved after the French Revolution has come the current notion of fundamental rights. These rights, together with such concepts as majority rule, periodic free elections, and the rule of law, are cornerstones of modern democratic nation-states.

Eugène Delacroix's Romantic painting *Liberty at the Barricades* (1830) captures the spirit of France's revolutionary period, when the people rallied behind the nation's tricolor flag to assert their fundamental rights against hereditary monarchs.

Constitution of Hungary (1948, significantly revised in 1989), Chapter I, General Provisions, Article 8: "(1) The Republic of Hungary recognizes the inviolable and inalienable fundamental human rights; to respect and to protect thereof shall be a primary duty of the state. (2) In the Republic of Hungary the rules touching fundamental rights and obligations shall be determined by law, which, however, shall not limit the substantial contents of any fundamental right."

Constitution of South Korea (1948), Chapter II, Rights and Duties of Citizens, Article 10: "All citizens shall be assured of human worth and dignity and have the right to pursue happiness. It shall be the duty of the state to confirm and guarantee the fundamental and inviolable human rights of individuals."

Bundesgesetzblatt

1949	Ausgegeben in Bonn am 23. Mai 1949	Nr.

Inhalt: Grundgesetz für die Bundesrepublik Deutschland vom 23. Mai 1949 ....

Grundgesetz
für die Bundesrepublik Deutschland
vom 23. Mai 1949.

Der Parlamentarische Rat hat am 23. Mai 1949 in Bonn am Rhein in öffentlicher Sitzung festgestellt, daß das am 8. Mai des Jahres 1949 vom Parlamentarischen Rat beschlossene Grundgesetz für die Bundesrepublik Deutschland in der Woche vom 16.—22. Mai 1949 durch die Volksvertretungen von mehr als Zweidritteln der beteiligten deutschen Länder angenommen worden ist.

Auf Grund dieser Feststellung hat der Parlamentarische Rat, vertreten durch seine Präsidenten, das Grundgesetz ausgefertigt und verkündet.

Das Grundgesetz wird hiermit gemäß Artikel 145 Absatz 3 im Bundesgesetzblatt veröffentlicht:

Präambel

Im Bewußtsein seiner Verantwortung vor Gott und den Menschen,

von dem Willen beseelt, seine nationale und staatliche Einheit zu wahren und als gleichberechtigtes Glied in einem vereinten Europa dem Frieden der Welt zu dienen, hat das Deutsche Volk

in den Ländern Baden, Bayern, Bremen, Hamburg, Hessen, Niedersachsen, Nordrhein-Westfalen, Rheinland-Pfalz, Schleswig-Holstein, Württemberg-Baden und Württemberg-Hohenzollern,

um dem staatlichen Leben für eine Übergangszeit eine neue Ordnung

I. Die Grundrechte

Artikel 1

(1) Die Würde des Menschen ist unantastba zu achten und zu schützen ist Verpflichtung staatlichen Gewalt.

(2) Das Deutsche Volk bekennt sich daru unverletzlichen und unveräußerlichen Mens rechten als Grundlage jeder menschlichen Ge schaft, des Friedens und der Gerechtigkeit i Welt.

(3) Die nachfolgenden Grundrechte binden setzgebung, Verwaltung und Rechtsprechung unmittelbar geltendes Recht.

Artikel 2

(1) Jeder hat das Recht auf die freie Entfa seiner Persönlichkeit, soweit er nicht die Recht derer verletzt und nicht gegen die verfass mäßige Ordnung oder das Sittengesetz verstöß

(2) Jeder hat das Recht auf Leben und kö liche Unversehrtheit. Die Freiheit der Perso unverletzlich. In diese Rechte darf nur auf G eines Gesetzes eingegriffen werden.

Artikel 3

(1) Alle Menschen sind vor dem Gesetz gle

(2) Männer und Frauen sind gleichberechtig

(3) Niemand darf wegen seines Geschle seiner Abstammung, seiner Rasse, seiner Sp seiner Heimat und Herkunft, seines Glaubens, s religiösen oder politischen Anschauungen be teiligt oder bevorzugt werden.

Artikel 4

(1) Die Freiheit des Glaubens, des Gew und die Freiheit des religiösen und weltans

G

Gag Rule. *See* Cloture; Debate

Gazette

In many countries laws passed by the legislature and approved or assented to by a president or monarch must be published in an official gazette before they can become effective. A daily record, similar to a journal, the term is derived from the Latin *gaza* (treasure) and possibly from the Italian *gazzetta* (a Venetian coin that was the price of a newspaper-like publication).

In Germany the official gazette in which a law must be published is the *Bundesgesetzblatt,* whose name is a combination of *Gesetz* (law or statute) and *Blatt* (paper). The Spanish word *gaceta* refers to an official newspaper, and in French a *gazette* is an official bulletin.

Constitution of Germany (1949), VII, Legislative Powers of the Federation, Article 82, Promulgation and Effective Date of Legal Provisions: "(1) Statutes enacted in accordance with the provisions of this Basic Law [the constitution] shall, after countersignature, be signed by the federal president and promulgated in the Federal Law Gazette. Ordinances shall be signed by the agency which issues them and, unless otherwise provided by statute, shall be promulgated in the Federal Law Gazette *(Bundesgesetzblatt).*"

Constitution of Ireland (1937), Signing and Promulgation of Laws, Article 25.4.2: "Every bill signed by the president under this constitution shall be promulgated by him as a law by the publication by his direction of a notice in the *Iris Oifigiúil* stating that the bill has become law."

General Welfare

Jeremy Bentham, the English jurist and philosopher who coined the word *utilitarianism* in 1801, called the obligation to minister to general happiness—the general welfare—paramount to and inclusive of every other obligation. The preamble to the U.S. Constitution (1789) declares that one purpose of the document is to promote the general welfare; however, in Article 1, Section 8, Congress is given the power not to pass laws promoting the general welfare but to "lay and collect taxes . . . to pay the debts and provide for the common defense and general welfare of the United States. . . . " James Madison, in essay 41 of *The Federalist* (1788), asserts that while this language seems excessively broad with respect to the powers granted to Congress, it is not, because those powers are enumerated and limited elsewhere in the Constitution. Congress's

The German and other constitutions require that acts passed by the legislature and approved by the head of state be published in an official gazette for them to have legal effect. The name of this gazette name combines the words *law* and *paper.*

Free public health services are among the benefits that derive from constitutional directives that governments provide for the general welfare. In Brazil this has included immunization programs that bring health-care providers to rural areas.

powers in relation to this provision have since been interpreted to include spending money to promote the general welfare as well as raising money for that purpose.

Some constitutions use terms such as *welfare of the people* to refer to the general welfare or the public good.

Constitution of the Philippines (1987), Article II, Section 5: "The maintenance of peace and order, the protection of life, liberty, and property, and the promotion of the general welfare are essential for the enjoyment by all the people of the blessings of democracy."

Constitution of India (1950), Part IV, Directive Principles of State Policy, Article 38(1): "The state shall strive to promote the welfare of the people by securing and protecting as effectively as it may a social order in which justice, social, economic, and political, shall inform all the institutions of the national life."

Good Behavior

In law *good behavior* means orderly and lawful conduct. William Blackstone, the eighteenth-century commentator on English law, notes that "justices are empowered to bind over to the good behavior towards the king and his people all [those] *that be not of good fame*" [Blackstone's emphasis].

Constitutional phrases such as *during good behavior*

and *except in the case of misbehavior* are sometimes used to indicate a life-tenure position to which a person is entitled unless he or she should misbehave in some way that would warrant removal. Life-tenure positions, which are most often found in the judiciary, are a means of ensuring that judges will not have to please the public or other officials to remain in office and thus can be independent and unfettered by public opinion.

Article 2, Section 4, of the U.S. Constitution (1789) provides that the president, the vice president, and all civil officers (thus excluding the military and members of Congress) may be removed from office on impeachment and conviction for treason, bribery, and other high crimes and misdemeanors—actions contrary to good behavior.

Constitution of the United States of America (1789), Article III, Section 1: " . . . The Judges, both of the supreme and inferior Courts, shall hold their Offices during good Behavior, and shall, at stated Times, receive for their Services, a Compensation, which shall not be reduced during their Continuance in Office."

Constitution of Liberia (1968), Chapter VII, The Judiciary, Article 74: "The chief justice and the associate justices of the supreme court and the judges of subordinate courts of record shall hold office during good behavior. They may be removed upon impeachment and conviction by the legislature based on proved misconduct, gross breach of duty, inability to perform the functions of their office, or conviction in a court of law for treason, bribery, or other infamous crimes."

Constitution of Kenya (1963), Chapter IV, The Judicature, Part 1, The High Court and the Court of Appeals, Section 62(3): "A judge of the high court may be removed from office only for inability to perform the functions of his office (whether arising from infirmity of body or mind or from any other cause) or for misbehavior, and shall not be removed except in accordance with this section."

Gorbachev, Mikhail Sergeyevich

The initiator of *perestroika* and *glasnost,* Mikhail Sergeyevich Gorbachev (b. 1931) introduced amendments to the Soviet Union's 1977 constitution that resulted in dramatic changes in the country and a new Russian constitution in 1993.

Born in Privolnoye in Krasnogvardeishy District on March 2, 1931, Gorbachev began his career in 1946 as a machine operator and in 1952 joined the Communist Party of the Soviet Union. In 1955 he was graduated from Moscow State University with a degree in law and later earned a second degree as an agricultural economist. Rising rapidly up the hierarchical ladder of the Communist Party, by 1982 he was being groomed by Yuri V. Andropov, then the party's general secretary and head of the Union of Soviet Socialist Republics (U.S.S.R.), to be Andropov's successor.

After succeeding to Andropov's position in 1985, Gorbachev slowly embarked on a program of economic and political reform. Realizing that the Soviet Union was

Mikhail Gorbachev's political and economic innovations in the Soviet Union led not only to its dissolution in 1991 but also to the development of new constitutional democracies in the U.S.S.R.'s former states.

falling behind many of the world's highly industrialized countries and that the quality of life was eroding, he instituted *perestroika*, an economic restructuring of Soviet society that decentralized day-to-day economic decisions, established a limited market mechanism to improve the quality and distribution of goods, and permitted cooperatively owned small businesses and foreign investment in the Soviet Union. His other major reform initiative was *glasnost,* or "openness in the interests of socialism," as he called it.

Two months after being elected chairman of the Presidium of the Supreme Soviet on October 1, 1988, General Secretary Gorbachev initiated major revisions to the "Brezhnev" constitution of 1977, named for the Soviet leader Leonid I. Brezhnev. The changes, which provided for a separation of powers between the executive and legislative branches, included the creation of a parliamentary system of government somewhat along the lines of the French model, as well as contested elections and increased judicial independence. Later amendments in 1989 and 1990 created a multiparty system, broadened the direct election process, and extended rights of private ownership of property and businesses. Institution of the multiparty political system required the abrogation of Article 6 of the Soviet constitution, which had given the Communist Party a monopoly on political power.

In the second half of the 1980s, *glasnost*—undoubtedly more than Gorbachev intended—energized Soviet society, which had been intellectually isolated for some seventy years. In 1990 he officially became president of the U.S.S.R. The tidal wave of economic and political changes, which he had both stimulated and attempted to control, however, forced him to resign the position on December 25, 1991. The collapse of the Soviet empire occurred shortly thereafter. Although it may be argued that when Gorbachev ascended to power the Soviet Union was already destined to disintegrate, the radical changes embodied in the amendments he initiated to the 1977 constitution are unlikely to have occurred so soon or so dramatically.

Gorbachev failed in his attempt to save the Soviet political and economic system by changing it, but he accomplished a dramatic constitutional revolution not only in the Soviet Union but also in many former members of the union and its Eastern European satellites. In 1996 he ran for and decisively lost election as president of Russia.

Government

The concept of government, which initially referred only to judicial rather than to political activities, predates the concept of the state described by Jean Bodin and Niccolò Machiavelli in the sixteenth century. As early as the thirteenth century, the term *governing*—to rule with authority, from Greek and Latin words meaning to steer—was used in England. By the 1500s government was accepted as the action of exercising authority over subjects or inferiors.

Jeremy Bentham, the English jurist and philosopher who died in 1832, believed that the business of government is simply to promote the happiness of society through punishment and reward. Jean-Jacques Rousseau had theorized a half century earlier that each sovereign moral person creates government. In such a basic system, a second moral person is subservient to the first. As the process expands, many subservient persons will act in government capacities on behalf of the entire group of sovereign moral persons, all of whom have delegated their sovereign authority to the government.

One meaning of government today, however, is the tangible machinery of the nation-state as created under the terms of national constitutions. Governments undertake numerous functions and historically have taken on many forms. The spectrum ranges from the absence of government—anarchy—to unlimited or unchecked government—totalitarian dictatorship, absolute monarchy, or autocracy. Between these two ends lie many other forms of constitutional or limited government.

Governments may also be categorized according to the number of rulers: a single ruler indicates a monarchy, several rulers an oligarchy, and many rulers a democracy. A government by an elite class is an aristocracy; by religious leaders, a theocracy; by the wealthy, a plutocracy or timocracy.

Another distinction can be made between a legitimist government, such as that of Monaco, and a popular sovereignty, which today includes many nation-states. Governments may be unitary, federal, or confederated. They may be presidential, as in the United States; parliamentary, as in the United Kingdom; or presidential-style parliamentary, in which the president takes the role of a monarch rather than that of the head of a coequal executive branch of government, as in Germany.

A country's political structure is also its government—for example, communist, socialist, or democratic. When applied to the current administration or political party in power under a multiparty system, the term may mean a particular party, such as the Democratic Party in the United States or the Labour Party in the United Kingdom; it may also refer to party ideology, such as liberal or conservative. Sometimes the government in a parliamentary system may be described as a coalition government when no single party has a majority of the seats in the parliament; or, in the case of a presidential system, the administration (the executive branch) may be held by one party and the legislature by another.

Written constitutions do not often stipulate a particular type of government, except to refer to the nation-state as a democracy or republic. Some constitutions, such as those in countries dominated by the Communist Party or the Arab Ba'ath Party, may specify that the political system is a single-party one; other constitutions note that the system is a multiparty one. "The constitution is in fact the government," Aristotle states in *The Politics,* but some modern constitutions mask the true nature of the government, calling it a multiparty democracy when in fact it is dominated by a single party or a military strongman or junta.

Constitution of France (1958), Title I, On Sovereignty, Article 2: "France is a republic . . . [i]ts principle is government of the people, by the people, and for the people."

Constitution of Spain (1978), Title III, Concerning the Cortes Generales [parliament], Chapter II, Concerning the Drafting of Bills, Article 82: "1. The Cortes Generales may delegate to the government the power to issue rules with the status of law on specific matters not included in the foregoing article."

Government Bill

The process of enacting legislation begins with the introduction of a bill. Some national legislatures, such as the U.S. Congress, restrict to legislators the right to introduce bills. Legislation proposed by the president or any government official except a member of Congress must be introduced in the House of Representatives or Senate by a member or members on that person's behalf. A bill for the executive, legislative, or judicial branch—a government bill—theoretically takes no precedence over any other draft legislative proposal.

In the model parliamentary system of government, as in the United Kingdom, however, the head of government (the prime minister) and the cabinet ministers are members of the legislature and therefore may introduce bills for the government. Such bills are called government bills to distinguish them from legislation introduced by parliamentary members on their own.

In some constitutions special provisions are necessary to allow the government to introduce bills directly in the legislature, and sometimes these bills may be treated differently from bills introduced on their own by legislators, other public officials or bodies, or, where initiative procedures are authorized, the public.

Constitution of Romania (1991), Title III, Public Authorities, Chapter I, Parliament, Section 3, Legislation and Procedure, Article 73: "(1) The legislative initiative lies with the government, deputies, senators, as well as no fewer than 250,000 citizens having the right to vote. . . . (3) The government shall exercise its legislative initiative by introducing bills in one of the chambers."

Constitution of France (1958), Title V, On Relations Between Parliament and the Government, Article 42: "The discussion of government bills shall pertain, in the first assembly to which they have been referred, to the text presented by the government. An assembly, given a text passed by the other assembly, shall deliberate on the text that is transmitted to it."

Governor

During the days of the British Empire a governor was a representative of the English monarch or Crown in the nation's dominions and colonies. He was the head of the local executive branch of government and likely had a governor-general above and lieutenant governors below him in authority.

Both political science and constitutional theory distinguish between governors and the governed, as between rulers and those ruled. But in constitutions the term *governor* refers specifically to the position of the chief executive of a constituent state or province in a nation-state with a federal form of government.

The constitutions of some federal nations set forth the criteria for the selection and duties of governors—from the Old French word *gouverneur,* which has a similar form in Spanish and Italian—while others are silent on the matter, leaving the form of government up to the individual states or provinces. All heads of the executive branches of state governments in the United States are called governors. In Austria the equivalent of a governor is called a *Landeshauptmann.*

Constitution of Pakistan (1973), Part IV, Provinces, Chapter I, The Governors, Article 101: "There shall be a governor for each province, who shall be appointed by the president after consultation with the prime minister."

Constitution of Mexico (1917), Title IV, Responsibilities of Public Officials, Article 108: "The governors of the states, the deputies of local legislatures, and the magistrates of the superior courts of local justice shall be responsible for violations of this constitution and federal law, as well as for mismanagement of funds and federal resources."

Governor-General

Since at least the sixteenth century, the chief executive who represents the English monarch in the Crown's territory has been known as the governor-general. Today the term is used exclusively for the representative of the United Kingdom's sovereign in Australia, Canada, and New Zealand. Although originally these positions were held by British subjects residing in the dominions, they are now generally filled by citizens of the countries in which they hold office.

Like the monarch, the governor-general's role is ceremonial; his or her actions are directed by an elected prime minister, who represents the majority party in the country's parliament. The governor-general's assent is formally required to validate enacted laws, and as the representative of the monarch he or she is the nominal head of the armed forces. A formal council advises the governor-general, although the only advice that matters is that of the prime minister and the cabinet of ministers.

Constitution of Canada, Constitution Act (1867), III, Executive Power, Section 10: "The provisions of this act referring to the governor general extend and apply to the governor general for the time being of Canada, or other [sic] the chief executive officer or administrator for the time being carrying on the government of Canada on behalf and in the name of the queen, by whatever title he is designated."

Constitution of Australia (1901), Chapter II, The Executive Government, Section 68:"The command in chief of the naval and military forces of the commonwealth is vested in the governor-general as the queen's representative."

Grievance

In William Shakespeare's play *The Tragedy of Romeo and Juliet* (1595), Benvolio remarks on seeing his friend Romeo: "See where he comes. So please you, step aside. I'll know his grievance, or be much denied." A belief that one has been wronged, afflicted unjustly, oppressed, injured, or distressed is a common human concern. Trade unions, for instance, often form grievance committees to hear the complaints of workers, which may be presented to the management of a business to seek relief.

Constitutions likewise may address individuals' grievances by granting them the right to petition the government peacefully to present grievances or wrongs to be redressed. The right to publicly object or demonstrate may not be enforced, however, even when constitutionally authorized. The 1982 constitution of the People's Republic of China grants to citizens the right to demonstrate and make complaints against the government, but in 1989 a demonstration in Tiananmen Square in Beijing ended in a massacre by government troops.

Constitution of the Philippines (1987), Article III, Bill of Rights, Section 4: "No law shall be passed abridging the freedom of speech, of expression, or of the press, or the right of the people to peaceably assemble and petition the government for redress of grievances."

Constitution of Germany (1949), I, Basic Rights, Article 17: "Everyone shall have the right individually or jointly with others to address written requests or complaints to the competent agencies and to parliaments."

Griffith, Samuel Walker

Although Sir Henry Parkes of New South Wales became known as the "Father of the Federation," Sir Samuel Walker Griffith (1845–1920) of Queensland played the major role in drafting the original bill that set in motion the development of the 1901 Australian constitution.

Born in Glamorgan, Wales, in 1845, Griffith moved to Australia in 1854 and studied law at Sydney University. In 1867 he began the practice of law in Queensland, soon becoming a leading barrister in Brisbane and a powerful force in Queensland politics.

At the 1891 constitutional convention in Sydney, Parkes and Griffith were united in support of a federal constitution like the U.S. Constitution (1789). Parkes was the host and president of the convention, but Griffith drafted the final version of the proposed new constitution bill. The document combined American constitutional concepts, especially ideas concerning relations between the federal and state governments, with the British parliamentary system.

The 1891 document that Griffith drafted became the basis for discussions at later constitutional conventions held in Adelaide, Sydney, and Melbourne in 1897 and 1898. After a number of amendments the constitution was accepted by the Australian people in a second referendum held in 1899. The proposed constitution still had to pass the British Parliament, which it did after further changes by the secretary of state for the colonies, Joseph Chamberlain, an avowed imperialist.

Appointed chief justice of Queensland in 1893, Griffith became first chief justice of the high court of Australia in 1900, a position he held until 1919. He died a year later. Griffith's position on the court precluded him from taking part in the 1897–98 constitutional conventions but allowed him to have a significant impact through his decisions on the relationship between the new national government and the constituent states of Australia, especially in matters involving legislative validity.

Sir Samuel Walker Griffith (top) wrote the first draft of the 1901 Australian constitution, and Sir Henry Parkes (bottom) successfully led the movement for a federal nation-state like the United States but headed by the British monarch.

Habeas Corpus

The English writ of habeas corpus ("you have the body") predates Magna Carta (1215) and was established in England by the seventeenth century as the proper means of challenging arbitrary or illegal imprisonment. A number of types of writs begin with this Latin phrase, but the preeminent writ is *habeas corpus ad subjiciendum*, which is directed to the person who detains another in custody and requires him or her to produce the detainee in court to receive whatever judgment the court or judge may render.

The Habeas Corpus Act of 1679 liberated "our bodies ... from arbitrary imprisonment ... ," said William Blackstone, the eighteenth-century commentator on the laws of England. Alexander Hamilton, in essay 84 of *The Federalist* (1788), points to the U.S. Constitution's habeas corpus clause as one of many examples of express constitutional rights that were also included in the earlier constitution of his home state of New York.

Constitution of the United States of America (1789), Article I, Section 9: "The Privilege of the Writ of Habeas Corpus shall not be suspended, unless when in Cases of Rebellion or Invasion the public Safety may require it."

Constitution of India (1950), Part III, Fundamental Rights, Article 32, Remedies for Enforcement of Rights Conferred by this Part: "(2) The supreme court shall have power to issue directions or orders or writs, including writs in the nature of *habeas corpus*. . . ."

Constitution of Brazil (1988), Title II, Fundamental Rights and Guarantees, Chapter II, Individual and Collective Rights and Duties, Article 5: "All persons are equal before the law, without any distinction whatsoever, Brazilians and foreigners residing in the country being insured of inviolability of the right to life, to liberty, to equality, to security, and to property, on the following terms: . . . LXVIII—'habeas corpus' shall be granted whenever a person suffers or is in danger of suffering violence or coercion against his freedom of locomotion, on account of illegal actions or abuse of power. . . ."

Hamilton, Alexander

In his writings Alexander Hamilton (1755–1804) left a legacy of original, profound, and still relevant constitutional thought, and his vision of the United States as an industrial nation with a strong central government came to pass.

Born on the island of Nevis in the British West Indies on January 11, 1755, Hamilton was the illegitimate son of a Scotsman and a French Huguenot physician's

In addition to acting on legislation, the British House of Commons has occasionally been the site of criminal trials before the High Court of Parliament, which serves as the supreme court of criminal jurisdiction in the kingdom.

Although his vision of a strong central government based on the British model was rejected, Alexander Hamilton argued persuasively for adoption of the U.S. Constitution. His views were published contemporaneously in *The Federalist* (1788).

daughter. After working as a clerk in a trading firm from eleven to thirteen years of age, he immigrated to New York City in 1773 and attended what is now Columbia University.

A pamphleteer for the American revolutionary cause, Hamilton joined the Continental Army, serving first as a lieutenant colonel and an aide-de-camp to General George Washington and then as the head of a line regiment at the Battle of Yorktown in 1781.

After serving a term in the Continental Congress, Hamilton concluded that the fledgling nation needed a stronger central government. At a national conference called by the Virginia legislature, he and James Madison led the delegates beyond their mandate, getting them to recommend a national meeting on the inadequacies of the Articles of Confederation (1781).

Hamilton represented New York at the Constitutional Convention in Philadelphia in 1787. His proposal for a government similar to the British model found little favor with his colleagues, but as soon as the new document was drafted he began an ardent and aggressive campaign for its adoption. Under the name Publius he wrote essays on constitutional thought in collaboration with Madison and John Jay; these were collectively published in 1788 as *The Federalist.* New York adopted the new national Constitution in 1788, largely as a result of Hamilton's efforts.

Over Thomas Jefferson's objection on the grounds of unconstitutionality, Hamilton, the new nation's first secretary of the treasury, created the First Bank of the United States, a quasi-public financial institution that strengthened the country's credit. He had a major impact on the young nation-state as a virtual prime minister in Washington's administration and as the leader of the country's first political party, the Federalist Party.

Hamilton and Jefferson were always philosophically opposed: Hamilton urged a strong, active, central government in support of industry, while Jefferson counted more on the self-reliance of the agrarian sector, with government playing a minimal role. Hamilton's political philosophy, grounded in "an eternal and immutable law, which is indispensably, obligatory upon all mankind . . . "—rather than Jefferson's—became accepted in the United States. On July 11, 1804, Hamilton was mortally wounded in a duel with Aaron Burr, a political rival who was offended by Hamilton's attacks on his character.

Head of Government

All modern democracies have a chief executive officer for the country who heads the government and ensures that laws are executed, that government programs are developed and presented to the legislature for action, and that government officials are appointed and supervised. There are two basic types of heads of government, as well as a number of variations.

In the presidential form of government, as in the United States, which has a strict separation of powers, a constitutionally limited Congress, and an independent judiciary with some form of judicial review, the president is the elected head of the executive branch and serves as both head of state and government. Following the U.S.

Margaret Thatcher, British prime minister from 1979 to 1990, was the first woman to head the government of a major industrialized Western country.

model, a number of constitutions prescribe this system.

The other basic type of government conforms to the British-style parliamentary system, the Westminster model, in which there is a head of state (the monarch) and a separate head of government (the prime minister). A variation on this model is a republic with both a president who is head of state and a prime minister, premier, or chancellor who is head of government.

In a parliamentary monarchy—for example, the government of Denmark—the head of state is nonpolitical, and the prime minister, as head of government, is also the leader of the majority party or a coalition of parties in the parliament. The prime minister is elected first as a member of the parliament and then selected by the majority party or a coalition of parties to run the government. He or she performs all the executive functions of government but does not act as the formal head of state, who represents the country and who assents to laws passed by the legislature.

In a presidential-style parliamentary government, the executive powers and duties of the head of government may be distributed between the president and the prime minister.

Unwritten constitutions, such as the United Kingdom's, and even some written ones, such as Australia's, do not mention the head of government (the prime minister); the position is simply accepted by tradition or convention. Other constitutions detail the duties of the head of government and his or her relationship to the head of state and the legislature.

Constitution of Singapore (1959), Part V, The Government, Chapter 2, The Executive, Article 24: "(1) There shall be in and for Singapore a cabinet which shall consist of the prime minister and such other ministers as may be appointed. . . . (2) Subject to the provisions of this constitution, the cabinet shall have the general direction and control of the government and shall be responsible to parliament."

Constitution of Romania (1991), Chapter III, The Government, Article 106: "(1) The prime minister shall direct government actions and coordinate activities of its members, under observance of the powers and duties incumbent on them. Likewise, he shall submit to the chamber of deputies or the senate reports and statements on government policy to be debated with priority."

In 1980 Vigís Finnbogadóttir of Iceland became the world's first popularly elected female head of state.

Head of State

Plato, who regarded the state, or polity, as a reflection of the human soul, equated the just person with the just state. The works of later political philosophers, including Jean-Jacques Rousseau, mirror this image of the state as a great being or person. A head of state, historically the sovereign or monarch, is the embodiment of the nation-state today, with all its people, culture, and diversity.

In many countries, particularly in Western Europe and Asia, the head of state is still a monarch who is succeeded on death by an offspring or, if there is none or none who qualifies for the position, by another member of the royal family. Except for Canada, where the British monarch is the nominal head of state, no major nations in the Western Hemisphere have a monarch as head of state. On the Arabian peninsula, Saudi Arabia and Kuwait are also examples of countries with a monarch as head of state.

Most nation-states today have presidents as head of state, either in conjunction with a separate head of government—as in parliamentary systems, such as in Ireland—or as both head of state and government—as in presidential governments, such as in the United States. Presidents are generally chosen by election, either directly by popular vote or indirectly by an electoral college. Sometimes the president may be chosen by the parliament alone or in conjunction with other electors, as in Germany and Indonesia.

The duties of a head of state are often ceremonial, such as officially opening the session of the legislature, receiving foreign dignitaries, and making state visits to foreign countries. To varying degrees the head of state has symbolic or real power to assent to laws enacted by the legislature in order for them to be considered valid. In a parliamentary system of government the head of state also generally appoints the prime minister or head of government, although he or she is almost automatically the leader of the majority party in the parliament or the leader of a coalition of parties. The head of state may make other official appointments and perform other official acts on the recommendation or at the direction of the head of government or on his or her own, depending on the powers granted by the country's constitution.

Constitution of Taiwan (1947), Chapter IV, The President, Article 35: "The president shall be the head of state and shall represent the Republic of China in foreign relations."

Constitution of Belgium (1831), Heading III, Concerning the Authorities, Chapter II, Concerning the King and His Ministers, Section I, Concerning the King, Article 62: "The king may not simultaneously be the head of another state save with the consent of both houses [of parliament]."

Health

After honoring the gods and honoring the soul, Plato in *The Laws* ranked honoring the body. For Aristotle, health was a necessity—the first of four attributes cities would be fortunate to have. Many centuries later John Stuart Mill, in his 1863 essay on utilitarianism, concludes that the desire for health is a part of the general desire for happiness. The English word *health* is derived from the Old English word *hælp* and the Old High German word *helida* (whole or hale). The term for *health* in German today is *Gesundheit,* in French *santé,* and in Spanish *salud.*

Many modern constitutions, as part of a general goal of creating a better life for a nation's citizens, include provisions and even whole sections devoted to the policies and powers of the state with respect to aspects of health, including maternity and child care, sanitation, the environment, and health insurance.

Constitution of the Netherlands (1814), Chapter 1, Fundamental Rights, Article 9: "2. Rules to protect health, in the interest of traffic and to combat or prevent disorders, may be laid down by act of parliament."

Constitution of Poland, Constitutional Provisions Continued in Force Pursuant to Article 77 of the Constitution Act (1992), Chapter 8, Fundamental Rights and Duties of Citizens, Article 70: "1. Citizens of the Republic of Poland shall have the right to health protection and to assistance in the event of sickness or the inability to work."

High Court

A high court may be a supreme court or a court above or below a supreme court. The United Kingdom has a High Court of Chancery, a High Commission Court, a High Court of Justice, and a High Court of Parliament. References to a supreme court of criminal jurisdiction can be found as early as the fifteenth century; according to William Blackstone, the eighteenth-century commentator on the laws of England, it is the High Court of Parliament. Since 1875 the High Court of Justice, together with the Court of Appeals and the Crown Court, has made up the United Kingdom's Supreme Court of Judicature. The justices of the High Court of Justice include the lord chancellor and lord chief justice.

The term *high court* itself implies the existence of lower, or inferior, courts that are bound by the decisions of the superior high court. Many constitutions, especially those of former dominions or colonies of the United Kingdom, contain provisions relating to the composition, jurisdiction, and position in the judicial branch's hierarchy of high courts and high court divisions of the judicature.

Constitution of Bangladesh (1972), Part VI, The Judiciary, Article 94: "(1) There shall be a supreme court for Bangladesh (to be known as the supreme court of Bangladesh) comprising the appellate division and the high court division. . . . (3) The chief justice, and the judges appointed to the appellate division, shall sit only in that division, and the other judges shall sit only in the high court division."

Constitution of Zambia (1991), Part VI, The Judicature, Section 94: "(1) There shall be a high court for the republic which shall have, except as to proceedings in which the industrial relations court has exclusive jurisdiction under the Industrial Relations Act, unlimited or original jurisdiction to hear and determine any civil or criminal proceedings under any law and such jurisdiction and powers as may be conferred on it by this constitution or any other law. (2)(a) The chief justice shall be *ex officio* a judge of the high court. (b) The other judges of the high court shall be such puisne [lower ranking] judges as may be prescribed by parliament."

House

As early as the eleventh century in England, the word *house*—from the Old English *hús*—meant a dwelling. By the sixteenth century it referred to the building in which a deliberative or legislative body met. Today a house of parliament or congress is a legislative chamber or subdivision of the whole parliament or congress.

Bicameral legislatures generally have an upper and a lower house. In a parliamentary system of government, the upper house, like the British House of Lords, is generally less representative of the people; it may not be subject to elections or at least not as often as the lower house, and its members may not be elected strictly on the basis of population. A parliament's lower house, which is generally more representative, is where most of the political power resides.

In a presidential system, such as in the United States, both houses of the legislature must vote to enact laws, although the constitution assigns certain individual functions to each house. In the United Kingdom, on the other hand, laws are enacted only by the lower house; the upper house functions primarily as a brake on the legislative process and as a court of appeals made up of judges called law lords.

The parliament of the Netherlands is divided into first and second, rather than upper and lower, chambers. Norway and Iceland have semibicameral legislative bodies, in which the upper and lower chambers are created after the general election of all members. A legislature's two houses may meet and act together jointly for certain purposes as provided for in their constitutions.

Constitution of the Netherlands (1814), Chapter 3, The States General, Section 1, Organization and Composition, Article 51: "1. The states general [parliament] shall consist of a second [lower] chamber (Tweede Kamer) and a first [upper] chamber (Eerste Kamer). . . . 4. The two chambers shall be deemed a single entity when they meet in joint session."

Constitution of India (1950), Part V, The Union, Chapter II, Parliament, Article 79: "Constitution of Parliament. There shall be a parliament for the union which shall consist of the president and two houses to be known respectively as the council of states and the house of the people."

Housing

Both Plato, in *The Laws*, and Aristotle, in *The Politics*, address governments' concern about housing, and they agree to a large extent on the need to build housing for security in the event of war. Construction of walled cities and defense fortifications have been an integral part of government activities throughout history. Only relatively recently, however, have national governments taken a positive role in the housing needs of their citizens.

The relationship between having decent dwellings and a country's economic progress and the health and security of its citizens has led some drafters of constitutions to make special provisions for residential housing. Some constitutions regard adequate housing as a fundamental right, while others merely state that improving the country's housing conditions is a goal.

Chronic shortages in housing have led to subsidized housing developments in many countries, including those in Europe after World War II, and an emphasis in some constitutions on housing as a national problem.

Constitution of Honduras (1982), Title III, Declarations, Rights, and Guarantees, Chapter IX, Housing, Article 179: "The state shall promote, support, and regulate the creation of systems and mechanisms for the utilization of internal and external resources to be used for solving the housing problem."

Constitution of Portugal (1976), Part I, Fundamental Rights and Duties, Section II, Rights, Freedoms, and Safeguards, Chapter II, Social Rights and Duties, Article 65, Housing: "1. Everyone shall have the right for himself and his family to a dwelling of adequate size satisfying standards of hygiene and comfort and preserving personal and family privacy."

Immigration

Citizens of ancient Athens left their city-state while serving in military campaigns, as ambassadors, and on trade missions; aliens came into Athens under the same circumstances. Aristotle relates in *The Politics* that resident aliens were citizens of Athens in a qualified sense but could not participate fully in community life. In ancient Rome a *civis sui juris* had all the privileges and duties under Roman law, unlike a *civis alien juris*. With the expansion of the Roman Empire, citizenship was extended to many of the conquered peoples, some of whom immigrated to Rome, the center of culture, intellectual activity, and political power.

During the discovery and exploration of the New World, many areas in North and South America were host to European immigrants, most of whom formed new political societies based on their European heritage and intermarried with the indigenous populations. Today, with national territorial jurisdictions largely stable, the influx of foreigners or aliens into a country to reside permanently and perhaps acquire citizenship there is an important concern of national governments. Constitutions may expressly provide for the regulation of immigration and for the rights and duties of immigrants seeking to make a new home.

The exodus of citizens leaving a country and seeking to live permanently elsewhere is called emigration.

Constitution of Austria (1920), The Federal Constitution, Chapter I, General Provisions, Article 10: "1. The *Bund* [federation] has powers of legislation and execution in the following matters: . . . 3. regulation and control of entry into and exit from the federal territory; immigration and emigration; passports; deportation, turning back at the frontier, expulsion, and extradition from or through the federal territory. . . ."

Constitution of Argentina (1853), First Part, Declarations, Rights, and Guarantees, Article 20: "Foreigners enjoy in the territory of the nation all of the civil rights of citizens; they may engage in their industry, commerce, or profession; own real property, purchase it and alienate it; navigate the rivers and coasts; freely practice their religion; make wills and marry in accordance with the laws. They are not obliged to assume citizenship nor to pay forced extraordinary taxes. They may obtain naturalization [citizenship] by residing two continuous years in the nation; but the authorities may shorten this term in favor of anyone so requesting, on asserting and proving services to the republic."

Immunity

The U.S. Constitution (1789), Article 4, Section 2, provides that "the Citizens of each State shall be entitled to all the Privileges and Immunities of Citizens of the

Immigrants, such as these at Ellis Island, have been required to undergo health inspections at the port of entry into a country.

several States." Alexander Hamilton, in essay 80 of *The Federalist* (1788), recommends that to ensure such privileges and immunities the national judiciary preside over all cases in which a state or its citizens are opposed to another state or its citizens.

Derived from the Latin word *immunitas* (exemption), immunity more commonly denotes freedom or exemption from a service or an obligation. In constitutions it is often paired with privilege and is most often mentioned in relation to legislators' immunity from being arrested for certain crimes and actions during legislative debates. The head of state in many parliamentary-type governments is often granted constitutional immunity from any legal responsibility for his or her acts.

Constitution of Jordan (1952), Chapter Four, Executive Power, Part I, The King and His Prerogatives, Article 30: "The king is the head of state and is immune from any liability and responsibility."

Constitution of Ghana (1992), Chapter Ten, The Legislature, Privileges, and Immunities, Article 116 (4): "Where a member refuses to render an apology [for defaming any person], the speaker shall suspend that member for the duration of the session of parliament in which the defamatory statement was made and a member so suspended shall lose his parliamentary privileges, immunities, and remuneration. . . . "

Impeachment

In the law impeachment is a criminal proceeding against a public official before a quasi-political court initiated by a written accusation called articles of impeachment. The English word *impeach* (to challenge or accuse) derives from the Latin *impedio* (hinder or hamper), and later the Middle English words *enpechen* and *empesche* had the same meaning. The correlative of *impeach* in German is *anklagen,* in French *mettre en accusation,* and in Spanish *demandar o acusar formalmente.*

In the United Kingdom impeachment is a prosecution by the House of Commons before the House of Lords of any person, whether a peer or commoner, for treason or other high crimes and misdemeanors. It is also a complaint of a public offense against a minister of the Crown first initiated in the House of Commons and then prosecuted by it in the House of Lords, which tries the matter. William Blackstone, the eighteenth-century commentator on English law, states that because the lower house brings the charge on behalf of its constituents, it is not impartial enough also to try the case.

High public officials can similarly be removed from office for violations of the constitution, gross misconduct, and high crimes. Various impeachment procedures have been established in different countries. Because impeachment is such a drastic measure, when it is brought against a president or another high official of the executive branch, constitutions generally require that the two other major branches—the legislative and judicial—be involved in the process.

Richard M. Nixon, the thirty-seventh president of the United States, resigned in 1974 rather than face an impeachment trial in the Senate over the Watergate affair.

Constitution of Bulgaria (1991), Chapter 4, President of the Republic, Article 103: "(2) Impeachment requires a motion from no less than one-quarter of the national representatives and is supported by the national assembly if more than two-thirds of the national representatives have voted in its favor. (3) The constitutional court considers charges formulated against the president or the vice president within one month of their filing. The president or the vice president loses his power if it is proved that he has committed treason or violated the constitution."

Constitution of Finland, Act on the High Court of Impeachment (1922), Section 1: "The high court of impeachment shall hear charges against a member of the council of state, the chancellor of justice . . . , the parliamentary ombudsman . . . , or the president or a member of the supreme court or of the supreme administrative court, for proceeding in an unlawful manner in an official act."

Incapacity. *See* Disability

Incidental Powers

Constitutions are about power: where it resides, who exercises it, and under what conditions and limits it may be exercised. Incidental powers are ones that depend on primary or principal powers. As broad outlines of the distribution of powers and rules for exercising them, constitutions often specifically provide only for major powers; however, to exercise some major powers, an official or institution must also be able to exercise certain unexpressed minor but necessary powers.

The U.S. Constitution (1789), Article 1, Section 8, refers to Congress's incidental powers as those "necessary and proper for carrying into Execution the foregoing" enumerated powers. In essay 33 of *The Federalist* (1788), Alexander Hamilton argues that this language is unnecessary and does no more than reiterate the axiomatic truth that the power to do a thing includes any and all powers required to accomplish it. The framers of many modern constitutions seem to agree with Hamilton. Consequently, few contain express language granting incidental powers.

Constitution of Argentina (1853), Chapter IV, Powers of Congress, Article 68: "Congress shall have power: . . . 28. To enact all laws and regulations that may be necessary to carry out the foregoing powers, and all others granted by the present constitution to the government of the Argentine nation."

Constitution of Liberia (1986), Chapter V, The Legislature, Article 36: "The legislature shall have the power: . . . (k) to make all other laws which shall be necessary and proper for carrying into execution the foregoing powers, and all other powers vested by this constitution in the government of the republic, or in any department or officer thereof."

Incompatibility

The medieval Latin word *incompatibilis* was used with respect to certain benefices, such as ecclesiastical offices and feudal estates. The English term *incompatibility,* derived from the Latin as well as the French word *incompatibilité* (inconsistency), in common parlance means that certain things, usually just two, do not fit together or that one thing excludes another.

In law incompatibility implies the incapability of existing or being exercised at the same time. A landlord and a tenant may not be the same person at the same time with respect to the same property, for example, and two government functions may be incompatible by their nature or by law. In constitutions incompatibility generally refers to the latter definition: certain offices may not be held at the same time by the same person. Incompatibility may also refer to the ineligibility of certain persons for certain positions in the government because of their status or past activities.

Constitution of Germany (1949), V, The Federal President, Article 55, Incompatibilities: "(1) The federal president may not be a member of the government nor of a legislative body of the federation or the *Land* [constituent state]. (2) The federal president may not hold any other salaried office, nor engage in an occupation, nor belong to the management of the board of directors of an enterprise carried on for profit."

Constitution of Honduras (1982), Title V, Branches of the Government, Chapter I, Legislative Branch, Article 199: "The following may not be elected deputies [to the national congress]: 1. The president of the republic and presidential designates of the republic. . . . 13. Delinquent debtors of the national treasury. These incompatibilities and disabilities shall affect those holding one of the above mentioned positions. . . . "

Indemnification. *See* Compensation

Independence

In Roman private law *libertas* (independence or freedom) was one of three degrees of personal status, along with *civitas* (citizenship) and *familia* (family, domestic servants, and family property). Freed slaves, or freedmen, came to be called *libertini*, although their relationship to their former masters was never completely terminated or consistent.

Independence is inextricably linked to the concept of nation-state sovereignty. A country cannot be fully sovereign unless it is fully independent. Theoretically, nation-state sovereignty is an absolute concept: all nation-states possessing sovereignty are completely independent, except for international obligations and ties accepted by custom or agreed to by treaty.

Newly independent nation-states, at least since the United States proclaimed its independence from Britain in 1776, have marked the occasion of their independence by adopting a new constitution to provide for internal governance and external relationships. A number of constitutions acknowledge the fact of their independence as a prerequisite for the sovereign authority to establish a constitutional government.

Constitution of Malaysia (1963), Part I, The States, Religion, and the Law of the Federation, Article 4, Supreme Law of Federation: "(1) This constitution is the supreme law of the federation and any law passed after Merdeka [Independence] Day which is inconsistent with this constitution shall, to the extent of the inconsistency, be void."

Constitution of Syria (1973), Preamble: "The Arab masses, however, did not consider political independence a final objective and the end to all struggle and sacrifices. They regard it rather as a means of enhancing their struggle and an advanced stage in the battle against colonialism, Zionism, and exploitation. . . . "

Ineligibility. *See* Incompatibility; Qualification

Inferior Court

Commenting on rural courts, Plato states in *The Laws* that apart from officials such as kings, whose decisions are final, no judge may hold court and no official may be a judge without being liable to be called to account for his actions, thereby establishing a hierarchy of judicial decision making. William Blackstone, the eighteenth-century commentator on the laws of England, ranked the English courts from the highest—the High Court of Parliament—to the lowest—the Court of Clerk of the Market.

In law the term *inferior court* denotes any court subordinate to the chief appellate tribunal in a judicial system. It is also used to designate a court with special, limited, or statutory jurisdiction that must prove its jurisdiction for its judgments to be valid.

Article 1, Section 8, of the U.S. Constitution (1789) grants Congress the power "to constitute Tribunals inferior to the supreme Court." Alexander Hamilton, in essay 81 of *The Federalist* (1788), comments that this language eliminates the necessity of bringing every case under national jurisdiction to the Supreme Court by authorizing in each state and district of the country additional courts with national jurisdiction. In addition to providing for a supreme court, many constitutions establish an entire judicial system with subordinate or inferior courts.

Constitution of Japan (1889, significantly revised in 1947), Chapter VI, Judiciary, Article 76: "The whole judicial power is vested in a supreme court and in such inferior courts as are established by law."

Because of the hierarchical structure inherent in most judicial branches of government, many countries such as France have a complex network of inferior (subordinate) courts that administer justice on a daily basis.

Constitution of Kenya (1963), Chapter IV, The Judicature, Part 2, Other Courts, Article 65(1): "Parliament may establish courts subordinate to the high court and courts-martial, and a court so established shall, subject to this constitution, have such jurisdiction and powers as may be conferred on it by any law."

Infringement

For William Blackstone, the eighteenth-century commentator on English law, counterfeiting of coins or the royal signature constituted a treason and "a break of allegiance, by infringing the royal prerogative." As now used in constitutions, the term *infringement* generally refers to the rights of an individual—whose entitlements have been elevated to the same status as the monarch's prerogative in Blackstone's time.

In law an infringement is a breaking into, a trespass, or an encroachment. It is derived from the Latin word *infringo* (to break off, crush, or weaken) and is translated in French as *transgresser*, in German as *verletzen*, and in Spanish as *infringir* or *violar*.

Constitution of Canada, Constitution Act (1982), Part I, Canadian Charter of Rights and Freedoms, Section 24(1): "Anyone whose rights or freedoms, as guaranteed by this charter, have been infringed or denied may apply to a court of competent jurisdiction to obtain such remedy as the court considers appropriate and just in the circumstances."

Constitution of Sweden, Freedom of the Press Act (1992), Chapter 1, On the Freedom of the Press, Article 9: "Notwithstanding the provisions of the present act, rules laid down in law shall govern . . . 2. bans on the publication, within the framework of the professional provision of credit information, of any credit rating which improperly infringes the personal integrity of a private subject, or which contains incorrect or misleading statements; liability to pay compensation for such publication; and correction of incorrect or misleading statements. . . ."

Inhabitant

In England the use of the word *inhabitant*—from the Latin *habitatio* (residence)—to mean a permanent resident has been standard since the sixteenth century. The French words *résident* and *habitant* are synonymous, but in German and Spanish the two terms have different meanings.

Some constitutions make a distinction between an inhabitant, who may be an alien and not necessarily a citizen, and a resident or citizen. Citizenship implies formal recognition that a person belongs to a nation-state and has all the rights and duties that stem from that relationship. An inhabitant, however, may be someone who simply resides, either temporarily or permanently, in the jurisdiction of a nation-state. Alternatively, the term may imply a more fixed, permanent abode than that of a resident. A constitution may require certain periods of residency for a citizen to be eligible to run for certain offices.

The term *domicile* is used in some constitutions with reference to the inviolability of the home, but it has a special meaning in law as a permanent or principal place of residence to which a person intends to return, even though he or she may have been absent for some time.

Constitution of Panama (1972), Title III, Individual and Social Rights and Duties, Chapter 4, National Culture, Article 76: "The state recognizes the right of every individual to participate in the culture of the nation, and shall foster the participation of all inhabitants of the republic in national culture."

Constitution of the United States of America (1789), Article I, Section 3: "No Person shall be a Senator who shall not have attained to the Age of thirty Years, and been nine Years a Citizen of the United States, and who shall not, when elected, be an Inhabitant of the State for which he shall be chosen."

Inherent Powers. *See* Prerogative

Initiative

An initiative is a procedure for implementing direct democracy, a concept derived from the form of democracy used in ancient Athens, in which citizens assembled periodically and functioned as a legislative body. The Athenian leaders found that it was not always easy to get citizens to participate, however, and they resorted to paying for attendance. The size of the population and territory of most modern nation-state democracies precludes the Athenian style of direct democracy. Consequently, practices such as the initiative, referendum, plebiscite, and recall have been instituted under various constitutions to allow for some workable aspects of direct democracy in addition to the more standard procedures of modern representative democracy.

Voters, in addition to elected representatives or other constitutionally authorized officials, may use an initiative to propose legislation or amendments to the constitution and to approve them. Usually the process begins with a petition signed by a required number of eligible voters, which asks that a proposed law be considered. The petition is then presented to the elected legislature. In the case of an indirect initiative, the legislature has an opportunity to act on the measure; but if the legislature does not approve the proposal, it is then submitted to the voters to decide. In the case of a direct initiative, the proposal is submitted directly to the voters once the required signatures are obtained.

Constitution of Switzerland (1874), Chapter III, Revision of the Federal Constitution, Article 121: "Partial revision [of the constitution] may be carried out either by means of a popular initiative or in accordance with the forms laid down for federal legislation."

Constitution of the Philippines (1987), Article VI, Legislative Department, Section 1: "The legislative power shall be vested in the congress of the Philippines, which shall consist of a senate and a house of representatives, except to the extent reserved to the people by the provision on initiative and referendum."

Insurrection. *See* Rebellion

International Law

Customary rules, such as the unwritten laws of warfare, and the terms of treaties that nations accept as legally binding on themselves, such as the 1945 charter establishing the United Nations, make up the main body of international law. Such agreements among the international community of sovereign nation-states are not enacted by a supernational legislature or enforced by a supernational police force, but as long as sovereign countries agree to be bound by them and conduct their relations accordingly, they can be just as effective as any other type of law.

Whether public international law—*droit des gens* in French and *Volkerrecht* in German—is law at all is problematic because the subjects of the law are equal, independent, and sovereign nation-states that, by

The International Court of Justice at The Hague, in the Netherlands, applies international law to the settlement of disputes.

definition, are above any other law but their own. Once the technicalities are dispensed with, however, international law, like so many other social conventions that cannot be legally enforced, provides an expedient and efficient means of resolving multinational and international problems. Pragmatism, rather than legal philosophy, divine revelation, or raw power, is the gravamen of international law.

A number of constitutions now include some references to international law, particularly with respect to its applicability to domestic institutions of government and its implications for standards of human rights. This trend may signal a general relaxation in the formerly strict reliance of most nation-states on the principle of absolute sovereignty in international relations.

Private international law is simply another name for conflict of laws—the effort to decide which laws apply in situations where more than one legal jurisdiction is involved.

Constitution of Romania (1991), Title I, General Principles, Article 3(2): "The frontiers of the country are sanctioned by an organic law, under observance of the principles and other generally recognized regulations of international law."

Constitution of Portugal (1976), Fundamental Principles, Article 8, International Law, 1: "The rules and principles of general or ordinary international law shall be an integral part of Portuguese law."

The Congress of Vienna (1814–15) tried to restructure post-Napoleonic Europe to ensure peaceful international relations.

International Relations

International relations are the interaction and interdependence of all nation-states under international law, including interaction with regional and world associations of nation-states. Foreign affairs or foreign relations activities tend to be more narrowly involved with country-to-country interaction. To join the United Nations, a country must enter into a treaty similar to an agreement with one or more other countries; thus, although the processes are similar to those relating to foreign affairs, the scope of international relations often is broader.

International relations are traditionally entrusted to the executive branch of government, but the legislative branch often must confirm treaties and representatives appointed to international bodies.

Some constitutions now include specific language concerning the duties and powers of officials and institutions with regard to international relations and aspects of international law resulting from such relations.

Constitution of Germany (1949), V, Federal President, Article 59, Authority to Represent the Federation in Its International Relations: "The federal president shall represent the federation in its international relations. He shall conclude treaties with foreign states on behalf of the federation. He shall accredit and receive envoys."

Constitution of Colombia (1991), Title VII, Concerning the Executive Branch, Chapter 8, Concerning International Relations, Article 224: "In order to be valid, treaties must be approved by the congress. However, the president of the republic may give temporary effect to provisional treaties of an economic or commercial nature negotiated through international organizations. In such a case, as soon as a treaty enters into force provisionally, it must be sent to the congress for approval. If the congress does not approve the treaty, its application will be suspended."

Interpellation

In most parliaments legislators may direct questions to members of the government, the prime minister, and the cabinet ministers—about how they have conducted themselves, for example. This formal process called interpellation is a formidable practice that requires the ministers of government to justify their actions to the legislative body that is responsible for approving their appointments and continuation in office. After the questioning period a general debate may ensue, following which a vote may be taken on a motion to censure or approve a minister on the basis of his or her reply.

In a presidential system of government, with its stricter separation of powers, cabinet members are primarily responsible to the elected head of the executive branch, the president. But a parliamentary system is based on making government ministers accountable directly to the majority in the legislature and, therefore, indirectly to the voters who elected them. Interpellation is a way of calling executive branch officers to account to their supervisor for their actions. Along with regular elections, it is the heart of the process of accountability in a parliamentary system of government.

The 1814 constitution of the Netherlands provides for both a questioning of ministers and state secretaries by one or more members of either chamber of the legislature and a right of inquiry *(enquête)*, which allows the legislature to conduct inquiries into alleged abuses or to obtain information. Interpellation in France has come to mean the action of interrupting the legislature's order of business by asking a government minister for an explanation about his or her area of responsibility.

In Anglo-American civil law an interpellation refers to a condition by one party to an agreement that he or she will not be bound by the agreement beyond a certain period of time. In early England the term referred to a citation or summons, although this meaning is now obsolete.

Constitution of Sweden, Instrument of Government (1974), Chapter 12, Article 5: "Under provisions laid down in the Riksdag Act, any member of the Riksdag may submit an interpellation or put down a question for a minister in any matter concerning the minister's performance of his duties."

Constitution of Slovakia (1993), Chapter Five, Legislative Power, Section One, The National Council of the Slovak Republic, Article 80: "(1) A deputy [legislator] may interpellate the government of the Slovak Republic, a member of the government of the Slovak Republic, or the head of any central body of state administration in matters of their jurisdiction. The deputy must receive a response to an interpellation within thirty days. (2) The national council of the Slovak Republic shall debate the response to an interpellation and may link it with a vote of confidence."

Constitution of France (1958), Title V, On Relations Between Parliament and the Government, Article 49: "The national assembly [lower house of the parliament] may question the responsibility of the government by the vote of a motion of censure. Such a motion shall be admissible only if it is signed by at least one-tenth of the members of the national assembly. The vote may only take place forty-eight hours after the motion has been filed; the only votes counted shall be those favorable to the motion of censure, which may be adopted only by a majority of the members comprising the assembly."

Interstate

Because states or provinces in federal nation-states are at best semisovereign, the relationship among them and between a state and the federal government is often expressly described in their national constitutions. Relations among these constituent states as well as among nation-states themselves are referred to as interstate relations.

Interstate commerce is trade among the constituent states of a federal nation-state. The U.S. Constitution (1789), for example, gives to Congress the power to regulate commerce with foreign nations and among the several states. This power over interstate commerce has been progressively broadened by interpretation by Congress and the Supreme Court, thereby expanding the power of the national government over the states.

Constitution of Russia (1993), Part I, Chapter 3, Organization of the Federation, Article 79: "The Russian Federation may participate in interstate associations and delegate to them part of its functions in accordance with international treaties unless this entails a restriction of human and civil rights and freedoms or is contrary to the fundamentals of the constitutional system of the Russian Federation."

Constitution of Switzerland (1874), Chapter I, General Provisions, Article 62: "All transfer taxes on the moving of property inside Switzerland and all preemption rights of citizens of one canton [constituent state] against citizens of other cantons are abolished."

Interstate Commerce. *See* Interstate

Invasion

In the section of *The Laws* dealing with the protection of the territory of his proposed colony of Magnesia, Plato requires that, as far as practical, nothing be left unguarded against an invasion. The word *invasion*—an external threat to the security of a nation-state—derives from the Latin *invado* (to enter or attack), and the same word with the same meaning is found in English, French, and Spanish.

In law an invasion may be an encroachment on the rights of another, such as an invasion of privacy, or more generally an incursion by a foreign army into the territory of another nation-state for the purpose of conquest or plunder. Constitutional provisions regarding invasions generally refer to armed aggression by one or more nation-states in which the aggressor enters the territory of another nation-state without permission, intending to capture a portion of the territory or otherwise harm the invaded state.

Constitutions sometimes express in detail the measures that must or may be taken by the executive and legislative branches of government in the event of an invasion. The U.S. Constitution (1789), for example, provides for Congress to call out the militia to suppress insurrections and repel invasions, for the government to suspend the writ of habeas corpus in the case of invasion, for the states to take action if invaded, and for the federal government to protect the states against invasion.

Constitution of Mexico (1917), Title I, Chapter I, Individual Guarantees, Article 29: "In the event of invasion, serious disturbance of the public peace, or any other event which may place society in great danger or conflict, only the president of the United States of Mexico, in agreement with the office holders of the secretary of state, the administrative departments, and the attorney general of

In the fourth and fifth centuries the Huns, a fierce and barbaric Asiatic tribe led by Attila, invaded Europe, wreaking death and devastation in their path.

the republic, and with the approval of the congress of the union, or during the adjournment of the latter, the permanent committee, may suspend throughout the country or in a determined place the guarantees which may present an obstacle to a rapid and smooth confronting of the situation. . . ."

Constitution of Turkey (1982), II, Functions and Powers of the Turkish Grand National Assembly, F, Declaration of State of War and Authorization to Permit the Use of Armed Forces, Article 92: "If the country is subjected, while the Turkish grand national assembly is adjourned or in recess, to sudden armed aggression and it thus becomes imperative to decide immediately on the use of armed forces, the president of the republic can decide on the use of the Turkish armed forces."

Inviolability

"Our constitution . . . unites the most perfect security of the subject's liberty with the most absolute inviolability of the sacred person of the sovereign," declared England's Bishop Horsley in a late-eighteenth-century sermon.

The concept of sovereignty as it developed in Europe up to 1650 was based on the majesty and supremacy of the sovereigns, or monarchs, who ruled burgeoning nation-states. Because the power of the sovereign was fused with the power of the state, the sovereign was held to be above the law and therefore inviolable—not subject to any accountability for his or her acts and protected by the full might of the country from personal harm. Any injury to the sovereign was equated with treason. According to William Blackstone, the eighteenth-century commentator on the laws of England, it was also treason to violate the monarch's companion, eldest unmarried daughter, or the wife of the sovereign's eldest son and heir.

Especially in constitutions of limited monarchies and presidential-style systems of governments, in which the president serves essentially in the role of a limited monarch, inviolability—derived from the Latin *inviolatus* (unharmed)—still refers to protection of the head of state from accountability for his or her acts and even his or her person. Certain fundamental rights of individuals may also be deemed inviolable.

Constitution of Thailand (1991), Chapter II, The King, Section 6: "The king shall be enthroned in a position of revered worship and shall not be violated."

Constitution of Peru (1993), Section I, Concerning the Individual and Society, Chapter I, Fundamental Rights of the Individual, Article 2: "Every individual has the right: . . . 9. to the inviolability of his home. . . . 10. to the inviolability and secrecy of private documents and communications."

Involuntary Servitude. *See* Forced Labor

Islamic Law

Like the early Chinese emperors who ruled under a "mandate of heaven," the leaders of Islamic nation-states believe that the Qur'an, the holy book of the religion of Islam—rather than a secular constitution—is the only truly supreme law. Together with the Sunnah (the teachings of the prophet Muhammad, the founder of Islam), the Qur'an provides the framework for *shari'a* (Islamic law), whose principles became solidified as law to a great extent in the tenth century and remain little changed.

Adherents of Islam (meaning submission to God) accept the Qur'an as the word of God as revealed to Muhammad in the Arabic language. Saudi Arabia and Libya, for example, claim the Qur'an as their true constitution, and the Iranian constitution expressly states that the Qur'an has supremacy over its provisions. In these and other Islamic countries, the Qur'an's constitutional influence can be seen in various aspects, from the requirement that key members of the government be Muslims (those who submit) to references that the holy book be considered a source of law for deciding cases before the courts.

Three general categories of Islamic influence on constitutions are exemplified by Turkey, Egypt, and Iran. Turkey is a secular country that is nevertheless greatly influenced by the Islamic religion. Egypt's constitution is less neutral than Turkey's toward the tenets of Islam and Islamic law. Iran is an outright theocracy in which the supreme law of its constitution is subordinate to the will of the Islamic religious leaders. In Saudi Arabia, a

Islamic judges such as this one from southern India apply the law based on the Qur'an and teachings of the prophet Muhammad, who died in the seventh century.

preconstitutional monarchy, the Islamic religion and the state are fused in the emir (king).

References to Islamic law are generally found in constitutional sections dealing with the judicial system, including provisions relating to the *shari'a,* or *qadi* (sometimes spelled *khadi),* courts, and in parts dealing with the basis of legislation.

Constitution of Egypt (1971), Part One, The State, Article 2: "Islam is the religion of the state and Arabic its official language. Islamic jurisprudence is the principal source of legislation."

Constitution of Iran (1979), Preamble, Mass-Communications Media: "They [Muslims] may then hope for success in building an ideal Islamic society that can be a model for all people of the world and a witness to its perfection (in accordance with the Qur'anic verse . . . 'Thus We made you a median community, that you might witness to men' [2:143])."

Constitution of Libya, Declaration on the Establishment of the Authority of the People (1979), Article II: "The holy [Qur'an] is the constitution of the Socialist People's Libyan Arab Jamahiriya ["state of the masses"]."

Constitution of Pakistan (1973), Part VII, The Judicature, Chapter 3A, Federal Shariat Court, Article 203D (amended in 1982): "(1) The court may, either on its own motion or on the petition of a citizen of Pakistan or the federal government or a provincial government, examine and decide the question of whether or not any law or provision of law is repugnant to the injunctions of Islam, as laid down in the holy Qur'an and the Sunnah of the holy prophet, hereinafter referred to as the injunctions of Islam. . . . "

Ito Hirobumi

Ito Hirobumi (1841–1909) had a singular impact on the constitutional development of his native Japan and that of other Asian countries by introducing to Japan the first Western-style constitution in Asia.

Ito was born in what is today Yamaguchi Prefecture in 1841 during the Tokugawa shogunate. The young Ito became an active member of the Sonnō Jōi movement for uniting Japan under imperial rule and repelling foreign intervention. In 1863 he was awarded samurai status and sent to England to study. While abroad, Ito became receptive to Western influences.

On January 3, 1868, troops surrounded the imperial palace in Kyoto as the sixteen-year-old emperor, Mutsuhito, proclaimed the end of the Tokugawa shogunate as an imperial surrogate. With the restoration of the Meiji dynasty, Ito became a *san'yō* (junior councillor) responsible for foreign affairs. In 1870 he traveled to the United States to study the currency system. Rapidly rising through the ranks, he again traveled to the United States and Europe. A political crisis in 1881 gave him unchallenged leadership of the government.

After a year and a half studying under leading constitutional scholars in Europe, especially in Prussia, in 1883 Ito and others began work on a Western-style constitution for the empire of Japan. He also worked on an imperial household law, based on the British Peerage Act (1884), to increase the prestige of the emperor's household. In 1885, while serving as chairman of the constitutional commission, Ito became the first prime minister under a cabinet-style government.

While in Europe, Ito had studied the constitutions of Prussia and France's Third Republic and heard lectures on representative government by the English philosopher Herbert Spencer in London. Having paid particular attention to the Prussian constitution and rejecting the supremacy of the legislature exemplified by the British model, Ito concentrated power in the hands of the executive branch acting in the name of the emperor. A legislature, the imperial Diet, was created with an upper house of peers and a lower house of representatives. Although consent of the legislature was required for laws, the power of the emperor sanctioned them.

The new constitution, the first Western-style constitution in Asia, was promulgated on February 11, 1889. It represented, at the least, an attempt to bring to Japan the form of a modern Western-style government, and it had an impact on other countries in Asia, particularly China.

Ito Hirobumi was assassinated on a tour of Manchuria in 1909. His comment on the government he helped create indicates his guiding principle: "[The imperial ancestors] have shown that the purpose of a monarchical government is to reign over the country and govern the people, and not to minister to the private wants of individuals or of families. Such is the fundamental basis of the present constitution." In 1947, after World War II, the 1889 Japanese constitution was significantly revised to transfer sovereignty from the emperor to the people and to make the elected parliament the supreme legislative authority.

Ito Hirobumi, who drafted the 1889 Western-style constitution of Japan, studied the constitutions of Prussia, Great Britain, and France's Third Republic.

J

Jefferson, Thomas

Thomas Jefferson (1743–1826) had a significant although indirect influence on the U.S. Constitution, but as the author of the Declaration of Independence he may have done more to chart the course of the fledgling nation than any other person.

An uncommonly multitalented person, Jefferson was born on April 13, 1743, in Shadwell, Albemarle County, in colonial Virginia. Peter Jefferson, a self-educated surveyor and mapmaker, insisted on a classical education for his son, which earned Thomas's express gratitude. Jefferson studied at local grammar and classical schools and attended the College of William and Mary in Williamsburg, where George Wythe, a Virginia lawyer, guided his legal education into the broader fields of history, culture, and morality. Admitted to the Virginia bar in 1767, Jefferson two years later became a member of the lower house of the Virginia legislature, the House of Burgesses.

In addition to his career in politics, Jefferson found time to become a proficient musician, scientist, agriculturalist, architect, and philosopher. With Benjamin Franklin, Jefferson led the Enlightenment movement in the United States. His personal philosophy was rooted in the empiricism of Francis Bacon, the harmonious laws of the physical universe of Sir Isaac Newton, and the concept of the consent of the governed espoused by John Locke. President John F. Kennedy is said to have told a gathering of Nobel laureates in the White House that never before had there been such an array of diverse genius in one place—except when Thomas Jefferson had dined there alone.

In the spring of 1775 Jefferson was appointed by the Virginia legislature to be a delegate to the Second Continental Congress meeting in Philadelphia. One of the Congress's more radical members, he was assigned to the committee to draft formal reasons for severing ties with Great Britain, serving with Franklin and John Adams, among others. Jefferson's superior talents ensured his role as the principal author of the Declaration of Independence, signed on July 4, 1776. He subsequently returned to Virginia to help reform its laws, drafting the Statute of Virginia for Religious Freedom, which was enacted after much controversy in 1786. Jefferson served as governor of Virginia from 1779 to 1781 and returned to Congress, where he helped draft the Northwest Ordinance; this legislation guaranteed political liberties and eventual statehood for those who left the states to settle the Northwest Territory.

In 1785 Jefferson succeeded Franklin as minister to France, where he spoke of limiting the monarchy. He became secretary of state in the first cabinet under the 1789 U.S. Constitution, vice president in 1797, and president in 1801, ending the domination of the Federalist Party and becoming the founding father of the present-day Democratic Party. As secretary of state he organized that

The concept of justice is often represented by a woman wearing a blindfold to symbolize impartiality, holding a scale to weigh the guilt or innocence of the accused, and wielding a sword to mete out punishment to the guilty.

department on an annual budget of less than $10,000. In his spare time as vice president and presiding officer of the Senate, he compiled *A Manual of Parliamentary Practice for the Use of the Senate of the United States,* which is still used today. As president, he worked to restrict the scope of the new nation's federal government, approved the purchase of the vast territory of Louisiana in 1807, and signed into law a ban on the importation of slaves in 1808.

Isolated in France for five years until 1790, Jefferson was neither a drafter nor a signer of the U.S. Constitution, but his debates with Alexander Hamilton and his friendship with James Madison, the father of that document, framed and sculpted its substance. Jefferson most profoundly influenced the country's development as author of the Declaration of Independence, which, along with the Constitution and the Bill of Rights—the first ten amendments guaranteeing rights to the people and the states—is a cornerstone of American democracy.

The revolutionary words and concepts of the Declaration of Independence not only served as a philosophical superstructure for the supreme law of the United States that became effective in 1789; they also have informed other documents of constitutional stature in countries around the world. For example, the concept of the equality of all individuals engendered in Jefferson's language that "all men are created equal" is reflected in Article 1 of the French Declaration of the Rights of Man and of the Citizen (1789), which states, "All men are born and remain free, and have equal rights." Jefferson expressed the notion of natural rights in the phrase "they are endowed by their Creator with certain inalienable rights; that among these is life, liberty, and the pursuit of happiness." Article 10 of the 1948 South Korean constitution states, "All citizens shall be assured of human worth and dignity and have the right to pursue happiness." Article 10 of the 1995 Ethiopian constitution includes the statement, "Human rights and freedoms are inviolable and inalienable." The U.S. Declaration of Independence's theoretical transfer of sovereignty from a monarch and parliament to the people is confirmed by the language that "to secure these rights, governments are instituted among men, deriving their just powers from the consent of the governed." Article 39 of the 1917 Mexican constitution reflects this theme by stating, "The national sovereignty resides essentially and originally in the people. All public power arises from the people and is instituted for their benefit."

Although he was in France during the U.S. Constitutional Convention in 1787, Thomas Jefferson's ideas helped shape the document that was adopted in 1789.

Jefferson's social as well as political philosophy influenced the framers of the American Constitution. He urged self-reliance, diligence, and common sense as qualities necessary in those who govern; promoted the right of every person to acquire property, thus increasing independence and responsibility; made education a primary requirement for popular sovereignty; and argued for institutions to ensure an "aristocracy of virtue and talent."

Whereas Hamilton saw the need for a strong, central, elitist government, Jefferson believed that with checks and balances, freedom of religion and the press, and the other guarantees of the Bill of Rights (1791), "the government that governs least, governs best." Their differences led to the two-party system, which organizes elections and the executive and legislative branches of government after elections, an unwritten element in the broader concept of the Constitution of the United States.

While Jefferson was in France, letters from Madison kept him informed of the constitutional drafting process. Jefferson was particularly unhappy with the lack of a bill of rights in the basic document and the fact that the president could succeed himself indefinitely. (Today the U.S. president is limited by the Twenty-second Amendment, ratified in 1951, to two four-year terms.) Many of Jefferson's other concerns were incorporated in the document, however. As Madison stated in *The Federalist* (1788), a collection of contemporaneous writings explaining and supporting the proposed Constitution, Jefferson showed in the Virginia constitution that he supported the concepts of the separation of powers and of checks and balances. In Jefferson's words, "An *elective despotism* [Jefferson's emphasis] was not the government we fought for; but one which should not only be founded on free principles, but in which the powers of government should be so divided and balanced among several bodies of magistracy as that no one could transcend their legal limits without being effectually checked and restrained by the others."

Retiring in 1809 to Monticello, his personal architectural masterpiece in Charlottesville, Virginia, Jefferson devoted the rest of his life to studying, farming, and founding the University of Virginia. He died at Monticello on July 4, 1826, the fiftieth anniversary of the Declaration of Independence.

Jefferson left an impressive legacy of constitutionalism not only to his fellow Americans but also to the citizens of the world. His works with major constitutional relevance include "A Summary View of the Rights of British America" (1774); the Declaration of Independence (1776); *Notes on the State of Virginia* (1782), his only book; and the Statute of Virginia for Religious Freedom (1786).

Joint Committee

A joint committee, sometimes called a joint commission, is a group of members from both the upper and lower houses of a legislature, generally equal or nearly equal in number. A joint legislative committee's responsibility may be ad hoc—for example, to conduct investigative hearings or resolve legislative issues about which the two bodies disagree—or permanent. Express directions for when and how joint committees are formed and what their functions will be may be included in a constitution.

The U.S. Constitution (1789) does not provide for legislative committees; these are organized by the two political parties, with the majority party naming a chairperson who has the power to determine the committee's agenda. Congressional committees and subcommittees and their chairs have been known to wield tremendous political power on occasion. Conference committees, which are a type of joint legislative committee created to reach a compromise on legislation passed in a different form by each house, however, are organized with "managers" from each house selected by the party leaders (the Speaker in the House of Representatives and the majority leader in the Senate). These managers must vote separately to approve any compromise.

Constitution of South Africa (1994), Chapter 4, Parliament, Money Bills, Section 60(4): "The national assembly shall not pass a bill referred to in subsection (1) unless it has been considered and reported on by a joint committee of both houses. . . . "

Constitution of the Philippines (1987), Article VI, Legislative Department, Section 18: "There shall be a commission on appointments consisting of the president of the senate, as ex officio chairman, twelve senators, and twelve members of the house of representatives, elected by each house on the basis of proportional representation from the political parties or organizations registered under the party-list system represented therein."

Joint Session

A joint session, sometimes called a plenary session, is a sitting of the two houses of a bicameral or semibicameral legislature. The U.S. Congress sits in joint session on noncontroversial occasions, such as when the president of the United States delivers the annual State of the Union message or when foreign dignitaries address Congress.

In other countries, however, the constitution may require a joint session of the legislative houses to resolve specific problems that the framers believed could not be adequately handled by the two chambers separately. The 1901 Australian constitution, for example, contains a unique provision for a joint sitting of the two houses of its parliament that is seldom invoked. When the requirement was used in 1974, it precipitated a constitutional crisis that was solved by an unusual and much-debated assertion of power by the governor-general, whose role traditionally is limited to acting ceremonially on behalf of the monarch.

Constitution of Australia (1901), Chapter I, The Parliament, Part V, Powers of Parliament, Section 57: "If the house of representatives passes a proposed law, and the senate rejects or fails to pass it, or passes it with amendments to which the house . . . will not agree, and if after an interval of three months the house . . . in the same or next session, again passes the proposed law with or without any amendments which have been made, suggested, or agreed to by the senate, and the senate rejects or fails to pass it, or passes it with amendments to which the house . . . will not agree, the governor-general may dissolve [both houses] simultaneously. . . . If after such dissolution [and subsequent elections] the house . . . again passes the proposed law . . . and the senate [rejects it as before], the governor-general may convene a joint sitting of the members of the senate and the house of representatives."

Constitution of Norway (1814), Article 76: "When a bill from the Odelsting [lower house of the semibicameral legislature] has twice been presented to the Lagting [upper house] and has been returned a second time as rejected, the Storting [both houses together] shall meet in plenary session, and the bill is then decided by a majority of two-thirds of its votes."

Journal

The journals of the British Parliament are the records of business conducted but not of speeches made; they date from 1509 and 1547, respectively, in the upper and lower houses. The journals of the upper house, the House of Lords, are considered public records, but those of the lower house, the House of Commons, are not. Copies of the journals—from the word *diurnal,* derived from *diurnus* (daily) in Latin—are admissible in court as evidence of parliamentary actions. In Canada journals are the official and permanent record of the proceedings of the lower house of parliament, also called the House of Commons.

The U.S. Constitution (1789) requires that each house of Congress keep journals of its proceedings and publish them from time to time, except for parts that they determine are to be kept secret. Individual votes for and against any issue must be entered in the daily journal if at least one-fifth of the members of each house present so demand. The president's objections to any bill passed by both houses and returned unsigned are also to be entered in the journals.

Generally, publication of a law in a journal—unlike in a gazette, or official legal publication—is not an official act promulgating a law. The 1987 Haitian constitution, however, requires publication of laws in its official gazette, which is called the *Journal Officiel.* This same French term is used in the 1958 French constitution to refer to a journal that includes a daily record of parliamentary debates.

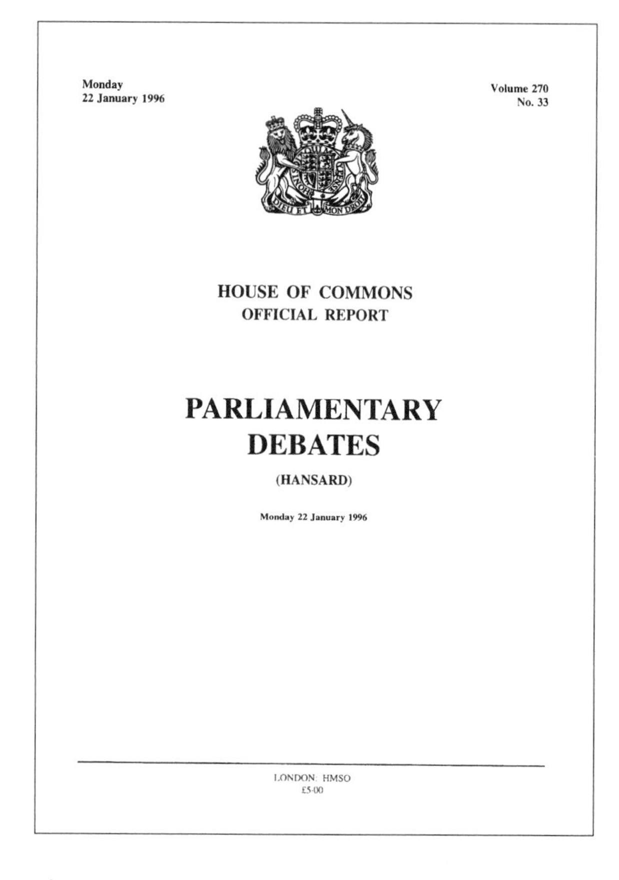
Monday
22 January 1996

Volume 270
No. 33

HOUSE OF COMMONS
OFFICIAL REPORT

PARLIAMENTARY
DEBATES

(HANSARD)

Monday 22 January 1996

LONDON: HMSO
£5·00

The *Hansard* is the official report or journal of the activities of the lower house of the British Parliament, the House of Commons, but not of the members' speeches.

Constitution of France (1958), Title IV, The Parliament, Article 33: "The meetings of the two assemblies [the national assembly and the senate] shall be public. An *in extenso* report of the debates shall be published in the *Journal Officiel.*"

Constitution of Sweden, Riksdag Act (1974), Chapter 2, Meeting of the Chamber, Article 16: "A complete record shall be kept of proceedings in the chamber. No one shall be entitled to speak without his remarks being entered in the record. A decision may not be changed when the record is approved."

Juan Carlos I de Borbón y Borbón

Born a Spanish prince, Juan Carlos de Borbón y Borbón (b. 1938) has steadfastly adhered to the goal of a democratic Spain, making that concept a reality.

When a 1929 attempt to return to a constitutional monarchy was rejected and the Spanish republic was proclaimed in 1931, Juan Carlos's family moved in exile to Rome, where he was born on January 5, 1938. He did not visit his native Spain until ten years later. After being graduated from the San Isidro School in Madrid, studying at military colleges and academies, and qualifying as a military pilot, he finished his studies at Madrid's Complutense University, specializing in constitutional and international law, economics, and taxation.

The republican constitution of 1931 had been repealed in 1939 by the military leader and de facto chief of state General Francisco Franco y Bahamonde, who replaced the constitution with fundamental laws of his own. Franco's fascist regime survived World War II, but internal problems resulted in some changes. On July 22, 1969, the Spanish parliament, at Franco's invitation, designated Juan Carlos as king and successor to Franco as chief of state.

On November 20, 1975, Franco was declared dead, and two days later Juan Carlos I was invested as the king of Spain. The new monarch began a carefully orchestrated reign with a view toward stabilizing the political system, reducing tensions, and leading the nation toward a more democratic form of government. By some accounts he played a leading role in selecting Aldolfo Suárez Gonzáles to head the government in mid-1976, a crucial period in the transition to a constitutional democracy. In June 1977 the first democratic elections since 1936 were held, and on December 6, 1978, a draft of the current constitution of Spain was approved by referendum.

Juan Carlos I's dedication to the principles of constitutionalism and democracy smoothed the way for Spain's adoption of a constitutional monarchy in 1978.

Although Juan Carlos I did not direct the drafting of the document, on the opening day of the newly elected parliament—July 22, 1977—he personally expressed his recognition of the sovereignty of the people, thus retaining only a symbolic role as the head of state and the traditional embodiment of national sovereignty. He also acknowledged that the monarch should have no political role in the government.

Since World War II a number of former European monarchies have chosen republics as their form of government—Italy in 1948, Greece in 1975, and Portugal in 1976. Spain, where republican governments have failed to provide the necessary stability to ward off dictatorship, is an exception. The fact that Juan Carlos I saw his role in Spain's government as analogous to other monarchs in successful European constitutional monarchies has placed Spain on a course similar to that taken by such historically stable and prosperous countries as the United Kingdom, the Netherlands, Sweden, and Denmark.

Judge

To establish a court is to elect officials, suggests Plato in *The Laws,* adding that a judge, "although strictly he is no official," becomes important on the day he gives his verdict. Aristotle, in *The Politics,* observes that because the soul is more important than the body, warriors, administrators of justice (judges), and deliberators are more essential to the state than those who provide the necessities of life. In Roman law a *judex,* from which the word *judge* is derived, was a layman chosen from a panel of senators and other officials who tried civil cases after a proceeding before the praetor, who helped frame the issues for trial.

Judges played an important role in the development of the common law in England. Working without a written code of references, English judges developed a body of jurisprudence that was applied by looking to previously decided cases to determine what rules of law applied to a new case. This concept of precedent, together with the principle of *stare decisis* (to let a former ruling or decision in a similar case stand unless the facts of the new case warrant a different outcome) is the essence of pragmatic, stable English common law, which has influenced the judicial systems of many countries.

To judge in a court of law is to apply the law to disputes between parties. In some cases a jury of lay people is required to judge the factual issues, but in others a judge may have to make determinations of both legal and factual issues. In the American and similar judicial systems, judges in matters of first instance

To symbolize their judicial authority, judges in the courts of law in Great Britain wear wigs traditionally made of horsehair.

preside over trials in which facts are presented by the parties. Appellate judges hear cases on appeal and rule only on legal arguments related to the disposition of the matter by a lower court.

With varying degrees of detail, almost all constitutions provide for the selection, independence, and tenure of judges, especially those who sit on the highest courts of the nation-state.

Constitution of Zimbabwe (1979), Chapter VIII, The Judicature, Article 83: "A judge of the supreme court or the high court, including an acting judge, shall, before entering upon his office, take and subscribe before the president or some person authorized by the president in that behalf the oath of loyalty and the judicial oath in the forms set out in schedule 1. . . . "

Constitution of Singapore (1959), Part VII, The Judiciary, Article 98: "(1) Subject to this article, a judge of the supreme court shall hold office until he attains the age of sixty-five years or such later time not being later than six months after he attains that age, as the president may approve. (2) A judge of the supreme court may at any time resign his office by writing under his hand addressed to the president, but shall not be removed from office except in accordance with the following provisions of this article."

Judicature. *See* Judiciary

Judicial Branch

One of the three major divisions of government identified by Montesquieu in *The Spirit of the Laws* (1748), the judicial branch of government generally consists of the courts—the judiciary—and other legal and administrative personnel related to judicial functions.

The judicial branch—derived from the Latin word *judicialis,* a combination of *judex* (judge) and *judicium* (trial, verdict, or court)—is essentially charged with interpreting and applying the law to cases and controversies. In some constitutions, however, it is given additional responsibilities, such as reviewing elections, participating in impeachment proceedings, giving opinions on legal matters, including constitutional issues, interpreting the constitution in the course of adjudicating cases, and declaring laws and actions by government officials unconstitutional and thus null and void. Some constitutions include the prosecutorial functions in the judicial rather than the executive branch. The highest judge—for example, the chief justice in many countries—often heads the administration of the judicial branch.

Constitutions use various terms—*judicial power, the judicature, the courts,* and so forth—to refer to the judicial branch and often contain provisions designed to insulate it from the other branches of government, which are considered more political in nature and therefore more properly responsive to the ebb and flow of public opinion. This policy is based on the principle that the courts should be the impartial arbiters of disputes in accordance only with the law and accepted rules of jurisprudence. To enhance the independence of the courts, judges may be appointed for life during good behavior and be given protection from salary reductions and transfers, and the budget for the judiciary may be considered separately by the legislature.

Constitution of Peru (1993), Section II, Concerning the Government and the Nation, Chapter VIII, The Judicial Branch, Article 138: "The power to administer justice emanates from the people and is exercised by the judicial branch through its hierarchical organs based on the constitution and the law. . . . "

Constitution of Bulgaria (1991), Chapter 6, The Judicial Branch, Article 117: "(1) The judicial branch protects the rights and legitimate interests of citizens, juridical persons, and the state. (2) The judicial branch is independent. Judges, court assessors, prosecutors, and investigators are guided strictly by law in the exercise of their functions. (3) The judicial branch has a separate budget."

Judicial Council

The method of selecting, nominating, and confirming judges differs among countries and among states within some countries. In some states of the United States judges are elected; in others they are appointed. At the national level in the United States and most other countries judges are appointed. As a part of the appointment process some constitutions provide for consultation with or the recommendation of a judicial council or commission.

A judicial council, in addition to participating in the appointment process, may also be assigned a role by the constitution in the administration of the judicial branch of government. Such duties include involvement in the assignment of judges, their compensation, and their removal. The composition and independence of a judicial council or commission may have a direct bearing on the independence of a nation's judicial system.

Rather than a judicial council, the United Kingdom has a single individual, called the lord chancellor, who is responsible for appointing and supervising judges. In a number of countries, such as the United States, judges are appointed in a process of nomination by the chief executive and confirmation by the legislative branch.

Constitution of Spain (1978), Title VI, Concerning the Judicial Power, Article 122: "2. The general council of the judiciary is the latter's governing body. An organic law shall set up its statutes and the system of incompatibilities applicable to its members and their functions, especially in connection with appointments, promotions, inspection, and the disciplinary system."

Constitution of Nigeria (1989), Chapter VII, The Judicature, Part I, Federal Courts, A, The Supreme Court of Nigeria, Section 229: "2. The appointment of a person to the office of a justice of the supreme court shall be made by the president on the advice of the federal judicial service commission, subject to confirmation of such appointment by the senate."

Judicial Review

Unlike the process of constitutional review, under which a separate judicial body in the court system or an extrajudicial body determines the constitutionality of laws and actions, judicial review is the determination of constitutionality by ordinary courts of law. Through judicial review a court may review legislation and the actions of government officials for conflicts with the national constitution. Finding a law or an act unconstitutional, such a court can declare it null and void.

The concept of judicial review is not fully accepted in countries where the legislature is supreme, such as the United Kingdom, although the validity of administrative actions and legislation delegating authority to the executive branch may be examined by the courts. Judicial review as practiced in the United States and countries modeled strictly on the U.S. Constitution (1789) is based on the supremacy of the constitution, rather than the legislature, and the doctrines of the separation of powers and checks and balances, which require that adherence to the constitution be enforced by one branch against the others.

Although the concept of judicial review is recognized in countries such as Canada and Japan, the courts there may focus mainly on administrative rather than legislative actions. In such cases the courts investigate and determine if fairness and due process have been applied to the discretionary actions of government officials.

In contrast to decisions of special constitutional review bodies that may void an unconstitutional law *erga omnes* (for all), judicial review technically affects only the parties before the court. In countries that practice judicial review, however, the legal principle of *stare decisis* (adhering to precedent) and the hierarchy of the court system ensure that the decisions of the supreme court will be followed in lower courts and thus apply to everyone.

Constitutions may or may not expressly provide for judicial review. The U.S. Constitution does not mandate it, but in 1803 the U.S. Supreme Court in *Marbury v. Madison* declared that judges were bound by their oath of office to act as guardians of the Constitution as the supreme law of the land. Even in countries whose constitutions explicitly authorize judicial or constitutional review, this power may be critically limited and its application in practice may not be effective.

A number of parliamentary governments that have in the past eschewed judicial review, such as Belgium, are now using it to a limited extent because they have entered into treaties that take precedence over parliamentary law, guaranteeing their own citizens certain internationally or regionally recognized human rights. Courts in these countries therefore can declare legislation that conflicts with the treaty provisions to be unconstitutional.

Constitution of Ghana (1992), Chapter Eleven, The Judiciary, Article 130: "(1) Subject to the jurisdiction of the

The concept of judicial review, by which courts ensure adherence to a written constitution, was initiated by the U.S. Supreme Court, which is housed today in Washington, D.C., in Cass Gilbert's 1935 Classical Revival building.

high court in the enforcement of the fundamental human rights and freedoms as provided [for] in . . . this constitution, the supreme court shall have exclusive original jurisdiction in—(a) all matters relating to the enforcement or interpretation of this constitution; and (b) all matters arising as to whether an enactment was made in excess of the express powers conferred on parliament or any other authority or person by law or under this constitution."

Constitution of Honduras (1982), Chapter XII, The Judicial Branch, Article 319: "The supreme court of justice shall have the following powers and duties: . . . 12. To declare laws to be unconstitutional in the manner and in the cases provided for in this constitution. . . . "

Judiciary

Judicium in Latin means trial or verdict, and the English word *judiciary,* recorded in England as early as the seventeenth century, comes from a related Latin word, *judicarius.* Both the judiciary and judicature are collective names for courts and judges or for the judicial branch of government itself and may refer to the administration of justice.

In constitutions modeled on the U.S. Constitution (1789), the judiciary is part of the general constitutional scheme of checks and balances against the excesses of the coequal executive and legislative branches of government and a guardian of the constitutionality of laws and actions of government officials where judicial review power exists. In addition, the judiciary provides an impartial forum for settling disputes between individuals, between individuals and the state (either the national government or a constituent state in a federal system of government), and between a state and another state as well as between a state and the national government in a federal system.

Constitution of Iraq (1970), Chapter IV, Institutions of the Iraqi Republic, Section IV, The Judiciary, Article 60: "(a) The judiciary is independent and is subject to no other authority save the law. . . . (c) The law determines [how courts are established], their levels, jurisdiction and conditions for the appointment, transfer, promotion, litigation, and dismissal of judges and magistrates."

Constitution of Israel, Basic Law: Judicature (1984), Chapter One, Basic Provisions, Judicial Power, 1: "(a) Judicial power is vested in the following courts: (1) the supreme court; (2) a district court; (3) a magistrate's court; (4) another court designated by law as a court."

Jurisdiction

The legal scope of forums of justice such as tribunals or courts of law is called jurisdiction, from the Latin words *jus* (right or law) and *diction* (speaking). Many constitutions, including the U.S. Constitution, establish the jurisdictions of the courts, which may be limited to the amount of money, types of action, or types of crimes involved.

Original jurisdiction means that a court has the authority to hear cases in the first instance; appellate jurisdiction is the authority to rule on cases previously decided by lower courts. Concurrent jurisdiction indicates that one court has the same authority as another. Some constitutions and legislation implementing constitutional authority may separate courts into jurisdictional areas such as admiralty, bankruptcy, criminal, domestic, labor, and religious law. Courts may be given other functions, including trying cases involving the impeachment of high government officials and reviewing election procedures and the constitutionality of laws and actions.

Territorial jurisdiction refers to the geographic area over which a country or other political subdivision, such as a state or county, or an entity such as the Vatican has authority to exercise government functions.

Constitution of Ghana (1992), Chapter Eleven, The Judiciary, Article 125(5): "The judiciary shall have jurisdiction in all matters civil and criminal, including matters relating to this constitution, and such other jurisdiction as parliament may, by law, confer on it."

Constitution of Mozambique (1990), Chapter VI, The Courts, Section I, Article 167: "1. In the Republic of Mozambique there shall be the following courts: a) the supreme court and other courts of justice; b) the administrative court; c) courts-martial; d) custom courts; e) fiscal courts; f) maritime courts; g) labor courts. 2. Other than the courts specified in the constitution, no other court may be established with jurisdiction over specific categories of crimes."

Constitution of Hungary (1949, significantly revised in 1989), Chapter X, The Judiciary, Article 50: "(1) The courts of Hungary shall protect and guarantee the constitutional order, the rights and lawful interests of the citizens, and punish the perpetrators of criminal acts. (2) The courts shall review the legality of the decisions of public administration."

Just Compensation. *See* Compensation

Justice

What constitutes justice is an age-old question, one that has intrigued philosophers throughout history. Plato tried to define justice by demonstrating how just men behave in a just society. Aristotle believed that justice could exist to some extent in both oligarchies and democracies, because in both types of government freedom and wealth contribute to the good life of the state. In *The Federalist* (1788), James Madison sees justice as the end sought by government and civil society, while Alexander Hamilton argues that the administration of justice left to the constituent states by the U.S. Constitution protects the states from excessive encroachment by the national government.

In jurisprudence, justice—from the Latin words *jus* (law, legal status, right, or authority) and *justitia* (justice)—means giving to everyone what he or she deserves, and this is its general meaning in constitutions. A judge may also be called a justice, especially one on a supreme court.

Commutative justice refers to the honoring of contracts, regardless of the personal merits of the parties, while distributive justice entails the distribution of rewards and punishments based on personal merit. Judicial authorities under constitutions are most concerned with the quality and nature of justice as they interpret and apply the laws of the land in civil as well as criminal matters.

Even when constitutions conscientiously describe procedures to ensure justice for all, implementation is never perfect. Yet justice, along with security, order, and prosperity, is one of the generally acknowledged goals of democratic constitutions.

Constitution of Spain (1978), Preamble: "The Spanish nation, desirous of establishing justice, liberty, and security and promoting the good of its members, by virtue of its sovereignty proclaims its will to. . . . "

Constitution of Cuba (1976), Chapter XIII, Courts and the Attorney General, Article 120: "The function of administering justice springs from the people and is carried out in their name by the people's supreme court and the other tribunals which the law establishes."

K

Karamanlis, Constantine

Constantine Karamanlis (b. 1907) was a major architect of the current Greek system of government, which seeks to promote stability while maintaining democratic principles.

Karamanlis was born in Prote, Macedonia, in 1907 during the Turkish occupation, the eldest of seven children. When his father died, Constantine ("Costas") worked hard to put himself and three brothers through school, earning a law degree from the University of Athens in 1932. In 1935 he was elected to the Greek parliament as a populist and conservative monarchist.

When the dictator Ioannis Metaxas closed the parliament in 1936, Karamanlis rejected his offer of a ministerial post, declaring, "All dictatorships contain the seed of death." After World War II he was again elected to parliament and appointed minister of labor. Later he successfully headed other ministries, and in 1955 he became the first Macedonian premier. Karamanlis dominated Greek politics until 1963.

Military officers seized power in 1967, and the king fled the country. In July 1974, however, the military leaders asked Karamanlis, living in exile in Paris, to return and lead the government. In August he restored the 1952 monarchical constitution, which guaranteed civil rights.

Constantine Karamanlis's popularity and vision of democracy were key factors in the creation of the Greek constitution in 1975 after seven years of military rule.

After the downfall of the Ottoman Empire, Mustafa Kemal Atatürk, the "Father of Turkey," created the 1924 Turkish constitution and set his country on the path to democracy.

His return was compared to that of Charles de Gaulle, whose political style Karamanlis had carefully studied while in Paris.

In October 1974 Karamanlis formed the New Democracy Party, which won a solid victory in the November elections. The country voted in a referendum in December to abolish the monarchy, and Karamanlis released a draft of a new constitution, which was adopted on June 7, 1975. It provided for a president with the power to appoint and dismiss the premier, the parliamentary head of government, who was still to be the dominant political power; to dissolve the parliament; to veto laws; to issue legislative decrees; and to declare war and martial law.

Karamanlis served as president of Greece until 1985. When de Gaulle asked him why he had not created a more austere constitution, as de Gaulle had for France, Karamanlis answered, "You came to power after a parliamentary chaos and your people wished for a strong government. I came to power after a dictatorship and my people wished for freedom."

Kelsen, Hans

Hans Kelsen (1881–1973) significantly influenced the drafting of the 1920 Austrian constitution, which was reinstated after World War II. Its concept of a constitutional court has influenced many other national constitutions.

Kelsen was born on October 11, 1881, in Prague, Czechoslovakia. His family moved to Vienna in 1883, where his father began a lamp business. Although he preferred physics and mathematics, he chose to study law because of his family's poor financial condition and obtained a law degree in 1905.

Kelsen's major interest was the relationship between the law and the state. Using an approach derived from the works of Immanuel Kant, the late-eighteenth-century German philosopher, he reasoned that whereas physical laws rule in the world of the "is," the law he had studied was a part of the world of the "ought" and was based on acts of will. After several graduate fellowships, which allowed him to study in Heidelberg, he supported himself with odd jobs, including teaching, and finally settled down at the University of Vienna.

After World War I, Kelsen became an adviser to a

Hans Kelsen played a key role in drafting Austria's 1920 constitution, which includes his concept of a separate constitutional court to exercise constitutional review.

parliamentary committee charged with drafting a new constitution for the fledgling Republic of Austria. In addition to serving as a technical adviser, helping revise drafts by committee members of the political party coalition of Social Democrats and the Christian Socialists, he also introduced some of his own ideas. One of his major contributions, unique at that time in Europe, was the institution of the constitutional court. Such a body, apart from the regular judiciary, would have the authority to review the constitutionality of legislation. This idea was consistent with Kelsen's view of laws as a pyramid of successive legal norms, extending from municipal ordinances at the bottom to constitutional and even international law at the top.

Austria's new constitution was enacted on October 1, 1920, and Kelsen was appointed a judge on the new constitutional court. At about the same time he became an associate and then a full professor of constitutional and administrative law at the University of Vienna. A prolific writer, he continued to defend the need for constitutional review of legislation against attacks by those who supported the absolute sovereignty of the parliament. The court, he argued, was necessary to protect the rights of minorities. Kelsen also urged that constitutions be narrowly drawn to minimize political decisions by judges. A constant champion of democracy, he defended it against attacks by the ideological forces of the time—fascists, communists, and proponents of a corporate state. In 1938 Austria's constitution was abrogated by the occupying Nazi government, but it was restored after World War II.

Kelsen came to the United States in 1940 and taught at Harvard, the University of California, and the Naval War College before his death on April 19, 1973, in Berkeley, California. His other major contributions to constitutional development were his writings, which include a conceptual analysis of the relationship between the law and the state in his 1945 work *General Theory of Law and State*, and his *Pure Theory of Law*, published in English in 1967.

Kemal Atatürk

Unlike Turkish reformers before him, Kemal Atatürk (1881–1938) drew on the ideas of Jean-Jacques Rousseau, the French Revolution, and popular sovereignty to create a secular government in an Islamic country. Realizing that Western concepts of democracy were incompatible with the religion of his country, he wrought a change in thinking in Turkey unparalleled since the Turkish tribes were converted to Islam a thousand years before.

A Macedonian Muslim, Mustafa, as he was first called, was born in 1881 in Salonika, Rumeli, a part of the Ottoman Empire that at the time included Albania, Macedonia, and Thrace. Later he was called Kemal (perfection) because of his excellence in mathematics. In 1895 he began preparing for a military career, seeing action in 1905 against the insurgent Druze, a fanatical and warlike religious sect in Syria. In the same year he joined a secret revolutionary organization called the Fatherland and Freedom Society.

Kemal became an active revolutionary against the Ottoman sultanate, which was an absolutist regime ruled by a sultan or pasha who was traditionally held to be appointed by God. Under the sultan was a grand vizier, who led a coalition of the administrative, military, and judicial elements of the government.

Finding the leaders of the revolutionary movement too moderate, Kemal concentrated instead on his military career, distinguishing himself during World War I by earning the title of pasha for his service at Gallipoli. After the war Kemal was exiled for leading a national resistance movement against the harsh terms of the victorious European allies. In 1920 he set up a rival government, and a year later he convened a grand national assembly, which enacted a constitution.

The sultan was deposed in 1922, and Kemal, now also called Ghazi (victorious) for his military successes, was unanimously elected president of the new Turkish republic. The assembly, led by Kemal, adopted a new constitution in April 1924 based on the earlier one. However, it contained a provision making Islam the state religion. After consolidating his power in 1928, Kemal was able to have the provision removed, making Turkey a secular nation-state. The 1924 constitution significantly influenced subsequent Turkish constitutions, including the present document from 1982, making all of them reflections of Kemal's political vision for Turkey—for which he was called Atatürk (the "Father of Turkey").

Kemal's influence is acknowledged in the preamble of the Turkish constitution: "The direction of the concept of nationalism as outlined by Atatürk, the founder of the Republic of Turkey, its immortal leader and unrivalled hero. . . ."

Khomeini, Ayatollah Ruhollah

Under the leadership of the Ayatollah Ruhollah Khomeini (c. 1900–89), the 2,500-year-old Persian-Iranian monarchy came to an end in 1979 with the establishment of a theocratic republic under a constitution that conferred supreme power on Khomeini.

Ayatollah Ruhollah Khomeini's 1979 constitution for the theocratic Islamic Republic of Iran included the position of supreme leader, which he held until his death in 1989.

The son and grandson of mullahs (Islamic clergymen), Ruhollah was born at the beginning of the twentieth century in Khomeyn, or Khomein, Iran. His father died shortly after his birth, and he was raised by his mother, aunt, and older brother. Educated in Islamic schools, he settled in Qom in the early 1920s, taking the name of his hometown as his surname around 1930.

A persistent critic of the shah (king) of Iran, Khomeini used his position as a scholar and teacher in the Shi'a Islamic sect to denounce the shah's attempt to Westernize the country. He particularly decried the shah's land reform program, which took property from the religious estates, and his efforts to emancipate women. In the 1960s he was given the title of grand ayatollah, making him a supreme religious leader.

Exiled in 1964, Khomeini went to Iraq but continued to call for the overthrow of the monarchy. When Saddam Hussein forced him to leave Iraq in 1978, he took up residence in Paris. From there he maintained his efforts to foment rebellion through tape-recorded messages smuggled back into Iran. On January 16, 1979, the monarchy was toppled by Shi'a adherents of Khomeini, who returned in triumph on February 1 to head the revolution for which he had worked so long and hard.

Khomeini created a ruling revolutionary council of close religious associates as well as representatives of the political and military establishments. He believed, however, that his power was above that of any government and personally appointed officials and declared the nation's policies on important questions. Khomeini articulated a vision for the future government of his newly proclaimed Islamic Republic of Iran based on his convictions as an Islamic fundamentalist: "The fundamental difference between Islamic government, on the one hand, and constitutional monarchy and republics, on the other hand, is this: whereas the representative of the people or the monarch in such regimes engages in legislation, in Islam the legislative power and competence to establish laws belongs exclusively to God almighty."

Khomeini set in motion the process of drafting a new constitution to replace the 1906 monarchical document. A draft, released on June 18, 1979, was based on the previous constitution but included the newly created position of a strong president, modeled on the 1958 French constitution. A seventy-three-member assembly of experts, which met on August 18, 1979, to discuss the draft, modified it to create the position of supreme leader, for which only a *faqih* (expert in Shi'a religious jurisprudence) would be eligible. To no one's surprise Khomeini fit the requirements precisely, and he held the position until his death on June 3, 1989.

Khomeini left a legacy of a unique national constitution, which, according to its own terms, is subordinate to the Islamic faith. A key element of the constitution is a council of guardians, reminiscent of the nocturnal council in Plato's *The Laws*, that must pass judgment on the religious correctness of laws enacted by the legislature. Even after his death, amendments that Khomeini sought were put in place, and today a council of the highest religious leaders heads the country.

Kim Il Sung

As crafter of the constitution of North Korea that established a communist dictatorship, Kim Il Sung (1912–94) dominated the economic and political life of North Korea from after World War II until his death.

Kim was born Kim Song Ju on April 15, 1912, in Pyongannamdo, a northern province of Korea. The country was annexed by Japan in 1910, and his father, a middle-class schoolteacher, fled with his family to Manchuria in the mid-1920s.

Although the official North Korean accounts of Kim's early exploits are undoubtedly exaggerated, he was probably a communist guerrilla soldier in a unit in Manchuria between 1932 and 1941. Having taken refuge during World War II in Siberia, he received political and military training in the Soviet Union and became a member of the Soviet army during the remainder of the war. Afterward, in October 1945, he accompanied the Soviet army when it occupied what was to become North Korea.

With the backing of the Soviet Union, Kim emerged as the Communist Party leader in North Korea and became premier under a constitution ratified by a Korean supreme people's assembly on September 3, 1948.

From the end of World War II until his death in 1994, Kim Il Sung (right), shown here greeting Kang Young-hoon (left), prime minister of South Korea, dominated North Korea and oversaw the creation of the country's 1972 communist constitution.

This constitution was clearly modeled on the 1936 "Stalin" constitution of the Soviet Union, as were many other constitutions in countries dominated by the Communist Party after World War II. Following the Korean War, which lasted from 1950 to 1953, Kim purged all his potential rivals, and by 1961 he was in complete control of the communist Workers' Party of Korea and the government.

Kim oversaw the drafting of a new constitution, which was adopted on December 27, 1972. It created a new position of president, which Kim filled, and a central people's committee to control the bureaucracy and make policy. The supreme people's assembly was retained as the "highest organ of state power," although, in fact, Kim, as head of the Workers' Party of Korea, continued to rule as a dictator. On December 25, 1972, Kim explained the need for the new constitution to the supreme people's assembly: "Our realities today urgently demand the establishment of a new socialist constitution to legally consolidate the tremendous achievements of our people in the socialist revolution and in building socialism, and to lay down principles for political, economic, and cultural spheres of socialist society."

In 1992 the constitution was revised, again under Kim's direction. The Marxist-Leninist aspects were diminished while concepts that Kim found to be more reflective of North Korean socialist culture were emphasized, and a framework for dealing with noncommunist countries was created.

Since Kim's death on July 8, 1994, his son, Kim Jong Il, has succeeded to the position of communist dictator of North Korea.

Elizabeth II assumed the throne of the United Kingdom in 1952 on the death of her father, George VI.

King

The idea of kingship—the divine right to rule—probably developed in early human culture from the figure of the father as head of the household, the provider and protector, evolving through the clan leader into a sacral king who possessed divinity and great power and resided at the center of the universe. Derived from the Old English word *cyning, king*—along with *prince, emperor,* and *tsar*—is one title for a monarch. The Latin word for king is *rex,* the French is *roi,* the German is *könig,* and the Spanish is *rey.* The feminine form of *king* is *queen.*

The evolution of kingship is reflected in mythology and religion. The ancient Greeks worshiped a pantheon of gods and goddesses ruled over by a king of the gods, Zeus, later adopted by the Romans and known as Jupiter, whose name is a variant of *Zeus-pater* (Zeus-father). The Israelite king, according to Jewish and Christian religious texts, had a special relationship to God. After the Christian religion created hegemony in Europe, it became standard procedure for the head of the church to crown a king.

By the mid-sixteenth century the English king Henry VIII had broken with the Catholic Church, and in continental Europe Martin Luther initiated the schism between the Catholic and Protestant denominations. Kings were considered above the law, answerable only to God. William Blackstone, the eighteenth-century commentator on

English law, noted that the king, "from the excellence and perfection" of his person, was supposed by the law to be incapable of doing wrong.

Most kings today are constitutional monarchs; an exception is the king of Saudi Arabia, who rules without constitutional limits. Constitutions of constitutional monarchies often expressly state that the king or queen has certain powers or authority. Generally, however, in these countries the monarch by tradition may act only on the advice of the prime minister and the cabinet, and his or her acts are valid only if countersigned by a government minister.

Constitutional monarchies have acts of succession that determine how a new king will be chosen when the reigning monarch dies. Some specify that only a male heir may ascend to the throne, thus ensuring that a king rather than a queen will always be the monarch for the nation-state.

For the most part today kings and queens, like emperors, are ceremonial figureheads as heads of state, but they may hold a special place with respect to the state religion. In some Asian countries, for example, they are still considered to be divine in certain respects.

Constitution of Nepal (1990), Part 5, His Majesty, Article 27: "(2) His majesty is the symbol of the Nepali nation and the unity of the Nepali people. (3) His majesty shall abide by and protect this constitution for the best interest and progress of the people of Nepal."

Constitution of Belgium (1814), Heading III, Concerning the Authorities, Chapter II, Concerning the King and His Ministers, Section I, Concerning the King, Article 60: "The constitutional powers of the king are hereditary in the direct line of natural, legitimate heirs of H. M. Leopold Georges Chrétien Frédéric of Saxe-Coberg, from male heir to male heir, in order of primogeniture, to the perpetual exclusion of women and their descendants."

Koran.

See Islamic Law

L

labor

In ancient Athens the first duty of a man was to support himself and his family, and idleness was a punishable offense. In Egypt any man who could not show that he had earned an honest living the previous year was condemned to death. The concept of labor—human effort to accomplish some task—was the basis of John Locke's conclusion that the right of private property, the right to the fruits of one's own labor, is a natural right.

Organized labor and the trade union movement in the last few centuries have had a tremendous impact on world governments. The eighteenth-century English legal commentator William Blackstone placed "unlawful combinations among workmen" in the class of offenses against public trade. Workers (the proletariat), however, were the basis of the theory of communism espoused by the German economic theorist Karl Marx. In many countries the worker's relationship to the capitalist and to the state has been fertile ground for legislation, confrontation, agitation, and revolution.

Constitutions deal in different ways with the concept of work—from the Latin *labor* (work, toil, or distress), now *labour* in French and *trabajo* or *labor* in Spanish; both *Arbeit* (work) and *Mühe* (trouble or pain) are used in German. The 1948 Italian constitution states in Article 1: "Italy is a democratic republic founded on labor." Some provisions make work a right, some a duty. Others deal extensively with the treatment of workers, hours of employment, and wages and benefits. Provisions may guarantee work for all those who seek it or secure the rights of trade unions to bargain collectively and strike.

Constitution of Venezuela (1961), Title III, Duties, Rights, and Guarantees, Chapter IV, Social Rights, Article 84: "All persons have a right to work. The state shall seek to enable every fit person to obtain employment that will provide him a worthy and decent living. Freedom of labor shall not be subject to any other restrictions than those established by law."

Constitution of the United States of America (1789), Article IV, Section 2: "No person held to Service or Labour in one State, under the Laws thereof, escaping to another, shall, in Consequence of any Law or Regulation therein, be discharged from such Service or Labour, but shall be delivered up on Claim of the Party to whom such Service or Labour may be due."

Constitution of Poland, Constitutional Provisions Continued in Force Pursuant to Article 77 of the Constitution Act (1992), Chapter 8, Fundamental Rights and Duties of Citizens, Article 85: "Trade unions shall play an important public function in the Republic of Poland as mass

By successfully prosecuting the American Civil War from 1861 to 1865, President Abraham Lincoln refined the constitutional concept of federalism, ensuring the sovereignty of the U.S. Constitution and the life of the country itself.

An 1878 allegory depicts democracy and American labor (represented by Abraham Lincoln) triumphing over foreign interests.

organizations which take part in the formulation and implementation of tasks of social and economic advancement of the country; the trade unions shall represent the interests and rights of working people, and shall be a school of civic activity and involvement in the creation of civic [formerly "socialist"] society."

Language

Language has played an important role in shaping culture and politics. Derived from the Latin *lingua* and the French *langage*, the term *language* defines any means of conveying or communicating ideas but particularly means human speech and writing. Related to the idea of language are the Greek word *barbaros* (strange or unintelligible) and the Sanskrit word *barbara* (a stammerer, presumably one not able to speak the same language).

Many constitutions, including the U.S. Constitution (1789), do not mention language, but some do, either to establish an official national language or languages or to give special rights and privileges or protection to certain languages spoken within a nation-state. Both English and French are the official languages of Canada. The Belgian constitution was significantly amended in 1993 to reflect the influence of the French- and Flemish-speaking communities on the political structure of the country, making it more like a federal nation than the unitary nation it was when it became independent in 1830.

Constitution of South Africa (1994), Chapter 1, Constituent and Formal Provisions, Languages, Section 3(1): "Afrikaans, English, isiNdebele, Sesotho sa Leboa, Sesotho, siSwati, Xitsonga, Setswana, Tshivenda, isiXhosa, and isiZulu shall be the official South African languages at [the] national level, and conditions shall be created for their development and for the promotion of their equal use and enjoyment."

Constitution of North Korea (1972), Chapter III, Culture, Article 46: "The state defends our language from the policy of the imperialists and their stooges to destroy it, and develops it to meet the present day needs."

Constitution of Belgium (1831), Heading II, Concerning the Belgians and Their Rights, Article 23: "The use of languages spoken in Belgium is optional; it may only be regulated by law and only in the case of acts by the public authorities and legal matters."

law

The general science or system of rules of human conduct is known as law, from the Latin *jus.* Second only to the idea of a constitution itself, law is the most important concept or term used in constitutions. The concept of law, however, has developed uniquely in many countries and regions of the world, thus making comparative constitutionalism difficult without an understanding of what law means in the countries being compared.

In constitutions a law generally refers to a rule of behavior imposed by authority. A constitutional law is a fundamental or basic law that is considered supreme over all other laws; based on the consent of the governed in a nation-state, it may be adopted by a body representing the people, by a referendum of the people, by tradition and custom, or simply by acquiescence. A law or statute *(lex)* passed by a legislature differs from law that develops from common usage and custom, such as the English common law. Other subordinate laws referred to in constitutions include legislation enacted in accordance with constitutional procedures and laws called decree laws issued by a public official, also in accordance with constitutional procedures. A fiat of an absolute monarch, a dictator, or a military junta may also have the force of law.

Some rules of behavior that arise from custom and usage may be generally obeyed even though they cannot be enforced in a court of law. Although many constitutional rules of countries with unwritten constitutions are conventions or practices observed by custom and tradition, they are nonetheless controlling in the political arena even though they cannot be legally enforced.

The Old English word for law—*lagu*—was in use as early as 1000 A.D., according to the collected laws of Ethelred II ("The Unready"), an English king who reigned from 978 to 1016. Derived from such old northern European words as the Old Icelandic *lag* (something laid or fixed), it is the equivalent of the Latin words *lex* and to some extent *jus.* Today *law* translates as *rett* in Norwegian, *rätt* in Swedish, *ret* in Danish, *Recht* or *Gesetz* in German, *loi* or *droit* in French, *ley, derecho,* or *jurisprudencia* in Spanish, and *hōritsu* in Japanese.

A broad concept, law embraces many technical terms that bear directly or tangentially on constitutions. Natural law, for example, refers to the fundamental laws of God and nature that some theorists have postulated as the basis for all man-made laws, including constitutions. Not surprisingly, there are various notions about what constitutes natural law. Positive law, on the other hand, refers to laws created by governments.

Law and laws have been divided into many subcategories that sometimes find their way into constitutions. The common law—law derived from judicial rulings—is a major element of the unwritten constitution of the United Kingdom. The continental code law instituted originally by Napoleon has played a key role in the development of judicial institutions and practices in many countries. *Rahmengesetz* (skeletal law) and *Grundsatzgesetz* (basic law) inform the constitutional processes in Austria, Germany, and Switzerland. The sections on the judiciary in some constitutions may spell out the types of law certain courts or tribunals are responsible for applying—civil or criminal law, for example, or labor, admiralty, religious, or military law.

Constitution of China (People's Republic of China) (1982), Chapter Three, Structure of the State, Section VII, The People's Courts and the People's Procuratorates, Article 135: "The people's courts, people's procuratorates, and public security organs shall, in handling criminal cases, divide their functions, each taking responsibility for its own work, and they shall coordinate their efforts and check each other to ensure correct and effective enforcement of law."

Belva Lockwood became the first woman lawyer to be permitted to argue a case before the U.S. Supreme Court in 1879, forty-one years before women could vote.

Constitution of Iran (1979), Chapter I, General Principles, Article 2: "The Islamic republic is a system based on belief in: 1. the one God (as stated in the phrase . . . 'There is no god except Allah'), His exclusive sovereignty and the right to legislate, and the necessity of submission to His commands; 2. Divine revelation and its fundamental role in setting forth the laws. . . . "

Constitution of Norway (1814), B, The Executive Power, The King and the Royal Family, Article 17: "The king may issue and repeal ordinances relating to commerce, customs tariffs, all economic sectors and the police; although these must not conflict with the constitution or the laws passed by the Storting [parliament]. . . . "

Law Decree.

See Decree

Lay Judge

To assist with legal adjudications, some constitutions make special provision for lay judges, also called people's jurors, assistant judges, or assessors. They are not legal professionals but generally serve on an equal basis with other judges and are used when a jurisdiction lacks judges trained in the law. They also fill a desire to add a nonjudicial element to legal proceedings, one that juries provide in other situations.

The use of lay judges is more often found in constitutions of countries dominated by the Communist Party, although Switzerland has a high proportion of them in its lower and higher courts. Lay judges were formerly used in some states of the United States as assistant judges in courts of first instance.

Constitution of Cuba (1976), Chapter XIII, Courts and the Attorney-General, Article 124: "In the administration of justice, courts function in a collegiate form, and both professional and lay judges participate with equal rights and duties. Priority is given to the judicial functions assigned to the lay judges in view of their social importance and work schedules."

Constitution of Vietnam (1992), Chapter X, People's Courts and People's Organs of Control, Article 129: "As stipulated by law, in adjudicating trials at the people's courts participated in by people's jurors and at courts martial participated in by military jurors of justice, the people's jurors have the same power as judges."

Legal

In Roman law a *lex* was a statute to which the people consented by a simple yea or nay vote. In the last days of the Roman republic the emperor Augustus often used this procedure to obtain approval by mob vote for changes in criminal and private laws, keeping the form if not the substance of democracy.

Derived from *leges,* the plural of the Latin *lex* (law), and the French word *légal* (lawful or legitimate), *legal* refers to practices that are required or permitted by the law, recognized by a court of law, or implied in law. Although the word may be used in many contexts, in constitutions it generally connotes actions recognized as valid under the law or ones sanctioned by the law.

The basic organization of laws, including constitutional laws and the judicial process of a nation-state or other jurisdiction, is called the legal system. The study of the basis of laws and legal systems is known as legal theory.

Constitution of Bangladesh (1972), Part VI, The Judiciary, Chapter I, The Supreme Court, Article 102(2): "The high court division may, if satisfied that no other equally efficacious remedy is provided by law—(a) on the application of any person aggrieved, make an order—. . . (ii) declaring that any act done or proceeding taken by a person performing functions in connection with the affairs of the republic or of a local authority has been done or taken without lawful authority and is of no legal effect. . . ."

Constitution of Poland, Constitutional Provisions Continued in Force Pursuant to Article 77 of the Constitution Act (1992), Chapter 9, The Principles of Elections to the Sejm, to the Senate, and to the Presidency, Article 99: "Electoral rights shall be denied to persons pronounced incapable of legal actions by a final decision of a court on the grounds of mental illness or mental deficiency. . . ."

legislation

Plato propounds his theory of the origins of legislation in *The Laws*. As a community grows in size, representatives known as lawgivers are chosen to review the rules of all households or families and to propose to community leaders rules that would be good for common use. Plato's theory is an apt if simplified description of how modern parliaments work. Representatives—legislators or lawgivers—are chosen to enact laws by majority rule to be presented to the monarch or other head of state for assent, and such laws will apply to all citizens.

Legislation—Late Latin meaning "bringing of the law"—is a body of laws enacted by a legislature, generally with some involvement of the executive branch, although legislation enacted over the veto of the chief executive is an exception to that general requirement. Acts, statutes, and laws are the product of legislation.

At the time the U.S. Constitution was drafted in 1787, the British Parliament had become supreme and the monarch largely a figurehead. Therefore, in developing a new form of constitutional government, something other than a limited monarchy, the framers were seriously concerned about the possible excesses of oppressive legislation. The Senate, whose members' terms were to be three times longer than those of the members of the lower House of Representatives, and the president's veto power were considered necessary checks on rash or impulsive legislation passed by the lower house to curry favor with the general population.

Whether in a presidential or parliamentary system of government, the legislative process begins with the introduction into the legislature of a bill setting forth a proposed act or law. The bill is then generally assigned to a committee or one of its subcommittees consisting of selected legislators charged with reviewing and reporting to the other members on the bill's subject matter. After the committee members vote among themselves and report on the bill, a vote is taken by the full legislature. Constitutions modeled strictly after the U.S. Constitution require passage of identical bills in both houses of the legislature and the signature of the president before a statute can become effective. Other constitutions specify that the monarch, his or her representative, or the head of state assent to a law passed by the legislature, and in some cases the statute must appear in an official government publication before it becomes effective.

Different types of legislation may produce basic laws, constitutional laws, organic laws, and ordinary laws—all public laws that apply to the general population. Legislators may also pass private laws, which affect only specified persons, groups, or legal entities.

Constitution of Ecuador (1979), Second Part, Title I, The Legislative Function, Section II, The Enactment and Sanction of Legislation, Article 65: "The initiative for the enactment of legislation may come from the legislators, the national congress, the legislative commissions, the president of the republic, the supreme court of justice, the fiscal tribunal, or the contentious administrative tribunal."

Constitution of Syria (1973), Part Two, Powers of the State, Chapter II, Executive Power, (1) President of the Republic, Article 111: "2—The president of the republic shall assume legislative power when the people's council is in session if this is required by an extreme necessity relating to the country's national interest . . . provided that all legislation so issued shall be referred to the council in the first meeting held by the council after issuance of the legislation."

Legislative Branch

The households of the cyclopes in Homer's *Odyssey* are described by Plato, in *The Laws,* as having no laws and no council for debating: in the hollow caves each man lays down the law. In ancient Rome *leges facio* (to enact or make laws) referred to the process by which proposals of the king, before the days of the republic, and later of magistrates elected by the people were ratified by a vote of the people. Debating, deliberating, and enacting laws for nation-states are now the province of the legislative branch of government, one of the three major powers identified by Montesquieu in his *Spirit of the Laws* (1748).

The Senate and House of Representatives of the U.S. Congress, the elected bodies of the legislative branch of government, hold their sessions in the Capitol in Washington, D.C.

Under most constitutions the legislative branch consists of a parliament, an assembly, or a congress that is often divided into two houses or chambers. The lower house is generally more representative of the people, who elect its members by direct vote from districts or at large; the upper house is often less representative, more conservative in its makeup, and in federal governments generally represents the constituent states or provinces. The legislative branch also comprises staff and even specialized resources such as the Library of Congress and the Congressional Budget Office in the United States. Some legislative branches include an appointed ombudsman, who has authority to investigate the actions of public officials.

The legislative branch is generally not solely responsible for the passage of legislation. Many constitutions permit members of the executive and judicial branches, state or provincial legislators, or a sufficient number of voters to initiate legislative proposals. And in both parliamentary and presidential types of governments, the head of government or state must endorse most acts of the legislature before they become law.

Constitution of South Africa (1994), Chapter 4, Parliament, Legislative Authority of Republic, Article 37: "The legislative authority of the republic shall, subject to this constitution, vest in parliament, which shall have the power to make laws for the republic in accordance with this constitution."

Constitution of North Korea (1972), Chapter V, The Supreme People's Assembly, Article 73: "The supreme people's assembly is the highest organ of power of the Democratic People's Republic of Korea. The legislative power is exercised exclusively by the supreme people's assembly [controlled in fact by the Communist Party]."

Legislature

A lawgiver, warns Plato in *The Laws,* should never forget the aims of the state: to be free and wise and enjoy internal harmony. Aristotle, in *The Politics,* comments that a legislator should keep his eyes on two points—the people and the country—without ignoring neighboring states.

Derived from the Latin word *leges* (laws), a legislature is a government institution charged with making laws. It forms the major component of the legislative branch and can be divided into two general forms: parliaments and congresses.

In parliamentary systems of government, as in the United Kingdom, the head of government and the heads of executive branch departments or ministries generally are chosen by the majority party or a coalition of parties in the most representative body of the parliament; consequently, the legislative and executive branches must work in cooperation. Technically, the legislature consists of the parliament and the head of state, whose assent is required for all laws to be valid.

In presidential systems, as in the United States, the head of government is elected separately from the members of its congress. That body has at best some role in the confirmation of heads of executive branch departments, who are chosen by the chief executive or president. Consequently, the legislative and executive branches do not necessarily work cooperatively. Although the president's signature is required on most congressionally enacted laws, a congress may be able to pass a law that will become effective in spite of a presidential veto.

A legislature, whether a parliament or congress, is generally composed of elected representatives called members, deputies, representatives, congressmen, or senators. Some countries also elect alternates. Most legislatures are bicameral, having an upper and a lower chamber or house, but some are unicameral and a few semibicameral. It is not uncommon to find that the members (or some members) of the upper house are not elected by the people. Members of the lower house generally are directly elected and choose the head of government—a prime minister, for example—and other ministers, while the upper house tends to be more conservative and functions as a check on the possible excesses of the lower house.

Constitutions often prescribe in great detail the qualifications of the members of the legislature, its powers and duties, and its procedures for carrying out its functions of enacting laws and checking on the actions of the executive branch.

Constitution of the United Kingdom, Halsbury's Laws of England (1974, 4th ed.), Volume 8, Paragraph 817, Legislature and Executive Coordinated by Conventions: "The rules and principles [of convention] have been found from experience to be essential to the cooperation of the three parties in whom the legislative and executive functions of government are vested, namely the Crown, the [House of] Lords and the [House of] Commons."

Constitution of the United States of America (1789), Article I, Section 1: "All legislative Powers herein granted shall be vested in a Congress of the United States, which shall consist of a Senate and House of Representatives."

Constitution of the Czech Republic (1993), Chapter Two, Legislative Power, Article 19: "(1) Every citizen of the Czech Republic who is eligible to vote and has reached the age of twenty-one may be elected to the chamber of deputies. (2) Every citizen who is eligible to vote and has reached the age of forty may be elected to the senate."

Legitimacy

Constitutions of limited monarchies and particularly constitutional documents called acts of succession—provisions for a monarch's ascendancy on the death of the predecessor—often require that the successor be the legitimate heir apparent of the preceding monarch. Derived from the Latin word *legitimus* (legal, legitimate, or right), *legitimate* may refer to a child born in rather than out of wedlock as well as to whether a sovereign's government or title is in accordance with law.

Legitimists believe that power to rule a nation should be based not on the constitutional democratic process of elections but on the legal right of a monarch to inherit the title to the throne, just as an average citizen is entitled to inherit property on the death of another. Following the French Revolution in 1789, those who wanted to restore only the legitimate heirs of Louis XVI to the throne of France were successful twice: in 1814 with the restoration of Louis XVIII and in 1830 with the ascension of Louis Philippe, a liberal monarch. Today supporters of the continued reign of legitimate rulers such as Monaco's Prince Rainier III and his heirs are by definition legitimists.

Constitution of Monaco (1962), Title II, The Prince, The Devolution of the Crown, Article 10: "The succession to the throne shall take place after the death or abdication within the direct legitimate line of the reigning prince, by order of primogeniture, with the priority being given to males within the same degree of relationship. In the absence of legitimate descendants, an adopted child or an adopted child's legitimate descendants are eligible to succeed."

Constitution of Norway (1814), B, The Executive Power, the King, and the Royal Family, Article 6: "The order of succession is lineal, so that only a child born in lawful wedlock of the queen or king, or of one who is herself or himself entitled to succeed, and so that the nearest line shall take precedence over the more remote and the elder in the line over the younger."

Legitimate. *See* Legitimacy

Liability. *See* Obligation

Liberty

"The basis of a democratic state is liberty, which, according to the common opinion of men, can only be enjoyed in such a state—this they affirm to be the great end of every democracy," says Aristotle in *The Politics.* Although slavery was practiced in ancient Greece, a person wrongly enslaved could be "removed to freedom" by a friend.

In ancient Rome *libertas* was the status acquired by a freed slave. For most purposes this implied the status of a citizen, but the former slave retained a special relationship under Roman law vis-à-vis his or her former master. Originally, Roman citizens were divided into an upper class, the patricians, and a lower class, the plebeians. But under private law the major distinction was between the freeborn *(ingenui)* and freed persons *(libertini). Liberti,* however, referred to the status of the freed slave to his or her former master, who retained certain rights with respect to the property of the freed person as well as legal privileges.

In British colonial America, laws and legal rights were said to rest on liberties, a concept probably derived from English liberties, districts that were free from the jurisdiction of the sheriff. The literal meaning of *liberty* and

The Liberty Bell in Philadelphia, a major tourist attraction, is traditionally believed to have cracked while ringing in celebration of freedom in America.

freedom today is exemption from extraneous control. When used in constitutions, however, these terms do not mean unrestricted license to do whatever one pleases; rather, they imply some restraints. As Alexander Hamilton states in essay 1 of *The Federalist* (1788), "... noble enthusiasm of liberty is apt to be infected with a spirit of narrow and illiberal distrust.... [and] the vigor of government is essential to the security of liberty...."

In the modern civil state liberty theoretically includes the relinquishment of certain natural rights in exchange for the equal protection and opportunity afforded by the political community. As a Chinese government official remarked on the subject of the return of Hong Kong in 1997, "In every country, freedom has its limits and bounds." Just what constitutes such limits and bounds on individual liberty in order for a government to be both effective and democratic is the subject of much debate.

Among the list of specific liberties or freedoms, also referred to as rights, guaranteed to the people under constitutions are freedom of conscience, thought, speech, the press, and assembly. A seminal category of such guarantees is contained in the Bill of Rights (1791), the first ten amendments to the U.S. Constitution (1789).

Constitution of Cuba (1976), Preamble: "We, Cuban citizens, heirs and continuators of the creative work and the traditions of combativeness, firmness, heroism, and sacrifice fostered by our ancestors; . . . by the slaves who rebelled against their masters; [and] by those who awoke the national conscience and the Cuban longing for a homeland and liberty. . . ."

Constitution of Liberia (1986), Chapter III, Fundamental Rights, Article 20: "No person shall be deprived of life, liberty, security of the person, property, privilege, or any other right except as the outcome of a hearing and a judgment consistent with the provisions of this constitution and in accordance with due process of law."

Constitution of Italy (1948), Part One, The Duties and Rights of the Citizens, Title I, Civil Relations, Article 13: "Personal freedom is inviolable."

Lincoln, Abraham

The steadfast stand of Abraham Lincoln (1809–65) against the secession of Southern states was his greatest contribution to the viability of the federal constitution of the United States, tested during the country's Civil War.

Born in a log cabin in Hardin County, Kentucky, in 1809, Lincoln lived in an even more rustic three-sided shelter of logs and brush after his family moved to Indiana seven years later. Young Abe was skilled in using an ax and splitting rails for wood fences, a talent that came in handy when the family moved again, this time to Illinois, where trees were plentiful. Mostly self-taught up to this time, he started his career in a local business, managing a mill and store in New Salem.

During the 1832 Blackhawk War, Lincoln was elected captain of a group of volunteers. On his return home, he ran for the Illinois legislature but was defeated; in 1834, on his second try, he won election. During this time he studied law, was admitted to the bar in 1836, and practiced law until he was elected to Congress ten years later as a member of the Whig Party. A burning issue for the country was slavery, which he pronounced a "moral, social, and political wrong."

In 1856 Lincoln left the Whig Party for the new Republican Party. In 1860, when he was elected the party's first president of the United States, seven Southern, proslavery states withdrew from the Union. In his inaugural address Lincoln declared that secession was anarchy and that the Union could not legally be broken apart. The states were not sovereign; only the nation was truly sovereign, he said. By the terms of the Constitution, no state had the right to refuse to obey the supreme law of the land simply because it opposed the newly elected president.

The bloody Civil War that ensued from 1861 to 1865 was prosecuted by Lincoln to prove his conclusions about the meaning of a federal constitution. After a major Northern victory at the battle of Antietam in 1862, he issued an Emancipation Proclamation that, although it fell short of abolishing the institution of slavery throughout the United States, confirmed his conviction that the country "was conceived in liberty and dedicated to the proposition that all men were created equal."

During the war Lincoln took steps to suspend the writ of habeas corpus, although the constitutional provision for such an act is found in the article relating to the legislative branch of government. Strongly criticized for this action, he defended the measure as necessary to ensure that the laws of the Union, like liberty itself, survived such a "clear, flagrant, and gigantic case of rebellion."

Abraham Lincoln died from an assassin's bullet on April 14, 1865. Although he never wrote a word of any constitution, his role in defining the nature of constitutional federal governments has provided a precedent for such governments around the world. With the notable exception of the Soviet Union's constitution before its breakup in 1991, constitutions do not contain provisions for the secession of constituent states from a federal government or for the secession of any territory from a unitary nation-state. Lincoln's principle and the federal cohesion of Russia under its 1993 constitution were tested by the rebellion in the province of Chechnya that began in 1994.

List Voting. *See* Proportional Representation

Locke, John

The concepts of the consent of the governed as the basis for government and of the social contract between rulers and the ruled, formulated by John Locke (1632–1704), provide the philosophical underpinnings of modern democratic constitutions.

Born on August 29, 1632, in Wrington, Somerset, England, Locke was educated at Westminster School and Christ Church, Oxford. He became a friend of and an adviser to Lord Ashley, earl of Shaftesbury, whom he met at Oxford in 1662, and helped him draft a constitution for the English colony of Carolina in the New World.

Shaftesbury became a leader of the parliamentary opposition to the Stuart monarchy and was forced to flee to Holland, as did Locke in 1683. In 1690 Locke's most important work, *Two Treatises of Government*, was published anonymously to justify insurrection to counteract the growing absolutism of the Stuart monarch Charles II. The first treatise attacks arguments supporting the divine right of kings to rule, such as those espoused by the conservative political writer Robert Filmer in *Patriarcha*, published posthumously in 1680. The second treatise begins by describing human beings in a state of nature in which actions are free and unfettered—a theoretical state of equality that could have existed before governments were established. Unlike Thomas Hobbes's vision of brutishness, Locke sees people acting in accordance with the laws of nature but observes that the primitive social system is inherently unstable. Locke postulates that human beings left the state of nature and created a civil society by an act of consent—the social contract—to preserve lives, liberties, and property. A primary function of the state, he says, is to preserve property rights and make laws regarding the use and transfer of property.

John Locke's *Two Treatises of Government*, written to protest absolutism, provided philosophical support for the constitutional concept of the consent of the governed.

According to Locke, governments remain in a state of nature with respect to their relationships because there is no common sovereign to settle differences between nation-states. Even today international law, which deals with the relations among nation-states, lacks the enforcement capability of a national sovereignty. Moreover, he continued, when governments become tyrannical the social contract is abrogated and the system reverts to the state of nature, with the rulers no different from marauding bandits.

The political thought of John Locke, who died on October 28, 1704, was influenced by Descartes, Pierre Gassendi, and the Cambridge Platonists. He, in turn, influenced constitutionalism and constitution makers, especially in the United States and France.

Lower House

The lower house or chamber of a legislature—in the Netherlands called the second chamber—is generally the larger, more representative part of a bicameral body. It is also generally the chamber in a parliamentary form of government from which the chief executive (prime minister) and the members of the cabinet or other ministers are selected, and it usually has the power to initiate money bills. The members of the lower house are almost always elected directly, although various forms of proportional and list voting may be used.

The House of Representatives, the lower house of Australia's Parliament, is composed of 148 members elected from single-member electoral districts or constituencies for only a three-year term.

The prototypical lower house of a parliamentary system is the British House of Commons, composed of representatives elected from the country's counties, cities, and boroughs. The Commons historically represented knights, citizens, burgesses, and all subjects of the Crown other than high church officials, nobility, and peers, who are members of the upper house, the House of Lords.

The prototypical lower house of a presidential form of government is the U.S. House of Representatives, whose members are elected directly by the people from congressional or electoral districts in the states. Each state of the United States is entitled to at least one; the more populous states have proportionally more representatives.

The British House of Commons is far more powerful than the U.S. House of Representatives. For all intents and purposes it is the supreme ruling body for the United Kingdom because acts of Parliament in 1911 and 1949 stripped the House of Lords of any power to withhold consent to bills passed by the House of Commons. The U.S. House of Representatives, on the other hand, except for its singular authority to raise revenues, is roughly coequal with the Senate in the legislative process; furthermore, the legislative branch is only one of three coequal branches of the U.S. government.

Constitutions of nation-states with bicameral or semi-bicameral national legislatures usually detail the composition, qualifications of members, and powers and duties of the lower house. Unlike the constitutions of Iceland and the Netherlands, most constitutions generally do not specifically designate a division of the national legislature as a lower house or second chamber.

Constitution of Iceland (1944), Chapter Three, Article 32: "The Althing is divided into an upper and a lower house. One-third of the members sit in the upper house and two-thirds in the lower house."

Constitution of the Netherlands (1814), Chapter 3, The States General, Article 51: "1. The states general shall consist of a second chamber (Tweede Kamer) [lower house] and a first chamber (Eerste Kamer) [upper house]. 2. The second chamber shall consist of one hundred and fifty members."

M

Macdonald, John Alexander

Sir John A. Macdonald (1815–91) was the chief architect of the 1867 federal constitution of Canada, even though he personally favored a more centralized form of government.

Born in Glasgow, Scotland, on January 10 or 11, 1815, Macdonald moved to Kingston, Ontario, when he was five years old. At the age of fifteen he began his preparation for the legal profession with a prominent Kingston lawyer and was called to the Canadian bar in 1837. The following year, as a private in the local militia, he gained a reputation by defending accused rebels.

Macdonald began his political career in 1843 as an alderman in Kingston, and in 1844, at the age of twenty-nine, he was elected to Canada's legislative assembly. A conservative, he supported the British Crown and was named attorney general for Canada West, or Upper Canada. In 1856 he became the acknowledged leader of the Conservative Party.

In 1791 Britain had divided Quebec into Upper and Lower Canada, with the lieutenant governor for the former theoretically responsible to the governor of Quebec. This hierarchical system of government did not work well, and in the first half of the nineteenth century proposals surfaced for a "grand confederacy" of all the British provinces in North America. Following an 1839 report recommending the union of Upper and Lower Canada and a greater degree of self-government, submitted by Lord Durham, the former governor-general and lord high commissioner for Canada, the provinces were united by British proclamation in 1841.

The Civil War (1861–65) in the United States led Canadians to realize how difficult military mobilization would

James Madison's prominent role in formulating and promoting the 1789 constitution of the United States earned him the title "Father of the Constitution."

Even though he favored a unitary form of government, Sir John Macdonald had the leading role in drafting the 1867 federal-style constitution for Canada.

be with a legislature that required, in effect, a double majority of members from both Upper and Lower Canada, because the consent of both legislatures was necessary under the provisions of the political union of 1841. In 1864 Macdonald, although personally favoring a unitary form of government for Canada, took a leading role in drafting a federal system for what was to become the Canadian constitution. He saw to it that the federal or national government would be dominant over the provincial governments and that only Britain could amend the constitution. For his efforts he was rewarded with a knighthood and was chosen Canada's first prime minister under the new constitution, taking office on July 1, 1867.

Macdonald's government continued in power until his forced resignation in 1873. He was again elected prime minister in 1878, remaining in that position for the rest of his life. Macdonald's government dominated Canadian politics for a half century and set many goals for future generations of Canadians to achieve. He died on June 6, 1891, in Ottawa.

Machiavelli, Niccolò

In *The Prince,* Niccolò Machiavelli described the model for future European monarchs who would lay the groundwork for the development of the modern nation-state.

With the publication of *The Prince* in 1513, Niccolò Machiavelli (1469–1527) influenced the course of constitutional development in Europe for more than three centuries and shaped many national leaders from Napoleon to Mussolini.

Machiavelli was born in Florence, Italy, in Tuscany, in 1469 into an aristocratic if not well-to-do family. Little is known of his early life, but he evidently studied Greek and Roman classics. In 1498 he became chancellor and secretary to the second (lower) chancery of the Florentine republic. This position took him on a number of trips to other states, including Rome, and to France, during which he proved an astute observer of local political conditions.

Influenced by Rome's history of military greatness, Machiavelli helped organize a citizen militia in Florence in 1510. However, when another Tuscan town was sacked by a Spanish army, the Florentines were so frightened that they overthrew the republic and restored to power the former rulers, the Medici family. Machiavelli was fired, imprisoned, and tortured as a conspirator against the Medicis. Unable to obtain other employment, he turned to writing.

Between 1513 and 1514, after already beginning a treatise entitled *Discourses on Livy*, Machiavelli completed *The Prince,* the work for which he would become forever famous. A shrewd psychological analysis, *The Prince* set a new, if somewhat repellent, tone of reality for political science. Instead of focusing on the traditional moralistic theories, Machiavelli defined the new state in light of the cultural and scientific developments resulting from the Renaissance and linked it with the person of the ruler or monarch.

From the pages of *The Prince* emerged the model for future monarchs, emperors, and dictators—a ruthless and efficient autocrat. No dissolute tyrant, the new prince was, according to Machiavelli, the personification of the state and would preserve the state by whatever means while encouraging the goodwill of his people. The most immediate model for Machiavelli's prince was Cesare Borgia, who had carved out a state for himself in central Italy at the end of the fifteenth century and had died in 1507. But Machiavelli also reviewed the records of Romans with the political genius to seize power in a time of crisis with the consent of the citizens and who brought strength, stability, and order to the state, as Napoleon and Charles de Gaulle would later do in France.

The Florentine republic was restored in 1512, but Machiavelli had now become identified with the Medici regime and so was offered no new employment. He died in June 1527, leaving an impoverished family and a blueprint for absolutism.

Madison, James

Because of his great contributions to the development of the U.S. Constitution (1789), including the concept of checks and balances to thwart tyranny, James Madison (1751–1836) is known as the "Father of the Constitution."

Madison was born on March 16, 1751, on his family's plantation in Orange County, Virginia. He attended preparatory school, where he learned Latin and Greek, and was graduated from the College of New Jersey at Princeton in 1771. Like Thomas Jefferson, he became an admirer of the European Enlightenment movement and of the writers and philosophers John Locke, Isaac Newton, and Voltaire.

In 1776 Madison participated in the Virginia convention that supported independence from Great Britain and drafted a new constitution. A champion of religious freedom, Madison contributed to the document the phrase: "liberty of conscience for all." At the time this language was considered extremely liberal. He also worked hard for a national constitutional convention, which first met in Philadelphia in May 1787. Here he and Edmund Randolph developed the Virginia plan for the national government: a bicameral legislature with members of the lower house being elected from the states by population and members of the upper house being elected by members of the lower. Although compromise and changes were required, the Virginia plan became the foundation for the new Constitution.

Madison saw the need for a strong national government to protect the rights and interests of individual citizens and the nation as a whole. A weak government could not promote freedom, and Madison espoused a system of political checks and balances to moderate the competing interests of the country's factions and classes. In addition to helping draft the Constitution, he wrote convincingly to urge its adoption, particularly in essays 10 and 51 of *The Federalist* (1788), a collection of contemporary writings in support of the Constitution, which was ratified by all thirteen U.S. states and became effective in 1789.

A close friend of George Washington's, Madison drafted the first president's first inaugural address and helped him set up the new executive branch of the national government. In 1794 he married a widow, Dolly Payne Todd, who soon came to dominate the social scene in the nation's capital. Madison was also a close friend of Thomas Jefferson's and worked for his election as president in 1800, becoming Jefferson's secretary of state.

Finally elected president in 1808 and again, handily, in 1812, Madison got the opportunity to direct the government that he had significantly helped craft. With Jefferson he now led the new Democratic-Republican Party, later called the Democratic Party. A counterpoint to Alexander Hamilton's concept of the national government as primarily for the benefit of the wealthy and commercial interests, the new party's platform rested on the virtues of the average citizen, self-reliance, public education, and an agrarian economy.

An uncommonly popular president, Madison retired from the office in 1817 and died on June 28, 1836. His solution to the fears that a popular democracy would be unstable—a strong government with internal checks and balances and based on the consent of the people—has stood the test of time and has been adopted by many other countries.

Magistrate

In English law any person charged with the duties of government, from the sovereign on down, is a magistrate. In his writings the eighteenth-century legal commentator William Blackstone warned that assaulting or wounding a magistrate, an officer, or any other lawfully authorized person in the exercise of his duty was punishable by up to four years of penal servitude.

Today a magistrate—from the Latin *magistratus* (a magisterial rank or a person holding such an office)—is generally a lower-echelon public officer whose functions may be executive, legislative, or judicial. In the United States, magistrates are a class of inferior judicial officers, such as justices of the peace and police justices.

As referenced in constitutions, however, magistrates are generally judges, although for the most part not of the first rank.

Constitution of South Africa (1994), Chapter 7, The Judicial Authority and the Administration of Justice, Magistrates Commission, Section 109: "There shall be a magistrates commission established by law to ensure that the appointment, promotion, transfer, or dismissal of, or disciplinary steps against magistrates takes place without favor or prejudice, and that the applicable laws and administrative directives in this regard are applied uniformly and properly, and to ensure that no victimization or improper influencing of magistrates occurs."

Constitution of India (1950), Part VI, The States, Chapter VI, Subordinate Courts, Article 236: "Interpretation. In this chapter—(a) the expression 'district judge' includes [a] judge of a city civil court, additional district judge, joint district judge, assistant district judge, chief judge of a small cause court, chief presidency magistrate, additional chief presidency magistrate. . . . "

Magna Carta

The acknowledged foundation of constitutional liberty in the United Kingdom is Magna Carta, from the Latin phrase meaning great charter. Its history began in the early thirteenth century when the English king John and Pope Innocent III clashed over the choice of a new

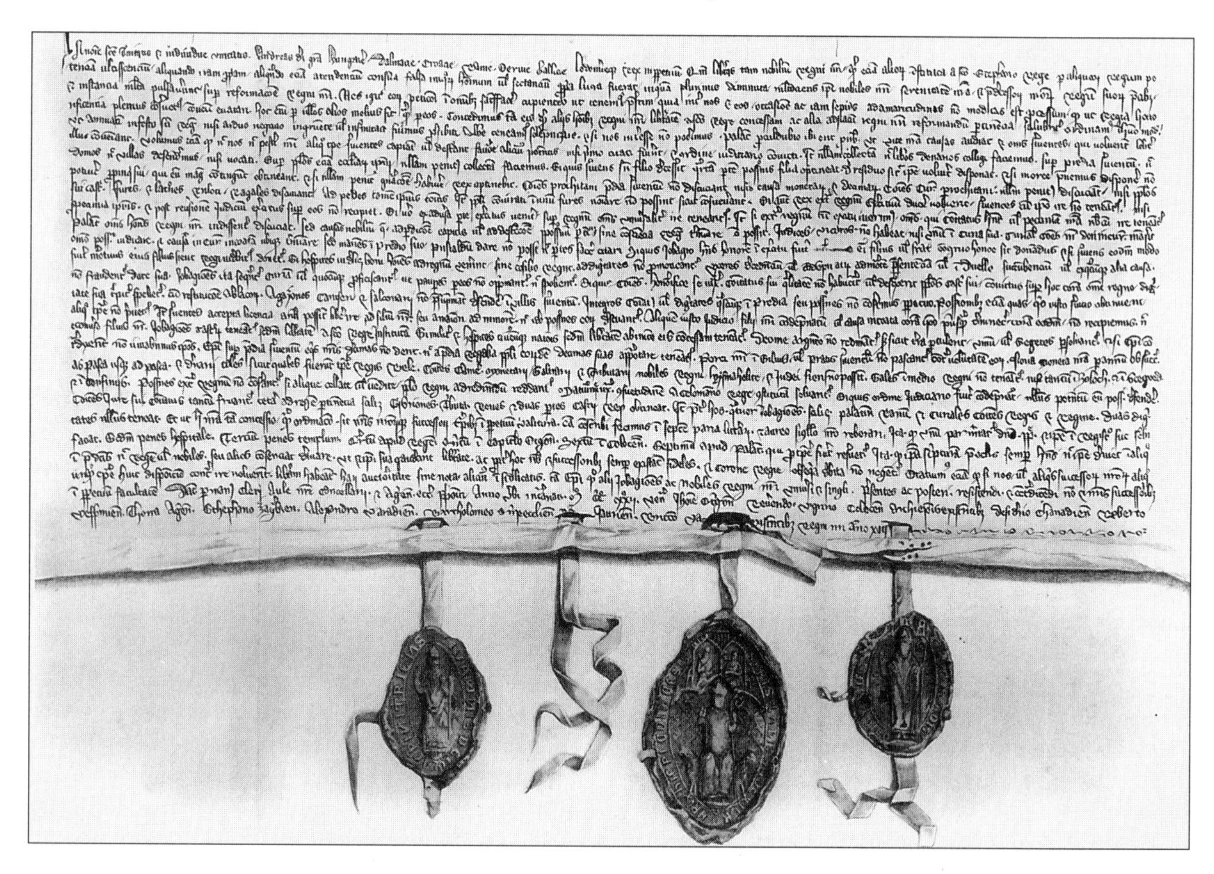

Although not as famous as the English Magna Carta of 1215, the Golden Bull was a similar document that Hungarian nobles forced their king to accept in 1222, curbing his power and enhancing their own, much as Magna Carta did.

archbishop of Canterbury. The pope won, and John was forced to pay an annual tribute to the Holy See in exchange for being allowed to remain king. This arrangement alienated John from his subjects, and when he attempted to mount a campaign to reclaim Normandy, the English clergy and the barons withheld their support, using it as a bargaining chip in 1213 to win concessions from him.

The basis for the barons' demands was a century-old charter of liberties granted on his coronation day, August 6, 1100, by Henry I, who reigned from 1100 to 1135. In 1214 the barons formed a confederacy and vowed war if the king refused to grant their demands. On June 15, 1215, at Runnymede, King John, abandoned by most of his supporters, placed his royal seal on the charter. Entitled The Great Charter of the Liberties of England and of the Liberties of the Forest, it contained a preamble and sixty-three clauses. In Magna Carta the king declared the church free and inviolate and granted all freemen certain rights, such as trial by a jury of peers and distribution of an intestate inheritance to one's nearest kin. Other rights and concessions were granted to nobles, widows, and the City of London.

King John soon began ignoring the document, which the pope had declared void. In the ensuing power struggle between the Crown and the barons, Magna Carta was reissued with a number of changes in 1217 by Henry III, who reigned from 1216 to 1272, and in 1225 he reissued it again. Between the reigns of Henry III and Henry IV, a span of nearly two hundred years, it was confirmed more than thirty times.

Magna Carta is the oldest known document of its kind, although a similar document, the Golden Bull of 1222, limited the power of the king of Hungary. A document of constitutional stature, Magna Carta provided guarantees to English subjects, albeit mostly for the nobility, and hastened the development of the royal courts at the expense of the local courts as well as the reduction in the power of the local sheriffs. Although much of the original document has been superseded and repealed, Magna Carta was an early harbinger of modern constitutionalism.

Constitution of the United Kingdom, Halsbury's Statutes of England and Wales (4th ed., 1985), Volume 10, Constitutional Law, Page 14, Magna Carta (25 EDW1) (as confirmed by Edward I, 1297), Preamble: "Edward by the grace of God King of England, Lord of Ireland, and Duke of Guyan, . . . [To all whom these present letters shall come, greetings.] We have seen the Great Charter of the Lord Henry sometimes King of England, our father of the liberties of England in these words: . . . "

Constitution of the United Kingdom, Halsbury's Statutes of England and Wales (4th ed., 1985), Volume 10, Constitutional Law, Page 15, Magna Carta (25 EDW1) (as confirmed by Edward I, 1297), Chapter 29, Imprisonment, etc contrary to law: "No freeman shall be taken or imprisoned, or be disseised [dispossessed] of his freehold, or liberties, or free customs, or be outlawed, or exiled, or any other wise destroyed; nor will we not pass upon him, nor [condemn him] but by lawful judgment of his peers, or by the law of the land. We will sell to no man, we will not deny or defer to any man either justice or right."

Mail. *See* Postal Service

Majlis

In the desert an Arab ruler may sit on his throne while holding a formal court, or *majlis*—an Arabic word that refers to an assembly or council, as well as a reception room. Now a term for a legislature in Islamic nations, it is spelled variously as *majelis, madijlis,* and *mezlis.*

The Majlis-e-Shoura-e-Islami (Islamic Consultative Assembly) is the name adopted for the Iranian national parliament; in 1906 Shah Muzza-far-ud-Din assented to the creation of a national council, the Majlis i Shora i Milli. In Pakistan the parliament is called the Majlis-e-Shoora, while in Egypt and Syria the people's assembly is known as the Majlis al-Sha'ab.

Constitution of Indonesia (1945), Chapter I, Form of the State and Sovereignty, Article 1(2): "Sovereignty shall be vested in the people and shall be exercised in full by the Majelis Permusyawaratan Rakyat."

Constitution of Pakistan (1973), Part III, The Federation of Pakistan, Chapter 2, The Majlis-e-Shoora (Parliament), Composition, Duration, and Meetings of Majlis-e-Shoora,

Article 50: "There shall be a Majlis-e Shoora (parliament) of Pakistan consisting of the president and two houses to be known respectively as the national assembly and the senate."

Majority Rule

An essential concept of democratic government is majority rule, under which officials are elected by the greatest number of citizens voting in an election and decisions are made and laws enacted by the greatest number of lawmakers present and voting. A rational and final way to settle disputes or decide issues, it is less disruptive than physical combat in determining which faction has the superior forces; it is also more pragmatic than requiring a consensus.

Like most basic constitutional concepts, majority rule is not an absolute principle. If it were, the majority of voters or legislators could destroy the minority. Many exceptions and safeguards for minority rights are built into constitutional governments. Some decisions, such as constitutional amendments, are often considered so important that supermajorities are required. On the other hand, some elections require that the winning candidate need receive only a plurality of the votes (more votes than for any other candidate but not necessarily more than half the total votes cast) rather than an absolute majority (more than half the total votes cast).

The concept of majority rule is found in almost all constitutions. If not explicitly stated, it can be recognized in the procedures described for the election of officials and the enactment of legislation.

Constitution of Thailand (1991), Chapter VI, The National Assembly, Part 4, Provisions Applicable to Both Houses, Section 142: " . . . if the house of representatives resolves to reaffirm the original [money] bill or the [money] bill considered by the joint committee by the vote of more than one-half the total members of the house of representatives, such bill shall be deemed approved. . . . "

Constitution of Indonesia (1945), Chapter III, The Executive Power, Article 6(2): "The president and the vice president shall be elected by the Majelis Permusyawaratan Rakyat by a majority vote."

Mandate

In ancient Rome an emperor's order issued to officials on his own initiative was called a *mandatum*. These orders, or *mandata*, generally directed to provincial governors, related primarily to military and administrative affairs, not to law. In addition, a *mandatum* was a form of contract by which one person undertook gratuitously to do some service requested by another.

In Anglo-American law a mandate is a contract by which a lawful business is committed to the management of another. Under the League of Nations (1920–46) mandates were used to give a member country the authority to govern and develop a particular territory; Palestine, for example, was a British mandate after World War I.

A mandate as expressed in constitutions now generally means a delegation of authority, especially from the voters to their representatives. The term may also refer to popular support for elected officials' policies or to a general authorization to them to carry out the will of the majority of the voters who put them in office.

Constitution of Israel, Declaration of Independence (1948): "This right [to Israel's national rebirth in its own country] was recognized in the Balfour Declaration of 2nd, November, 1917, and reaffirmed in the mandate of the League of Nations which, in particular, gave international sanction to the historic connection between the Jewish people and Eretz-Israel and to the right of the Jewish people to rebuild its national home."

Constitution of Ethiopia (1995), Chapter Six, The Federal Councils, Part One, The Council of Peoples' Representatives, Article 54, Members of the Council of Peoples' Representatives: " . . . 7. A council member may lose his mandate of representation upon loss of confidence by the electorate."

Mandela, Rolihlahla Nelson

In South Africa's first truly democratic elections, held in May 1994, Nelson Mandela (b. 1918) was elected president under a new constitution, which he almost single-handedly brought to fruition after many years of imprisonment by the apartheid government in his country.

Mandela, born on July 18, 1918, grew up in Qunu, in the Transkei district of Umtata. After his father's death in 1927, he moved to Great Place, Mqekezweni, attending school there and later in the Mqanduli and Ciskei districts. In 1939 he enrolled at Fort Hare University College, only to be expelled in 1940 for organizing a boycott of the student council.

Returning to his studies in Johannesburg, Mandela joined the African National Congress (ANC) and helped found the ANC Youth League. After receiving a suspended sentence for breaking segregation laws, he began a legal practice with Oliver Tambo, who would later become president of the ANC. In 1961 Mandela participated in an ANC mission to force by acts of sabotage a change in the South African policy of racial segregation called apartheid. Although some of his colleagues were arrested, he escaped and during the following year promoted his cause with black and white political leaders outside South Africa.

Mandela was finally arrested, however, and in November 1962 was sentenced to five years' imprisonment. In 1963 and 1964 he stood trial on additional charges, declaring in court, "I am prepared to die for what I believe." Sentenced instead to life imprisonment, he was not released until February 11, 1992, nine days after the ban against the ANC in South Africa was officially lifted. Shortly after his release he became deputy president and then president of the ANC. During his term he led a vigorous campaign to end once and for all the white minority rule in his country and to create a transitional constitution for all the people.

Nelson Mandela, after surviving thirty years as a political prisoner, was instrumental in fashioning the 1994 and 1996 constitutions of South Africa.

Clearly the dominant voice in the ANC and the country, Mandela worked through the Convention for a Democratic South Africa (Codesa), which included leaders of the ANC, the Inkatha Freedom Party, headed by Chief Mangosuthu Buthelezi, and the party still in power, the National Party, to draft a new constitution. Although the ANC wanted a document that would give power to a strong central government, Mandela, supported by the Inkatha Party, agreed to accept a federal form of government. This compromise led to the final acceptance of a new constitution, which was adopted on January 25, 1994, and became effective on April 27, 1994.

On May 24, 1994, Mandela committed the government to an ambitious reconstruction and development program to restore economic vitality to a nation-state that had finally—peacefully—achieved a true democratic political system. In a speech given to the National Press Club in Washington, D.C., on October 7, 1994, President Mandela affirmed: "Our experience of repression and of persecution has only strengthened the commitment to the rights of freedom of information, freedom of expression, and freedom of the press, not merely as constitutional rights, but as a daily reality."

Marshall, John

As part of his legacy to American constitutional law, John Marshall (1755–1835), chief justice of the United States for nearly a quarter century, articulated the concept of judicial review and confirmed the power of Congress in matters of foreign and interstate commerce and in the full exercise of its delegated powers.

The eldest of fifteen children, Marshall was born on September 24, 1755, in Fauquier County, Virginia. His

In his opinion in the 1803 case of *Marbury v. Madison*, U.S. Chief Justice John Marshall enunciated the concept of judicial review, which allows courts to invalidate unconstitutional acts.

family was not wealthy, so his education was limited. Although he did not attend college, he was able to sit in on law lectures for at least one month and was admitted to the Fauquier County bar in 1780. He fought in the American Revolution, during which he was promoted to the rank of captain. In 1783 Marshall married the daughter of the state treasurer of Virginia.

An able lawyer, Marshall was elected to the Virginia legislature in 1782 and was a member of the convention in Virginia that ratified the U.S. Constitution (1789). A representative to the U.S. Congress in 1799, in 1800 he was appointed secretary of state by President John Adams, after declining nominations to other positions. In January 1801 he was confirmed as the fourth chief justice of the U.S. Supreme Court.

Marshall's first case, after a fourteen-month furlough occasioned by Congress's postponement of the Court's sessions, was *Marbury v. Madison*. Marbury, along with others, was a last-minute appointee of President Adams to a federal judicial position. When Adams's Federalist Party was voted out of power, Thomas Jefferson, the new president in 1801, canceled the appointments. Marbury sought the Court's help under Section 13 of the Judiciary Act of 1789 to force James Madison, Jefferson's secretary of state, to restore his appointment. Presenting the opinion of a unanimous Court, Marshall held that although Marbury and his colleagues were entitled to their positions, Congress had unconstitutionally tried to confer on the Court the power to decide the matter. He ruled that Congress could not grant the judicial branch any more authority than was expressly set forth in the written Constitution.

Marshall's opinion confirmed the now widely adopted constitutional concept of judicial review, by which the courts serve as interpreters and protectors of the terms of the Constitution. In its purest form judicial review means that in the regular course of business courts of law can declare laws or actions by other branches of the government unconstitutional, with the Supreme Court having the final say in such matters. Other countries have adopted variations of this concept. In some, special courts in the judicial system or tribunals and councils outside the court system are given the role of interpreting or screening ordinary laws for constitutionality, although, as with many constitutional provisions, the role may not always be fully realized. In countries with unwritten constitutions, the supremacy of the legislature negates true judicial review powers in the courts.

Marshall served as chief justice until his death on July 6, 1835, in Philadelphia, after a stagecoach accident.

Martial law

Mars, the Roman god of war, lends his name as the base of the Latin word *martialis* (sacred to Mars). In common usage martial refers to the military or things pertaining to the military.

A form of military government instituted primarily when the security of a nation-state or region is seriously threatened, martial law has also been used unconstitutionally to maintain power. During a period of martial law, which is generally enforced by the military rather than by regular police, ordinary law is suspended, many constitutionally guaranteed rights may be suspended, and the dispensation of justice may depend on the character of the military officer in charge.

A number of constitutions specifically provide for the potential imposition of martial law or for a state of emergency, which may result in a similar suspension of regular law enforcement. Language may expressly indicate the conditions under which martial law can be invoked, how it will affect constitutional rights, and how long it can continue.

Constitution of Turkey (1982), Part Three, Fundamental Organs of the Republic, Chapter Two, Executive, III, Procedure Governing Emergency Rule, B, Martial Law, Mobilization, and State of War, Article 122: "During the period of martial law, the council of ministers meeting under the chairmanship of the president of the republic may issue decrees having the force of law on matters necessitated by the state of martial law."

Constitution of Peru (1994), Section IV, Concerning the Structure of Government, Chapter VII, Concerning the State of Emergency, Article 137: "Under [a state of emergency], constitutional rights relating to personal freedom and security, the inviolability of the home, and the freedom to assemble and move about within the territory . . . may be curtailed or suspended."

Member

A person who has been formally elected to take part in a legislature such as a parliament or congress is a member of that body. A member may also be known as a representative, deputy, delegate, or senator. In the United Kingdom the formal designation is member of Parliament (often abbreviated M.P.), and in the United States the official designation is member of Congress. For some legislative bodies, alternates as well as members are elected.

Constitutions often prescribe in detail the qualifications of legislators, duration of terms, privileges and immunities, functions, and conditions for continuing to hold office. Members of legislatures are often granted immunity from arrest for some violations of law, unless they are apprehended in *flagrante delicto* (the act of committing the crime), and for their remarks and actions during debates in legislative sessions.

In constitutions the word *member* may also refer to a member of a political party or government bodies such as boards, commissions, councils, and courts.

Constitution of New Zealand, Electoral Act (1956), Part II, The House of Representatives, Section 13: "Members of Parliament—Members of the House of Representatives shall be known and designated by the title of 'members of Parliament,' and in this act and all other acts the term 'member of Parliament' shall be construed accordingly."

Constitution of Thailand (1991), Chapter VI, The National Assembly, Part 3, The House of Representatives, Section 105: "A person having the following qualification has the right to be a candidate in an election: . . . (3) being a member either of a political party sending members to stand for election under section 106 or the political party under section 15. . . . "

Military. *See* Armed Forces

Militia

In some contexts constitutions use the term *militia*—derived from the Latin *militia* (military service or warfare)—for the concept of general control over a country's military and naval forces. However, the term may refer more specifically to the body of citizens in a nation-state enrolled for discipline as a military force but not actually engaged in military service. In this sense a militia is a citizen army rather than mercenaries or professional soldiers.

Article 1, Section 8, of the U.S. Constitution (1789) grants to Congress the power to call forth the militia to execute the laws of the Union, suppress insurrection, and repel invasions. Article 2, Section 2, however, designates the president as the commander in chief of the army and navy and of the militia of the several states when they are actually called into service. In essay 29 of *The Federalist* (1788), Alexander Hamilton argues that the power of the national government to command the militia of the states in times of emergency should alleviate the need for

An honor guard of state militiamen escorted U.S. President William Howard Taft on an official visit to the state of Ohio in 1909. These militia members, except when called to national service, are under the command of the state governor.

standing armies, which he considered dangerous to liberty.

To understand whether the term *militia* in a constitution refers to the general military or the militarily trained citizenry, the context and history of a particular constitutional document must be carefully examined.

Constitution of Canada, Constitution Act (1867), VI, Distribution of Legislative Powers, Powers of the Parliament, Section 91: " . . . (notwithstanding anything in this act) the exclusive legislative authority of the parliament of Canada extends to . . . 7. Militia, military and naval service, and defense."

Constitution of Argentina (1853), Second Part, Authorities of the Nation, Title I, Federal Government, First Section, The Legislative Power, Chapter IV, Powers of Congress, Article 67: "The congress shall have power: . . . 24. To authorize the summoning of the militia in all the provinces or part of them, whenever the execution of the laws of the nation may so require, and when necessary to suppress insurrection or repel invasion. To provide for the organization, equipment, and discipline of said militia, and the administration and government of such part of them as are employed in the service of the nation, leaving to the provinces the appointment of their respective chiefs and officers, and the duty of establishing in their respective militia the discipline prescribed by congress."

Constitution of the United States of America (1789), Amendment II (1791): "A well regulated Militia, being necessary to the security of a free State, the right of the people to keep and bear Arms, shall not be infringed."

Mill, John Stuart

A nineteenth-century champion of individual liberty and freedom, John Stuart Mill (1806–73), through his works *On Liberty* (1859), *Considerations on Representative Government* (1861), and "Utilitarianism" (1863), has been influential beyond the borders of his native Great Britain.

Born in London on May 20, 1806, Mill began his

education at an early age under the tutelage of his father, who taught him Greek at age three, Latin and arithmetic at eight, logic at twelve, and political economy at thirteen. Young Mill later began law studies but left these in 1823 to work for India House, headquarters of the British East India Company. The company was abolished in 1858, leaving Mill free to pursue his philosophy and politics.

Building on the political philosophy of his father and his father's friend, Jeremy Bentham, the English jurist and philosopher, Mill's writings underscored the liberal trend developing in Britain, which found its way into the constitutions of other countries that embraced the concepts of individual freedom and liberty exemplified by the U.S. Constitution (1789). He argued for personal liberty and freedom from government domination of and interference in an individual's pursuit of happiness. A major work, *On Liberty*, first published in 1859, is a defense of the individual's right to think and act independently. In it Mill argues cogently against both the accretion of power in government authorities and social tyranny, while seeking to improve conditions for working people and promoting suffrage for women.

John Stuart Mill's arguments in support of personal liberty and freedom from government interference have significantly influenced constitutional theory in many countries.

Concerning minority views Mill said: "If all mankind minus one, were of one opinion, and only one person were of the contrary opinion, mankind would be no more justified in silencing that one person, than he, if he had the power, would be justified in silencing mankind." Of freedom he said: "The only freedom which deserves the name is that of pursuing our own good in our own way, so long as we do not attempt to deprive others of theirs or impede their efforts to obtain it."

The Canadian Constitution Act of 1982 echoes Mill's views on limiting government interference in individual liberty and freedom. That document states: "1. The Canadian Charter of Rights and Freedoms [La Charte canadienne des droits et libertés] guarantees the rights and freedoms set out in it subject only to such limits prescribed by law as can be justified in a free and democratic society."

In 1865 Mill was elected to Parliament from Westminster and served a three-year term but was not reelected. He later moved to France, where he died in Avignon on May 7, 1873.

Minister

In Europe ministers—from the Latin word *minister* (servant or assistant)—historically were high officials appointed by a monarch to provide advice on the affairs of state and to carry out royal decisions through the government departments they headed. Absolute monarchs made all the important and final decisions; consequently, they alone were responsible for bad decisions.

With the evolution of constitutional monarchies, ministers began to be selected from the elected members of the parliament. Collectively the group of ministers was called the council of ministers, or cabinet; individually they became responsible for the policy decisions of the government or the Crown, as monarchs were reduced to figureheads representing the authority and stability of the nation-state. In the Netherlands amendments to the constitution in 1840 required ministers to be responsible for their actions; because all acts and royal decrees had to be signed by the monarch and countersigned by the relevant minister, the ministers could be held accountable. In presidential-style parliamentary systems, such as in Germany, the relationship between the president, as head of state, and the ministers is similar to that of a monarch.

In the United Kingdom cabinet ministers can and generally do dominate Parliament, from which they are chosen; moreover, because they are members of Parliament, they generally handle themselves well when questioned by their colleagues about the actions of their departments or ministries. French ministers, on the other hand, are barred from also being members of the parliament and may be chosen from outside the government. This situation is similar to that in the United States, where cabinet members, generally called secretaries, are selected by the president and confirmed by the Senate. Cabinet members may not be members of Congress while holding the position of secretary. This distinction is the result of a strict application of the constitutional principles of the separation of powers and of checks and balances.

The ministerial system in the United Kingdom is superimposed on a career civil service system, so that each department or ministry, in addition to having a minister as its head, also has a chief civil servant who continues in office regardless of which political party is in power. Department heads are called ministers of the Crown, with ministers of state ranking just below them.

Constitutions may spell out the qualifications and duties of ministers or rely on tradition and convention to determine the selection process and the role of ministers. The chief minister, who is generally the head of government, may be called the prime minister, chancellor, or premier.

Constitution of Denmark (1953), Part III, Section 13: "The king shall not be answerable for his actions; his person shall be sacrosanct. The ministers shall be responsible for the conduct of the government; their responsibility shall be determined by statute."

Constitution of Austria (1920), Chapter III, Federal Execution, A, Administration, 1, The Federal President, Article 67: "(1) Save as otherwise provided by the constitution, all official acts of the federal president shall be based on the recommendation by the federal government or the federal minister authorized by it. The law provides to what extent the federal government or the competent federal minister is herein dependent on recommendation from other quarters. (2) Save as otherwise provided by the constitution, all official acts of the federal president require for their validation the countersignature of the federal chancellor or the competent federal minister."

Ministry

The Latin word *ministerium* (service or occupation) has become the English *ministry,* the French *ministère,* and the German *Ministerium.* When used in constitutions of countries with parliamentary systems of government, the term generally refers to a department of government. In such countries the ministry of economic affairs, for example, would be the government department headed by a minister (a member of the cabinet) who is charged with the supervision of economic activities. He or she would act under the general supervision of the prime minister and would be subject to questioning by members of the parliament on the department's conduct.

Sometimes *ministry* may be used in a broader sense to include all the members of a government who came in with and will go out with the prime minister; "the second Gladstone ministry," for example, refers to the

The foreign minister representing India, Sadar Swaran Singh, speaks in 1971 at a meeting of the United Nations Security Council regarding the India-Pakistan War.

second government administration under the direction of the nineteenth-century British prime minister William Gladstone.

In the United Kingdom and in some other countries, the term designates the building in which the business of a specific ministry is conducted.

Constitution of Austria (1920), Chapter III, Federal Execution, A, Administration, 2, The Federal Government, Article 77: "(1) The federal ministries and the authorities subordinate to them shall perform the business of the federal administration. (2) The number of federal ministries, their competence, and their internal organization will be prescribed by federal law."

Constitution of Bangladesh, Part V, The Legislature, Chapter I, Parliament, Article 73A (added in 1975): "(1) Every minister shall have the right to speak in, and otherwise to take part in the proceedings of, parliament, but shall not be entitled to vote or to speak on any matter not related to his ministry unless he is a member of parliament also."

Ethnic, cultural, and linguistic minorities in many countries, such as the indigenous Nunivak people of Canada, are often given special protection in national constitutions.

Minorities

In constitutions minorities generally denote definable groups within the nation-state that contain fewer members than a larger group or groups called majorities. The actual number of people in a minority is not always as significant as the historical exclusion of members of that group from institutions of power or control, as in the case of women. Minority status is often based on factors such as religion, ethnicity, race, and language. Although a small ruling class or an undemocratically aristocratic class may qualify technically as a minority in a nation-state, only groups that are politically, socially, or economically disadvantaged are generally included in the constitutional definition of minorities.

Although based generally on the principle of majority rule, constitutions often contain provisions for developing the economic and political status of certain minorities and specifically protecting their rights. The constitution of India, for example, provides for a parliamentary system of government that is based on majority rule and was developed in England, but India has a long history of entrenched classes or castes that receive special consideration in its constitution. In contrast, during the formulation of the U.S. Constitution (1789), James Madison considered the Senate, the upper house of Congress, a protection for a minority—in this case, the wealthier citizens or property-owning classes—from the temporary errors and delusions of the more common people that might be expressed in the lower, more representative house.

Constitution of Pakistan (1973), Part II, Fundamental Rights and Principles of Policy, Chapter 2, Principles of Policy, Article 36: "The state shall safeguard the legitimate rights and interests of minorities, including their due representation in the federal and provincial services."

Constitution of Taiwan (1947), Chapter III, The National Assembly, Article 26: "The national assembly shall be composed of the following delegates: . . . 4. The number of delegates to be elected by various racial groups in frontier regions shall be prescribed by law. . . . "

Constitution of Finland, Parliament Act (1928), Chapter 4, Preparation of Matters, Section 52a (added in 1991): "The Sámi [Lapplanders] shall be heard in a matter of special consequence to them, as further provided in the procedure of parliament."

Monarch. *See* King; Monarchy

Monarchy

The modern nation-state is the result of the transformation of the European form of government known as a monarchy, which developed between the sixteenth and eighteenth centuries. The concept of nationalism so prevalent in the twentieth century is derived from the ideal of a relatively large and distinct territory with a centralized form of government like a monarchy—which comes from the Greek word *μοναρχία* (rule by one person).

Plato devotes an early section of *The Laws* to a comparison of monarchy and democracy, calling the two forms of government the "two mother constitutions." Aristotle, in *The Politics*, says that the rule of a household is a monarchy because every house has a single head but that constitutional rule is a government by freemen and equals.

A monarchy is a government in which all power is vested in a single individual, who may be called a king or queen, an emperor or empress, a sovereign, a monarch, or, in some Arabic countries, an emir or amir. The monarch and his or her government, especially in Europe and some former dominions of the United Kingdom, may also be referred to as the Crown. In a monarchy, the transfer of power is based on heredity. On the monarch's death, power is usually transferred to a close blood

A crown, such as this crown of Hungary, is the historical symbol of a monarch's authority to rule a nation or an empire.

relation, generally the oldest son or a daughter if there is no son. The procedure for the succession of power in a monarchy may be spelled out in constitutional acts of succession. In some cases, however, a small group may be designated to elect a successor from a restricted number of candidates—for example, only persons of royal lineage.

Dictatorships, autocracies, and totalitarian governments resemble historical absolute monarchies because they concentrate power in the hands of a single person, although a monarchy may be distinguished on the basis of its "legitimate" character—that is, the monarch's subjects accept the historical or so-called legitimate right of the monarch to rule them.

In Plato's and Aristotle's time, a true monarchy and a true democracy were incompatible forms of government, although certain elements of the two could be mixed. Today, however, many of the world's most democratic governments are constitutional monarchies, including emirates such as Kuwait—in which the monarch may be just as much a subject of the constitution, whether written or unwritten, as are the citizens.

Constitution of Norway (1814), A, Form of Government and Religion, Article 1: "The Kingdom of Norway is a free, independent, indivisible, and inalienable realm. Its form of government is a limited and hereditary monarchy."

Constitution of Kuwait (1962), Part I, The State and the System of Government, Article 4: "Kuwait is a hereditary amirate, the succession to which shall be in the hands of the descendants of the late Mubarak al-Subah. The heir apparent shall be designated within one year, at the latest, from the date of accession of the amir."

Constitution of Cambodia (1993), Chapter 2, The King, Article 10: "Cambodia's monarchy is of elected origin. The king shall not have the power to appoint his successor to the throne."

Money Bill

A money bill—also called a revenue, finance, or appropriations bill—is a legislative proposal that involves raising taxes or revenue or appropriating or expending public funds. Many constitutions provide special procedures for the introduction and enactment of money bills.

The U.S. Constitution (1789) expressly requires that bills raising revenues originate in the House of Representatives, although the Senate may propose or concur in amendments. Alexander Hamilton, in essay 66 of *The Federalist* (1788), notes: "The exclusive privilege of originating money bills will belong to the House of Representatives." By tradition, appropriations bills, like revenue or taxation bills, originate there as well.

The French constitution of 1958 requires finance bills to be submitted first in the lower house, or national assembly, and provides that the parliament must pass finance bills under conditions stipulated in an organic act.

Constitution of Malaysia (1963), Part IV, The Federation, Chapter 5, Legislative Procedure, Article 68, Assent to Bills Passed by the House of Representatives Only: "(1) Where a money bill is passed by the house of representatives and, having been sent to the senate at least one month before the end of the session, is not passed by the senate without amendment within a month, it shall be presented to the Yang di-Pertuan Agong [head of state] for his assent unless the house of representatives otherwise directs."

Constitution of Nepal (1990), Part 9, Legislative Procedure, Article 68: "(3) A finance bill denotes any or all matters concerning the following subjects: (a) imposition, collection, abolition, remission, alteration, or regulation of taxation; (b) any matter which relates to the preservation of the consolidated fund or any other government fund, the deposit of amounts in such funds, the appropriation or expenditure from these funds, or the reduction, increment, or cancellation of any such expenses; (c) matters relating to amendment in the laws concerning the raising of loans or to guarantees by his majesty's government or any matter in which his majesty's government has or is to take liability; (d) matters relating to the arrangement for keeping in deposit revenues, loan returns, and grants and their investments or audit of the accounts of his majesty's government; or (e) matters directly related to the above subjects. (4) In the case of disputes regarding the money bill, the decision made by the speaker shall be final."

Montesquieu, Charles-Louis de Secondat, Baron de La Brède et de

Through his writings Charles-Louis de Secondat, Baron de La Brède et de Montesquieu (1689–1755)—known simply as Montesquieu—has had a profound impact on constitutionalism and the constitutions of nation-states throughout the world, particularly the seminal 1789 Constitution of the United States.

Charles de Secondat was born near Bordeaux on January 18, 1689, to an aristocratic family. His early life was spent in the village of La Brède, but in 1700 he began a progressive education at Oratorian Collège de Juilly at Meaux. Once back in Bordeaux, he studied law and was admitted to practice before the Bordeaux *parlement* (court) in 1708. He inherited the presidency of the regional court, which he later sold, and the barony of Montesquieu.

In his early work *The Persian Letters* (1721), published anonymously, Montesquieu irreverently criticized European—that is, French—civilization but was nevertheless granted admission to the French Academy. Having traveled extensively in Europe, he was admitted also to the Royal Academy in England and in 1734 published an analysis of the grandeur and decline of Rome.

In 1748 Montesquieu published his most important and influential work, *The Spirit of the Laws,* which advanced the principles of constitutional separation of powers. In it he tried to show that the essence of law is in the necessary relationships that derive from the nature of things. By definition, because people, time, and places are different, diversity in the law is unavoidable and even reasonable. Having lived during the absolutist age of Louis XIV, he argued that when the three basic powers of government—the executive, legislative, and judicial—were combined, tyranny was possible. Autonomous judicial bodies, such as the *parlements,* were examples of independent powers that could frustrate despotic tendencies in an absolute monarchy and protect liberties.

Montesquieu's concepts laid the foundation for demands by other French intellectuals for an expanded political role after the death of Louis XV—among them the so-called *philosophes,* such as Jean-Jacques Rousseau and Voltaire, whose works led to the French Revolution of 1789. Montesquieu also influenced the adoption of popular sovereignty as a basis for constitutionalism. He died on February 10, 1755, during a trip to Paris.

In *The Spirit of the Laws,* Montesquieu describes the separation of the powers of government, an important and influential concept of modern constitutionalism.

Since his death, Montesquieu has continued to affect the constitutions of the world. In *The Spirit of the Laws* he declared: "A constitution can be such that no one will be constrained to do the things the law does not oblige him to do or be kept from doing the things the law permits him to do." Montesquieu's language is clearly echoed in the 1993 constitution of the Czech Republic, Article 2(4): "Every citizen may do whatever is not forbidden by law, and no one may be forced to do what the law does not enjoin."

Motion

A formal method by which a lawmaker submits a proposal for consideration and action, the term *motion*—derived from the Latin words *moveo* (to move) and *motus* (movement or motion)—appears in an entry in the Nottingham Record of 1605: "The mocion [variant spelling of motion] of 20 to be added to the Councell shalbe assented vnto."

The procedural rules of order for parliamentary-type sessions or meetings include numerous types of motions—from a move to adjourn to a suggestion to lay a matter "on the table"—as well as the type of action each motion requires. The British Parliament and the parliaments and congresses of other countries use the procedure to initiate actions such as votes on legislative measures, votes on the conduct of their own members, motions to censure, and motions on the conduct of other members of the government (motions of no confidence or motions to impeach high officials).

In legal practice a motion is a party's application to a court to obtain a ruling that the party seeks to resolve or advance his or her cause before the court, such as a motion to dismiss a pending case or to suppress evidence illegally obtained.

Constitution of Nepal (1990), Part 8, Legislature, Article 59, Vote of Confidence: "(2) In case one-fourth of the total members in the house of representatives so desire, they may move in writing a no confidence motion against the prime minister. But such no confidence motion shall not be moved more than once in the same session."

Constitution of Finland, Parliament Act (1928), Chapter 3, Initiation of Matters in Parliament, Section 31: "Parliament shall have the right to consider an initiative that has been duly submitted by a representative. Such an initiative may be: ... 2) A budget motion, containing a proposal for an appropriation or other decision to be included in the budget ... 3) a petitionary motion, containing a proposal for parliament to petition the government to undertake measures on a matter within its competence."

Municipality

Ancient Rome was a city-state similar to the Greek prototype of the city-state. During Roman hegemony there were Roman-, Italian-, and Greek-type cities throughout the empire, as well as some divergent types. The Roman colonies, with cities modeled after Rome, enjoyed full Roman civic rights. *Municipia* (self-governing towns), however, were Italian cities whose inhabitants, not being Roman citizens, enjoyed the forms of Italian, as opposed to Roman, civic life; they received from Rome the "Italian right" as a special favor that allowed them to avoid direct taxation. In French and Spanish the word for *municipality* is similar to the English word, but in German the concept requires two words—*Stadt* (town) and *Selbstverwaltung* (self-government or autonomy).

A municipality may be a city, a town, a borough, or an incorporated village, although the technical definition is a subordinate public entity authorized by a higher sovereignty or political subdivision to carry on government activities. A number of constitutions contain provisions regarding the status and authority of municipalities in the nation-state.

Constitution of Denmark (1953), Part VIII, Article 82: "The right of municipalities to manage their own affairs independently under the supervision of the state shall be laid down by statute."

Constitution of Brazil (1988), Title III, The Organization of the State, Chapter IV, The Municipalities, Article 29: "Municipalities shall be governed by organic law, voted in two readings, with a minimum interval of ten days between the readings, and approved by two-thirds of the members of the municipal chamber, which shall promulgate it, observing the principles established in this constitution, in the constitution of the respective state, and the following precepts."

Napoleon Bonaparte

Through his liberalizing influence, introduction of the Napoleonic code, and charismatic personality, Napoleon (1769–1821) significantly affected political, constitutional, and legal development throughout the world.

Napoleon Buonaparte (the spelling was later changed) was born on August 15, 1769, in Ajaccio, Corsica, the fourth of eleven children. That same year France annexed Corsica, and Napoleon's father, a descendant of Corsican nobility, was granted similar noble status by France. The young Buonaparte was educated at a boys school in Ajaccio and later at the military college of Brienne in Burgundy, where he was called the "little corporal" because of his small size. In 1784 he was appointed to the royal military school of Paris and afterward became a second lieutenant in the French army.

After the French Revolution in 1789 Napoleon spent some time in Corsica helping implement the consequent social and political changes. A power struggle with a local leader, however, forced him to flee to the mainland. In 1793 he became a captain in command of a republican army unit, winning national recognition at the siege of Toulon. Because of the political leanings of some of his acquaintances, he was imprisoned falsely for several days but was released in time to help defend the new government, called the Directory, against a royalist attack in 1795.

Made commander of the army, Napoleon conquered Egypt and reorganized its government. After several military setbacks in 1799 he returned to Paris. Finding popular discontent with the Directory, Napoleon overthrew the government in November 1799. Under a new French constitution, he became first consul, with virtually dictatorial powers. In 1804 he created the French Empire and set out on a series of victorious military campaigns in Europe. In the wake of his conquests Napoleon changed and liberalized governments.

Spain's first constitution in 1812 was based on the French revolutionary principles introduced there by Napoleon. In 1814 Norway's constitution was made possible by his defeat and the defeat of his ally, Denmark, whose political grip on the country was thus broken. As far away as Haiti, the liberalizing republican force on the constitutional process made itself felt. Simón Bolívar attended Napoleon's self-coronation as emperor of the French on December 2, 1804, and was inspired to free South America from the Spanish, resulting in the constitutions of Venezuela, Ecuador, Colombia, Peru, and Bolivia.

In addition, the Code Napoleon of 1804, officially called the Code civil des français, written at Napoleon's direction and consisting of 2,287 articles, gave to the countries of Europe in which it was introduced a unified legal system based on Roman law. This process also had an impact on European constitutional and

Napoleon Bonaparte's personality, conquests, and code of laws all led to important changes in the constitutional development of many countries. Despite his liberal influence on other nations, he proclaimed himself emperor of France in 1804.

legal development—for example, the Italian version of the code remains the foundation of Italian law today.

After his defeat at the hands of the duke of Wellington at Waterloo in 1815, Napoleon was exiled to the island of St. Helena, where he died on May 5, 1821.

Nation

A nation is an aggregate of persons closely associated by common descent, language, and history, usually occupying a definite territory as a separate political state. Derived from the Latin word *natio* (race or nation), the term was recorded in use in England by the beginning of the fourteenth century.

Many factors account for the formation and development of nations and for their dissolution, as the recent examples of the breakup of Yugoslavia and Czechoslovakia show. In *The Idea of Nationalism* (1944), Hans Kohn, professor of history at the City College of New York, uses the term *nation-state* simply to emphasize the nature of the totality of the state government apparatus within the territorial definition of a nation or country and distinguishes between the nation as a state and other states such as city-states and semisovereign constituent states of federal nation-states. Arab countries, on the other hand, may use the name Arab Nation to mean a coalition of Arab nation-states.

Nationalism is the movement to become a nation-state, as well as a theory supporting nation-states as the basis of government throughout the world. It began generally in Europe as *Volkgeist*, a German word for the cohesive forces of a common literature, folklore, language, and history. The idea of nationalism emanates from the human urge to belong to a social and political group larger than the family and community but smaller than all of humankind; as history documents, it can also create an "us against them" mentality.

Nearly two hundred sovereign and theoretically independent nation-states now coexist on the globe, including giants in area and population, such as the People's Republic of China, and the minuscule, such as the island Republic of Palau in the northern Pacific Ocean. Although some territorial jurisdictions are not exactly nation-states—the Vatican is under the control of the head of the Roman Catholic Church, and Tibet has been administratively absorbed into the People's Republic of China—almost all the people on Earth live in a nation-state or under the control of a nation-state.

Constitution of Argentina (1853), First Part, Declarations, Rights, and Guarantees, Article 1: "The Argentine nation adopts for its government the federal, republican, representative form, as established by the present constitution."

Constitution of Syria (1973), Preamble: "This constitution is based upon the following main principles: . . . 2—All achievements which have been, or may be, attained by any Arab country in the present state of dismemberment are bound to be inadequate and incapable of reaching their full dimensions. . . . Likewise, any danger from colonialism and Zionism menacing any Arab country is a danger that threatens the Arab Nation [all Arab countries] as a whole."

Constitution of Poland, Constitution Act (1992), Chapter 3, The President of the Republic of Poland, Article 30: "The president shall succeed to office upon making the following oath in the presence of the national assembly: 'Assuming, by the will of the nation, the office of the president of the republic of Poland, I do solemnly swear to be faithful to the provisions of the constitution; I pledge that I will steadfastly guard the dignity of the nation, the independence and security of the state, and also that the good of the homeland and the prosperity of its citizens shall forever remain my supreme obligation.'"

Nation-State. *See* Nation

National. *See* Citizenship; Nationality

National Anthem. *See* Symbol

Nationalism. *See* Nation

Nationality

Isocrates, an Athenian orator of the fourth century B.C., defined being Greek as sharing the Greek culture but not necessarily the Greek blood. As the Roman Empire began to expand beginning in the first century B.C., it was dominated by Roman citizens; the peoples they conquered were allowed to retain their culture but not their nationality, so that they owed allegiance to Rome.

A relatively new term in English usage, *nationality,* from the French *nationalité,* defines the relationship of belonging to a nation-state. Possessing nationality has become the criterion for claiming certain civil and political rights that flow from owing allegiance to a particular nation, such as voting, and carries reciprocal duties, such as paying taxes and defending the country. In some cases a national is considered of lesser status than a full citizen. Before 1924 Native Americans, for example, were considered to be nationals but not citizens of the United States.

As a legal status, nationality attaches to people and legal entities such as corporations based on their relationship to a particular nation. The nationality of a corporate business, for example, may depend on factors such as the country in which it is chartered or incorporated, the nationality of the majority of its stockholders, where it is headquartered, and where it conducts the majority of its business. Nationality always implies a legal nexus between the individual or legal entity and the nation that is recognized under international and municipal law, as distinct from an alien or a stateless person or entity.

Constitution of Kuwait (1962), Part III, Public Rights and Duties, Article 27: "Kuwaiti nationality shall be defined by law. No deprivation or withdrawal of nationality may be effected except within the limits prescribed by law."

Constitution of Israel, Law of Return (1950, as amended), Section 4A: "The rights of a Jew under this law and the rights of an *oleh* [a Jew immigrating into Israel] under the nationality law . . . [of 1952], as well as the right of an *oleh* under any other enactment, are also vested in a child and a grandchild of a Jew and the spouse of a grandchild of a Jew, except for a person who has been a Jew and has voluntarily changed his religion."

Natural Law

Throughout history the quest for immutable laws of human behavior akin to the laws of physics has engaged great minds. From the Greek Stoics of the third century B.C. to the Enlightenment philosophers of the eighteenth century A.D., "natural" laws governing human relationships have been propounded. In the thirteenth century St. Thomas Aquinas proposed that the basis of all positive law—laws created by human authority—was to be found in natural law, which he saw as a part of the eternal law of God. The theory of natural law culminated in the U.S. Declaration of Independence in 1776 and the French Revolution of 1789.

A general theory of human society, natural law encompasses political science, the law of associations, and constitutional law. A number of principles on which the U.S. Constitution (1789) is based are clearly derived from natural law. In essay 43 of *The Federalist* (1788), James Madison states that the proposed new constitution can be adopted by less than unanimous consent of the states because of self-preservation, which is the transcendent law of nature and nature's God and declares that the safety and happiness of society are the objects of all political institutions.

From natural law come natural rights, such as those embodied in constitutional bills of rights. Alexander Hamilton, a student of natural law, nevertheless opposed the U.S. Bill of Rights (1791) on the grounds that the new constitution required no qualifications because under it the people surrender nothing and retain everything. In defense of Hamilton's stand, the legal maxim that a person accused of a crime is presumed innocent until proven guilty is still applied vigorously by the courts in the United States, although it does not appear anywhere in the Constitution, including the Bill of Rights.

Although few constitutional documents refer expressly to natural law, many basic principles from individual rights and popular sovereignty to limitations on rulers owe their existence to the proponents of natural law.

Constitution of France (1958), Declaration of the Rights of Man and of the Citizen (1789) (incorporated by reference in the Preamble), Article 2: "The purpose of political association is to preserve the natural and inalienable rights of man, i.e., liberty, private property, the inviolability of the person, and the right to resist oppression."

Constitution of Liberia (1986), Preamble: "Acknowledging our gratitude to God, and acting within the exercise of our natural, inherent, and inalienable right to establish a framework of government for the purpose of promoting unity, stability, peace, concord and tranquillity, liberty, justice, and human rights under law with opportunities for political, social, economic, and cultural advancement for ourselves and our posterity. . . ."

Natural Rights. *See* Fundamental Rights; Natural Law

Naturalization

In *The Laws,* Plato sets the population of a new colony to be established at exactly 5,040 persons, because this number can be divided evenly by the numbers one through twelve, except for eleven. The populations of modern nation-states, however, cannot be so exactly controlled because of births and deaths and emigration and immigration. The aliens who immigrate into a country often wish to become citizens of their new homeland, a process called naturalization.

In the early days of the Roman Empire, citizens of Rome held a place of preeminence. In 212 A.D. the emperor Caracalla extended citizenship to all people under Roman control except for the lowest class, the *dediticii* (prisoners of war who had surrendered unconditionally). Later the practice was stopped when frequent attacks in the provinces by barbarians, as well as plague, famine, and civil wars, weakened the reins of the central government in Rome.

Citizenship is the formal link between the individual and the nation-state. To become a naturalized citizen of a country it is generally necessary to renounce any existing allegiance to another nation and to comply with a prescribed formal procedure of naturalization. In essay 43 of *The Federalist* (1788), James Madison comments that the new U.S. Constitution (1789) is an improvement over the Articles of Confederation (1781) because it authorizes the national government to provide uniform naturalization rules throughout the country.

Procedures for formal naturalization, also called registration, vary from country to country. Most constitutions authorize the legislature to establish such procedures by legislation.

To qualify to become citizens by naturalization, many immigrants, like these Chinese in 1881, have had to learn the language, customs, and laws of their adopted countries.

Constitution of Ecuador (1979), First Part, Title I, Ecuadorans and Foreigners, Section I, Nationality, Article 7: "The following are Ecuadorans by naturalization: 1—Those who have obtained the Ecuadoran nationality for having rendered relevant services to the country; 2—Those who have obtained a certificate of naturalization; 3—Those who have been adopted as children by Ecuadorans while minors . . . ; and 4—Those who are born abroad to foreign parents who later are naturalized in Ecuador, while being under age."

Constitution of Nigeria (1989), Chapter III, Citizenship, Section 28(2): "Any registration of a person as a citizen of Nigeria or the grant of a certificate of naturalization to a person who is a citizen of a country other than Nigeria at the time of such registration or grant shall be conditioned upon effective renunciation of the citizenship or nationality of any other country within a period of not more than twelve months from the date of such registration or grant."

Necessary and Proper Clause. *See* Incidental Powers

Nehru, Jawaharlal

The first prime minister of the constitutional government of independent India, Jawaharlal Nehru (1889–1964) secured democracy for one of the world's most populous and diverse nation-states.

Nehru was born into a wealthy and socially prominent family in Allahabad on November 14, 1889. Described by his sister Krishna as "shy and sensitive," this son of a Brahmin lawyer was educated at Harrow and at Trinity College in Cambridge, England. Admitted to the Inner Temple in London, he was later called to the bar and began practicing law in India in 1912.

In 1919 Nehru became active in the Indian National Congress Party. Imprisoned nine times for revolutionary agitation against the Raj, the British colonial regime, he was last released on June 15, 1945, just when the movement for independence from the British was picking up steam. The Indian National Congress, of which Nehru was president, viewed India as one multicultural country, but the congress's political rival, the Muslim League, considered it two nations—one Hindu and one Muslim.

Independence came at midnight on August 14, 1947. At that hour, addressing the constituent assembly established in December 1946 to draft a new constitution, Nehru declared: "A moment comes, which comes but

Jawaharlal Nehru, India's first prime minister (shown with his sister, Madame Pandit, and U.S. President Harry S. Truman in 1949), crafted India's 1950 constitution, which incorporated elements of the U.S. and British constitutions.

rarely in history, when we step out from the old to the new, when an age ends, and when the soul of a nation, long suppressed, finds utterance."

Considered by many to be the architect for the 1950 constitution of India, Nehru was able to craft it to reflect his vision for a democratic India. At the local level the traditional *panchayat* (councils) were strengthened. At the regional level more than five hundred princely states were abolished and twenty-six states or provinces with their own governors and legislatures were created. At the national level, drawing on the British parliamentary and American presidential models of government, a bicameral legislature, a prime minister, and a president were installed.

In 1947 Nehru became the first prime minister of India and served in that position until 1964. Throughout his life he urged a neutralist, nonaligned foreign policy, the abandonment of traditional discrimination practices, and the gradual modernization of India. He died in New Delhi on May 27, 1964.

No-Confidence Vote

In many parliamentary systems of government the cabinet, the government in office, may be terminated through a no-confidence vote by the members of the parliament. In the United Kingdom and France a vote to censure the government or the failure of the government to have a key policy bill approved by the parliament can lead to the resignation of the prime minister and the cabinet and to the dissolution of the parliament. New elections are then held to determine whether the old government will be restored to office or whether a new government will be formed by a new parliamentary majority.

A number of parliamentary governments specify in their constitutions the procedures for a vote of confidence for a newly installed government and for a vote of no confidence when a sufficient number of legislators question the government's performance.

Constitution of Japan (1889, significantly revised in 1947), Chapter V, The Cabinet, Article 69: "If the house of representatives passes a non-confidence resolution, or rejects a confidence resolution, the cabinet shall resign en masse, unless the house of representatives is dissolved within ten (10) days."

Constitution of Italy (1948), Part II, The System of the Republic, Title III, The Government, Section I, The Council of Ministers, Article 94: "The government shall win the vote of confidence of the two chambers [of the parliament]. Each chamber gives a vote of confidence or revokes it by means of a justified motion which shall be voted by roll-call."

Nomination

The term *nomination* appeared in England's Rolls of Parliament in the fifteenth century with respect to ecclesiastical appointments and today is used in constitutions to refer to proposing a candidate for elective office—for example, a nominee for president or for membership in the legislature. It also designates the first phase of the process by which the head of the executive branch appoints people to high positions in the government, which may also include a confirmation phase, usually by a legislative body or commission.

Many constitutions set forth nomination procedures particularly for the executive and judicial branches, and some also detail how candidates may be nominated to qualify for election and hold office if elected.

Constitution of New Zealand, Electoral Act (1956), Part II, The House of Representatives, Section 30, Public Servants May Become Candidates or Be Elected: "(1) Any public servant who desires to become a candidate for election as a member of parliament shall be placed on leave of absence for the purposes of his candidature. (2) That leave shall commence on such date as his controlling authority determines, being not later than nomination day, and, in the event of his nomination as a candidate, shall continue until the 7th day after polling day, unless he withdraws his nomination."

Constitution of Poland, Constitution Act (1992), Chapter 3, The President of the Republic of Poland, Article 47: "The provisions of article 46 [regarding the requirement for a countersignature for presidential acts] shall not apply to: ... (7) nomination of the prime minister and appointment of the whole council of ministers...."

Candidates for U.S. president and vice president are nominated by delegates from the states and other jurisdictions at national political party conventions that convene several months before the national election.

O

Oath

To assume office and begin their duties, many government officials are required by their constitutions to take an oath of office. An oath, a word derived from the Teutonic and Germanic languages, is an attestation in which a person signifies that he or she is bound to perform an act faithfully and truly. It often takes the form of a solemn appeal to God—or another deity or a revered person—as a witness to the truthfulness and honesty of a promise or undertaking; such an appeal also overtly or implicitly invokes divine retribution for failure or untruthfulness.

In *The Laws*, Plato requires anyone who wishes to add a write-in candidate to a prepared list of nominees for general in the military to first "swear his oath." Augustus Caesar had the troops of Rome's allies swear allegiance to him personally, rather than to Rome or the Senate. William Blackstone, the eighteenth-century commentator on the laws of England, classified the administration of unlawful oaths as a felony.

Constitution of Germany (1949), V, The Federal President, Article 56, Oath of Office: "On assuming his office, the federal president shall take the following oath before assembled members of the Bundestag and the Bundesrat [houses of the parliament]: 'I swear that I will dedicate my efforts to the well-being of the German people, enhance their benefits, avert harm from them, uphold and defend the Basic Law [the constitution] and the statutes of the federation, fulfill my duties conscientiously, and do justice to all. So help me God.' The oath may also be taken without religious affirmation."

Constitution of Iraq (1970), Chapter IV, Institutions of the Iraqi Republic, Section III, The President of the Republic, Article 59: "Vice president of the republic and ministers take the following oath before the president of the republic before assuming the responsibilities of their functions: 'I swear by God almighty, by my honor and by my faith to preserve the republican system, to commit myself to its constitution and laws, to look after the independence of the country, its security and territorial integrity, and to do my best earnestly and sincerely to realize the objectives of the people.' "

Objection

In a nation with a presidential system of government, the chief executive may oppose a bill that has been enacted by the legislature but that requires presidential approval to become law. By objecting to the proposed law the president exercises a constitutional power to veto the measure. Constitutions may require that a veto be accompanied by stated objections, comments, or reasons for withholding executive approval.

George Washington was the first president of the United States to take the oath of office prescribed by the 1789 Constitution.

Article 1, Section 7, of the U.S. Constitution (1789) requires that a bill that has passed both houses of Congress be presented to the president. If the president approves the bill, he must sign it; if not, the bill must be returned to the house in which it originated, together with the president's objections. In essay 73 of *The Federalist* (1788), Alexander Hamilton comments on the president's veto power, saying that a direct and categorical negative would be more harsh and more apt to irritate than a mere suggestion of argumentative objections to be approved or disapproved by Congress, which could override the veto if it disagreed with the president's objections.

In constitutional monarchies and presidential-style parliamentary governments, the sovereign or head of state is generally constitutionally powerless to withhold his or her consent to laws passed by the parliament.

Constitution of South Korea (1948), Chapter III, The National Assembly, Article 53: "(1) Each bill passed by the national assembly shall be sent to the executive, and the president shall promulgate it within fifteen days. (2) In the case of objection to the bill, the president may . . . return it to the national assembly with written explanation of his objections, and request it be reconsidered."

Constitution of Colombia (1991), Title VI, Concerning the Legislative Branch, Chapter 3, Concerning the Laws, Article 165: "Once a legislative bill is approved by both chambers, it will be transmitted to the government for its approval. Should the latter have no objections, it will approve the bill's promulgation as law; if it objects to it, the bill will be returned to the chamber in which it originated."

Obligation

An obligation is a debt or liability enforceable in a court of law. Legal action to enforce an obligation owed was an option for citizens of ancient Greece and Rome. Justinian, the sixth-century Byzantine emperor, defined *obligatio* in Roman law as a legal tie whereby one is subjected to having to make some performance in accordance with the law.

In constitutions the term encompasses many definitions. It may refer to a duty on the part of a citizen, such as an obligation to pay taxes, or a duty on the part of a government official or institution. It may mean a financial obligation, either a bond or another form of contracted debt. An obligation may also be the commitment of certain appropriated funds by a government agency, which is one of the phases in the budget cycle of budgeting, authorizing, appropriating, obligating, expending, and auditing.

Constitution of Turkey (1982), Part Two, Fundamental Rights and Duties, Chapter Four, Political Rights and Duties, VI, Obligation to Pay Taxes, Article 73: "Everyone is under the obligation to pay taxes according to his financial resources, in order to meet public expenditures."

Constitution of Malaysia (1963), Part XIII, Temporary and Transitional Provisions, Article 167, Rights, Liabilities, and Obligations: "(6) The attorney general shall . . . certify whether any right, liability, or obligation is by virtue of this article a right, liability, or obligation of the federation or of a state. . . . "

Offense

In their writings both Plato and Aristotle discuss offenses—general breaches of duty, law, propriety, or even etiquette—and crimes, along with their root causes and punishments. Plato defines theft from temples, subversion, and treason as capital offenses, actions that call for the death penalty. In ancient Rome an offense such as a crime was called a *delictum*, and in Roman law an obligation *ex delicto* merely required making satisfaction for the wrong.

Offenses in Anglo-American law include any crime or misdemeanor. William Blackstone, the eighteenth-century commentator on English law, warned that in indictments "words of art" must be used to express the precise idea of the offense alleged. By this he meant that to make a charge against an alleged offender in a court of law, exact legal terminology was required to trigger an action and a remedy familiar to the court, thus allowing the court to entertain the matter.

In constitutions offenses are usually crimes of which persons may be accused and for which they may be arrested, put on trial, convicted, and punished. Some constitutions provide immunity for members of the legislature from offenses or crimes committed during their incumbency except, however, where a member is apprehended by the authorities in *flagrante delicto* (the act of committing the offense).

Constitution of Uganda, Simplified Draft (1992), Chapter 5, Fundamental Human Rights and Freedoms, Article 13: "A person arrested for an offense shall be entitled to be released on bail unless tried within a reasonable time."

Constitution of Ethiopia (1995), Chapter Six, The Federal Councils, Part One, The Council of Peoples' Representatives, Article 54, Members of the Council of Peoples' Representatives, Section 6: "A member of the council shall not be arrested or charged with a crime without the permission of the council unless he is apprehended in *flagrante delicto*."

O'Higgins, Bernardo

A key figure in winning South America's independence from Spain, Bernardo O'Higgins (1778–1842) was also instrumental in the early constitutional development of his native Chile.

Born probably on August 20, 1778, in Chillán, Chile, Bernardo was the illegitimate child of Ambrosio O'Higgins and Isabel Riquelme, the daughter of a Chilean landowner. His father, although Irish, was a Spanish officer who became the governor of Chile and later the viceroy of Peru.

At the age of twelve Bernardo was sent to Lima for his secondary education and later studied in Spain and England. In London, along with other activists, he joined a secret Masonic lodge dedicated to winning independence for South America. There he also met General Francisco Miranda, who influenced the South American liberator Simón Bolívar.

When Ambrosio O'Higgins died, he left a large hacienda to Bernardo, who then took his father's surname and settled down in Chile to run the estate. After Napoleon invaded Spain in 1808, however, O'Higgins became deeply involved with the independence movement, and in 1814 he took over command of the Chilean revolutionary forces. Beaten in battle by the Spanish, he fled to Argentina, where he teamed up with José de San Martín, the Argentine general, statesman, and liberator. Together they liberated Chile in a decisive battle at Chacabuco on February 12, 1817.

Later that year O'Higgins was made *director supremo* (head) of the Chilean government. The revolutionaries had adopted a constitution earlier, in 1813, but the first two national charters after full independence were drafted and approved during the period of O'Higgins's leadership. The first, the Proyecto de Constitución Provisional para el Estado de Chile, was ratified by a plebiscite in 1818. In 1822 a new document, the Constitución Politîa para Estado de Chile, was approved by a constitutional convention after O'Higgins intervened. Near revolutionary in its liberal democratic provisions, seventeen articles detailed basic rights, including freedom

Bernardo O'Higgins, who helped liberate Chile from Spain's colonial empire, played a significant role in his country's early constitutional development after full independence.

for those born in Chile and equality before the law.

O'Higgins, however, alienated the landowners and the Catholic Church by abolishing titles of nobility and giving the government the power to make ecclesiastical appointments. He was forced into exile in Peru the following year. Although the 1822 constitution was scrapped by the junta that followed O'Higgins to power, it did become the model for a new Chilean constitution in 1833. A liberal ahead of his time who had always admired the British constitution, O'Higgins died in October 1842 in Peru, having left a legacy of constitutionalism in his native Chile.

Ombudsman

The institution of ombudsman originated in Sweden, where the word simply means an authorized representative. The position is established generally, but not always, in the legislative branch to hear, investigate, report, and take action on complaints of citizens against public officials. Ombudsmen are usually independent of direct executive branch oversight, however, so that they will be free to investigate and seek redress in the event of misconduct.

Many other countries, including Austria, Chile, and New Zealand, now have official government ombudsmen or equivalent positions. No such offices exist in the United Kingdom or United States, where legislators—members of Parliament or Congress or members of their staffs—often handle similar constituent complaints.

In addition to nation-states, some private organizations and other political organizations establish ombudsman positions. The European Parliament recently elected a Finnish delegate as the first "European ombudsman" to help citizens deal with the new European Union.

Constitution of Portugal (1976), Part III, Organization of Political Powers, Section III, Assembly of the Republic, Chapter II, Powers, Article 166 (added in 1992), Powers with Respect to Other Organs: "With respect to other organs, the assembly shall have the following powers: . . . i). To elect by a two-thirds majority of the members present where the majority is larger than the absolute majority of the members entitled to vote, ten judges of the constitutional court, the ombudsman [and other officials]. . . ."

Constitution of Nepal (1990), Part 12, Abuse of Authority Investigation Commission, Article 98, Duties, Powers, and Functions of the Abuse of Authority Investigation Commission: "(1) The abuse of authority investigation commission may itself make or let inquiries and investigations be made on the basis of information or on the complaint of any person received about the misuse of authority by improper or corrupt deeds of any person holding public office."

Order

In French law *ordre* is the priority of the claims of creditors with liens against the proceeds from a sale of real property. The English word *order,* which is derived from the French term, encompasses many definitions. An order can be a listing by rank or priority—for example, the order of the day for matters to be taken up by a legislative body. An order can also refer to a command, such as a military order, or a request, such as an order for goods or services.

In constitutions an order generally refers to an authoritative directive relating to parliamentary procedures in legislative proceedings or to a directive issued by the executive to subordinates or by a court to legal officers or parties under its jurisdiction. Standing orders, like standing rules, are ones that continue in effect even when a body is not in session; they may be changed only by a motion to reconsider.

In law an order is a command or authoritative direction such as that given by a court of law. Final orders terminate a court action, while interlocutory orders settle only some aspect of a matter before the court, not the cause itself.

Constitution of Kenya (1963), Chapter IV, The Judicature, Part 2, Other Courts, Section 65(2): "The high court shall have jurisdiction to supervise any civil or criminal proceedings before a subordinate court or court-martial, and may make such orders, issue such writs, and give such directions as it may consider appropriate. . . ."

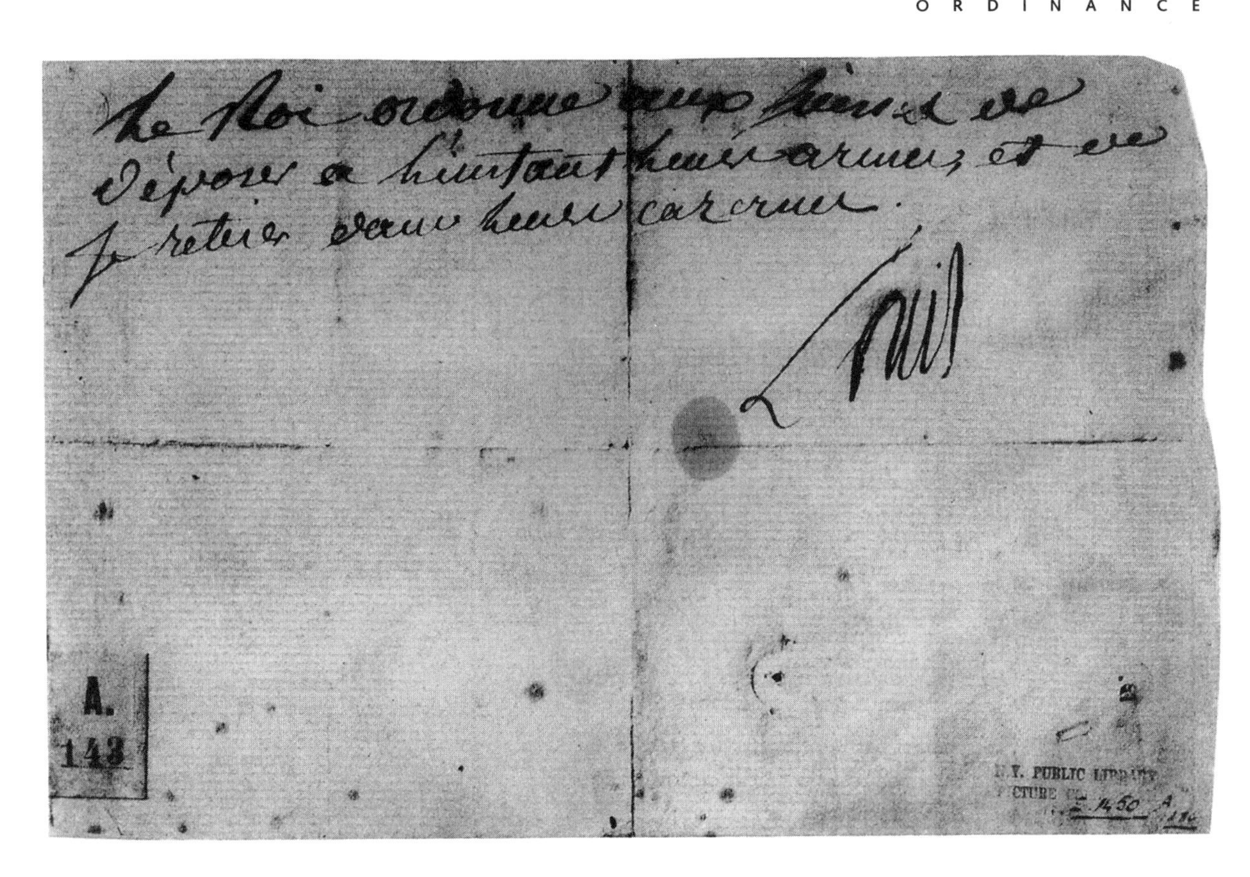

Le Roi ordonne aux Suisses de déposer à l'instant leurs armes et de se retirer dans leurs casernes.

Louis

The last royal order signed by Louis XVI was on August 10, 1792, just before angry Parisians stormed his palace and took the royal family prisoner. Refusing to acknowledge the authority of the revolutionaries, Louis was executed on January 21, 1793.

Constitution of Greece (1975), Part Three, Organization and Functions of the State, Section III, Parliament, Chapter Four, Organization and Functioning of the Parliament, Article 65: "1. Parliament shall determine the manner of its free and democratic operation by adopting its own standing orders.... 6. The standing orders shall determine the organization of the services of the parliament under the supervision of the speaker; all matters concerning its personnel shall likewise be regulated."

Order of Business. *See* Agenda

Order of the Day. *See* Agenda; Order

Ordinance

In contrast to a law—a legislative enactment by a national authority or by a semisovereign constituent state or provincial authority in a federal nation-state—an ordinance is generally a legislative enactment by a local authority. Because local governments are basically creations of a state or nation-state, they have no inherent sovereign power to enact laws; therefore, their legislative enactments are generally called ordinances to distinguish them from statutes enacted by sovereign or semisovereign bodies.

Constitutions may refer to ordinances variously to mean local or municipal enactments, as well as issuances by national authorities that have a status inferior to laws. A new law, for example, can override an old law, but a new ordinance cannot override an old law, just as a new law cannot override a constitutional provision.

Enactments of a general or even an organic character have also been designated as ordinances. The Ordinance for the Government of the North West Territory enacted by the U.S. Congress in 1787 guaranteed political liberties and eventual statehood for the northwestern territories of the United States. In England earlier in this century, before the House of Lords was deprived of its power to veto legislative proposals, all statutes had to be approved by both houses of Parliament and the monarch, while ordinances required only the approval of two of these three parliamentary authorities.

Constitution of Venezuela (1961), Title VII, The Judicial Power and Public Ministry, Chapter II, The Supreme Court of Justice, Article 215: "The powers of the supreme court of justice are: . . . 4. To declare the total or partial nullity of state laws, municipal ordinances, and other acts of the deliberative bodies of the states and municipalities that conflict with the constitution. . . ."

Constitution of France (1958), Title II, The President of the Republic, Article 13: "The president of the republic shall sign the ordinances and decrees decided upon in the council of ministers."

384 PUBLIC LAWS—CH. 512—AUG. 1, 1950 [64 STAT.

[CHAPTER 512]

AN ACT

August 1, 1950 [H. R. 7273] [Public Law 630]

To provide a civil government for Guam, and for other purposes.

Organic Act of Guam.

Be it enacted by the Senate and House of Representatives of the United States of America in Congress assembled, That this Act may be cited as the "Organic Act of Guam".

30 Stat. 1754.

SEC. 2. The territory ceded to the United States in accordance with the provisions of the Treaty of Peace between the United States and Spain, signed at Paris, December 10, 1898, and proclaimed April 11, 1899, and known as the island of Guam in the Marianas Islands, shall continue to be known as Guam.

Capital.

Powers of government; branches, etc.

SEC. 3. Guam is hereby declared to be an unincorporated territory of the United States and the capital and seat of government thereof shall be located at the city of Agana, Guam. The government of Guam shall have the powers set forth in this Act and shall have power to sue by such name. The government of Guam shall consist of three branches, executive, legislative, and judicial, and its relations with the Federal Government shall be under the general administrative supervision of the head of such civilian department or agency of the Government of the United States as the President may direct.

CITIZENSHIP

54 Stat. 1138. 8 U. S. C. §§ 601-605.

SEC. 4. (a) Chapter II of the Nationality Act of 1940, as amended, is hereby further amended by adding at the end thereof the following new section:

"SEC. 206. (a) The following persons, and their children born after April 11, 1899, are hereby declared to be citizens of the United States, if they are residing on the date of enactment of this section on the island of Guam or other territory over which the United States exercises rights of sovereignty:

"(1) All inhabitants of the island of Guam on April 11, 1899, including those temporarily absent from the island on that date, who were Spanish subjects, who after that date continued to reside in Guam or other territory over which the United States exercises sovereignty, and who have taken no affirmative steps to preserve or acquire foreign nationality.

"(2) All persons born in the island of Guam who resided in Guam on April 11, 1899, including those temporarily absent from the island on that date, who after that date continued to reside in Guam or other territory over which the United States exercises sovereignty, and who have taken no affirmative steps to preserve or acquire foreign nationality.

"(b) All persons born in the island of Guam on or after April 11, 1899 (whether before or after the date of enactment of this section), subject to the jurisdiction of the United States, are hereby declared to be citizens of the United States: *Provided*, That in the case of any person born before the date of enactment of this section, he has taken no affirmative steps to preserve or acquire foreign nationality.

Persons held not to be nationals of U. S.

"(c) Any person hereinbefore described who is a citizen or national of a country other than the United States and desires to retain his present political status shall make, within two years of the date of enactment of this section, a declaration under oath of such desire, said declaration to be in form and executed in the manner prescribed by regulations. From and after the making of such a declaration any such person shall be held not to be a national of the United States by virtue of this Act.

Laws providing for the government of a territory such as Guam, an island possession of the United States in the north Pacific Ocean, are called organic laws.

Organ

The organs of the body politic, analogous to plant and animal parts adapted for particular functions, include any of the various institutions created to fulfill vital government functions. An organ—in Latin *membrum*—is the constituent part of an organism or organization, and any discrete part therefore may be consider an organ.

Particularly in constitutions of nations dominated by the Communist Party, an organ is a specialized government institution other than those considered strictly a part of the executive, legislative, and judicial branches—for example, "people's organs of control."

Constitution of Vietnam (1980), Chapter X, People's Courts and People's Organs of Control, Article 137: "The supreme people's organ of control shall control the observance of law by the ministries and equivalent agencies and other government bodies, local administration agencies, economic and social organizations, people's armed forces units, and all citizens. It shall exercise the right of public prosecution and ensure the strict and uniform observance of law."

Constitution of Greece (1975), Part Three, Organization and Functions of the State, Section VI, Administration, Chapter Two, Status of Administrative Agents, Article 103: "3. Organic posts of specialized scientific and technical or auxiliary personnel may be filled by personnel hired on private law contracts. The terms of employment and the specific guarantees under which this personnel shall be employed shall be specified by law."

Organic Law

A constitution or a fundamental law of a political entity—one that defines or establishes the organization of government—is an organic law. Constitutions use *organic law* to mean laws enacted under a broad constitutional mandate that relate to the structure of a government.

The term may arise specifically regarding the organization and government of a state or territory. Legislative enactments of the U.S. Congress providing a government for a territory such as the island of Guam in the northern Pacific Ocean, for example, are called organic acts because they deal with the structure of the territorial government. Similarly, the powers of the District of Columbia, the federal capital district of the United States, are conferred by the U.S. Congress also by means of organic laws.

The organic theory of constitutions holds that constitutions are not created out of thin air by those who frame or draft them but evolve from a political community's existing practices and institutions.

Constitution of France (1958), Title II, The President of the Republic, Article 13: "An organic law shall determine the other posts to be filled in meetings of the council of ministers, as well as the conditions under which the power of the president of the republic to make appointments to office may be delegated by him and exercised in his name."

Constitution of Romania (1991), Chapter V, Public Administration, Section 1, Specialized Central Public Administration, Article 116(3): "Autonomous administrative authorities may be established by an organic law."

Organic Theory. *See* Organic Law

P

Paine, Thomas

The liberal republican writings of Thomas Paine (1737–1809) had a significant impact on the constitutional development of the United States and France, which in turn have influenced many constitutions around the world.

Paine, the son of a Quaker father and an Anglican mother, was born in Norfolk, England, on January 29, 1737. His father was a poor corset maker who nevertheless saw that his son got a basic schooling. At sixteen young Thomas ran away to become a sailor. On returning to England he worked at various jobs while continuing to educate himself. Between 1757 and 1759 he attended lectures on Newtonian astronomy.

Unhappy and unsuccessful in all that he tried, Paine immigrated to the American colonies in 1774 after meeting Benjamin Franklin in London. He became a writer and an editor for the *Pennsylvania Magazine*, using his pen to castigate slavery. In early 1776 *Common Sense*, a seventy-nine-page pamphlet Paine wrote calling for American independence from Great Britain, was instantly acclaimed by the American colonists. In it he attacked George III, calling him a "hardened, sullen tempered Pharaoh," and extolled the independence movement, saying, "The sun never shined on a cause of greater worth." He worked on the 1776 constitution of the state of Pennsylvania and served in George Washington's army during the Revolutionary War (1775–81).

After returning to England some years later, Paine wrote *The Rights of Man* (1791), in which he defended French democracy in reply to an attack on the French

A political gadfly born in England, Thomas Paine contributed to the early constitutional development of the republics of the United States and France.

Plato's works, such as *The Republic* and *The Laws*, explore the nature of justice and the state and have been the wellsprings of constitutional thought for centuries.

Revolution by Edmund Burke, the eighteenth-century British statesman and defender of the British monarchy. The work was another immediate success, and Paine donated the large income from its sale to the Society for Constitutional Reform. The British government soon banned *The Rights of Man* as seditious, and Paine fled to France, where in 1792 he was elected to the national convention to create a French constitution and appointed to the nine-member committee to draft the document.

At the convention Paine, in opposition to his own party's position, argued against executing King Louis XVI, and on December 28, 1793, the French revolutionary leader Maximilien François Marie Isidore de Robespierre had him arrested. Eleven months later he was released through American intercession, although he had earlier criticized President George Washington for not helping him.

Paine's last great work, *The Age of Reason* (1793), defended deism but attacked all "revealed" religions and was condemned as atheistic. On returning to the United States in 1802 he was shunned by old friends and compatriots and was even denied burial in a Quaker cemetery following his death on June 8, 1809.

Pardon

In ancient Athens a person who had committed an accidental homicide could be pardoned, or forgiven, with the unanimous consent of the victim's father, brothers, and sons. Once granted, the pardon could not be revoked. Roman law also provided for pardons for wrongs and crimes. William Blackstone, the eighteenth-century commentator on the laws of England, noted: "If neither pregnancy, insanity, non-identity, nor other plea will avail to avoid the judgement and stay the execution consequent thereupon, the last and surest resort is in the sovereign's most gracious pardon; the granting of which is the most amiable prerogative of the Crown."

A pardon is an act of grace that comes from the power to execute the laws and exempts an individual from any punishment required by law for a crime. In addition to the possibility of a pardon, a person accused of a crime may hope for a commuted, or lesser, sentence or a reprieve, which temporarily suspends a sentence.

The power to grant pardons is an inherent right of sovereignty, and many constitutions give the head of state (the monarch or president) the specific powers of pardon, clemency, and amnesty, although some limitation may be placed on the power—for example, the head of state may be prohibited from granting a general amnesty or pardon, only individual ones.

The U.S. Constitution (1789) gives to the president the power of the pardon for offenses against the United States, although he or she may not pardon anyone who has been or is being impeached. Alexander Hamilton, in essay 74 of *The Federalist* (1788), declares that "humanity and good policy conspire to dictate that the benign prerogative of pardoning should be as little fettered or embarrassed" as possible. State governors in the United States also have the power to grant pardons for offenses committed within their jurisdictions.

Constitution of Mexico (1917), Title III, Chapter III, Executive Powers, Article 89: "The powers and duties of the president are as follows: . . . XIV. To grant, according to law, pardons to prisoners convicted of crimes within the jurisdiction of the federal courts, and to those convicted of common crimes in the federal district. . . ."

Constitution of Spain (1978), Title II, Concerning the Crown, Article 62: "It is incumbent upon the king: . . . i) To exercise the right to grant pardons in accordance with the law, which may not authorize general pardons."

Parkes, Henry. *See* Griffith, Samuel Walker

Parliament

The French word *parlement*, derived from *parler* (to speak or discourse), historically referred to the French king's court of justice. But the English word *parliament* comes from the thirteenth-century Anglo-Latin term *parliamentum* (a consultation, discussion, or debate). The ancient Roman Senate was not a true parliament; it was constitutionally an advisory body consisting primarily of conservative aristocrats, although it had some executive and legislative powers during the Roman republic.

Supreme political power resides in the House of Commons of the British Parliament, which has been called the "Mother of all Parliaments." Members of the majority party and the "loyal opposition" party sit facing each other during sessions.

The earliest record of a parliamentary-type legislative body is the Icelandic Althing, which met as long ago as 930 A.D. Like the parliament that later developed in England, it had both legislative and judicial functions. Without a king or an executive institution, however, the Althing's decisions were difficult to enforce. This deficiency was remedied in the English version, which evolved into a legislative body with two houses or chambers, the upper House of Lords and the lower House of Commons, and a monarch or sovereign who, together with the two houses, had to approve all laws. The modern British Parliament, now the country's supreme governing body, consists of three estates, somewhat like the former Estates-Général in France: the lords spiritual (the high church officials) and the lords temporal (the peers of the realm), who are entitled to sit in the upper house, and the elected representatives of the commons, who make up the lower house.

Many constitutions describe their legislatures as parliaments, which are all in varying degrees modeled after the United Kingdom, or Westminster, model, particularly in the nation-states that were formerly dominions or colonies of the United Kingdom. The central features of any parliamentary system of government are an elected body of representatives, which fill either one or two houses of the legislature (the lower house generally being more representative and having the greater power); a government or council of ministers (cabinet) with a prime minister (head of government) approved by the majority of the members of the lower house or both houses and responsible to them; a maximum period between elections, although the more representative house in a bicameral parliament may be dissolved earlier if the government originally approved by it loses the confidence of the majority of its members and is forced to resign, initiating new elections; and a head of state (a monarch or president), who must, if only ceremonially, assent to bills passed by the parliament before they may become effective.

The major difference between a congress and a parliament is that a parliament is theoretically the relatively supreme branch of government. A congress, on the other hand, is one of at least three coequal branches of government, with an independently elected chief executive as the head of both state and government who can veto legislation passed by the congress, although generally vetoes can be overridden by a supermajority vote.

Constitution of Iceland (1944), Chapter One, Article 2: "The legislative power is jointly vested in the Althing (parliament) and the president of the Republic of Iceland."

Constitution of Malaysia (1957), Part IV, The Federation, Chapter 4, Federal Legislature, Article 44, Constitution of Parliament: "The legislative authority of the federation shall be vested in a parliament, which shall consist of the Yang di-Pertuan Agong [monarch] and two *majlis* (houses of parliament) to be known as the Dewan Negara (senate) and the Dewan Rakyat (house of representatives)."

Party System. *See* Political Party

Patent. *See* Copyright

Peace

Maintaining a state of peace—the opposite of war—is an express aim of many constitutions. As a state of tranquillity, peace—from the Latin *pax*, now *paix* in French,

A rally held in Washington, D.C., in 1922 to promote peace among the countries of the world attracted mostly women. Constitutions generally specify how peace, as well as war, is to be declared.

paz in Spanish, *Frieden* in German—is enjoyed by nation-states when good order is maintained internally and good relations are enjoyed with other nations. As with declarations of war, many constitutions assign the responsibility for making or concluding peace at the end of a war to one or more institutions of the national government, often the chief executive.

In law peace refers to offenses that, while not specifically injurious, damage the public's interest in some way, such as a breach of the peace or disturbing the peace. In his eighteenth-century commentaries on English law, William Blackstone devotes an entire chapter to offenses against the public peace.

Constitution of China (People's Republic of China) (1982), Chapter Three, Structure of the State, Section I, The National People's Congress, Article 62: "The national people's congress exercises the following functions and powers: . . . (14) to decide on questions of war and peace. . . . "

Constitution of Portugal (1976), Part III, Organization of Political Power, Section II, President of the Republic, Chapter II, Powers, Article 138, Powers in International Relations: "The president of the republic shall be competent in international relations to: . . . c. Declare war in the case of actual or imminent aggression and make peace at the proposal of the government after hearing the council of state and having obtained authorization of the assembly of the republic or, when the latter is not in session and it is impossible to call it into session at once, of its standing committee."

Constitution of the United States of America (1789), Article I, Section 6: "The Senators and Representatives shall . . . in all Cases except Treason, Felony and Breach of the Peace, be privileged from Arrest during their Attendance at the Session of their representative Houses, and in going to and returning from the same. . . . "

Permanent Committee. *See* Standing Committee

Petition, Right of. *See* Grievance; Redress

Plato

The constitutional constructs of Plato (ca. 427–347 B.C.) have been the touchstones for all subsequent major works of political philosophy.

Plato was born into an aristocratic Athenian family in approximately 427 B.C. His father died when he was young, and his mother then married a friend of Pericles, the leader of democratic Athens. At this time, the power and influence of Athens, which had fought off Persian invasions several times between 490 and 479 B.C., were beginning to wane. Sparta, Athens's nondemocratic rival, soon clashed with Athens over its arrogant and imperialistic policies.

Plato undoubtedly fought in the Peloponnesian War (431–404 B.C.), in which Sparta defeated Athens and subsequently established in the historic city-state a regime of rule by the "Thirty Tyrants." Democracy was restored a year later, but Plato seemed as disenchanted with it as with rule by the Tyrants, especially after the man he most admired as a great moralist and intellectual, Socrates, chose death over exile as punishment for his crimes against Athens. In his famous dialogue *The Republic*, Plato speaks through Socrates, who in Plato's text is the personification of wisdom and virtue.

Holding that all knowledge is obtainable through thought and discourse, Socrates sought to elicit from others the "true" general nature of concepts such as piety and justice by leading questions, a method of teaching known as the Socratic method. Plato adopted the general philosophical principles of Socrates as the basis for an ideal government. Plato's method of theorizing from general principles is often contrasted with that of his pupil, Aristotle, who instead sought knowledge by collecting, cataloguing, and analyzing empirical data.

In *The Republic*, Plato describes a system of government in which every aspect of a society ruled by philosopher-kings is controlled to ensure proper respect for and obedience to the laws. In *The Laws*, his final work, he attempts to create a constitution for a new utopian colony called Magnesia, using law as a supreme but acknowledgedly imperfect instrument not just for governing but also for moral salvation. The *dirigiste* constitutions of Portugal and Brazil today reflect this same desire to mold a whole society through the use of constitutional directives.

The modern constitutional concept of the rule of law would not be unfamiliar to Plato's Athenian in *The Laws*, who says: "Such people [the holders of high offices] are usually referred to as 'rulers,' and if I have called them 'servants of the laws' it is because ... [w]here the law is subject to some other authority and has none of its own, the collapse of the state, in my view, is not far off...."

Plebiscite

In the early days of ancient Rome the people were divided into two classes: the aristocracy, called patricians, and the commoners, called plebeians. The plebeians fought for equality with the patricians, and in 287 B.C. their struggle was ended with the *lex Hortensia*, which gave the *plebis scita* (resolutions of the plebeian assembly) the force of law.

Plebiscites have historically been revolutionary proposals, also called referendums, submitted to the people to bring about a radical change in their constitution. In the mid-nineteenth century Louis Napoleon submitted plebiscites to the French citizens to establish the Second Empire. The Swiss constitution authorizes similar direct popular votes on constitutional revisions.

Other questions or the selection of officials may also be submitted to the citizens in the form of a plebiscite or referendum. In some cases such votes are an extraconstitutional method of obtaining popular opinion about an important government decision, such as joining the European Union.

Constitution of Egypt (1971), Part Five, System of Government, Chapter One, The Head of State, Article 76: "The people's assembly shall nominate the president of the republic. The nomination shall be referred to the people for a plebiscite."

Constitution of the Philippines (1987), Article IX, Constitutional Commissions, C, The Commission on Elections, Section 2: "The commission on elections shall exercise the following powers and functions: (1) Enforce and administer all laws and regulations relative to the conduct of an election, plebiscite, initiative, referendum, and recall."

Plenary Session. *See* Joint Session

Pluralism

Pluralism is the theory that the state is just one of many centers of power in society and that a democracy can exist only as long as access to the political process is guaranteed to competing interest groups. Constitutions may also use the concept to acknowledge that the populations of some nation-states—for example, Canada and Belgium—are more ethnically, racially, religiously, or socially diverse than others. Pluralism in this sense is a country's recognition that it has separate ethnic, cultural, or linguistic differences within its jurisdiction and that these differences affect the structure and processes of the government.

Constitution of Brazil (1988), Title I, Fundamental Principles, Article 1: "The Federative Republic of Brazil, formed by the indissoluble union of the states and municipalities and of the federal district, is a legal democratic state and is founded on: I—sovereignty; II—citizenship; III—the dignity of the human person; IV—the social values of labor and of free enterprise; V—political pluralism."

Constitution of Ireland (1937), Article 18: "7.1. Before each general election of members of Seanad Éireann [upper house of the parliament] to be elected from panels of candidates, five panels of candidates shall be formed in the manner provided by law containing respectively the names of persons having knowledge and practical experience of the following interests and services, namely: (i) National language and cultural, literature, art, education, and such professional interests as may be defined by law for the purposes of this panel; (ii) Agriculture and allied interests and fisheries; (iii) Labor, whether organized or unorganized...."

Constitution of Belgium (1831), Heading III, Concerning the Authorities, Chapter I, Concerning the Houses of Parliament, Section III, Concerning the Community Councils, Article 59b: "1. There is a council and an executive of the French community and a council and an executive of the Flemish community, the composition and functioning of which are regulated by law."

Policy

Based on the Greek and Latin words for polity, meaning government or constitution, a policy is a course of action adopted and pursued by a government as well as by its individual agencies and institutions. Although all branches and facets of a government to some degree contribute to government policy making, constitutions usually assign major responsibility to the executive branch. This branch generally proposes and the legislative branch disposes—approves or disapproves of—programs and budgets, for example, to implement policy decisions formulated by the executive branch. Specialized policy areas such as foreign policy and economic policy may also be detailed in constitutions.

In a presidential system of government, the executive departments under the general supervision of the president develop policies—ways of handling the management of government operations and solving problems—and propose these to the president, who may reject or adopt and support them. The president and his or her staff may, of course, also develop policy initiatives on their own. Because government policies often require legislative action, the executive branch sometimes must develop public support for its policy initiatives.

In a parliamentary system of government, the role of policy formulation falls almost exclusively to the prime minister and cabinet, who then take their programs to the parliament, which translates them into laws and provides appropriations to fund their implementation. As long as the cabinet enjoys the confidence of the majority of the members in the parliament, its policy measures generally will be approved. Any serious differences between the parliamentary majority and the cabinet can result in the resignation of the cabinet and new parliamentary elections.

Constitution of Slovakia (1993), Chapter Six, Executive Power, Section Two, The Government of the Slovak Republic, Article 119: "The government [cabinet] makes decisions as a body ... d) on crucial measures for safeguarding the economic and social policy of the Slovak Republic ... g) on key issues of domestic and foreign policy. ..."

Constitution of North Korea (1972), Chapter VII, The Central People's Committee, Article 105: "The central people's committee establishes an internal policy commission, a foreign policy commission, a national defense commission, a justice and security commission, and other commissions which are to assist in its work."

Political Party

In a constitutional democracy a political party is a group of people, generally having a similar political philosophy, who are organized to nominate candidates for office and to contest elections. Each party's aim is to win elections and thereby temporarily gain and exercise control over government policy and personnel decisions. The losing party and its candidates become the opposition party, the party out of power. They criticize the actions and policies of the party in power in an attempt to influence the outcome of the next cycle of elections.

Political factions—groups of citizens for and against programs, personalities, and issues—are not a recent phenomenon. In ancient Greek city-states some citizens supported Pericles and others Philip of Macedonia; in ancient Rome some citizens advocated leniency and others harshness towards Carthage; and in Italy at the time of Dante Alighieri, the Guelf and Ghibelline families had their respective supporters in their struggles for power.

It was in England toward the end of the eighteenth century, however, that two political parties, the Tories and Whigs, barely distinguishable as conservative and liberal, emerged and vied for a majority in Parliament and the consequent right to form a government and direct national policy. The concept of modern political parties was further refined in the United States, particularly by Thomas Jefferson and Alexander Hamilton, who saw political parties as a grass-roots basis for obtaining electoral majorities for opposing political philosophies. Jefferson's philosophy, which emphasized agrarian and individual virtues, led to the formation of the Democratic-Republican Party, while Hamilton's, which embraced commercialism and a strong central government, led to the formation of the Federalist Party.

Political parties had not developed at the time the U.S. Constitution was drafted in 1787, and even today many other constitutional documents do not refer to political parties, although parties may play a significant role in government electoral and organizational processes. A number of constitutions, however, expressly acknowledge a multiparty system and detail the role of political parties in the processes of government.

Political parties in a two-party or multiparty democracy are different from ideological parties in countries dominated by a single party. A true political party seeks temporary power, albeit for as long as possible, in a political system that is predicated on contested elections and a continuing opposition from a party or parties out of power. In contrast, ideological parties such as the communists or fascists seek the termination of all other parties and the installation of one "true" political regime.

Constitution of Egypt (1971), Part One, The State, Article 5: "The political system of the Arab Republic of Egypt is a multi-party one, within the framework of the basic elements and principles of the Egyptian society as stipulated in the constitution (political parties are regulated by law)."

Constitution of Thailand (1991), Chapter II, The King, Section 12: "A privy councillor shall not be a member of the constitutional tribunal, senator, member of the house of representatives, government official holding a permanent position or receiving a salary, official of a state enterprise, or member or official of a political party, and must not manifest loyalty to any political party."

Grass-roots political party rallies, like this one held in 1964 in the West African nation of Cameroon, form the basis of strong democracies. The first political parties, the Whigs and the Tories, developed in England in the eighteenth century.

Constitution of Syria (1973), Part One, Fundamental Principles, Chapter 1, Political Principles, Article 8: "The Ba'ath Arab Socialist Party shall be the leader party in society and the state and shall lead a National Progressive Front that works to unite the capacities of the masses of the people to serve the interests of the Arab Nation."

Poll. *See* Election; Vote

Postal Service

For several centuries mail was transported between towns by post, with carriers riding continuously except for a change of horses along the way. Today the post, or mail—domestic and international written messages and parcels—is sent and received through a national government's postal service, although private enterprise is increasingly assuming the task of package delivery.

Federal nation-state constitutions in particular specify that the postal service falls exclusively within the jurisdiction of the national government. In essay 42 of *The Federalist* (1788), James Madison, arguing that post roads for carrying the mail should be placed under the jurisdiction of Congress, contends that nothing that facilitates intercourse between the states can be deemed unworthy of public care.

Some constitutions specifically guarantee individuals' right to privacy in their communications through the mail.

Constitution of Germany (1949), VII, Legislative Powers of the Federation, Article 73, Exclusive Legislative Power, Catalogue: "The federation shall have exclusive power to legislate in the following matters: . . . 7. postal and communication services. . . ."

Constitution of Belgium (1831), Heading II, Concerning the Belgians and Their Rights, Article 22: "The secrecy of letters is inviolable. The law shall determine which agents are responsible for the violation of secrecy in the case of letters sent by post."

Power

"Power, properly understood, is the ability to achieve purpose," wrote the Reverend Martin Luther King Jr., the American civil rights leader, in *Where Do We Go from Here: Chaos or Community?* (1967). "It is the strength required to bring about social, political, and economic changes. In this sense power is not only desirable but necessary in order to implement the demands of love and justice."

Power *(potestas* in Latin) is the possession of control or command over people or things. Supreme political power *(majestas* in Latin) is what constitutions are all

Even a flood did not deter this British letter carrier in Maidenhead from completing his rounds and delivering the post.

about, and political and social scientists have long tried to define it accurately. In French, political power is *puissance politique*, but legitimate power is *pouvoir*, which is exercised by a person or persons in the name of the state. Political power, as opposed to economic, social, or religious power, is generally associated with the ability to control or direct the resources of the state.

Although the concept of political power is often placed in the context of the master-slave relationship, modern political theory—derived from commentators as ancient as Aristotle—posits a consensual basis for it. The power of some to command the actions of others for a common purpose of the state rests constitutionally on the acceptance by the governed of the need for the governors to exercise such power for a limited purpose and for a limited time. The people of the state grant to the governors through a constitution the power or authority to exercise government powers, and such powers often include power over life and death—sending troops into combat and limiting or in some cases prohibiting capital punishment. In a broader sense, political power may also encompass the relative abilities of certain individuals, such as candidates for office and party leaders vying for office, to persuade others that they should receive grants of authority.

Political power may also reside outside the constitutional framework, in which people hold office in accordance with the constitution and exercise power in the name of the people or the state. By definition, a constitution limits power and often divides it among various government components. In Libya, by contrast, Colonel Mu'ammar al-Qadhafi rules without having a constitutional position in the government. The Saudi Arabian monarch also has unlimited power in all aspects of government, except to the extent that he limits himself in some way. Similarly, the German constitution of 1871, although it provided for a representative parliament, in fact left real power in the monarchy. In modern constitutional monarchies, however, to a large extent the power of the monarch is symbolic, with actual political power exercised by the legislature or through the executive and judicial officers it selects and supervises.

Constitutions that do not provide for a ceremonial monarch or president as head of state generally separate the powers of government into three roughly coequal branches: executive, legislative, and judicial. The powers granted to each branch are in most instances enumerated, and any powers not specifically granted are denied to that branch. But judicial decisions along with tradition and custom may expand the enumerated powers. Powers granted to the legislative branch in a limited monarchy or a parliamentary system differ to some extent from those in a presidential or congressional system, particularly in the selection and control of the executive branch members. Powers granted to the executive branch in parliamentary and presidential systems also vary significantly. The independence of the judicial branch is generally declared in written constitutions, but the powers of the judiciary, particularly to review and nullify unconstitutional acts of the other two branches, in fact may be quite limited.

Constitution of Peru (1993), Section IV, Concerning the Structure of Government, Chapter IV, Executive Branch, Article 118: "It is the duty of the president of the republic to: . . . 8. exercise the power of regulating laws without violating or distorting them and, within these limits, issue orders and resolutions."

Constitution of Nigeria (1989), Chapter I, General Provisions, Part II, Powers of the Federal Republic of Nigeria, Article 4: "(1) The legislative powers of the Federal Republic of Nigeria shall be vested in a national assembly for the federation which shall consist of a senate and a house of representatives."

Constitution of Japan (1889, significantly revised in 1947), Chapter VI, Judiciary, Article 76: "The whole judicial power is vested in a supreme court and in such inferior courts as are established by law."

Preamble

Perhaps the most significant constitutional preamble is the opening statement of the U.S. Constitution (1789). In essay 84 of *The Federalist* (1788), Alexander Hamilton declares that the phrase "We, the people . . . do *ordain* and *establish* this constitution . . . ." [Hamilton's emphasis] is a better recognition of popular rights than volumes of aphorisms or the concessions wrung from the English monarchs over the centuries as recorded in documents such as Magna Carta (1215) and the English Bill of Rights (1688).

Some constitutions dispense with a preamble, or introduction—from the Latin words *pre* (before) and *ambulo* (to walk)—but many written constitutions have some prefatory language that introduces the legal language of the document. The preamble to the U.S. Constitution contains only fifty-two words.

Although the constitutions of countries dominated by the Communist Party may mask the country's real power structure, their preambles often shed some light on the reason the party leaders decided to promulgate the document.

In the United Kingdom a preamble is also the part of a bill presented to Parliament that contains the reasons for and the intended effect of the proposed legislation. Such preambles are not essential to a bill and are often omitted; however, the language in a preamble may be helpful in interpreting the law itself.

Constitution of India (1950), Preamble (amended in 1977): "We, the people of India, having solemnly resolved to constitute India into a sovereign socialist secular democratic republic and to secure to all its citizens: justice, social, economic, and political; liberty of thought, expression, belief, faith, and worship; equality of status and of opportunity; and to promote among them all fraternity assuring the dignity of the individual and the unity and integrity of the nation; in our constituent assembly this twenty-sixth day of November, 1949, do hereby adopt, enact, and give to ourselves this constitution."

Constitution of Vietnam (1980), Preamble (amended in 1992): "Since 1986, the comprehensive national renovation undertaking initiated by the sixth congress of the Communist Party of Vietnam has had initial yet very important achievements. The national assembly decided to amend the 1980 constitution to meet the requirements arising from the new situation and tasks."

Constitution of the Czech Republic (1993), Preamble: "We, the citizens of the Czech Republic in Bohemia, Moravia, and Silesia, at the time of the renewal of an independent Czech state, loyal to the good traditions of the ancient statehood of the lands of the Czech Crown and the Czechoslovak statehood, . . . through our freely elected representatives, adopt this constitution of the Czech Republic."

Chou En-lai (shown with a group of American students) was the premier of the People's Republic of China from its inception in 1949 until his death in 1976.

Premier

In some countries the person who holds the position of prime minister is called the premier—from the Latin *primarius* (chief or of the first rank). The term *premier* is a title, not a functional description, because the duties and powers of a premier vary considerably. The 1958 constitution of the Fifth Republic of France, for example, refers to the head of government as the premier and to the head of state as the president; previously, under the Third and Fourth Republics, the head of government was called the president of the council of ministers. In the past the first prime minister of the British Crown (the prime minister of Great Britain) and of some of its former colonies were called premiers; today the chief minister of a state or province in Australia and Canada is still known as the premier.

Unlike today's British prime minister, who is a member of and elected by the lower house of Parliament and remains prime minister for as long as he or she commands a majority in Parliament, the French premier is chosen by the president; neither he nor the other government ministers are members of the parliament. In fact, it is constitutionally incompatible for a member of the French government (its cabinet) to be a parliamentary member. The first premier of the Fifth Republic, although not constitutionally required to do so, submitted himself and his cabinet to the parliament, just as a typical prime minister would do, and received a favorable vote of confidence. Since then other premiers have followed this precedent.

Constitution of France (1958), Title II, The President of the Republic, Article 8: "The president of the republic shall appoint the premier. He shall terminate the functions of the premier when the latter presents the resignation of the government."

Constitution of China (People's Republic of China) (1982), Chapter Three, The Structure of the State, Section III, The State Council, Article 86: "The state council [the highest organ of state administration] is composed of the following: the premier; vice premiers; the state councillors. . . . The premier has overall responsibility for the state council. The ministers have overall responsibility for the respective ministries or commissions under their charge."

Prerogative

In English law a prerogative is a discretionary power or will above and uncontrolled by any other power or will. It manifests itself particularly in the royal prerogative—the rights and capacities enjoyed by the sovereign—but it can be any special power, privilege, immunity, or advantage vested in an official or a government body, such as a legislature or court. In his eighteenth-century commentaries on English law, William Blackstone catalogued several felonies as immediately injurious to the royal prerogative, including serving a foreign prince, embezzling or destroying the sovereign's arsenal, deserting the sovereign's armies in time of war, and offenses relating to coinage.

Monarchs in constitutional monarchies are still accorded limited royal prerogatives. These rights in the United Kingdom, for example, now stem from the sovereign's preeminence as recognized by the common law and modified to some extent by statute. They include the monarch's immunity from civil and criminal proceedings; exemption from the operation of statutes or custom; titular supremacy over the church, armed forces, and state; recognition as the source of all honors; and special privileges in relation to property rights. The royal prerogative has been limited over the centuries by documents such as Magna Carta (1215), the Petition of Right (1628), the Bill of Rights (1688), and the Act of Settlement (1700).

Under the doctrine of inherent powers as recognized by the U.S. Supreme Court, the executive branch of the U.S. government has its own "prerogative powers," especially with respect to foreign affairs in protecting the security and well-being of its citizens.

Constitution of the United Kingdom, Halsbury's Laws of England (4th ed., 1974), Volume 8, Constitutional Law, Paragraph 806, Sources of Powers and Duties: "The specific legal sources of governmental powers and duties are the specific sources of law, that is to say: . . . (2) that part of the common law which relates exclusively to the sovereign, and is called the royal prerogative; (3) prerogative rules and orders made and issued by the Crown, acting in exercise of the power entrusted to it by virtue of the common law, and embodied in 'orders in council,' treaties, charters, proclamations relating to the colonies or dependencies, and other executive documents. . . . "

Constitution of the Netherlands (1814), Chapter II, The Government, Section I, The King, Article 32: "Upon assuming the royal prerogative the king shall be sworn in and inaugurated as soon as possible in the capital city, Amsterdam. . . . "

Constitution of Thailand (1991), Chapter II, The King, Section 9: "The king has the prerogative power to create titles and confer decorations."

President

According to most constitutions, the head of state is called a monarch or president. A president may be either a surrogate monarch in a parliamentary system of government, with the traditional ceremonial duties of a monarch and varying degrees of real power, or the chief executive and head of government as well as head of state in a presidential system. The term *president* derives from the Latin words *praesideo* (to guard or direct) and *praesidere* (to sit before or preside over).

The presidency created by the U.S. Constitution (1789) was modeled somewhat on the governorships of the constituent states. Historically the appointed governor or lieutenant of a province or national division was called a president, and the term was used in England in this context as early as the fourteenth century. Alexander Hamilton makes it clear in essay 69 of *The Federalist* (1788) that the person in whom executive power is vested under the U.S. Constitution is, unlike the monarch of Great Britain, an elected position rather than a hereditary one, although the incumbent could be reelected every four years if the voters so desired. (However, the term of the U.S. president was limited by constitutional amendment in 1951.)

A president is generally the commander in chief of the armed forces in addition to being the head of state and government. He or she also appoints or nominates high officials in both the executive and judicial branches, confers honors, and grants pardons. A president is usually the head of the political party that sponsored his or her election to office, but he or she may not always be able to command a majority of the members of the legislature as a prime minister must be able to do.

U.S. President Jimmy Carter meets with El-Hadj Omar Bongo, the president of the Republic of Gabon, in 1977.

In governments that are only presidential in style, however, the president generally functions more as a monarch or ceremonial head of state, while a prime minister who has the support of a majority of the legislators—and therefore holds supreme political power—serves as the head of government. This type of system has many variations in which the relative powers of a president vis-à-vis a prime minister vary greatly. The power of an incumbent president, like that of a prime minister, may depend to some extent on his or her personal popularity and character.

In some constitutions the presiding officers in judicial and legislative bodies also may be referred to as presidents. And under the 1978 Spanish constitution, which establishes a limited monarchy, the position of prime minister is called the president.

Constitution of Mozambique (1990), Part III, Organs of State, Chapter II, The President of the Republic, Article 117: "1. The president of the republic is the head of state, embodying national unity, representing the nation domestically and internationally, and overseeing the correct operation of state organs. 2. The head of state shall be the guarantor of the constitution. 3. The president of the republic shall be the head of government. 4. The president of the republic shall be commander in chief of the armed and security forces."

Constitution of Finland, Constitution Act (1919), V, Courts of Law, Section 54: "The supreme court shall comprise a president and the requisite number of supreme court justices."

The Press

The first successful daily newspaper was started in London in 1702, after which newspapers quickly increased in circulation and influence. In Germany the first weekly publications of public opinion appeared after 1720. The constitutional reforms in Great Britain and the American colonies are attributable in large part to the reformers'

Johann Gutenberg's invention of movable type in the mid-fifteenth century led to the mass production of written text and the spread of democratic ideas, a freedom secured in documents such as the U.S. Bill of Rights (1791).

ability to disseminate written information rapidly among the population. One hundred twenty thousand copies of Thomas Paine's pamphlet *Common Sense,* printed in early 1776, were sold in three months, inciting Americans to revolt against Britain. The framers of the U.S. Constitution initially debated whether to include a guarantee of freedom of the press in the original document, which became effective in 1789; this guarantee was not included until the Bill of Rights was adopted in 1791.

The notion of a free press is predicated on the right of uncensored publication: prohibiting the government from reviewing material before dissemination and exercising prior restraint of expression. This does not mean that publishers are not to be held legally responsible for libel, obscenity, or incitement to crime after publication. Like other freedoms, freedom of the press is not absolute; often it must be weighed against other rights and obligations. The rights of a person accused of a crime, for example, can be jeopardized by publication of a misleading account of the crime, and a government's international negotiations or defense plans may be put at risk by irresponsible journalism. However, a free press, like free speech, contributes greatly to the interchange of ideas, especially the political ideas on which a constitutional democracy depends.

Because a hallmark of a totalitarian government is state control of the press—newspapers, periodicals, and other media—many constitutions give special protection to a free press. Sweden's Freedom of the Press Act, enacted in 1766 and revised most recently in 1992, is one of the country's basic constitutional documents.

"The time, it is to be hoped, is gone by, when any defense would be necessary of the 'liberty of the press' as one of the securities against corrupt or tyrannical government," wrote John Stuart Mill in *On Liberty* (1859). Plato suggested otherwise in *The Republic,* preferring that the state supervise poets and compel them to implant the image of good spirits in their poems.

Constitution of Portugal (1976), Part I, Fundamental Rights and Duties, Section II, Rights, Freedoms, and Safeguards, Chapter I, Personal Rights, Freedoms, and Safeguards, Article 38, Freedom of the Press and Mass Media: "1. Freedom of the press shall be safeguarded. 2. Freedom of the press shall involve: a. The freedom of expression and creativeness for journalists and literary collaborators as well as a role for the former in giving editorial direction to the concerned mass media, save where the latter belong to the state or have a doctrinal or denominational character. . . ."

Constitution of Jordan (1952), Chapter Two, Rights and Duties of Jordanians, Article 15(ii): "Freedom of the press and publication shall be ensured within the limits of the law."

Prime Minister

In a true parliamentary system of government, as in the United Kingdom, the head of government is called the prime minister. Similar designations include premier, chancellor, and president of the council of ministers. The title, from the Latin words *primus* (first) and *minister* (servant), originally referred to a sovereign ruler's principal minister among many ministers. In Great Britain the position ultimately became identified with the leader of the political party that won a majority in the House of Commons, the lower house of Parliament.

The head of state, such as a monarch or president, usually ceremonially designates the prime minister, but the prime minister's power and authority to head the government actually stem from his or her support by a majority of the members of the legislature. Once selected, based on the political party's relative voting strength in the parliament, the prime minister then nominates the remaining members of the cabinet to serve in the government with the confidence of the parliamentary majority. In a coalition government the selection process may be more complicated.

The prime minister generally functions as the chief executive of the government except under constitutions that entrust this role to a head of state. He or she is responsible for developing the government's legislative program and having it approved by the parliament; keeping the head of state advised on important matters; presiding over meetings of the council of ministers or cabinet and generally supervising the ministers; and presenting, as a formality, official acts to the head of state for assent. The prime minister bears the ultimate responsibility to the

The Right Honorable John Major, member of Parliament, was appointed prime minister of the British Parliament, first lord of the treasury, and minister for the civil service of the United Kingdom government in 1990.

parliament for all government actions. If the prime minister loses the confidence of the majority in parliament, he or she and the cabinet must resign and stand for reelection in new parliamentary elections. To continue in office the prime minister's supporters must be elected to a majority of the seats in the new parliament.

There are many variations of the United Kingdom model of parliamentary government (known as the Westminster model), and varying degrees of power are entrusted to a prime minister. The political power and duties of a prime minister in a Westminster-model parliamentary government are generally not spelled out in written constitutional documents but flow from tradition and well-established custom. Some written constitutions, like France's 1958 document, do not allow the prime minister, there called a premier, and the cabinet to be members of the parliament; others, like the 1993 Peruvian constitution, permit the president to appoint and remove the prime minister at will. Australia's 1901 written constitution and others make no mention of the position of prime minister, which, as in the United Kingdom, is a creature of custom.

Crown Prince Asfa Wossen, the heir apparent to the throne of Ethiopia, declared himself emperor in 1989.

Constitution of Singapore (1963), Part V, The Government, Chapter 2, The Executive, Article 28: "(1) The cabinet shall not be summoned except by the authority of the prime minister. (2) The prime minister shall, so far as is practicable, attend and preside at meetings of the cabinet and, in his absence, such other minister shall preside as the prime minister shall appoint."

Constitution of Kuwait (1962), Part IV, Powers, Chapter II, The Head of State, Article 56: "The emir shall, after the traditional consultations, appoint the prime minister and relieve him of office. The emir shall also appoint ministers and relieve them of office upon the recommendation of the prime minister."

Prince

In the first century B.C. Gaius Julius Caesar Octavianus, called Augustus, came to be known by the Latin term *princeps* (first citizen), from which the English word *prince* is most likely derived. A prince is generally a sovereign, a ruler, a monarch, or even a king. Niccolò Machiavelli, writing in early-sixteenth-century Florence, describes in *The Prince* his ideal supreme ruler: ruthless, efficient, and defiant, one who personifies the state and uses his autocratic power to further the interests of the state and himself.

Used in England as early as the thirteenth century, the term prince was applied even to female sovereigns, including Elizabeth I. It has come to refer to any male member of a royal family and in the United Kingdom to the son or grandson of a king or queen, sometimes called a "prince of the [royal] blood." The heir apparent to the throne is often given the title of prince; for example, the Spanish heir apparent is called the Prince of Asturias.

The word *prince* is not used in many modern constitutions, except in those of some limited monarchies and in the constitution of the Principality of Monaco.

Constitution of Monaco (1962), Title I, The Principality—The Public Powers, Article 3: "The executive power is derived from the high authority of the prince. The person of the prince is inviolable."

Constitution of the Netherlands (1814), Chapter Two, Government, Section I, The King, Article 24: "The title to the throne shall be hereditary and shall vest in the legitimate descendants of King William I, Prince of Orange."

Constitution of the United States of America (1789), Article I, Section 9: " . . . no Person holding any Office of Profit or Trust . . . shall, without the Consent of the Congress, accept of any present, Emolument, Office, or Title, of any kind whatever, from any King, Prince, or foreign State."

Privacy

Few people throughout history have had the luxury of a truly private aspect to their lives or privacy (from the Latin *privatus)* as we know it today. Even Plato warns in *The Laws* against excluding a citizen's private life from legislation. But by the nineteenth century John Stuart Mill wrote, "Nobody desires that laws should interfere with the whole detail of private life."

It is only in the last half century that privacy—the right to conduct one's personal affairs without government interference and to protect personal information from dissemination—has been acknowledged as a protected personal freedom. Although the U.S. Constitution (1789) does not specifically mention the right of privacy, the U.S. Supreme Court has found support for a general right of privacy in the language of the First, Fourth, and Ninth Amendments (1791).

English courts have long held that if no remedy at common law exists for a violation of the right of privacy, then equity—the more flexible branch of English jurisprudence—may be invoked to prevent injury.

Many constitutions now include the right of privacy or language to this effect in the enumeration of individual rights and freedoms that are to be protected by the government.

Pro-choice demonstrators in Washington, D.C., stress a woman's right to privacy against government interference.

Constitution of South Africa (1994), Chapter 3, Fundamental Rights, Privacy, Article 13: "Every person shall have the right to his or her personal privacy, which shall include the right not to be subject to searches of his or her person, home, or property, the seizure of private possessions or the violation of private communication."

Constitution of Sweden, Instrument of Government (1974), Chapter 2, Fundamental Rights and Freedoms, Article 3: "No record about a citizen in a public register may be based without his consent solely on his political opinions. Citizens shall be protected to the extent determined in detail by law against any infringement of their personal integrity resulting from the registration of information about them by means of electronic data processing."

Private.

See Privacy; Public

Privilege

Although equality among all citizens is a basic principle of democratic constitutionalism, most constitutions extend privileges and immunities to various classes of citizens, most notably to heads of state, members of the legislature, the disabled, women, children, and formerly oppressed or disadvantaged classes. The Latin word *jus* (law or legal status) also can mean privilege, which is adapted from the Latin *privilegium* (private or secular law).

Under general parliamentary procedures a member of a body has the right to raise a point of personal or constitutional privilege that takes precedence over all other business. A bill of privilege in the upper house of the British Parliament is a petition by a peer to be tried by his or her peers, and a writ of privilege demands the release of a privileged person from arrest in a civil matter.

Article 1, Section 6, of the U.S. Constitution (1789) states that members of Congress, except in certain cases, are privileged from arrest during sessions of their respective houses. The Fourteenth Amendment (1868) prohibits the states from making or enforcing any law abridging the privileges and immunities of U.S. citizens, a provision added specifically to protect U.S. citizens formerly held in slavery.

Constitution of Denmark (1953), Part VIII, Section 83: "All privileges by legislation attached to nobility, title, and rank shall be abolished."

Constitution of Zimbabwe (1979), Chapter V, Parliament, Part 4, Senate and House of Assembly, Section 49 (amended in 1989): "Subject to the provisions of this constitution, an act of parliament may make provision to determine and regulate the privileges and immunities and powers of parliament and the members and officers thereof. . . . "

Constitution of Malaysia (1957), Part XII, General and Miscellaneous, Article 153(2): " . . . the [monarch] shall . . . ensure the reservation for Malays and natives of the states of Sabah and Sarawak of such proportion as he may deem reasonable of positions in the public service . . . and of scholarships, exhibitions and other similar educational or training privileges or special facilities. . . . "

Privy Council

In Great Britain the privy council (from the medieval Latin *concilium privatum)* was a body of advisers to the sovereign selected by the sovereign, together with others included by custom, such as princes of the blood, archbishops, present chief officers of the government, and past ministers of state. The council grew out of the *curia regis* (king's council) of the Norman rulers. Later, this council split into what became Parliament and the courts, with a small "continual council" that acted as a superior court of appeals.

As vice president of the United States and president of the Senate, Thomas Jefferson in 1801 compiled a manual of procedure for the Senate that is still used today.

The privy council in the United Kingdom, consisting of about three hundred people who hold or have held high office, now functions ceremonially only on certain occasions to sign proclamations, such as at the ascension of a new king or queen. The judicial committee, however, consisting of the lord chief justice, lord justices of appeal, the attorney general, lord advocate, and others, still serves as the country's highest court of appeals and until recently was the highest court of appeals for many members of the British Commonwealth. Canada has its own privy council to the monarch, consisting of cabinet ministers and others, but its role is also only ceremonial.

Constitution of Australia (1901), Chapter III, The Judicature, Section 73: "(iii) . . . But no exception or regulation prescribed by the parliament shall prevent the high court from hearing and determining any appeal from the supreme court of a state in any matter in which at the establishment of the commonwealth an appeal lies from such supreme court to the queen in council [the privy council]." [The Australia Act of 1986 terminated the possibility of appeals from Australian courts to the privy council in the United Kingdom.]

Constitution of Canada, British North America Act (1867), Title II, Union, Section 3: "It shall be lawful for the queen, by and with the advice of her majesty's most honorable privy council, to declare by proclamation that . . . the provinces of Canada, Nova Scotia, and New Brunswick shall form and be one dominion under the name of Canada. . . . "

Procedure

In law *procedure* has two meanings. In the broader sense it is the legal machinery that confers rights and duties and imposes the rules of substantive law. In the narrower sense it is that part of law governing the process of initiating and seeing through to conclusion a legal claim or action in a court of law.

Procedures—from the French *procédure* (practice or proceedings)—cited in constitutions often refer to the rules by which a legislature or other government body conducts its business, but the term ordinarily means a system or method of proceeding. Some constitutions provide detailed instructions on rules of procedure for bodies such as legislatures, while others simply authorize a body to establish its own rules of procedure.

Constitution of Venezuela (1961), Title V, The National Legislative Power, Chapter IV, Common Provisions, Article 156: "The requirements and procedures for the installation and other sessions of the chambers [of the legislature], and for the functioning of their committees, shall be determined by the regulations."

Constitution of Austria (1920), Chapter III, Federal Execution, A, Administration, 1, The Federal President, Article 60(1): "Detailed provisions about the electoral procedure and possible compulsory voting will be established by a federal law."

Procurator

Especially in countries dominated by the Communist Party, constitutions may use the terms *procurator* or *procuratorate* in sections on the courts to refer to the legal representative of the state in judicial, particularly criminal, matters. A procurator (derived from Latin and French words meaning a manager or an agent) does not function as an independent prosecutor under true constitutional systems, which attempt to maintain a strict separation between legal enforcement authorities and the judicial branch of government.

In Scottish law a procurator in *rem suam* is a person acting under a procuration (a power of attorney).

Constitution of Vietnam (1976), Chapter X, People's Courts and People's Organs of Control, Article 138: "The formation of the control committees, the problems that the chief procurators of the people's organs of control have the power to decide on, and the important issues the control committees must discuss and decide based on the views of the majority are defined by law."

Constitution of China (People's Republic of China) (1982), Chapter III, The Structure of the State, Section VII, The People's Courts and the People's Procuratorates, Article 129: "The people's procuratorates of the People's Republic of China are state organs for legal supervision."

Promulgate

To put a new law, ordinance, decree, or even a new constitution into effect is to promulgate it, from the Latin *promulgo* (to publish). Promulgate in French is *promulguer*, in Spanish *promulgar*, and in German *verkünden* or *verbeiten*.

Constitutions may or may not expressly require that a law be promulgated or published to become effective. The U.S. Constitution (1789) requires only that a bill be passed by both houses of Congress and signed by the president or that, in the case of a bill vetoed by the president, it be passed again in each house by a two-thirds majority vote.

Constitution of Zambia (1991), Part IV, The Executive, Article 44(3): "Subject to the provisions of this constitution dealing with assent to laws passed by parliament and the promulgation of such laws . . . the president shall have power to—(a) sign and promulgate any proclamation which by law he is entitled to proclaim as president. . . ."

Constitution of South Africa (1994), Chapter 5, The Adoption of the New Constitution, Adoption of the New Constitutional Text, Article 73(13): "A new constitutional text adopted in terms of this chapter shall be assented to by the president and shall upon its promulgation [in 1996] be the constitution of the Republic of South Africa."

Proportional Representation

The most common system of voting for legislators, as used in the United States and United Kingdom, simply requires that the successful candidate in any one constituency receive a plurality, or most, of the votes cast. But since the mid-nineteenth century this method has been criticized as not being truly democratic because it allows for only one winner and therefore only one view of issues from each electoral district, thus tending to create a narrow two-party political system. Another criticism is that the votes for the losing candidates are wasted—that is, the people who voted for the losing candidates have no representation. To counteract these effects, proportional representation methods have been adopted in a number of countries.

There are two basic types of proportional voting: (1) the party list method, or list voting, which emphasizes the role of political parties, uses multimember constituencies in which seats are distributed as closely as possible in accordance with each party's total popular vote, and (2) the single transferable voting method, which emphasizes the candidates rather than the parties. Under this method each constituency elects several members to the legislature, and candidates with or without party affiliation can get on the ballot. Each voter then ranks the candidates according to his or her own preferences. The votes are tabulated on the basis of the number of first-place rankings, and then an electoral quota is determined according to one of several formulas. If no candidate attains the quota of the first-place votes, the candidate with the fewest first-place votes is dropped and the second-place votes on his or her ballots are then distributed to the other candidates respectively as first-place votes. This process continues until all the seats for a particular constituency are filled.

Some constitutions specify that voting is to be by proportional representation only, and some actually indicate the type of proportional voting method to be used.

Constitution of Portugal (1976), Part III, Organization of Political Power, Section III, Assembly of the Republic, Chapter I, Status and Election, Article 155, System of Election: "1. Members of the assembly shall be elected by the system of proportional representation according to the Hondt highest average method. 2. The conversion of votes cast into effective suffrages shall not be limited by law through any requirements as to a minimum national percentage of the votes."

Constitution of Iceland (1944), Chapter Four, Article 43: "The Althing [parliament] shall elect, by proportional representation, three salaried auditors, who shall annually audit the national revenue and expenditure accounts. . . ."

Prorogue. *See* Adjournment

Prosecution

William Blackstone, the eighteenth-century commentator on the laws of England, described prosecution as a manner of formal accusation against an alleged offender resulting from a finding of fact by an inquest or a grand jury or without such a finding. In criminal law prosecution—from the Latin *prosequi* (to pursue or present)—is the action of bringing a person accused of a crime to trial to determine his or her guilt or innocence.

Under constitutions that maintain a strict separation of powers, such as the U.S. Constitution (1789), the office of public prosecution is generally located in the executive branch, although in the United States under certain circumstances special prosecutors or independent counsels may be authorized by the other branches of government to investigate public officials. Some constitutions include the public prosecution function in the judicial branch, which makes the possibility of independence in ordinary criminal matters problematic.

Constitution of Egypt (1971), Part Five, System of Government, Chapter VI, The Socialist Public Prosecutor, Article 179: "The socialist public prosecutor shall be responsible for taking procedures which secure the people's rights, the safety of the society and its political system, the preservation of the socialist achievements, and commitment to the socialist behavior. The law shall define his other competences. He shall be subject to the control of the people's assembly [legislature] in accordance to what is prescribed by law."

Constitution of Bulgaria (1991), Chapter 6, The Judicial Branch, Article 129: "(1) Judges, prosecutors, and investigators are appointed, promoted, demoted, transferred, or dismissed by the high judicial council."

Prosecutor General. *See* Solicitor General

Protection. *See* Security

Provision

In England enactments of the "king in council" were historically designated as provisions. To reform certain abuses, English barons in 1259 issued their own body of ordinances and declarations entitled the Provisions of Westminster. During the reign of Edward I (1272–1307), royal enactments became known as statutes.

In the broadest constitutional sense a provision—from the Latin *providus* (prudent) and *privideo* (to foresee or provide for)—is simply a portion of written language dealing with a particular subject, usually designed as an article or a section. Typically, however, a provision is a clause or division in constitutional documents or a proviso, a clause that creates a stipulation or condition.

A transitional or transitory provision is one that lasts just for a period of transition, generally between a previous constitutional document and a new one. Constitutions may also include temporary provisions, supplementary or additional provisions, and special provisions. The Canadian and Indian constitutions have schedules, which are similar to supplementary provisions. Some constitutions have final or concluding provisions.

Constitution of Nepal (1990), Part 21, Transitional Provision, Article 129: "The Making of Laws Prior to the First Session of the Parliament: His majesty, after commencement of this constitution and prior to the holding of the first session of the parliament, shall have power to make and promulgate necessary laws with the advice and by the consent of the council of ministers."

Constitution of Malaysia (1957), Eighth Schedule, Article 71, Provisions to Be Inserted in State Constitution, Part I, Final Provisions: "1. Ruler to act on advice (1) In the exercise of his functions under the constitution of this state or any law or as a member of the conference of rulers the ruler shall act in accordance with the advice of the executive council or of a member thereof acting under the general authority of the council. . . ."

Public

In the ancient Greece of Plato and Aristotle, public life, at least for free men, encompassed a broad range of important activity. Later in Rome the concept of *res publica* (commonwealth) evolved from *res* (a thing or matter) and *publica* (of the state). This concept reflected the fact that a large segment of the population, not just a ruling house or family, took an interest in the government. In contrast to *res publica, res privata* was a private fund of the Roman emperors acquired from confiscated property and used to buy the loyalty of the army.

Today the word *public*—derived from the Latin terms *publicus* (of the state) and *populus* (the people)—has the broad meaning of being outside the house or family, such as speaking in public, and a narrower meaning in reference to the government, such as public office or public funds. It may also refer to quasi-government or nonprofit operations, such as a public corporation or public broadcasting.

Constitutions vary widely in their use of the term *public*, and specific meanings can be gleaned only from the context and history of particular provisions. Some constitutions distinguish between public property and private property and between public laws, those that affect citizens at large, and private laws, which affect only certain individuals.

Constitution of Italy (1948), Part One, The Duties and Rights of the Citizens, Title I, Civil Relations, Article 28: "Government and public agencies' officials and employees are directly liable, pursuant to criminal, civil, and administrative laws, for the acts carried out in violation of the rights [set forth in preceding articles]. In such cases civil liability is extended also to the state and public agencies."

Constitution of Libya, Constitutional Proclamation (1969), Chapter I, The State, Article 4: "Work in the Libyan Arab Republic is a right, a duty, and an honor for every able-bodied citizen. Public functions are the duty of those who are put in charge of them. The goal of the state employees in discharging their duties is to serve the people."

Public Service. *See* Civil Service

Publication

Derived from the Latin *publicare* (to publish), publication is the act of making a thing public, offering it to the public, or making it accessible to public scrutiny. As early as the fourteenth century one common meaning of publication in England was to print and distribute materials such as books or pamphlets to the public at large, free or for a price. The publication in the nineteenth century of material supporting the lawfulness of tyrannicide resulted in the Government Press Prosecutions of 1858, infringing, at least for a while, the right of publication by private individuals in the United Kingdom.

In constitutions publication may refer to the right of a free press or of expression—that is, the right to publish material without prior restraint—as well as to steps required to make government acts or documents available for public scrutiny.

Constitution of Israel, Basic Law: The Knesset (1958), Section 28: "The publication of proceedings taken and utterances made at an open meeting [of the parliament] is not restricted and does not entail any criminal or civil liability; provided that the chairman of the meeting may, in such manner as has been prescribed by the rules, prohibit the publication of anything the publication of which may, in his opinion, prejudice the security of the state."

Constitution of Chile (1980), Chapter V, National Congress, Article 72: "Promulgation [of enacted laws] must always be made within a period of ten days from the date on which such promulgation should be in order. Publication shall occur within five working days following the date on which the decree of promulgation is totally processed."

Constitution of the United States of America (1789), Article I, Section 9: "No Money shall be drawn from the Treasury, but in Consequence of Appropriations made by Law; and a regular Statement and Account of the receipts and Expenditures of all public Money shall be published from time to time."

Punishment

John Stuart Mill concluded in *On Liberty* (1859) that when a person's actions are prejudicial to the interests of others, he is accountable and may be subjected to social and legal punishment. Forms of punishment dating to ancient Athens included fines, disenfranchisement, imprisonment, and exile; executions were rare except in such cases as the murder of an Athenian by an alien. In

In many countries such as China, caning has been a historically acceptable form of legal punishment for criminals.

the Roman military, punishment included flogging, dishonorable discharge, and execution. In the eighteenth century William Blackstone, the commentator on the laws of England, noted that earlier a woman convicted of treason was burned alive and that a man who committed high treason was disemboweled alive.

In criminal law punishment is any pain, penalty, or suffering inflicted by legal authority based on a court's judgment and sentencing of a person for a crime or an offense committed or for an omission of duty enjoined by law. In constitutions punishment and restrictions on punishment, such as the prohibition of the death penalty or cruel and unusual punishment, are usually set forth in the section dealing with the rights and duties of citizens or with the jurisdiction and authority of the courts. Constitutions also generally specify punishment for violation of the qualifications and rules of legislative bodies and for certain crimes of public officials, such as treason.

Punishment springs from good principles, Aristotle suggests in *The Politics*, adding that it would be better if individuals and the state could do without it.

Constitution of Singapore (1963), Part IV, Fundamental Liberties, Article 11(1): "No person shall be punished for an act or omission which was not punishable by law when it was done or made, and no person shall suffer greater punishment for an offense than was prescribed by law at the time it was committed."

Constitution of Nicaragua (1987), Title IV, Rights, Duties, and Guarantees of the Nicaraguan People, Chapter I, Article 39: "In Nicaragua the penitentiary system is humane, and it has as a fundamental objective the transformation of the interned in order to reintegrate him or her into society. The progressive stages within the penitentiary system shall promote family unity, health care, education and cultural advancement, and productive occupation with financial compensation for the interned. Sentences have a reeducational character."

Qadhafi, Mu'ammar Abu Minyar al-

After seizing power in Libya in 1969, the dictator Mu'ammar Abu Minyar al-Qadhafi (b. 1942) replaced the Libyan constitutional monarchy with his own concept of direct democracy based on Islamic socialism.

Mu'ammar al-Qadhafi was born in 1942 near Surt, Libya. The son of a Bedouin farmer, he attended school in Sebha and became a devout Muslim. While a student at the University of Libya in 1961, he was identified as one of the instigators of an Arab unity demonstration. He was graduated from the university in 1963 and from the Libyan military academy in 1965.

While in Sebha, Qadhafi formed a secret society called the Free Officers, named after a similar group created by Gamal Abd al-Nasser in Egypt, which planned to overthrow the government of King Sayyid Muhammad Idris. In August 1969, while in Turkey for medical treatment, King Idris announced his intention to abdicate the throne. On September 1, 1969, the Free Officers took control of the Libyan army barracks and the radio station without significant resistance.

In December 1969 a ruling revolutionary council headed by Qadhafi issued a constitutional proclamation declaring Libya to be a part of the Arab Nation and dedicated to "the realization of socialism through the application of social justice." The document established the revolutionary command council as the supreme executive and legislative authority in the country. Qadhafi held the posts of commander of the armed forces and chairman of the council.

After taking steps to expel all non-Arab Libyans and nationalize foreign-owned oil interests, Qadhafi began a campaign in 1974 to instill his personal concept of Islamic socialism throughout the country. His vision of true democracy was described in *The Green Book* (so titled because green is the traditional color of the Islamic religion), published in two volumes in 1976 and 1980. In it Qadhafi claims that direct democracy is superior to representational democracy as practiced in most nation-states of the world because it does not allow a majority to rule the minority, which is dictatorship in disguise.

In 1979 the Declaration on the Establishment of the Authority of the People was issued, ostensibly to put Qadhafi's political philosophy into practice. It established as the chief law-making body a general people's congress, whose more than one thousand delegates meet about two weeks every year. Leaders of Qadhafi's political network, originally called the Arab Socialist Union, maintain a working majority in the congress.

In some ways Qadhafi's singular form of "democracy" draws on the ideas of Jean-Jacques Rousseau, who noted that the English were sovereign only when they went to the polls; between parliamentary elections they were at the mercy of those whom they had elected. In fact, Qadhafi is a dictator who rules by controlling the armed forces.

Colonel Mu'ammar al-Qadhafi's *Green Book* promotes his own concept of direct democracy, in contrast to the representational democracy on which most modern constitutional governments are based.

Qualification

Writing in the eighteenth century, William Blackstone, the commentator on English law, was able to justify property ownership as a necessary condition or qualification for being able to vote. Although this standard has been eliminated as a prerequisite for exercising one's democratic privileges, most constitutions do enumerate certain qualifications for voters, such as age, citizenship, and residency requirements.

They also specify qualifications for elected officials, including the president and vice president and members of the legislature, as well as for appointed officials, such as judges. Cabinet ministers may be required to be members of the legislature also—or they may be barred from holding dual positions—and judges may be to have a certain level of judicial training and experience. The U.S. Constitution (1789) indicates qualifications for presidential and vice presidential electors and members of Congress (which each house may judge for itself), as well as for president and vice president, but prohibits religious qualifications. Some constitutions, however, require adherence to a particular religious faith for holding certain government positions. Iran's 1979 constitution goes so far as to require specialized religious training and status for designated officials.

In addition to qualifications, constitutions often list disqualifications—from the French *disqualifier* (to render incapable)—that make a person ineligible or unfit to vote or hold an elective or appointive office in the government. The U.S. Constitution refers to certain disqualifications resulting from impeachment of public officials and barring senators and representatives from holding other offices. France's constitution disqualifies members of the parliament from holding certain other offices that are deemed incompatible with their parliamentary duties.

Constitution of Venezuela (1961), Title III, Duties, Rights, and Guarantees, Chapter VI, Political Rights, Article 111: "All Venezuelans who have reached eighteen years of age and who are not subject to civil interdiction or political disqualification are voters. Voting in municipal elections may be extended to foreigners, under such residence and other requirements as the law may establish."

Constitution of Kenya (1963), Chapter III, Part 1, Composition of Parliament, Article 43(2): "No person shall be qualified to be registered as a voter in elections to which this section applies—(a) if, under any law in force in Kenya, he is adjudged or otherwise declared to be of unsound mind. . . . "

Constitution of Bangladesh (1972), Part V, The Legislature, Chapter I, Parliament, Article 66(1): "A person shall . . . be qualified to be elected as, and to be a member of parliament, if he is a citizen of Bangladesh and has attained the age of twenty-five years."

Constitution of Pakistan (1973), Part III, The Federation of Pakistan, Chapter 1, The President, Article 41(2): "A person shall not be qualified for election as president unless he is a Muslim of not less than forty-five years of age and is qualified to be elected as a member of the national assembly."

Constitution of Honduras (1982), Title V, Branches of Government, Chapter VI, The Executive Branch, Article 239: "A citizen who has held the office of president under any title may not be president or a presidential designate. Any person who violates this provision or advocates its amendment as well as those that directly or indirectly support him shall immediately cease to hold their respective offices and shall be disqualified for ten years from holding any public office."

Queen.

See King; Monarch

Question

Members of a legislature, usually but not always a parliament rather than a congress, have the right to question a member of the government (the council of ministers or the cabinet or a lesser government official). This right of asking questions, sometimes called interpellation, is one means by which a parliament exercises its supervision over the government, which a majority of its members are supposed to support.

In Belgium, for example, questions and interpellations

reflect the parliament's constitutional right to call the government to account over policy and legislative proposals, which may lead to a vote of no confidence and the resignation of the prime minister and the cabinet.

A motion made by a member of a parliament, when repeated by the chairman of that body, is also called a question. To "move the previous question" is a subsidiary parliamentary motion that means to close debate and takes precedence over all other subsidiary motions except a motion to table or set aside a measure.

A constitutional question, another kind of question, is an issue that the constitution may charge the courts with answering by interpreting the constitution itself. A political question, on the other hand, is a controversial matter that the courts tend to avoid answering by finding that the constitution requires that it be answered by either the executive or legislative branch or by the people themselves.

Constitution of Finland, Parliament Act (1928), Chapter 3, Initiation of Matters in Parliament, Section 37: "If a representative wishes to put a question to a member of the council of state on a matter within the competence of the member, he shall submit the question in writing worded in precise terms to the speaker, who shall forward it to the member of the council of state. A question may also be asked when the parliamentary session has been interrupted."

Constitution of Colombia (1991), Title VI, Concerning the Legislative Branch, Chapter 1, Concerning Its Structure and Functions, Article 135: "Each chamber [of the congress] will have the following powers: . . . 4. To determine the holding of sessions reserved on a priority basis in order to deal with oral questions by the congressmen addressed to the ministries and the answers of the latter."

Quorum

Parliamentary rules generally require, in the absence of a specific rule, that a majority of the members of a body be present—creating a quorum—to transact business validly. Such a requirement is reasonable because as long as a majority of the members are present and agree to conduct business, even if every one of the absent members did not want to participate, they could be outvoted. Important business, however, may be postponed if only a minimal quorum is present simply because it may be prudent to make such decisions with more than a bare majority of the members present.

As used in constitutions, a quorum is the number of legislators necessary to conduct business or in some cases the number of members necessary to pass certain types of legislation—for example, proposed amendments to the constitution, which may require that a greater number of members be present. As early as the fifteenth century the term *quorum* referred to certain justices of the peace in England. The Latin phrase *Quorum vos . . . unum* ("of whom we will that you . . . be one") was used in certain commissions designating members of a body.

The upper house of the British Parliament, the House of Lords, has more than four hundred members, but only three members constitute a quorum; and in the lower house, the House of Commons, which has nearly seven hundred members, forty members constitute a quorum. The U.S. Constitution (1789) provides that a majority of the members of each house of Congress creates a quorum for conducting business.

Constitution of Japan (1889, significantly revised in 1947), Chapter IV, The Diet (Parliament), Article 56: "Business cannot be transacted in either house unless one-third or more of the total membership is present."

Constitution of Romania (1991), Title III, Public Authorities, Chapter I, Parliament, Section 1, Organization and Functioning, Article 64: "The chamber of deputies and the senate shall pass laws, and carry resolutions and motions, in the presence of the majority of their members."

Qur'an. *See* Islamic Law

SUPPLEMENT

TO THE

Independent Journal,

New-York, July 2, 1788.

In our Independent Journal of this Morning, we announced the Ratification of the New Conſtitution by the Convention of Virginia: For the gratification of our Readers, we publiſh the following particulars, received by this day's poſt:—

Ratification of the New Conſtitution, by the Convention of Virginia, on Wedneſday laſt, by a Majority of 10:---88 for it, 78 againſt it.

WE the delegates of the people of Virginia, duly elected, in purſuance of a recommendation of the General Aſſembly, and now met in Convention, having fully and fairly inveſtigated and diſcuſſed the proceedings of the Federal Convention, and being prepared as well as the moſt mature deliberation will enable us to decide thereon, DO, in the name and on behalf of the people of Virginia, declare and make known, that the powers granted under the Conſtitution being derived from the people of the United States, may be reſumed by them whenſoever the ſame

With theſe impreſſions, with a ſolemn appeal to the ſearcher of hearts for the purity of our intentions, and under the conviction, that whatſoever imperfections may exiſt in the Conſtitution, ought rather to be examined in the mode preſcribed therein, than to bring the UNION into danger by a delay, with a hope of obtaining amendments previous to the ratification:

We the ſaid delegates, in the name and in behalf of the people of Virginia, do by theſe preſents aſſent to and ratify the Conſtitution, recommended on the 17th day of September,

R

Ratification

An act of ratification—confirmation by giving consent—was recorded in England as early as the fourteenth century. Derived in part from the medieval Latin *ratificatio* (the act of sanctioning), ratification in law is the adoption of an action or a contract made by a person who would not otherwise have been bound by it.

Constitutions may require that international treaties and agreements negotiated by the executive branch of government be approved by the legislative branch, a process called legislative ratification. They may also specify that an action of one official or branch be confirmed or ratified by another.

States or provinces of federal nation-states or their voters additionally may be required to ratify, or approve, constitutional amendments or revisions. Article 5 of the U.S. Constitution (1789) dictates that amendments be ratified by the legislatures of three-fourths of the states or by conventions in three-fourths of the states, "as the one or the other Mode of Ratification may be proposed by the Congress."

Constitution of Lebanon (1926), Chapter IV, The Executive Power, Article 52: "The president of the republic shall negotiate and ratify treaties. . . . Treaties involving a charge upon the finances of the state, commercial treaties and, in general, treaties which cannot be denounced at the expiration of each year shall not be definitive until they have been adopted by the chamber [of deputies]."

Constitution of Mexico (1917), Title III, Chapter II, The Legislative Branch, Section III, Powers of Congress, Article 73: "The Congress has the power: . . . III. To form new states within the borders of existing ones. . . . 7. If the legislatures of the states whose territory is involved have not given their consent, the ratification [by a majority of the legislatures of the states] . . . must be passed by two thirds of the legislatures of the other states. . . . "

Reading

Before legislative votes are taken, specific periods are often allotted for discussion, questions, and debate related to a proposed measure—a process variously called reading or debate.

Constitutions that detail the procedures for the legislature may specify a certain number of readings of a bill, usually not more than three, before a final vote is taken. As a general rule, the first formal reading is perfunctory, after which a vote is taken to submit the matter to a specialized committee of the legislature. The committee is instructed to review the proposal and report to the full

The ratification of the U.S. Constitution by the Commonwealth of Virginia was announced in the *Independent Journal* newspaper in New York City on July 2, 1788. All thirteen former colonies ratified the document, Rhode Island being the last.

The Boxer Rebellion in 1900 was an attempt by members of a secret society to rid China of the influences of foreign governments. The rebels besieged the diplomatic offices of the British, French, Japanese, and Russians.

body with a recommendation for action. The second reading, after the committee's report has been made, is when real debate is possible, after which another vote is taken. The matter, along with any amendments, is then scheduled for a third and final reading, also usually perfunctory, and a third and final vote. Of course, not all legislative bodies follow this general outline all the time.

Constitution of Portugal (1976), Part III, Organization of Political Power, Section III, Assembly of the Republic, Chapter II, Powers, Article 171, Discussion and Voting: "1. Discussion of bills shall include two readings. 2. Voting shall include voting on first reading, voting on second reading, and a final, global vote. 3. Where the assembly so decides, the texts approved on the first reading shall be submitted to the committees for a vote on second reading, without prejudice to avocation by the assembly and to the latter's final vote for global approval."

Constitution of Ecuador (1979), Second Part, Title I, Legislative Function, Section II, The Enactment and Sanction of Legislation, Article 67: "Approval of bills calls for discussion in two debates; before the first debate takes place, the project will be read and the legislators may make any remarks. No law or decree project can be discussed without the text having been delivered to each legislator fifteen days in advance. . . . If during the course of the first debate, observations to the project should be presented, it will go back to the commission that originated it so that they can inform exclusively on those observations."

Rebellion

Patriots historically have sought to set limits on the power of rulers, asserts John Stuart Mill in *On Liberty* (1859), noting that specific resistance or general rebellion is justifiable if these limits are infringed.

Rebellion is the deliberate, organized resistance by force of arms to the authority, laws, and actions of officials of the legitimate government. Most constitutions avoid direct reference to rebellion, which, like revolution or secession, can destroy the basic order that the constitution seeks to create. Albert Camus, the twentieth-century existentialist, nonetheless suggests in *The Rebel* (1951) that "rebellion is one of man's essential dimensions."

Insurrection connotes a more limited and less organized event than rebellion. Either one may lead to a revolution and eventually a complete change in the basis of government. As internal uprisings, both may trigger emergency powers and actions, such as a declaration of martial law, during which the government attempts to restore peace and internal security. In essay 16 of *The Federalist* (1788), Alexander Hamilton argues: "As to those partial commotions and insurrections which sometimes disquiet society ... the general government could command more extensive resources for [their] suppression [than the constituent states]." Constitutional documents often incorporate provisions for such breaches of internal security, although they may not expressly mention the terms *rebellion* or *insurrection.*

Constitution of the United States of America (1789), Article I, Section 9: "The Privilege of the Writ of Habeas Corpus shall not be suspended, unless when in Cases of Rebellion or Invasion the public Safety may require it."

Constitution of the Philippines (1987), Article VII, Executive Department, Section 18: "The president shall be the commander in chief of all the armed forces of the Philippines and whenever it becomes necessary, he may call out such armed forces to prevent or suppress lawless violence, invasion, or rebellion."

Recall

Elected officials may be removed—recalled—from office before the expiration of their terms, a power that some constitutions grant to the voters. Along with the popular initiative and the referendum, recall is an important procedural device for the practice of direct democracy.

A diplomat is also subject to recall by being summoned to his or her home country and relieved of diplomatic duties. Constitutions may use the term in this sense or to mean the dismissal of any government official.

Constitution of Uganda, Simplified Draft (1992), Chapter 8, The Legislature (Parliament), Article 9: "Voters may recall an elected member on grounds and according to procedure which will be set out in the law regarding this matter."

Constitution of Russia (1993), Part One, Chapter 4, The President of the Russian Federation, Article 83: "The president of the Russian federation shall: . . . l) appoint and recall, after consultations with the corresponding committees or commissions of the houses of the federal assembly, diplomatic representatives of the Russian federation in foreign countries and international organizations."

Recess

In parliamentary procedures a recess—derived from the Latin word *recedere* (to recede) and the French words *recez* and *recès*—is an adjournment of a body for a limited time during its session. Constitutions may refer to a recess as a period when a legislature is not in session or the period between sessions of a continuous legislative body. The final adjournment of a legislative body before the convening of a new body after general elections, however, is called adjournment *sine die.*

A similar practice of taking short breaks in the proceedings is also common in courts of law.

Constitution of Ecuador (1979), Second Part, Title I, Legislative Function, Section II, The Enactment and Sanction of Legislation, Article 65: "If a bill regarding the economy were presented by the president of the republic and he qualified it as urgent, the national congress, or during its recess, the plenary of legislative commissions, must approve, reform, or refuse it in a period no longer than fifteen days. . . . "

Constitution of the United States of America (1789), Article II, Section 2: "The President shall have Power to fill up all Vacancies that happen during the Recess of the Senate, by granting Commissions which shall expire at the end of their next Session."

Reconsideration

A motion to reconsider a parliamentary action may be made only by a member who voted on the prevailing side and only on the same day as the first vote. If a motion to reconsider is carried, the matter is reopened for discussion and a new vote. No issue may be reconsidered twice unless it has been materially amended.

Under a constitution that grants the head of government the power to veto legislative proposals, legislatures may also reconsider a bill after it has been returned unapproved. The reconsideration procedure gives the legislature a chance either to accept the executive's veto or to attempt to override it by repassing the measure in accordance with the constitutionally prescribed procedures. Such procedures generally require repassage of the proposed legislation by a supermajority or after new legislative elections have been held.

Constitution of Romania (1991), Title III, Public Authorities, Chapter I, Parliament, Section 3, Legislation and Procedure, Article 77(2): "Before promulgation, the president of Romania may return the law to parliament for reconsideration, and he may do so only once."

Constitution of Taiwan (1947), Chapter V, Administration, Article 57: "2. If the legislative *yuan* [body] does not concur in any important policy of the executive *yuan* [the cabinet], it may, by resolution, request the executive *yuan* to alter such a policy. With respect to such resolution, the executive *yuan* may, with the approval of the president of the republic, request the legislative *yuan* for reconsideration."

Constitution of the United States of America (1789), Article I, Section 7: "Every Bill which shall have passed the House of Representatives and the Senate, shall, before it become a Law, be presented to the President of the United States; If he approve he shall sign it, but if not he shall return it, with his Objections to that House in which it shall have originated, who shall enter the Objections at large on their journal, and proceed to reconsider it. . . . "

Record. *See* Journal

Redress

Constitutional redress—from the French word *redresser* (to put right or straighten)—governs the right of the people to peacefully assemble or demonstrate publicly to bring to the attention of others and government officials wrongs that the demonstrators believe should be addressed by the government and corrected. It specifically relates to the right of individuals to petition their government orally or in writing to present grievances and request that what they perceive as wrong be made right.

Only a few constitutions, including the U.S. Constitution (1789), use the actual term *redress,* but most constitutions of modern democratic nation-states provide some guarantee of the people's right to bring their concerns directly to the attention of the government and seek satisfaction for wrongs done to them.

Constitution of Liberia (1986), Chapter III, Fundamental Rights, Article 17: "All persons, at all times, in an orderly and peaceably manner, shall have the right to assemble and consult upon the common good, to instruct their representatives, to petition the government or other functionaries for the redress of grievances and to associate fully with others or refuse to associate in political parties, trade unions, and other organizations."

Constitution of Mexico (1917), Title I, Chapter I, Individual Guarantees, Article 8: "Public officials and employees respect the exercise of the right of petition, provided it is made in writing and in a peaceful and respectful manner; but this right may only be exercised in political matters by citizens of the republic."

Referendum

One method of presenting a government proposal to the voters for their approval or disapproval is a referendum, a term derived from the Latin *refero* (to propose or refer). In some cases, such as a plebiscite, a popular vote on a measure may be optional or advisory. Four referendums were held in the United Kingdom in the 1970s regarding relations with the European Common Market, Scotland, Wales, and Northern Ireland.

In a number of constitutions, notably the Swiss, referendums are specifically authorized in certain instances so that the government can determine the opinion of the people before deciding how to proceed on an important national issue. In some cases the question of whether to submit a matter for referendum is discretionary, in others mandatory. With respect to constitutional amendments, however, the results are generally but not always binding.

In international law a referendum is a communication by a diplomat to the home country to seek advice or instructions on how to handle a matter that he or she does not want to decide independently.

Constitution of Switzerland (1874), Chapter III, Revision of the Federal Constitution, Article 120: "If one section of the federal assembly decides on a total revision of the federal constitution and the other does not consent or if 100,000 Swiss citizens entitled to vote demand the total revision . . . the question whether such a revision should take place or not must be submitted in both cases to the vote of the Swiss people."

Constitution of France (1958), Title II, The President of the Republic, Article 11: "The president of the republic, on the proposal of the government during (parliamentary) sessions, or on joint motion of the two assemblies, published in the *Journal Officiel,* may submit to a referendum any bill dealing with the organization of governmental authorities, entailing approval of a community agreement, or providing for authorization to ratify a treaty that, without being contrary to the constitution, might affect the functioning of (existing) institutions."

Registration of Citizenship. *See* Naturalization

Regulation

Regulations and rules are, in general, guides to conduct or behavior. However, a regulation—from the Latin *regula* (a wooden ruler or a model or pattern)—more specifically refers to an official guideline for some government or private-sector activity that a government authority is charged by law to oversee.

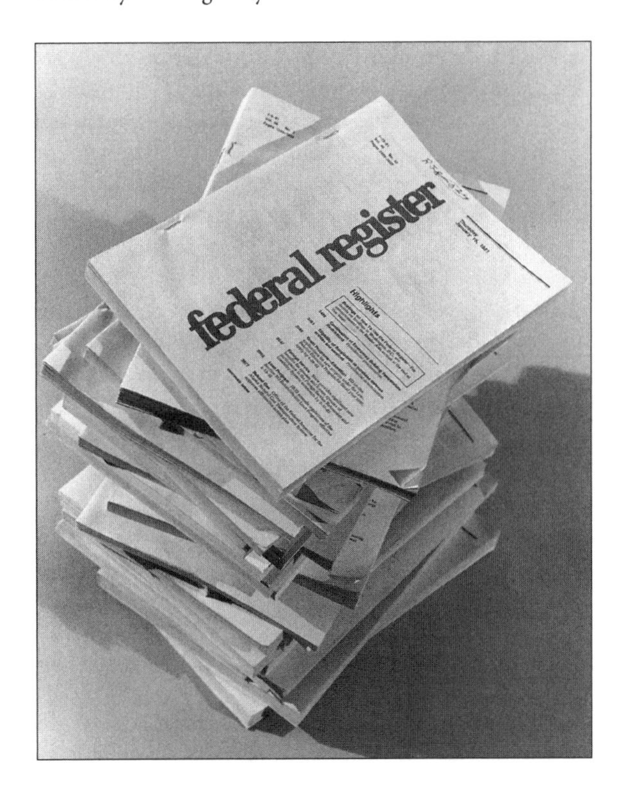

A large stack of the *Federal Register,* the daily publication that contains new federal regulations, is evidence of the massive volume of U.S. government regulations.

Government regulations, like directives, may be internal, prescribing the official work schedule for employees or the priority for handling an agency's various functions. They may also be external, affecting some areas of the private sector; for example, an agency charged with the protection of the environment may issue regulations for acceptable air pollution by privately owned factories.

Constitutional documents often use the term *regulation* to mean a guideline that supplements a law but that itself does not have the same force as law, although failure to comply with it may be punishable by law. In constitutions a regulation generally has a narrower focus than a law and relies on the discretion and expertise of the issuing authority rather than on legal norms, the usual basis for enacted laws. In other cases, however, a regulation may be synonymous with a law or rule.

Constitution of Austria (1920), Chapter IV, Legislation and Execution by the *Länder*, A, General Provisions, Article 95: "(1) The legislation of the *Länder* [states] is carried out by the *Landtage* [state legislatures]. Their members are elected on the basis of proportional representation by equal, direct, secret, and personal suffrage of all male and female federal nationals who, in accordance with the *Landtag* electoral regulations are entitled to vote and who have their domicile in the *Land* [state] concerned."

Constitution of Bangladesh (1972), Part VI, The Judiciary, Chapter I, The Supreme Court, Article 107(1): "Subject to any law made by parliament the supreme court may, with the approval of the president, make rules for regulating the practice and procedure of each division of the supreme court and any court subordinate to it."

Religion

From the beginning of recorded history, religion and rulers have been intertwined. The ancient historical and mythological development of the father figure into the sacral king, endowed to a greater or lesser extent with divinity and power, led to the personification of the king of the gods, such as the ancient Greek god Zeus. The pharaohs of ancient Egypt, the kings of Israel favored by the biblical God, and the concept of the divine right of kings—all are examples of religion's tremendous influence on political processes and government institutions, as well as on the constitutions of states and empires throughout history. After the French king Louis XVI was beheaded on January 21, 1793, some people believed that not only was the theory of the divine right of kings dead, but God as well. The Holy Roman Empire, a symbol of the alliance between church and state in feudal Europe for nearly one thousand years, was finally dissolved in 1806 by Napoleon.

Some modern constitutions—Thailand's, for example—still acknowledge the divinity of their countries' rulers. Many others deal with religious matters, including designation of an official state religion, selection of religious leaders, and profession of certain religious beliefs as a prerequisite for important government positions. Some countries, particularly those where Islam is predominant, make special constitutional provision for religion in the functioning of the government. Iran, a theocracy, has a written constitution that acknowledges the Qur'an, the holy book of Islam, as the supreme law of the land and requires proficiency in religious teachings for many government positions.

Other constitutions strive for religious accommodation. In Lebanon an unwritten constitutional practice called "confessionalism" requires that the major political positions be allocated on the basis of the relative number of adherents to the major religions in the country.

Many constitutions now expressly guarantee religious freedom and neither authorize nor prohibit any particular religion or religious denomination. This constitutional right is based on the concept of the separation of church and state, whose purpose is to prevent the use of the power of the state to coerce or punish religious behavior.

Constitution of Russia (1993), Part One, Chapter 1, Principles of the Constitutional System, Article 14: "1. The Russian Federation shall be a secular state. No religion shall be declared an official or compulsory religion. 2. All religious associations shall be separate from the state and shall be equal before the law."

Constitution of Greece (1975), Part One, Fundamental Provisions, Section II, Relations of Church and State, Article 3(3): "The text of the Holy Scripture shall be maintained. Official translation of the text into any other form of language, without the prior sanction by the Autocephalous Church of Greece and the Great Church of Christ in Constantinople, is prohibited."

A contemporaneous satirical etching from 1792 portrays in an unflattering manner the French clergy, who opposed the adoption of France's first constitution, which was promulgated by a legislative assembly on September 13, 1791.

Constitution of Finland, Constitution Act (1919), X, Public Office, Section 87: "The president shall appoint: 1) the chancellor of justice and the assistant chancellor of justice; 2) the archbishop and the bishops as well as the chancellor of the university. . . ."

Removal

The power to dismiss or discharge an appointed official is often vested in the person or institution given the power of appointment—generally, the executive branch of government, with or without confirmation of the appointment by another branch, usually the legislature.

The U.S. Constitution (1789) gives the president the power to appoint ambassadors, judges, and other officers, with the advice and consent of the Senate. The Senate's consent should be necessary "to displace as well as appoint," asserts Alexander Hamilton in essay 77 of *The Federalist* (1788), in part to contribute to the administration's stability. The U.S. Supreme Court, however, has upheld the president's unrestricted right to remove the officers appointed by him, except for members of certain independent regulatory commissions, whom the president may remove only for causes specified by Congress.

Under the U.S. Constitution, the president can be removed from office for certain impeachable offenses, after which his or her duties are assumed by the vice president. In parliamentary systems of government, the removal of the head of government (the prime minister) or the cabinet ministers is a responsibility of the legislature.

Constitution of Panama (1972), Title VI, The Executive Branch of Government, Chapter 1, The President and the Vice-Presidents of the Republic, Article 178: "Functions which may be exercised by the president of the republic by himself are: 1. To appoint and remove freely the ministers of state. . . . "

Constitution of the United Kingdom, Halsbury's Laws of England (4th ed., 1974), Volume 8, Paragraph 819, Principal Conventions: "The paramount convention is that the sovereign must act on the advice tendered to her by her ministers, in particular the prime minister. She must appoint as prime minister that member of the House of Commons who can acquire the confidence of that house, and must appoint such persons to be members of the ministry and cabinet as he recommends. . . . Civil servants are not responsible to the House. . . . Accordingly they are not to be dismissed upon a change of ministry but are removable only for misconduct or inefficiency."

Representation.

See Proportional Representation; Representative

Representative

Representative government, a hallmark of modern democratic nation-states, is one in which the citizens who are eligible to vote and do so elect from among themselves citizens to represent them for some period of time in the decision-making processes of governing. The size of nations today makes impractical the direct democracy of ancient city-states, where citizens actually assembled from time to time to participate in decisions of governing.

A person elected to the lower and more representative body of some bicameral legislatures is called a representative, meaning a person who acts for another or stands in his or her stead. The U.S. Constitution and others specifically refer to members of the lower house as representatives. However, persons elected to the lower house of Australia's bicameral parliament and to New Zealand's unicameral parliament, both of which are called the House of Representatives, are referred to as members of parliament rather than representatives. Other constitutions may refer to legislative members as deputies or delegates.

Persons elected or appointed to upper houses of a legislature are also technically representatives but are not generally referred to as such. If an upper house is called the senate, the members are always referred to as senators. In the United Kingdom representative peers are elected at the commencement of each new session of Parliament to represent Scotland and Ireland in the House of Lords.

Constitution of Ethiopia (1995), Chapter Six, The Federal Councils, Part One, The Council of Peoples' Representatives, Article 54, Members of the Council of Peoples' Representatives: "4. Members of the council are representatives of the Ethiopian peoples as a whole. They are governed by: a. The constitution; b. the will of the people; and c. their conscience."

Constitution of the Philippines (1987), Article VI, Legislative Department, Section 5(2): "The party-list representatives shall constitute twenty *per centum* of the total number of representatives including those under the party list."

Representative Democracy

For his new state of Magnesia proposed in *The Laws,* Plato provides for a form of representative democracy to be achieved by the election of various government and military officials who will act on behalf of the rest of the citizens. In ancient Rome citizens voted by groups in *comitia* (assemblies)—the upper class in groups called centuries, the lower class by tribes. The subsequent Roman republic, however, was primarily an aristocracy whose power centered in a consultative body called the Senate, although the plebeians (lower-class citizens) had popular political assemblies that sought to defeat the aristocracy by legislation or armed conflict.

Before the end of the seventeenth century, natural law theorists had concluded that it was possible for the people to be "represented" in the exercise of their political rights by an assembly of estates or classes and that the collective power of the people was bestowed by the act of election. James Madison, in essay 10 of *The Federalist*

(1788), points out that representation is the distinction between republican and direct democracies; he contends that in the former public views can be refined by passing through a chosen body of citizens.

Almost every modern national constitution provides for some form of representative democratic government. Both the widely used parliamentary model of government of the United Kingdom, sometimes called the Westminster model, and the presidential, or consensus, model of the United States are examples of representative rather than direct democracy. The constitution of neither country provides for popular referendums, initiatives, or recalls—the chief modern procedures for direct democratic participation in government decision making.

Under the U.S. Constitution (1789), citizens elect 435 members of the House of Representatives every two years from electoral districts based on population, although every constituent state is guaranteed at least one representative. The British Parliament is based on the principle of the assembly of estates: the upper house, the House of Lords, contains the estates of the clergy and the nobles or peers of the realm, who are unelected, while the lower house, the House of Commons, numbers nearly seven hundred elected members representing the third estate, the commoners. Today the head of government (the prime minister) is selected exclusively from the lower, more representative house, and only the lower house may enact laws.

In 1922 seven women were elected to represent their states in Congress. Although a majority of citizens are women, the ratio of elected women to men has not increased significantly.

Constitution of Japan (1889, significantly revised in 1947), [Preamble]: "We, the Japanese people, acting through our duly elected representatives in the Diet [parliament]. . . ."

Constitution of Ethiopia (1995), Chapter Two, Fundamental Principles of the Constitution, Article 8, Sovereignty of the People, Section 3: "They [the nations, nationalities and peoples of Ethiopia] exercise, in accordance with this constitution, their sovereignty through their elected representatives and through direct democratic participation."

Representative Government.

See Representative; Representative Democracy

Republic

A government that selects its head of state by any means other than heredity is a republic. Plato, in his dialogue entitled *The Republic,* constructs a city-state in which the rulers are the best older men, chosen for their devotion to the state and assisted by lower-class guardians or soldiers. To Aristotle republicanism was government based on citizens acting as free agents, with a distinct role allowed for a meritorious aristocracy who would serve the many and be constrained by them. In the republic of ancient Rome, citizens participated in making important decisions of the government; Roman legions even went into battle carrying standards emblazoned with "SPQR" (the Senate and People of Rome). In the eighteenth century Thomas Jefferson defined a pure republic, the system practicable for a large population, as a government of divided powers exercised by representatives for a short period to ensure that they expressed the will of their constituents.

The modern definition of a republic is a form of government in which the business of governing is open to all citizens. A republic differs from an oligarchy or a monarchy, in that its governors are not invested for life with their powers, and from a pure democracy, in that all citizens do not participate in every decision of government. The term may also signify a nation that uses the word *republic* in its official title regardless of whether the government actually conforms to republican principles.

Constitution of France (1958), Title I, On Sovereignty, Article 2: "France is a republic, indivisible, democratic, and social."

Constitution of Ethiopia (1995), Chapter One, General Provisions, Article 1, Nomenclature of the State: "This constitution establishes a democratic federal state. Reflecting this structure the Ethiopian state shall be known as the Federal Democratic Republic of Ethiopia."

Requirement. *See* Qualification

Resignation

Human history, to a great extent, has been the record of the struggle of certain individuals to acquire and retain the power to rule over others. However, the voluntary relinquishment of power by those chosen to rule is a hallmark of modern democratic governments. The fifth-century B.C. farmer Cincinnatus is reported to have left his plow to accept the dictatorship of Rome and, having led its army to victory, resigned his office sixteen days later to return to his farm.

Today national governments can be divided into dictatorships and those in which power is regularly relinquished by elected officials in accordance with the directives of constitutions. Resignation—adapted from the Latin *resignare* (to cancel or give up)—is an important step in the relinquishment of government power so that it may be bestowed again on others or the same person or persons, depending on the outcome of elections.

The transfer of power in parliamentary governments such as in the United Kingdom depends on the concept of the resignation of the prime minister and his or her cabinet when the government loses the confidence of a majority of the elected members of Parliament. In presidential systems, as in the United States, the president and other elected officials do not have to formally resign, because their power expires on certain dates in accordance with constitutional provisions.

Some constitutions also mention resignations in regard to the voluntary relinquishment of power by key government officials. In presidential systems, when a president resigns before his or her constitutional term of office expires, the vice president generally succeeds to the position. Special constitutional provisions may also be made in the case of resignation of other officials, such as the speaker of a legislative body.

Constitution of Ecuador (1979), Second Part, Title II, The Executive Function, Section I, The President of the Republic, Article 75: "The functions of the president of the republic terminate definitively and his post is left vacant: . . . c) by acceptance of his resignation by the national congress. . . ."

Constitution of Turkey (1982), Part Three, Fundamental Organs of the Republic, Chapter Two, Executive, II, Council of Ministers, E, Formation of Ministries and Ministers, Article 113: "A minister who is brought before the supreme court by decision of the Turkish Grand National Assembly shall lose his ministerial status. If the prime minister is brought before the supreme court, the government shall be considered to have resigned."

Resolution

Under general parliamentary procedures, a resolution is similar to a motion except that it is presented in writing, may contain a preamble or an introduction, and is much more descriptive, often including clauses beginning with "Whereas ... " and concluding with "Therefore be it resolved. . . . " In legislative bodies a resolution or resolve, unlike a bill that can become a law, expresses a determination, a decision, an opinion, or an intention of a majority of the members. Some constitutions expressly prescribe the use of legislative resolutions as a means of accomplishing certain actions other than by enacting laws.

A simple resolution is one passed by a single house or chamber of a bicameral legislature, while a joint resolution is one passed by both houses. In the United States,

SIXTH CONGRESS OF THE FEDERATED STATES OF MICRONESIA

THIRD REGULAR SESSION, 1990 C. R. No. 6-99, C.D.1

A RESOLUTION

To ratify and accede to the Vienna Convention on Consular Relations, done at Vienna on April 24, 1963.

1 WHEREAS, consular relations have been established between
2 peoples since ancient times; and
3 WHEREAS, one of the primary consular functions is to serve the
4 needs of citizens of a sovereign nation; and
5 WHEREAS, another primary consular function is to assist foreign
6 nationals who wish to visit our Nation; and
7 WHEREAS, it is of great benefit to both our Nation and to
8 nations which seek to provide consular services in the Federated
9 States of Micronesia to be in agreement as to what functions,
10 privileges, and immunities are attributes of consular relations; and
11 WHEREAS, most nations of the world have joined in an
12 international convention on consular relations, privileges and
13 immunities; and
14 WHEREAS, the Federated States of Micronesia will contribute to
15 and benefit from participation in uniform international consular
16 practices by acceding to the Vienna Convention on Consular Relations;
17 now, therefore,
18 BE IT RESOLVED by the Sixth Congress of the Federated States of
19 Micronesia, ~~Third~~ Fourth Regular Session, 1990, that pursuant to
20 section 2(b) and 4 of article IX of the Constitution of the Federated
21 States of Micronesia, the Congress hereby ratifies and accedes to the
22 Vienna Convention on Consular Relations, 1963; and
23 BE IT FURTHER RESOLVED that upon receipt of this resolution the
24 Secretary of External Affairs shall, when appropriate, lodge with the
25 Secretary General of the United Nations, as depository, an Instrument

Draft resolutions introduced into the Congress of the Federated States of Micronesia are typical in form and resemble those presented to many other national legislatures.

where joint resolutions require approval by the president, Congress may also issue a concurrent resolution—one that is passed by a single house and concurred in by the other but that does not require the president's approval. The U.S. Supreme Court, however, held in the 1983 *Chadha* case that the use of a concurrent resolution to veto the president's exercise of powers delegated to him by Congress violates the separation of powers inherent in the U.S. Constitution.

Constitution of Jordan (1952), Chapter Five, The Legislative Power, The National Assembly, Part III, Provisions Governing Both Houses, Article 90: "No senator or deputy may be removed from his office except by a resolution of the house to which he belongs, provided that other than the case of disqualification and combination of offices as prescribed in this constitution and in the electoral law, the resolution . . . must be taken by a two-thirds majority of the house."

Constitution of Greece (1975), Part Three, Organization and Functions of the State, Section III, Parliament, Chapter Four, Organization and Functioning of the Parliament, Article 68: "A parliamentary resolution adopted by the absolute majority of the total number of members shall be required in order to set up investigation committees on matters related to foreign policy and national defense."

Resulting Powers. *See* Currency

Revenue

In 1690 John Locke described the annual income of the English government as revenue. Similar to taxes, which are one source of government income, revenue—related to the French word *revenu* (revenue, profit, or income)—is a broad term that includes all public money that the state or government collects from whatever source and in whatever manner.

Constitutions generally entrust to the legislature the power to raise revenue—to take money from the citizens for public use—because an elected legislative body, representative of the people and dependent on them for reelection, is less likely to authorize excessive or unnecessary revenue-raising measures. "All Bills for raising Revenue shall originate in the House of Representatives," states Article 1, Section 7, of the U.S. Constitution (1789). The lower house is considered the more representative chamber because its members are elected more frequently than senators. Article 1, Section 9, prohibits giving any preferences in commerce or revenue to ports of one state of the United States over another.

Constitution of Pakistan (1973), Part III, The Federation of Pakistan, Chapter 2, The Majlis-e-Shoora (Parliament), Financial Procedure, Article 78(1): "All revenues received by the federal government, all loans raised by that government, and all moneys received by it in repayment of any loan, shall form part of the consolidated fund, to be known as the federal consolidated fund."

Constitution of South Korea (1948), Chapter IV, The Executive, Part 2, The Executive Branch, Section 4, The Board of Audit and Inspection, Article 99: "The board of audit and inspection shall inspect the closing of accounts of revenues and expenditures each year and report the results to the president and the national assembly in the following year."

Revision. *See* Amendment

Revolution

Some political revolutions, such as the American (1776), French (1789), and Russian Revolutions (1917), have been violent upheavals signaling fundamental changes in how people are governed in a nation-state. Other, more subtle revolutions have also significantly affected governments and constitutions, among them the 1688–89 Glorious Revolution, when the English monarchy was restored but limited by a bill of right for Parliament. Even unsuccessful revolutions like the uprisings in Hungary (1956) and Czechoslovakia (1968) shed light on the basic instability of a government. Where a rebellion implies a refusal to obey government authority, however, a revolution is an organized attempt to change the actual basis for government authority.

During the Russian Revolution of 1917, soldiers fought in the courtyard of the Winter Palace of Tsar Nicholas II, an autocrat who ruled while ignoring the legislative Duma.

In one sense revolution is anathema to constitutional government because it implies that constitutional processes have failed to satisfy the needs and aspirations of the people; most constitutional documents thus avoid using the term. Some constitutions, however, are actually founded on revolution and may express this fact in a preamble or government structure by calling a body or an institution "revolutionary."

Constitution of Cuba (1976), Preamble: " . . . and having decided to carry forth the triumphant revolution of the Moncada and the Granma, of the Sierra and of Girón under the leadership of Fidel Castro, which sustained by the closest unity of all revolutionary forces and of the people, won full national independence. . . . "

Constitution of Iraq (1970), Chapter IV, Institutions of the Iraqi Republic, Section I, The Revolutionary Command Council, Article 37: "The revolutionary command council is the supreme institution in the state, which on July 17, 1968, assumed the responsibility to realize the public will of the people by removing the authority from the reactionary, individual, and corruptive regime, and returning it to the people."

Riding. *See* Electoral District

Right

Most constitutions achieve at least two ends: (1) they create a structure and procedures for the transmission and exercise of power, and (2) they guarantee rights. In general a right is a person's ability to pursue a course of action under the protection of the law. Rights may be

UNIVERSAL
DECLARATION
of
HUMAN RIGHTS

ON DECEMBER 10, 1948, the General Assembly of the United Nations adopted and proclaimed the Universal Declaration of Human Rights, the full text of which appears in the following pages. Following this historic act the Assembly called upon all Member countries to publicize the text of the Declaration and "to cause it to be disseminated, displayed, read and expounded principally in schools and other educational institutions, without distinction based on the political status of countries or territories."

Many constitutions contain an express list of individual rights, and on December 10, 1948, the United Nations adopted the Universal Declaration of Human Rights.

based on custom and formally defined and protected by constitutions, laws, courts, and other authorities. The English word *right* is derived from Old English, and its correlative in French is *droit*, in German *Rechts*, and in Spanish *derecho* (right or law).

The rights of some citizens against absolute monarchs were won incrementally beginning in England in the thirteenth century with Magna Carta. Culminating in the eighteenth century, the modern concept of individual and minority rights was developed by natural law theorists. They asserted that positive law (as enacted by governments) is limited by principles of natural or inherent law and detailed the objective rights of individuals that are beyond the reach of positive law—rights that the state cannot take away. Immanuel Kant, the eighteenth-century German philosopher, theorized that the state's role could be reduced to simply securing an internal "system of right" and providing protection against external enemies.

The U.S. Bill of Rights, added to the U.S. Constitution in 1791, represents a formal expression of citizens' rights. Since its adoption this list comprising the first ten amendments to the Constitution has inspired many documents that guarantee state protection of rights and freedoms of individuals and groups, including international and regional declarations of rights and national constitutions. Modern constitutional documents refer to many types of rights—human rights, civil rights, minority rights, equal rights, political rights, the right of privacy, rights of the accused, substantive rights, procedural rights, natural rights, fundamental rights, and property rights, for example.

Constitution of Ireland (1937), Fundamental Rights, Private Property, Article 43: "1.1. The state acknowledges that man, in virtue of his rational being, has the natural right, antecedent to positive law, to the private ownership of external goods. 1.2. The state accordingly guarantees to pass no law attempting to abolish the right of private ownership or the general right to transfer, bequeath, and inherit property."

Constitution of South Africa (1994), Chapter 3, Fundamental Rights, Application, Section 7(4)(a): "When infringement of or threat to any right entrenched in this chapter is alleged, any person [acting on his or her own behalf or on behalf of others, including the public interest, and an association] shall be entitled to apply to a competent court of law for appropriate relief, which may include a declaration of rights."

Roll Call Vote. *See* Yeas and Nays

Rousseau, Jean-Jacques

Jean-Jacques Rousseau (1712–78) did not live to see his progressive social ideas materialize in the French Revolution of 1789, but his concepts of popular sovereignty and the general will have survived as the keystones of most modern nation-state constitutions.

Nine days after Rousseau's birth on June 28, 1712, in Geneva, his mother died. A precocious child, he was reading French novels with his father at the age of three, and at thirteen he completed his formal education. Apprenticed unsuccessfully on several occasions, he lived most of his adult life from hand to mouth or with the support of others, including the British philosopher David Hume.

A man of paradoxical genius, Rousseau wrote operas, novels, and entries for Denis Diderot's famous *Encyclopédie* in the 1750s, in addition to works of philosophical criticism and inquiry. One of his abiding themes was that the social order of civilized society, which was based on the ownership of private property, produced inequality and unhappiness. Proclaiming that "the fruits of the earth belong to everyone and the earth to no one," he, like Darwin a century later, lent support to the socialist movement. His *L'Emile ou de l'education (Emile: Or, On Education)* (1762) set forth progressive ideas about education.

Rousseau's companion work to *L'Emile* was his constitutionally influential *Social Contract* (1762), which contained the key notions of popular sovereignty and the general will. In it Rousseau proposed that government as it existed was not based on the sovereignty of the people, nor was society the result of a social contract by all the people. The people should both create laws and follow them, he suggested, and government should be the instrument through which their collective will was translated into action.

Other philosophers and writers, such as Immanuel Kant and Leo Tolstoy, and political activists such as Maximilien François Marie Isidore de Robespierre, were particularly influenced by Rousseau's ideas, which shaped much of the post–French Revolution democratic movement in Europe. His impact, not unlike that of Voltaire's, can be seen in the development of European democracies—for example, in the 1814 Norwegian constitution and the 1831 Belgian constitution. Although his broad view of democratic government was not adopted completely, his enlightened views on fundamental rights and equality are still enshrined in many constitutional documents of democracies today.

Rousseau did not hesitate to criticize democratic institutions as well. In *The Social Contract* he said of the British Parliament, "[The English people are] only free during parliamentary elections: once the members of parliament have been elected [the people] lapse back into slavery, and become nothing." The modern constitutional concepts of recall and referendum are attempts to relieve this problem identified by Rousseau. Rousseau died on July 2, 1778, in a hospital near Paris.

Jean-Jacques Rousseau's ideas of popular sovereignty gave support to the French Revolution in 1789 and to many constitutional documents around the world.

Rule

A rule—from the Old French words *riule* and *rule*—is generally an established guide or regulation. In constitutions a rule generally refers to guidelines or regulations made in accordance with law that have a legal effect within a certain ambit. Rules of procedure for a legislature or other government body, for example, apply only to them and must be made in accordance with the constitution and organic laws. Similarly, administrative rules apply within the jurisdiction of an administrator or administrative body and must be made in conformity with constitutional and statutory provisions.

In law a rule of a court may be a command to an official or a party before the court, or it may refer to a decision by the court on a point of law arising during a trial. Court rules are also regulations governing court procedures made pursuant to constitutional and statutory authority.

Constitution of the United States of America (1789), Article I, Section 5: "Each House may determine the Rules of its Proceedings, punish its Members for disorderly Behavior, and, with the Concurrence of two-thirds, expel a Member."

Constitution of Syria (1973), Part Two, Powers of the State, Chapter 1, Legislative Power, Article 61: "The council [legislature] shall be convened in three regular sessions annually; and it may be convened in extraordinary sessions. The council's internal rules shall specify the dates and durations of the sessions."

Rule of Law

The rule of law is a basic concept embodied in modern constitutionalism and reflected in the constitutional documents of genuinely democratic countries, although elements of it may be found in other societies and in times past. In any legal system the rule of law implies that there are limitations on the powers of the rulers, whether legislators, executives, or judges, and that there are safeguards against abuse of power or law.

Although often held to be a purely Anglo-American concept, the rule of law most likely originated in medieval days, when the law of God was believed to rule the world. Later, the idea became embodied in the theory of natural law, which was thought to be so fundamental and unalterable that even sovereign governments were subject to it. The development of English common law provided a stable system of protection for some individual rights against the monarch and some abuses of his or her power, although even today in the United Kingdom the monarch, lesser royalty, and peers of the realm receive deferential treatment under the country's constitution and laws. Thus, the rule of law, which postulates the equality of all citizens except for those democratically chosen to govern for a limited and accountable period of time, is not yet fully established in the United Kingdom.

Underpinning the rule of law are substantive laws enacted by governments to protect against private coercion; a government bound by the same substantive laws and not only the constitution; certainty, generality, and equality in substantive laws, to the extent possible; substantive laws that accurately reflect social values; impartial and honest law enforcement; accessibility to the courts of law; and a general public attitude supportive of the rule of law.

The rule of law is expressly acknowledged in some constitutions, as well as in international declarations and conventions on rights and freedoms including the Universal Declaration of Human Rights (1948) and the European Convention for the Protection of Human Rights and Fundamental Freedoms (1950).

Constitution of Bangladesh (1972), Preamble: "Further pledging that it shall be a fundamental aim of the state to realize through the democratic process a socialist society, free from exploitation—a society in which the rule of law, fundamental human rights and freedom, equality, and justice, political, economic, and social, will be secure for all citizens."

Constitution of Bulgaria (1991), Chapter I, Fundamental Principles, Article 4(1): "The Republic of Bulgaria is a state based on the rule of law. It is governed according to the constitution and the laws of the country."

Rules of Procedure.

See Procedure

GENERAL SCOTT.

THE HERCULES OF THE UNION,

SLAYING THE GREAT DRAGON OF SECESSION.

S

Sadat, Mohamed Anwar El

Anwar Sadat (1918–81) gave his native land of Egypt peace with Israel and a multiparty constitution, but assassins denied him the opportunity to enjoy for long the fruits of his achievements.

Born in Mit Abul-kum, Egypt, on December 25, 1918, Mohamed Anwar El Sadat was raised by his maternal grandmother. Two years after Egypt was unilaterally declared independent by the British in 1922, his family moved to Cairo, where he was educated. From 1937 to 1938 he attended the military academy and the following year, along with Gamal Abd al-Nasser, established the Free Officers against the British, who still dominated much of Egypt's affairs.

Active in the anti-British movement, in 1945 Sadat participated in a plot to assassinate the pro-British prime minister, Mustafa Nahhas. In January 1946 he was arrested for an assassination attempt on a government official and was imprisoned for two years. On July 23, 1952, as a member of the Free Officers, he took part in the military takeover of the government, announcing the coup to the Egyptian people on the radio. A key leader in the revolutionary government led by Nasser, he became the acting president when Nasser died on September 28, 1970, and was elected president shortly thereafter.

General Winfield Scott of the U.S. Army combats the many-headed monster of the Southern states, whose secession from the Union precipitated the American Civil War in 1861.

In 1980 President Anwar Sadat promoted democracy in Egypt by supporting an amendment to the 1972 constitution that permitted multiparty political activity.

At home Sadat continued to work for a multiparty government. The stated objectives of the 1952 revolution had included the eradication of imperialism, feudalism, and monopoly and the establishment of a strong national army, social justice, and a sound democratic life. By 1971 Sadat believed that all these goals except the last had been attained. Establishing a constitutional democratic government, he thought, would legitimize his power and restore confidence in his leadership.

On May 20, 1971, Sadat called for the creation of a permanent constitution and set forth thirteen basic principles to be included, among them that the state, like individuals, should be subject to the power of the law and that sovereignty should be for the people only. Although the constitution provided limited guarantees for individual rights and freedoms, it retained a single political party structure, the Arab Socialist Union.

In March 1973 Sadat made himself prime minister and supreme commander of the armed forces and military governor of Egypt. On October 6 of that year Egypt and Syria made a surprise attack on Israel, but ten days later, faced with advancing Israeli troops, Sadat proposed a peace conference. Reelected president in October 1976, he continued the peace process with Israel, which culminated in the Camp David Accords, signed on September 17, 1978. In December he shared the Nobel Peace Prize with Menachem Begin, prime minister of Israel.

In July 1976 Sadat had agreed to permit *manabir* (divergent political platforms) within the Arab Socialist Union, which could develop into true competing political parties. In 1980 the electorate approved by 99.9 percent amendments authorizing a multiparty political system, expanding the role of the press, and establishing a Shoura Assembly to be consulted on major initiatives to preserve the goals of the 1952 and 1971 revolutions.

In May 1980 anti-Coptic unrest forced Sadat to appropriate extraordinary powers, including those of the prime minister, who had just resigned. His assassination by young religious extremists on October 6, 1981, prevented him from seeing the long-term results of his impact on the Egyptian constitution. His understanding of the importance of Egypt's new constitution, however, is evident in his speech to the constituent committee of the Democratic National Party on August 14, 1978: "Explain to the people that in all great nations the constitution is sacred ... [and it] stands for stability, security, safety, rights, and obligations."

St. Augustine's description of separate spiritual and temporal worlds in *The City of God*, written in the fifth century, influenced the relationship between church and state in Europe.

St. Augustine

St. Augustine (354–430) influenced constitutional development primarily through his work *The City of God* (ca. 420), which set the doctrinal stage for the development of church and state for nearly a millennium and a half.

Augustine was born in Tagaste, Souk-Ahras, in what is now Algeria, on November 13, 354. His mother was a devout Christian, but his father embraced Christianity only when near death. The young Augustine learned Latin grammar and literature in Tagaste and Madaura and studied rhetoric in Carthage. Still unbaptized, he took a mistress and fathered a son.

Influenced by reading Marcus Tullius Cicero, the

By defining the separate roles of the Christian church and the state in the thirteenth century, St. Thomas Aquinas contributed to constitutional development in Europe.

Roman statesman and orator of the first century B.C., Augustine adopted the Persian religion of Manichaeanism and opened a school of rhetoric in 373. He later lost his faith in Manichaeanism, however, and journeyed to Rome and Milan in 383. In 387 he became a baptized Christian and later an ordained priest and bishop in Algeria.

A prolific writer, Augustine drew on the Greek and Roman classics, especially Plato. He wrote as a theologian, not as a political scientist or constitutional theorist, and his works reflect fundamental world changes that occurred during his lifetime: Rome was sacked by the Visigoths, signaling the end of the Roman Empire. During the ensuing Dark Ages the church's writings, including Augustine's, would become the repository of classical knowledge.

In *The City of God* Augustine's vision of society encompasses a temporal world—Rome, which had adopted Christianity as the official religion—and a spiritual world—Heaven, including God, the angels, and the saved, whose representative on earth is the church. Like Plato, Augustine was interested in justice, which he saw as a right relationship between humans and God, from which would follow a right relationship among humans. According to Augustine, the justice of the spiritual world is lacking in the earthly sphere; therefore, government must be instituted to maintain peace and justice, because those things are necessary for the soul to come to know God. If justice on earth is taken away, he says, kingdoms are no more than excuses for "great robberies." The origins of worldly peace and justice are found in just rulers who serve those whom they command and who rule from a sense of duty, not power. These concepts formed the philosophical foundations for the later development of Europe's monarchical governments.

Although Augustine clearly espoused some of the classical constitutional concepts regarding the just state and the just citizen, he also condoned slavery and supported the primacy of the church. He died in 430, having elucidated the uneasy relationship between religion and the state in Western thought, a relationship that still causes friction today in many countries of the world.

St. Thomas Aquinas

As Italy emerged from the Dark Ages on its way to the Renaissance, St. Thomas Aquinas (ca. 1224–74) helped restore reason as the foundation for understanding government and explicated the roles of spiritual and temporal leadership.

Thomas Aquinas was born probably in 1224 at his family's castle between Naples and Rome. The youngest son of a minor noble who was an official of Frederick II, emperor of Germany and king of Naples, he was educated first by Benedictine monks at a nearby monastery. After studying in Naples he joined the Dominican order in 1244 against his family's wishes. His family abducted him, but he returned to the order to study in Paris and Cologne from 1245 to 1252.

Quickly attaining the status of master of theology, Aquinas taught in Paris for seven years, but opposition by secular teachers led to his return to Italy. Between 1252 and 1273 he produced an encyclopedic volume of works. Unlike Augustine, he criticized Plato and his concept of a world of intelligible forms, building instead on the works of Aristotle, particularly *The Politics* and *The Ethics*, although many of Aristotle's ideas were in conflict with church dogma.

Aquinas's views on politics are found mainly in his greatest work, *Summa Theologica*, which he began about 1266, and the short fragment *On Kingship*. Challenging Augustine's conclusion that political association and government were the result of evil and sin, he derived from Aristotle the notion that society and government are a necessary consequence of natural human social instincts. Dominion of one person over another was slavery and wrong, but Aquinas posited that dominion as a manner of governing free people was clearly compatible with a state of innocence.

Drawing on Aristotle, Aquinas concluded that secular government is necessary and that the organization of secular government must be based on the superior morality and wisdom of the ruler for the benefit of the ruled. But, he maintained, secular government must still be subject to the church, because good government is only the intermediate end to what he saw as the ultimate end—the salvation of souls.

An elitist like Aristotle, Aquinas stressed the constitutional idea of a limited monarchy whose end was to ensure temporal, as opposed to spiritual, peace and welfare. He viewed favorably the concept of a mixed constitution, combining elements of monarchy, aristocracy, and popular participation. For Aquinas, divine justice did not negate human justice, a derivation of natural reason. St. Thomas Aquinas, who was known as the "Angelic Doctor," died of an illness in March 1274 at the Cistercian monastery at Fossanuova. He was canonized in 1323.

Salary. *See* Compensation

Schedule. *See* Provision

Science

Science and technology have created a world that is far different from that of even the recent past. Science—from the Latin *scientia* (knowledge)—may be "pure" (theoretical) or "applied," in which case its fruits often advance technology. Technology, which comes from a Greek phrase meaning "the science of art," refers to the branch of knowledge that deals with industrial arts.

Some constitutions have sought to promote and protect scientific and technological activities by providing private citizens with patent protection for inventions and scientific creations—for example, laser technology and genetic engineering. In contrast, the 1992 constitution of Vietnam gives the state the leading role in scientific and technological development. Other constitutions treat science and technology in a more general way by declaring a policy of encouraging development of

The phonograph and other inventions of Thomas Edison brought to the world the practical benefits of science, a subject specifically addressed in some constitutions.

and investment in science and technology, as in the 1992 amendments to the Taiwanese constitution.

Constitution of Brazil (1988), Title VIII, Social Order, Chapter IV, Science and Technology, Article 218: "The state shall promote and foster scientific development, research, and technological expertise."

Constitution of Egypt (1971), Part Two, Basic Constituents of the Society, Chapter I, Social and Moral Constituents, Article 12: "The society shall be committed to safeguarding and protecting morals, promoting genuine Egyptian traditions and abiding by the high standards of religious education, moral and national values, historical heritage of the people, scientific facts, socialist conduct, and public morality within the limits of the law."

Seal. *See* Symbol

Search and Seizure.

See Unreasonable Search and Seizure

Secession

In ancient Rome the lower-class plebeians would occasionally undertake an action similar to a strike or boycott, withdrawing to a place outside the city to force the upper-class patricians to redress their grievances. Secession—from the Latin *secessio* (withdrawal)—is the action by which constituent states or provinces secede from, or leave, a federation or federal nation-state. It has historically been viewed as unconstitutional and generally is not tolerated by a national government. As evidenced by conflicts such as the American Civil War (1861–65) and the secessionist war in the Russian province of Chechnya during the 1990s, central governments will use whatever force is necessary to thwart attempts at secession.

Some constitutions contain language designed to serve notice that secession is unacceptable, even though the term itself is rarely used. The indivisibility of the federal system is often expressed in the preamble or the first section of a written constitution. Unitary states with unwritten constitutions, such as the United Kingdom, may also be faced with the possible loss of territory under their jurisdiction but are presumed to have more flexibility in dealing with such situations. The resolution of Northern Ireland's status, for example, may be less intractable than if it were an equal member in a federal nation-state with a written constitution declaring the federation indissoluble.

The constitution of the Soviet Union, before its breakup in 1991, contained unique provisions allowing for secession.

Constitution of Australia, Commonwealth of Australia Constitution Act (1901), (Preamble): "Whereas the people of New South Wales, Victoria, South Australia, Queensland, and Tasmania, humbly relying on the blessings of almighty God, have agreed to unite in one indissoluble federal commonwealth. . . . "

Constitution of Nigeria (1989), Chapter I, General Provisions, Part I, Federal Republic of Nigeria, Section 2(1): "Nigeria is one indivisible and indissoluble sovereign state to be known by the name of the Federal Republic of Nigeria."

Secrecy

Keeping some activities of the state or government secret has been standard operating procedure in all countries, and in times of war the reasons for secrecy—from the Latin *secretus* (separate, remote, or secret)—increase. One who is entrusted with private or secret information is often called a secretary, a title now used in the United States and some other countries for cabinet members. During the Roman Empire imperial secretariats were often composed not of Roman citizens but of freedmen, or former captives, who were personally loyal to the emperor.

With the development of the concept of popular democracy, however, the need for a sovereign people to know what its government does in order to make wise choices in elections and referendums conflicts with the traditional practice of government secrecy. Article 1, Section 5, of the U.S. Constitution (1789) nonetheless expressly authorizes the houses of Congress to withhold publication in their journals of proceedings "such parts as may in their judgment require secrecy." The secrecy necessary for government activities obviously increases in the arena of foreign affairs and in wartime.

The secrecy of the voting booth or the secret ballot, on the other hand, is a device that protects the democratic election process. In many constitutions secrecy may refer to secret balloting either in general elections or in specific internal procedures for selecting certain officials, to aspects of national security, or to guarantees for individuals with respect to personal data and communications.

Constitution of Turkey (1982), Part Three, Fundamental Organs of the Republic, Chapter Two, Executive, I, President of the Republic, B, Election, Article 102: "The president of the republic shall be elected by a two-thirds majority of the total numbers of members of the Turkish grand national assembly and by secret ballot."

Constitution of Colombia (1991), Title II, Concerning Rights, Guarantees, and Duties, Chapter 2, Concerning Social, Economic, and Cultural Rights, Article 74: "Professional secrets are inviolable."

Constitution of Russia (1993), Part One, Chapter 2, Human and Civil Rights and Freedoms, Article 23: "1. Each person shall have the right to inviolability of private life, personal and family secrecy, and the protection of honor and good reputation."

Section. *See* Article

Security

In *The Laws,* Plato places the city's security—from the Latin *securus* (carefree or tranquil)—in the hands of generals, company commanders, tribe leaders, members of the executive, city wardens, and market wardens; for internal security he relies on a nocturnal council, so called because it meets before dawn. John Stuart Mill, in his 1863 essay "Utilitarianism," says that security—freedom from apprehension—is "to every one's feelings the most vital of all interests."

Both the personal security of the individual citizen and the general security of the nation-state itself are constitutional concerns, the latter obviously of paramount importance to many framers of modern constitutional documents. Political, social, and economic progress is of little satisfaction if the citizens and territory of a country are not secure. Security involves defense against both external and internal threats but may result from diplomacy as well as military might. The collapse of the Soviet Union and other dictatorships proved that the security of a nation-state depends as much on the security of individual citizens from the oppression of the state as on the protection of a country as a whole from outside aggression.

Constitution of Algeria (1976), Title I, General Principles Governing the Algerian Society, Chapter III, The State, Article 23: "The state is responsible for the security of every citizen. It assures their protection abroad."

Constitution of Austria (1920), Chapter I, General Provisions, Article 10(1): "The *Bund* [federal government] has powers of legislation and execution in the following matters: . . . 7. the maintenance of peace, order, and security, excluding the local public safety administration. . . . "

Constitution of Spain (1978), Title One, Concerning Fundamental Rights and Duties, Chapter II, Concerning Rights and Liberties, Article 17: "1. Everyone has a right to freedom and security. No one may be deprived of his freedom except as laid down in this article and in the cases and in the manner provided by the law."

Self-Amendment. *See* Unamendable Provision

Semibicameral Legislature

A unicameral legislature has a single house or chamber and may be called a parliament, a congress, an assembly, or a majlis. A bicameral legislature has two houses or chambers. Both the British Parliament and the U.S. Congress have upper and lower houses, although these two bicameral legislative bodies function quite differently.

Two countries, Norway and Iceland, have adopted a

hybrid form of bicameral legislature in which the members of the national legislature are elected together to form one body, which then divides itself into an upper and a lower house. The upper house has fewer members than the lower house, but, like the U.S. Senate, it plays a role in enacting legislation together with the lower house. Unlike the U.S. Congress but like some other legislatures, both the Norwegian and the Icelandic semibicameral legislatures may be constitutionally required to meet and act together in a plenary session.

Constitution of Iceland (1944), Chapter Three, Article 32: "The Althing [legislature] is divided into an upper and a lower house. One-third of the members sit in the upper house and two-thirds in the lower house. Should the number of members be such as to make impossible a division by thirds the odd members shall sit in the lower house."

Constitution of Norway (1814), C, Rights of Citizens and the Legislative Power, Article 73: "The Storting [legislature] nominates from among its members one-fourth to constitute the Lagting [upper house], the remaining three-fourths to constitute the Odelsting [lower house]. This nomination shall take place at the first session of the Storting that assembles after a new general election, whereafter the Lagting shall remain unchanged at all sessions of the Storting assembled after the same election, except insofar as any vacancy which may occur among its members has to be filled by special nomination."

Senate

The Roman Senate was a council or an assembly of citizens charged with the highest deliberative functions in the government. Originally a legislative and an administrative body elected by the upper-class citizens, the patricians, it was later composed of appointees and members who had formerly held high office in the government. The term *senate*—from the Latin *senatus* (a

Julius Caesar, according to William Shakespeare's tragic play, was assassinated in the Senate in 44 B.C. by some of his fellow Romans, who feared that he would be tempted to accept a monarch's crown and end the republic.

council of old men)—was also used for other similar bodies in the ancient world; for example, Lacedaemon, also called Sparta, at one time was said to be ruled by a king and senate.

A number of constitutions create an upper house of the national legislature that is called a senate or a related term. It generally has fewer members than the corresponding lower house and stricter qualifications for membership, including a higher minimum age. In addition, its role in all aspects of legislative enactment may be limited, although it may have special functions such as confirming executive appointments or trying high officials on impeachment charges. The senate's role in legislation related to money bills may also be limited because of its less representative nature.

James Madison is presumed to have written essay 62 of *The Federalist* (1788), in which the stated qualifications for members of the U.S. Senate compared to members of the House of Representatives include being older and having held citizenship for a longer period of time. The U.S. Senate, the first established under a modern constitution, also reflects the Roman Senate in its conservative nature; its members are elected for six years, rather than two years as are members of the lower house, and are elected at large in each state to represent the interests of the state as opposed to simply the people's interests.

Constitution of the Czech Republic (1993), Chapter Two, Legislative Power, Article 16: "(1) The chamber of deputies has 200 deputies, elected for a term of four years. (2) The senate has 81 senators, elected for a term of six years. One third of the senators is elected every second year."

Constitution of France (1958), Title V, The Parliament, Article 24: "The parliament shall comprise the national assembly and the senate. The deputies to the national assembly shall be elected by direct suffrage. The senate shall be elected by indirect suffrage. It shall insure the representation of the territorial units of the republic. French nationalists living outside France shall be represented in the senate."

Constitution of Italy (1948), Part II, The System of the Republic, Title I, The Parliament, Section I, The Chambers, Article 59: "He who has been the president of the republic is senator by right for life, unless he waives this right. Five persons who honored the republic for very high merits in the social, scientific, artistic, and literature fields may be appointed senators for life by the president of the republic."

Separation of Church and State

Throughout the history of humankind, the fusion of church (religion) and state (government) has been the rule rather than the exception. As typical heads of state, monarchs—if not revered as gods themselves—were ordained by God or at the least looked on as "defenders of the faith." Both Plato and Aristotle embraced the union of church and state, with Plato prescribing harsh punishment for impiety and Aristotle going so far as to suggest that the expense of religious worship should be a public charge.

As the concept of natural law developed in Europe in the sixteenth century, after the Reformation, it became difficult to reconcile the supremacy of the church and the supremacy of the head of a sovereign state. Hugo Grotius, the seventeenth-century Dutch jurist and statesman, admitted the influence of the spiritual world, arguing that ecclesiastical as well as lay matters should be entrusted to the political sovereign as the highest of all authorities. But the biblical advice to "render unto Caesar that which is Caesar's" and the foundations laid by St. Augustine in his fifth-century work *The City of God*, written after the Roman Empire had embraced Christianity, have kept open the debate on the wisdom of fusing the nation-state with a particular religion. The Thirty Years' War (1618–48) in Europe between Protestants and Catholics did not help resolve the question.

The framers of the U.S. Constitution in 1787 were particularly mindful of the debate: the U.S. president was to be nothing like the British monarch, who remains the head of the Church of England. The Americans therefore prohibited any religious test for political office and, in the First Amendment, barred the national government from making any "law respecting an establishment of religion." The tension over the issue continues in the United States, however, in the context of issues such as officially sanctioned prayer in public schools, government support for religious schools, and abortion rights.

The manner in which national constitutions deal with the concept of the separation of church and state varies widely. Some constitutions proclaim complete freedom of religion, while others designate a state church. A few, such as the Irish and Spanish constitutions, stop short of merging church and state but acknowledge the leading role of a particular religion (Catholic) in the nation. Iran's constitution makes the country a theocratic state. In Israel, a democratic state with an unwritten constitution, the Jewish religion plays more than a passive role in politics, although other faiths are tolerated.

The Cuban constitution has undergone an explicit change in the state's relationship to religion. Before 1992 it provided: "It is illegal and punishable by law to oppose one's faith or religious belief to the revolution; to education; or to the fulfillment of one's duty to work, defend the homeland with arms, show reverence for its symbols and fulfill other duties established by this constitution." Since 1992 it states simply: "The law regulates the activities of religious institutions."

Constitution of Bulgaria (1991), Chapter 1, Fundamental Principles, Article 13: "(1) There is freedom of religion. (2) Religious institutions are separate from the state. (3) The Eastern Orthodox religion is the traditional religion of the Republic of Bulgaria. (4) Religious communities and institutions or religious convictions may not be used in the pursuit of political objectives."

Constitution of Cambodia (1993), Chapter 3, The Rights and Obligations of Cambodian Citizens, Article 43: "Cambodian citizens of both sexes shall have the right to belief. The freedom of religious belief and practices shall be guaranteed by the state on condition that they do not affect other beliefs, orders, and public security. Buddhism is the state religion."

Constitution of Turkey (1982), Part Two, Fundamental Rights and Duties, Chapter Two, The Rights and Duties of the Individual, IV, Freedom of Religion and Conscience, Article 24: "No one shall be allowed to exploit or abuse religion or religious feelings, or things held sacred by religion, in any manner whatsoever, for the purpose of personal or political influence, or for even partially basing the fundamental, social, economic, political, and legal order of the state on religious tenets."

Separation of Powers

Plato saw danger in unchecked power concentrated in one person, adding in *The Laws* that a balance of power is needed among the ruling elements of a state. In *The Spirit of the Laws* (1748), the eighteenth-century political and legal theorist Montesquieu identifies the executive, legislative, and judicial functions in the British constitution as separate powers common to all governments.

James Madison quotes Montesquieu in essay 47 of *The Federalist* (1788) to the effect that there can be no liberty where a nation's legislative and executive powers are fused in one person or body or where the judicial power is not separated from the other two. He points out that the principle of separation of powers does not prevent one branch of government from having some control over another; each can do so through the principle of checks and balances.

The notion of the separation of government powers has had a different history in continental Europe, especially in France, than in the United States. Constitutional framers in France feared judge-made law, while the framers of the U.S. Constitution (1789) were wary of popularly elected legislatures, fears that led to an acknowledgment of the supremacy of the legislative branch in France and to an acceptance of judicial review of the Constitution in the United States.

Constitutions seldom refer expressly to the separation of powers principle, but it is obvious from the structure of government institutions and, in the case of constitutions based on the U.S. model, the emphasis on the independence of the judiciary and some form of judicial review, whereby ordinary courts are empowered to review the constitutionality of laws and government actions.

Like the principle of checks and balances, the requirement that the powers of a democratic government be separated is criticized by some as resulting in government weakness, inefficiency, and inability to act responsively and decisively when necessary. This criticism, however, cannot refute the success of such governments or deny their stability compared with totalitarian governments.

Constitution of Liberia (1986), Chapter I, Structure of the State, Article 3: "Consistent with the principles of separation of powers and checks and balances, no person holding office in one of these branches [the legislative, executive, and judicial] shall hold office in or exercise any of the powers assigned to either of the other two branches. . . ."

Constitution of Panama (1972), Title I, The Panamanian State, Article 2: "[Public power] is exercised by the state, in conformity with this constitution, through legislative, executive, and judicial branches of government which act within limits and separately, but in harmonious cooperation."

Session

A sitting of a court, legislature, council or commission, or another official body for the purpose of transacting business is a session, derived from *sessio parliamenti* (a sitting of parliament) in Old English law. A session may be the period of time during any one day in which such a body transacts business; the entire period of time from the first convocation to the final adjournment *sine die;* or the day-to-day meetings of a legislative body. The term *session* appeared in the records of the British Parliament as early as 1444.

Most constitutions define the period of a complete legislative session as running from the time the members first convene after a general election to the date on which the term of the legislature expires by law or is replaced after new elections.

Constitution of India (1950), Part V, The Union, Chapter II, Parliament, General, Article 85, Sessions of Parliament, Prorogation and Dissolution: "(1) The president shall from time to time summon each house of parliament to meet at such time and place as he thinks fit, but six months shall not intervene between its last sitting in one session and the date appointed for its first sitting in the next session."

Meetings of legislatures in many small countries, such as this Panamanian congress session in 1926, often take place in an informal setting. Panama's constitution was revised two years later, and a new constitution was adopted in 1972.

Constitution of Sweden, Riksdag Act (1974), Chapter I, Sessions, Article 2: "The Riksdag [parliament] shall convene in ordinary session on the first Tuesday in October each year in which a general election to the Riksdag is not held, unless the Riksdag has fixed another day in September or October when the session shall begin, on proposal from the speaker's conference at the preceding session. If an extra election has been declared before the day fixed, and if, on account of the election, the Riksdag has not assembled in session by July at the latest, no session shall start in accordance with this paragraph."

Constitution of the United States of America (1789), Article I, Section 5: "Neither House, during the Session of Congress, shall, without the Consent of the other, adjourn for more than three days, nor to any other place than that in which the two Houses shall be sitting."

Shari'a. *See* Islamic Law

Sihanouk, Norodom

King Norodom Sihanouk (b. 1922) has come full cycle from being made king of Cambodia in 1941, abdicating in 1955, and again becoming the country's constitutional monarch in 1993.

Prince Norodom Sihanouk was born on October 31, 1922, in the Cambodian capital of Phnom Penh, a French protectorate since 1863. His education began at a French day school in the capital, but he was later sent to secondary school in Saigon, Vietnam, another part of French Indochina. His schooling was cut short in 1941, when he was called back to be crowned king of Cambodia to placate the French, who thought that the rightful heir to the throne was too headstrong. France had already fallen to the Germans, and although Japanese armed forces had entered Cambodia, Japan permitted Vichy France to continue to administer the country. In March 1945, with the Japanese pulling out, Sihanouk proclaimed Cambodia an independent country, but when the French returned after the war, he caved in to their demands. In January 1946 France made Cambodia an

Norodom Sihanouk abdicated the throne of Cambodia in 1955 to head a political party but returned as the country's monarch under a new constitution in 1993.

autonomous state but retained considerable control over the government.

Siding with the progressive elements in the country, Sihanouk abdicated in 1955. Over the next five years, as the head of the Popular Socialist Community Party, which he had founded, he often served as premier of the government. In 1960, after the death of his father, who had been installed as king, he nominally abolished the monarchy and became the head of state.

On March 18, 1970, Lieutenant General Lon Nol and Prince Sisowath Sirik Matak overthrew the government,

Early Roman slave auctions were part of the long and pernicious history of human enslavement. A number of modern constitutions contain provisions expressly prohibiting the practice of slavery and making it a crime.

causing Sihanouk to set up a government in exile in China. Sihanouk returned in 1975 only to be placed under arrest while the head of the Cambodian Communist Party, Pol Pot, presided over an internal blood bath. Vietnam then invaded Cambodia and set up a government called the People's Republic of Kampuchea. In 1987, supported by Indonesia, Sihanouk negotiated with pro-Vietnamese forces, but the effort failed.

China agreed in 1988 to stop supporting the Cambodian communists, the Khmer Rouge, and the following year Vietnam agreed to withdraw its troops from Cambodia. The major factions in Cambodia later formed an interim supreme national governing council, and in November 1991 they agreed to recognize Sihanouk as the Cambodian head of state, at least until 1993.

Sihanouk took an active role in reestablishing a constitutional government, which with the help of the United Nations was installed on September 21, 1993. The same day a new constitution of the Kingdom of Cambodia, establishing Norodom Sihanouk as the monarch of his country for the second time, went into effect. "Cambodia is a kingdom," states Article 1 of the constitution, "whose king shall comply with the constitution and a multi-party, liberal democratic system. The Kingdom of Cambodia is an independent, sovereign, peaceful, neutral, and permanently non-aligned state."

Simple Majority. *See* Absolute Majority

Sitting. *See* Session

Slavery

The practice by which one person owns another as property was generally accepted in the ancient world and even condoned by religions and philosophers. Plato decrees in *The Laws* that in his new colony anyone in his right mind who wishes may seize his own slave and, within limits, treat him as he likes. At the outset of *The Politics,* Aristotle makes clear that those who can use their minds to "foresee" are by nature lords, while those who can use their bodies to give effect to such "foresight" are subjects and by nature slaves. In ancient Rome slaves were at the bottom of the social ranks; the second-century Roman historian Tacitus despised even freed slaves as base newcomers who were trying to live above their station.

Slavery continued for many centuries throughout the world. Not until 1807 was the slave trade abolished in the British Empire, and not until late in 1865, after the Civil War, did the U.S. Constitution (1789) prohibit slavery under the Thirteenth Amendment. Today a number of constitutions specifically proscribe slavery, but many others do not directly address the subject.

Constitution of the United States of America (1789), Amendment XIII (1865): "Neither slavery nor involuntary servitude, except as a punishment for crime whereof the party shall have been duly convicted, shall exist within the United States, or any place subject to their jurisdiction."

Constitution of Liberia (1986), Chapter III, Fundamental Rights, Article 12: "No person shall be held in slavery or forced labor in the republic, nor shall any citizen of Liberia nor any person resident therein deal in slaves or subject any other person to forced labor, debt bondage, or peonage; but labor reasonably required in consequence of a court sentence or order conforming to acceptable labor standards, service in the military, work, or service which forms part of normal civil obligations or service exacted in cases of emergency or calamity threatening the life or well-being of the community shall not be deemed forced labor."

Constitution of Singapore (1959), Part IV, Fundamental Liberties, Article 10(1): "No person shall be held in slavery."

Social Security

To pacify socialist agitators, Chancellor Otto von Bismarck had legislation enacted between 1883 and 1889 to provide protection and benefits for German workers. In 1911 the United Kingdom's National Insurance Act, based on the German model, established a broad-based program for protecting all workers against sickness and

Elderly American citizens can be insured by Medicare, a program of old age health insurance coverage that became a part of the U.S. Social Security system in 1966. Many constitutions now identify such entitlement programs.

unemployment. Social security—a state-sponsored program insuring workers and their families for illness, disability, unemployment, and old age—is now a fixture in almost all nation-states, and numerous recent constitutions explicitly state the rights and benefits of the people with respect to social security programs.

The basic social welfare legislation in the United States is the Social Security Act of 1935, which created a program of social insurance, public assistance, and child health and welfare services. When challenged a few years later, it was held constitutional by the U.S. Supreme Court on the grounds that Congress had broad powers to "promote the general welfare" under Article 1, Section 8, of the Constitution (1789).

Constitution of Honduras (1982), Title III, Declarations, Rights, and Guarantees, Chapter VI, Social Security, Article 142: "Every person is entitled to the security of his economic means of support in the event of work disability or inability to obtain remunerated employment. Social security services shall be furnished and administered by the Honduran social security institute and shall cover cases of sickness, maternity, family allowance, old-age, orphanhood, lockout, work injury, involuntary unemployment, occupational disease, and other contingencies affecting the capacity to produce."

Constitution of Cuba (1976), Chapter VI, Fundamental Rights, Duties, and Guarantees, Article 46: "By means of the social security system the state assures adequate protection to every worker who is unable to work because of age, illness, or disability."

Social State. *See* Socialism

Socialism

The term *socialism* was first used in the early nineteenth century to describe the theory or policy of social organization that advocates the ownership of the means of production—labor, capital, and land—by the whole community; the goods and services created are to be managed and distributed in the interests of all the people. Socialists' ideas are derived from Jean-Jacques Rousseau and the French Revolution (1789); however, while liberals emphasized liberty and democrats stressed equality, socialists focused on fraternity, or the brotherhood of the common people. Unlike socialism, capitalism emphasizes a free marketplace, or the unfettered rights of the individual to negotiate for labor and capital as well as goods and services.

Socialism has taken a number of paths: through utopian and Christian socialism, as well as into anarchy and communism. It has been a powerful political force especially in the twentieth century, particularly in Europe. The more virulent forms of socialism, such as Nazism, which grew out of the National Socialist Party in Germany (1933–45), and communism, as defined by the Communist Party worldwide, are all but defunct or in rapid decline. A number of political parties retain the word *socialist* in their names, however. The Socialist Party in France is still active, for example, having some time ago shed its association with the communists. Some constitutions still allude to the social state or socialism as a premise for the political organization and goals of the nation-state.

Constitution of Portugal (1976), Preamble: "The constituent assembly affirms the Portuguese people's decision to defend their national independence, safeguard the fundamental rights of the citizens, establish the basic principles of democracy, secure the primacy of the rule of law in a democratic state and open the way to socialist society, respecting the will of the Portuguese people and keeping in view the building of a freer, more just, and more fraternal country."

Constitution of Turkey (1982), Part One, General Principles, II, Characteristics of the Republic, Article 2: "The Republic of Turkey is a democratic, secular, and social state governed by the rule of law. . . . "

Solicitor General

The title of solicitor general can be traced to the sixteenth century in England, where the position of king's solicitor was first mentioned a century earlier. In English law a solicitor practices law before the courts of equity, rather than the common law courts.

The socialist movement never made a significant impact on U.S. politics, although Socialist Party candidates regularly ran for elective offices. Socialism and socialist parties have had a greater impact on many European countries.

The name has come to signify the legal position that is second in the realm—an assistant to and a deputy of the attorney general. In the United States the solicitor general, a position under the Department of Justice, helps decide which legal cases the federal government should appeal to the Supreme Court and supervises the presentation of federal appeals before the Court.

A solicitor general differs from a prosecutor general in that the latter is responsible for overseeing the government's cases brought in the name of the state or the people against persons accused of crimes.

Constitution of Zambia (1991), Part IV, The Executive, Section 55: "(1) There shall be a solicitor general of the republic whose office shall be a public office and who shall, subject to ratification by the national assembly, be appointed by the president. . . . (3) Any power or duty imposed on the attorney general by this constitution or any other written law may be exercised or performed by the solicitor general—(a) whenever the attorney general is unable to act owning to illness or absence; and (b) in any case where the attorney general has authorized the solicitor general to do so."

Constitution of Russia (1993), Part One, Chapter 7, Judicial Power, Article 129: "The prosecutor general of the Russian federation shall be appointed and dismissed by the federation council [upper house of the parliament] on the recommendation of the president of the Russian federation."

Sovereign.

See King; Monarchy; Sovereignty

Sovereignty

The modern concept of national sovereignty—the right to govern and set rules for citizens or subjects—developed from the change in relations within and between European political entities beginning in the sixteenth and seventeenth centuries, after the Holy Roman Empire, the unity of Christianity, and feudalism all declined. The rise of differentiated nation-states and the reintroduction of Roman legal concepts in Europe led to the adoption of the theory of sovereignty espoused by Jean Bodin in *De Republica* (1576). He asserted that absolute political power or sovereignty *(majesta* in Latin) resided most frequently in an individual monarch who is above the laws of the state but subject to divine law, the laws of nature, and the laws of nations or international law. In some national constitutions, sovereignty rests today with the nation, the people, or a single institution such as the legislature.

Under international law sovereignty is the principle that a nation-state must be treated equally with all other nation-states, regardless of size or military power. Nations today consist of specific territory in which they have jurisdiction over people and property, subject only to restrictions agreed to under international law but not to the jurisdiction of any other state. Because this concept is related to the older notion that a monarch holds his or her kingdom as a personal estate, rules for acquiring sovereignty have been adapted from the Roman law rules for acquiring property.

According to proponents of natural law, the nature of sovereignty has changed from a negative—being without constraint—to a positive—being a supreme power that undergirds both popular sovereignty and constitutional, or limited, monarchies. A transfer of territory from one sovereign authority to another, based on international law, transfers all instruments of political power, and laws under the former sovereignty that are in conflict with the constitution of the new sovereignty cannot be enforced.

Constitution of Turkey (1982), Part One, General Principles, VI, Sovereignty, Article 6: "Sovereignty is vested in the nation without reservation or condition. The Turkish nation shall exercise its sovereignty through the authorized organs as prescribed by the principles laid down in the constitution. The right to exercise sovereignty shall not be delegated to any individual, group, or class. No person or agency shall exercise any state authority which does not emanate from the constitution."

Constitution of Monaco (1962), Title IV, The Public Domain, The Public Finances, Article 34: "The assets of the Crown are applied to the exercise of sovereignty. They are inalienable and imprescriptible. Their composition and the rules regarding them are determined by the statutes of the sovereign family."

Constitution of Mozambique (1990), Part I, Basic Principles, Chapter I, The Republic, Article 8: "1. The Republic of Mozambique acknowledges and shall honor the sacrifices made by those who gave their lives for the national liberation struggle and for the defense of the country's sovereignty. 2. The state shall guarantee the special care and protection of both those who suffered permanent injury in the national liberation struggle and in the defense of independence, sovereignty, and territorial integrity as well as the orphans and other dependents of those who died in this cause."

Speaker

The use of the title *speaker* for the presiding officer of the lower house of the British Parliament was documented in the fourteenth century, while the title *lord speaker* for the upper house, the House of Lords, was recorded in the seventeenth century by the English diarist Samuel Pepys. Today the lord chancellor is the presiding officer of the House of Lords, but he or she is never referred to by the title of speaker.

The presiding officer of the German parliament is called the president, as in many French- and Spanish-speaking countries. But elsewhere the presiding officer and administrative head of a legislative body, usually the lower house

Japan's Western-style 1889 constitution included a parliament with a speaker, who looks on here as the military leader Hideki Tojo addresses the members before the war with the United States that began in 1941.

or chamber, is still often called the speaker. In the United Kingdom, as in U.S. House of Representatives, the speaker of the House of Commons is elected by the members from among their number at the start of each new session. However, the British speaker, as a channel of communication between the lower house and both the upper house and the sovereign, must be approved by the lord chancellor. No nominee has failed to win approval since 1678.

In the United States the Speaker of the House of Representatives, who is always from the majority party, is its most powerful and influential member and often serves as a political voice of the majority party. He or she recognizes members wishing to speak, interprets and applies the rules, decides questions of order, selects members of certain committees, and refers bills to committees.

In some countries the speaker may not vote on measures except in the case of a tie, and in others the speaker does not have to be a member of the legislative body.

Constitution of Singapore (1959), Part VI, The Legislature, Article 40(1): "When parliament [a unicameral body] first meets after any general election and before it proceeds to the dispatch of any other business, it shall elect a person to be speaker, and, whenever the office of speaker is vacant otherwise than by reason of dissolution of parliament, shall not transact any business other than the election of a person to fill that office."

Constitution of Sweden, Instrument of Government (1974), Chapter 5, The Head of State, Article 6: "The Riksdag [parliament] may appoint someone on the government's recommendation to serve as temporary regent [head of state when the monarch is unavailable for stated reasons]. The speaker, or if he is prevented from attending, one of the deputy speakers shall serve as temporary regent on the government's recommendation, when no other competent person is in a position to serve."

Speech

The histories of ancient Greece and Rome record the names of great orators such as Demosthenes and Marcus Tullius Cicero. But Plato was not an advocate of free speech in Greece, and the Roman emperors were not above exercising censorship over the expression of personal opinions.

Roman censors, in addition to taking the census, also policed the manners and morals of the citizens. In the eighteenth century William Blackstone, the commentator on English law, discussed offenses of speech, including spreading false news or false prophesies and administering unlawful oaths.

The U.S. Bill of Rights (1791), comprising the first ten amendments to the Constitution (1789), unconditionally guarantees the right of free speech. The U.S. Supreme Court, however, has found some utterances beyond the protection of the constitutional language—for example, yelling "Fire!" in a crowded theater. Subsequent national constitutions likewise have included in their bills or lists of the people's fundamental rights the right of free speech or its equivalent, free expression. But even today the United Kingdom has no document comparable to the U.S. Bill of Rights to guarantee the right of free speech to its subjects. The 1688 English Bill of Rights extracted from the monarch certain rights for Parliament, not for the citizenry.

In the United States an amendment to the Constitution to prohibit desecration the U.S. flag has been proposed and defeated in Congress; opponents contend that such a measure could inhibit symbolic speech such as burning the flag to protest government policies. Other areas in which freedom of speech in democratic societies faces the challenge of censorship include government security and the dissemination of pornography in the conventional media as well as the Internet now globally linking personal computers.

Constitution of the United States of America (1789), Amendment I (1791): "Congress shall make no law . . . abridging the freedom of speech. . . ."

Constitution of Japan (1889, significantly revised in 1947), Chapter III, Rights and Duties of the People, Article 21: "Freedom of assembly and association as well as speech, press, and all other forms of expression are guaranteed. No censorship shall be maintained, nor shall secrecy of any means of communication be violated."

Constitution of Canada, Constitution Act (1982), Part I, Canadian Charter of Rights and Freedoms, Fundamental Freedoms, Section 2: "Everyone has the following fundamental freedoms: . . . (b) freedom of thought, belief, opinion, and expression, including freedom of the press and other media of communication. . . ."

Stalin, Joseph

At the time the ruthless communist dictator Joseph Stalin (1879–1953) died, the 1936 constitution of the Soviet Union, drafted under his direction, had spawned many similar undemocratic constitutions in countries dominated by the Communist Party.

Iosif Vissarionovich Dzhugashvili, who would later take the name Stalin, was born the son of a cobbler in Gori, Georgia, on December 21, 1879. The young Stalin studied for the ministry in Tiflis until being expelled in 1899 for his subversive views. In 1901 he joined an underground revolutionary Marxist movement, was later arrested, and was sent to Siberia. After escaping, he systematically stole money to support the movement.

Not a proponent of constitutionalism, the dictator Joseph Stalin created a constitution for the Soviet Union in 1936 that became a model for many countries dominated by the Communist Party.

As a protégé of the Communist Party leader Vladimir Lenin from 1912, Stalin rose rapidly in the party hierarchy following the 1917 Russian Revolution and became its general secretary in 1922. But Lenin, who died in early 1924, favored Leon Trotsky to succeed him as leader of Soviet Russia, fearing that Stalin was too ruthless. Lenin's assessment proved astute: by the early 1930s Stalin had become dictator of the Soviet Union, having eliminated all his rivals. As the leader of the Communist Party there, he remained the absolute ruler of the vast Union of Soviet Socialist Republics and a powerful influence on the Soviet satellite countries in Eastern Europe.

During his two-decade-long dictatorship, Stalin oversaw every aspect of Soviet life, including the drafting and implementation of what became known as the "Stalin" constitution of 1936. A 1918 constitution of the Russian Soviet Federated Socialist Republics had formally recognized the Bolshevik communists as the ruling party of the dictatorship of the proletariat, or workers, in alliance with the peasants.

The dictatorship of the proletariat, which according to Karl Marx was to precede a withering away of the state, had been installed by Lenin after the 1917 revolution. The 1918 constitution, on paper, vested supreme state power in an All-Russian Congress of the Soviets, consisting of representatives, called deputies, from local soviets (councils) throughout Russia. In 1924 a new supreme law confirmed the union of the Russian Soviet Federated Socialist Republic with the Ukrainian, Belorussian, and Transcaucasian republics, or the Union of Soviet Socialist Republics. The new document established as the supreme state authority a central executive committee, in place of the Congress of Soviets, and two other bodies—the soviet of the union, which was to represent the republics, and a soviet of nationalities.

In 1934 Stalin initiated a series of political purges whose victims included many of the Communist Party leaders during the 1917 revolution. Although economic conditions improved during 1935 and the early part of 1936, an increase in political tensions led to harsher laws, including the punishment of all close family members of traitors to the homeland. It was in this climate of brutal repression that the "Stalin" constitution was drafted and "adopted" on December 5, 1936. A large collective, some members of which were later killed, actually prepared the document, but there is no doubt that Stalin had to approve every aspect. The new constitution, he ordered, should "register" the gains of socialism rather than prescribe "future achievement."

The 1936 constitution was a matter of form only; the true supreme law of the land was the directives of the Communist Party and its head, Stalin. Nevertheless, the constitution did significantly change the apparent form of the government of the U.S.S.R. and, indirectly, that of many countries dominated by the Communist Party throughout the world. Today, however, even the remaining communist-controlled countries, such as China, North Korea, and Vietnam, have greatly customized their constitutions so that they no longer reflect much of Stalin's 1936 model. Stalin died, apparently from natural causes, on March 5, 1953.

Standing Committee

In parliamentary procedures standing committees are bodies appointed under an organization's bylaws to function year-round. The English word *stand* is related to the Latin *status* (fixed) but also has an Anglo-Saxon and a Scandinavian root *(standan).*

In the United Kingdom standing committees are permanent committees appointed to deal with all matters within a particular sphere during the existence of the appointive body. In the United States standing committees are regular committees of a legislature that consider bills and, in some cases, appointments of certain high government officials within designated areas of government, such as the treasury and foreign affairs. Both houses of the U.S. Congress together number nearly forty such committees. Under some constitutions a standing or permanent committee may be authorized to act on behalf of a legislature when it is not in session.

An ad hoc committee is one appointed for some special purpose, such as to investigate a matter or resolve differences in bills passed by the houses of a bicameral legislature; it is disbanded after it completes its work.

Constitution of China (People's Republic of China) (1982), Chapter Three, The Structure of the State, Section I, The National People's Congress, Article 57: "The national people's congress of the People's Republic of China is the highest organ of state power. Its permanent body is the standing committee of the national people's congress."

Constitution of Finland, Parliament Act (1928), Chapter 4, Preparation of Matters, Section 41 (amended in 1983): "If parliament is unanimous on the election, it shall elect the members and deputy members of the standing and temporary committees."

Standing Order. *See* Order

State

The concept of the state—what it is and what it ought to be—has been the subject of intellectual inquiry for much of recorded history. Plato, in *The Laws,* analyzes and contrasts the ideal and the real state *(polis),* and Aristotle, in *The Politics,* suggests that every state is a community established with a view to some good and that the best state aims at the greatest good. Perhaps the most well known ideal state is Utopia, the literary creation of the early-sixteenth-century English statesman and author Sir Thomas More. The term is derived from the Latin *status* (state or condition) and is related to *civitas* and *republica,* which refer to a political state.

A political community occupying a definite territory, a state has a definable government organization and some degree of internally and externally recognized sovereignty. The ancient Greek city-states were states, but because of their small size and interrelationship with other Greek-speaking polities they are generally not viewed as nations or nation-states by today's standards. Groups of tribes of indigenous Indians in North America were considered nations among themselves and by European settlers, but they generally lacked the defined territory to be considered states.

In constitutions the word *state* has three basic meanings: (1) a nation-state; (2) a political subdivision of a nation-state with a federal form of government; and (3) the combined institutions of sovereign political power usually referred to as "the state." This last meaning may be used with respect to a legitimate or constitutional monarchy, a military dictatorship, a theocratic republic, or a popular democratic republic. The constitution of India, for example, uses the word in all three senses in the same document.

The U.S. Constitution (1789) also uses *state* in the more general sense to mean a condition. Article 2, Section 3, for example, provides that the president shall "from time to time give to the Congress Information of the State of the Union. . . . "

Constitution of India (1950), Part II, Citizenship, Article 9: " . . . No person shall be a citizen of India . . . if he has voluntarily acquired the citizenship of a foreign state."

Constitution of India (1950), Part V, The Union, Chapter IV, The Union Judiciary, Article 150: " . . . The accounts of the union and the states shall be kept in such a form as the president may, on the advice of the comptroller and auditor general of India prescribe."

Constitution of India (1950), Part IV, Directive Principles of State Policy, Article 38: "(1) . . . The state shall strive to promote the welfare of the people. . . . "

Constitution of Israel, Basic Law: The Knesset (1958), Section 1: "The Knesset is the parliament of the state."

Statute

A statute is a law that contains one or more provisions and is enacted at one time by a sovereign legislature. Unwritten laws are not statutes. Most constitutions avoid using the word *statute* and use simply *law* instead, but exceptions can be found. *Statute* is derived from the Latin *statuo* (to set up, settle, or decide) and is related to the French *statut* (statute, decree, regulation, or bylaw).

In the United Kingdom a statute is another term for an act of Parliament. In the United States it refers to laws enacted by Congress or legislatures of the constituent states—both public and private laws passed in each legislative session that are collected, numbered consecutively, and used as a legal reference.

In legal theory an important distinction is made between a statute and a law: a statute is the written embodiment of the intention and will of the legislators to enact a law, but it is the resulting law that affects people's behavior—those subject to it, those who have the power to interpret and apply it, such as judges, and those who enforce it, such as the police. Some legal theorists conclude

Sir Thomas More tried to describe a perfect state and society in his 1516 work *Utopia*. The concept of the state—the authority and machinery of a sovereign government—has become merged with the concept of the nation.

that law cannot exist in the abstract but only when someone applies it to a specific situation.

Constitution of the United Kingdom, Halsbury's Laws of England (1974, 4th ed.), Volume 8, Constitutional Law, Paragraph 806, Sources of Powers and Duties: "The specific legal sources of governmental powers and duties are the specific sources of law, that is to say: . . . (6) subordinate legislation made by the Crown, government departments, local authorities or other bodies on whom legislative powers have been conferred by statute. . . . ”

Constitution of New Zealand, New Zealand Constitution Bill (1986), Part V, Miscellaneous Provisions, Section 25: “United Kingdom enactments ceasing to have effect as part of the law of New Zealand—As from the date of the commencement of this act the following enactments of the parliament of the United Kingdom, namely . . . (b) Sections 2 to 6 of the Statute of Westminster 1931 (22 Geo. V, c.4) . . . shall cease to have effect as part of the law of New Zealand.”

Subject.

See Citizen

Succession

The transition of power from one head of state to another is usually addressed in constitutional provisions that describe succession on death or abdication in the case of a monarch or death, disability, resignation, or removal in the case of a president.

Many constitutional monarchies have an act of succession that establishes how a new monarch can become vested with the power of the former monarch on his or her death or abdication. Constitutions in which the head of state is elected for a term of office also usually specify the process of succession—from the Latin *successio*—when an incumbent president dies or otherwise must relinquish the office.

Constitution of the United States of America (1789), Article II, Section 1: “In Case of the Removal of the President from Office, or of his Death, Resignation, or Inability to discharge the Powers and Duties of said Office, the Same shall devolve on the Vice President. . . . ”

Constitution of the United States of America (1789), Amendment XXV (1967), Section 1: “In case of the removal of the President from office or of his death or resignation, the Vice President shall become President.”

Constitution of Nicaragua (1987), Title VIII, Organization of the State, Chapter III, Executive Branch, Article 149: “If the president and the vice president of the republic are permanently absent, the president of the national assembly, or whoever is next in the order of succession under law shall assume the functions of the president.”

Constitution of Denmark, The Succession to the Throne Act (1953), Section 2: “On the demise of a king the throne shall pass to his son or daughter so that the son takes precedence [over] a daughter, and where there are several children of the same sex the eldest child shall take precedence [over] a younger child.”

Constitution of Monaco (1962), Title II, Devolution of the Crown, Article 10: “The succession to the throne shall take place after the death or abdication within the direct legitimate line of the reigning prince, by order of primogeniture, with priority being given to males within the same degree of relationship.”

Suffrage

By the sixteenth century the word *suffrage* was used in England in the sense of a vote either for or against a nomination or a question in controversy. “People of Rome, and people’s tribunes here, I ask for your voices and your suffrages,” says the hero of William Shakespeare’s *Tragedy of Titus Andronicus* (1588). In modern constitutions suffrage—from the Latin *suffragium* (vote or ballot)—may refer to either the act of voting or the right or privilege of casting a vote.

Many classes of people have historically been disqualified from participating in government decision making—deemed ineligible or unfit to vote or hold an elective or appointive office. Often only the absolute ruler had any political authority to make such decisions because his or her word was law. In the democracy of ancient Athens and the republic of ancient Rome, only adult male citizens who were not otherwise disqualified by their misconduct were eligible to participate in governing. Today the right of suffrage has been expanded generally to all citizens in a nation-state over a certain age, usually eighteen or twenty-one years, generally with certain other qualifications and disqualifications.

Although most nations now grant both men and women the right to vote in all public elections on an equal basis, in some countries many obstacles still prevent women, other minorities, and the economically disadvantaged from fully exercising political rights including the right to vote. The right of women to vote at a national level began when the governor-general of New Zealand assented to a women's suffrage bill at 11:45 A.M. on September 19, 1893; on November 20 of that year the women of New Zealand voted in the national elections. Finnish women gained suffrage in 1906, when Finland was still under Russian rule. In 1920 the Nineteenth Amendment to the U.S. Constitution (1789) extended the vote to American women.

Constitution of France (1958), Title II, The President of the Republic, Article 6: "The president of the republic shall be elected for seven years by direct universal suffrage."

Constitution of Germany (1949), III, The Federal Parliament (Bundestag), Article 38, Elections (2): "Anyone who has attained the age of eighteen years shall be entitled to

Women in the United States had to campaign vigorously to counteract organized opposition to the movement to ratify the Nineteenth Amendment to the Constitution in 1920 giving them suffrage—the right to vote.

vote; anyone who has attained majority shall be eligible for election."

Constitution of the United States of America (1789), Amendment XIX (1920): "The right of citizens of the United States to vote shall not be denied or abridged by the United States or by any State on account of sex."

Sukarno

Sukarno (1901–70), a leader in the Indonesian movement to achieve independence from the Dutch, became the country's first president and played an influential role in developing and later reinstating the nation's 1945 constitution.

Sukarno was born June 6, 1901, in Surabaja, East Java, into a relatively well established family. His father, a Muslim schoolteacher, arranged for him to study at the Hooger Burger School with children of Dutch and high Indonesian officials. While attending school, Sukarno lived with H.O.S. Tjokroaminoto, a religious and political leader who had founded an Indonesian independence group called the Sarekat.

Committed to independence for his country, which had been a Dutch colony since the early seventeenth century, Sukarno joined the Young Java group and honed his impressive skills as a speaker, an organizer, and a writer. An excellent student, he was one of the first eleven Indonesian students admitted to a Dutch technical college and was graduated as an engineer. His later activities in support of the independence movement led to his arrest on December 29, 1929. During his trial, he gave his "Indonesia accuses" speech, in which he leveled specific charges against the Dutch rule in Indonesia for more than three hundred years. He was imprisoned following the trial and again in 1933.

Immediately after the Japanese surrender in August 1945, which ended World War II, Sukarno and his associate Mohammed Hatta, as leaders of the independence movement, issued a brief but formal declaration of independence. By late September of that year, a constitution had been drafted, installing Sukarno as president and creating a cabinet directly responsible to him. It was not until the Linggadiati Agreement in 1946 that the Dutch gave de facto recognition to the new Republic of Indonesia, although they subsequently abrogated the agreement. Finally in 1949 the Dutch were forced to cede their sovereignty to the Indonesians.

After leading Indonesia to complete independence from the Dutch in 1949, President Sukarno by decree reinstated the 1945 constitution, which contains his five basic principles of the Indonesian nation.

Sukarno was sworn in as president on December 27, 1949, under a second, federal constitution. The following year, however, Indonesia became a unitary state under a new provisional constitution, which set up an inadequate parliamentary government structure. In 1955 the country became divided over what the basis of the Indonesian nation-state should be: the Islamic religion or Sukarno's five principles—one deity, humanity, popular sovereignty, nationality, and social justice—set forth in his *Pantja Sila (Five Principles)*. After declaring martial law in 1957, Sukarno by decree reinstated his 1945 constitution, which made his election dependent on a majority vote of the

People's Consultative Assembly. Under the 1945 constitution his executive authority was independent of the parliament, except for approval of laws enacted, declarations of war and peace, and the proclamation of treaties, and he was made commander in chief of the armed forces.

Sukarno served as president of the Indonesian republic from 1945 to 1967. The question of whether his five principles or the Islamic religion would become the base of the Indonesian nation-state is answered in the preamble to the 1945 document: "... [the] constitution of the sovereign Republic of Indonesia ... is based on the belief in the one and only God, just and civilized humanity, the unity of Indonesia, democracy guided by the inner wisdom of deliberations amongst representatives, and the realization of social justice for all the people of Indonesia."

Sun Yat-sen

Sun Yat-sen (1866–1925), who worked unceasingly during the early part of the twentieth century to bring his own brand of Western constitutionalism to the people of China, is today venerated in both the People's Republic of China and Taiwan.

Sun Yat-sen was born in a coastal village in Kwangtung Province, near the Portuguese colony of Macao. Educated in both Chinese and Western-style schools, he attended college in Hawaii. He returned to China to study in 1883 and later obtained a medical degree in Hong Kong in 1892. Two years later, concerned about China's fate at the hands of Western powers, he founded in Honolulu the Hsing-chung hui, a secret society for regenerating China and developed his three basic political goals: nationalism, democracy, and the people's well-being—his formula for a strong, independent, democratic, and prosperous China.

After the reorganized Hsing-chung hui's planned uprising against the Manchus in Canton, led by Sun, failed in 1895, he fled to Japan and then traveled extensively. Donning Western-style clothes, he posed as a Japanese and returned to Hawaii, afterwards going to San Francisco and England, where he was kidnapped and then rescued by the dean of his Hong Kong medical school. His exploits gained him an international reputation. Before leaving England he acquainted himself with the works of the German communist theorist Karl Marx and the American tax reformer Henry George.

Sun continued to travel but returned to Japan in July 1905 to organize the T'ung-meng hui (Revolutionary Alliance). He and his supporters tried ten times during the next sixteen years to seize power from the corrupt imperial Manchu government. Finally, in 1911, his forces were successful, and on December 29, 1911, he was chosen president of the new Chinese republic. Five constitutions were adopted during the next few years, but according to Chinese scholarship the provisional constitution of 1912 was the most respected. It was influenced greatly by the three principles of Sun, who was familiar with Western constitutional documents and was known to quote the U.S. Declaration of Independence.

In 1912 Sun was forced to turn over the presidency to a military strongman, Yüan Shih-kai, who tried to declare himself emperor. Five years later, after the death of his

Sun Yat-sen aided the development of constitutionalism in China at the beginning of the twentieth century, but it survives today only in Taiwan.

successor, Sun returned and was chosen to lead the Chinese military government in Canton. He became president in 1921, spending the years until his death in 1925 trying to unite the feuding warlord regimes. To eliminate the power of the warlords and foreign influences of countries such as Japan, he allied his political party, the Kuomintang, with the local Chinese communists, for which he is venerated by the mainland Chinese communist regime. Although his democratic ideals were only briefly realized while he lived, Sun's efforts are memorialized in the preamble to the constitution of Taiwan: "The National Assembly of the Republic of China, by virtue of the mandate received from the whole body of citizens, in accordance with the teachings bequeathed by Dr. Sun Yatsen in founding the Republic of China. . . . "

Supermajority. *See* Absolute Majority

Supremacy Clause

Many written constitutions expressly state, in a supremacy clause, that they are the supreme law of the nation-state—the paramount authority. Article 6 of the U.S. Constitution (1789) declares: "This Constitution, and the Laws of the United States which shall be made in Pursuance thereof; and all Treaties made, or which shall be made, under the Authority of the United States, shall be the supreme Law of the Land; and the Judges in every State shall be bound thereby, any Thing in the Constitution or Laws of any State to the Contrary notwithstanding." This language binding judges to the Constitution laid the groundwork for judicial review by the U.S. courts and their guardianship of the Constitution, which is critical for enforcing its supremacy.

In unwritten constitutions, such as those of the United Kingdom, Israel, and New Zealand, parliaments reign supreme—from the Latin *supremus* (highest or last)—because without the supremacy of a written constitution, the national lawmakers are the highest constitutional authority and can change the constitution simply by a majority vote in the legislature. The eighteenth-century English jurist Sir Edward Coke described the supremacy of the British Parliament as "so transcendent and absolute, that it cannot be confined, either for causes or persons, within any bounds."

The constitutions of Iran and Libya are notable exceptions in that they acknowledge the Qur'an as the supreme law of the nation-state.

Constitution of Bulgaria (1991), Chapter 1, Fundamental Principles, Article 5(1): "The constitution is the supreme law, and no other law may contradict it."

Constitution of Nepal (1990), Part I, Preliminary, Article 1: "Constitution as the Fundamental Law. (1) This constitution is the fundamental law of Nepal and all laws inconsistent with it shall, to the extent of such inconsistency, be void."

Supreme Court

The concept of a supreme court—a court that makes final decisions—is not new. In ancient Athens a disputant dissatisfied with a magistrate's decision could appeal to a higher authority, who would rehear the matter and render a judgment that superseded that of the magistrate. For most of human history, however, the final say in any dispute lay with a single person, the ruler or monarch, should he or she choose to exercise the authority. Even today in Saudi Arabia the courts will defer to the king and the royal family in legal matters.

According to William Blackstone, the eighteenth-century commentator on English law, the supreme court in criminal matters was the High Court of Parliament, and even today the courts of the United Kingdom acknowledge Parliament's supremacy over them. France's courts likewise do not constitute a coequal branch of government. Its supreme court of appeals is called the Cour de Cassation, and the 1958 French constitution created a high council on the judiciary, presided over by the president of the republic, that nominates judges for the Cour de Cassation and the court of appeals and disciplines the nation's judges. Germany has a federal supreme court for civil and criminal matters, the Bundesgerichtshof, but also administrative, tax, labor, and social courts, all of which are generally under the constitutional court, the Bundesverfassungsgericht.

The Supreme Court created by the U.S. Constitution

in 1789 was unique then, but many subsequent constitutions have established similar, if not identical, supreme courts at the apex of their national judicial branch. Such courts generally make final determinations in all cases, both appellate and those for which the supreme court has original jurisdiction, are coequal with and independent of any other branch of government, and are responsible for the administration of the national court system. Under some constitutional structures, a so-called supreme court may in fact have only limited jurisdiction and exist along with a separate high court.

Constitution of Indonesia (1945), Chapter IX, The Judiciary Power, Article 24: "(1) The judiciary power shall be exercised by a supreme court and such other courts of law as are provided for by law. (2) The composition and powers of these legal bodies shall be regulated by law."

Constitution of Colombia (1991), Title VIII, Concerning the Judiciary, Chapter I, Concerning General Provisions, Article 233: "The judges of the constitutional court, the supreme court of justice, and of the council of state [highest administrative court] will be elected for a period of eight years."

Swearing In. *See* Oath

ARGENTINA

Symbol

The use of a symbol—from the Latin *symbolus* (sign, token, or ticket)—as a summary of a religious belief of a Christian church or sect to distinguish it from a non-Christian church or sect can be traced back as far as the third century. Today a symbol is generally something that stands for something else: a crown may represent a monarch or monarchy, and a cross may represent a Christian church.

In some constitutions symbols of the nation-state are expressly described. These symbols include flags, seals, and even national anthems. Article 2 of the 1958 French constitution, for example, states: "The national anthem is the 'Marseillaise.'" The words and music of the German national anthem are included as an appendix to the official English translation of the 1949 German constitution.

The constitutions of many countries specify in varying degrees of detail the symbols of the nation, such as the national flag, seal, and even the anthem.

Constitution of the Czech Republic, Chapter One, Basic Provisions, Article 14: "(1) The state symbols of the Czech Republic are the large and small state emblems, the state colors, the state flag, the banner of the president of the republic, the state seal, and the state anthem. (2) The state symbols and their use are determined by law."

Constitution of New Zealand, Seal of New Zealand Act (1977), Section 3, Use of Seal (1): "The seal of New Zealand shall be the seal to be used on any instrument that is made by her majesty or her successors, or by the governor-general, on the advice of a minister of her majesty's government in New Zealand or on the advice and with the consent of the executive council of New Zealand."

T

Tax

Throughout history the collection of taxes by the government has been a source of benefit but also dissatisfaction among citizens. Ancient Greece and Rome both had tax laws; in Rome tax collectors were called publicans. Taxes—compulsory monetary contributions to support the operations of government—are levied on people and property, including income and commodities, as well as on transactions.

In Middle English *taxe* and *taske* (task) were nearly synonymous, but as early as the fourteenth century *tax* came to mean an assessed money payment. By the eighteenth century William Blackstone, the commentator on English law, wrote that a tax on land had superseded previous methods of judging the worth of property and of people with respect to their property.

The British colonists' resentment over taxes levied on them by the British Parliament was a key factor in the American Revolution (1775–83). In essay 10 of *The Federalist* (1788), James Madison notes that "the apportionment of taxes on various descriptions of property is an act which seems to require the most exact impartiality" and cautions that the dominant party in a legislature will be tempted to reduce the taxes on its members and place them instead on the minority party.

Unlike the voyages of discovery in the New World, planting the flag of the United States on the moon, an unclaimed territory, did not confer U.S. sovereignty over it.

Constitutions may limit the power to raise taxes by granting it to the more representative body of a bicameral national legislature, such as the U.S. House of Representatives. Among other references to taxation in the U.S. Constitution (1789) are Article 1, Section 2, which provides that representatives in the House and taxes are

Democratic governments today often have to make an effort—such as putting up explanatory signs—to justify the need for taxes to voters who have to pay them.

to be apportioned among the states; and the Twenty-fourth Amendment (1964), which prohibits the loss of voting rights for failure to pay a poll tax or other tax.

Constitution of China (People's Republic of China) (1982), Chapter Two, The Fundamental Rights and Duties of Citizens, Article 56: "It is the duty of citizens of the People's Republic of China to pay taxes in accordance with the law."

Constitution of Sweden, Instrument of Government (1974), Chapter 1, Basic Principles of the Constitution, Article 4: "The Riksdag [parliament] is the foremost representative of the people. The Riksdag enacts laws, determines taxes, and decides how public funds shall be used."

Constitution of North Korea (1972), Chapter II, Economy, Article 33: "The state abolishes taxation, a hangover of the old society."

Technology. *See* Science

Tenure. *See* Term

Term

Lawyers, says Rosalind in William Shakespeare's *As You Like It* (1600), "sleep between term and term and . . . perceive not how time moves." A century and a half earlier the Rolls of Parliament recorded an action in 1454 "by Bille in Michell' terme last past." Taken from the Latin *termino* (limit, determine, or end), the word as used in constitutions now generally refers to a fixed or set period of time. Like tenure, a term is the length of time an official, especially an elected official, may hold office. Sessions of courts and legislatures are also called terms.

The U.S. Constitution (1789) expressly sets forth the terms of office for the president, vice president, and members of each house of Congress, although an effort was initiated in the 1990s to introduce term limits for legislators, so that a person could not run again after serving a certain number of terms. Term limits were noted in the first century B.C. by Marcus Tullius Cicero, the Roman statesman and orator, who related that consuls and praetors were barred from holding certain positions until five years after their terms of office had expired.

Among the many other meanings of *term* are the conditions of an agreement and the period of time for which an interest in property may be held under certain conditions, such as the term of tenancy or a life estate.

Constitution of Argentina (1853), Second Part, Authorities of the Nation, Title I, Federal Government, Second Section, The Executive Power, Article 78: "The president of the nation ceases in his authority on the same day on which his term of six years expires; no event that may have interrupted it shall be reason for completing the term later."

Constitution of Thailand (1991), Chapter X, The Constitutional Tribunal, Article 204: "If the office of a member of the constitutional tribunal . . . becomes vacant upon any other reason than the vacation term, the senate or the house of representatives, as the case may be, shall appoint a new member. . . ."

Territory

Because a nation-state's territorial sovereignty is of critical importance, numerous constitutions contain provisions describing the extent and limits of their jurisdiction over territory—land or country belonging to a state or ruler. The word *territory* has its root in the Latin *terra* (earth, land, or region), but it may also have been derived from the Latin *territo* (to terrify), signifying land that people were afraid to enter.

An important legal principle is *terra manus vacua occupanti conceditur* ("land lying unoccupied is given to the first occupant"). Under international law a nation-state may acquire territory by unilateral occupation, by having it ceded by another state, by gift, by prescription (simply using it over a long period of time), and by operation of nature, such as a river that creates land by depositing silt.

International law also prescribes a nation's jurisdiction

over territorial waters. Countries adjacent to water always extend their authority on land to some extent over the outlying seas or waters. Before the advent of modern ballistic missiles, the extent of a country's territorial seas—three miles—was predicated on the customary range of cannon shot; today, however, many nations claim up to two hundred miles as their territorial waters.

In their constitutions some nations even include extraterritorial jurisdiction or historically coveted territory. Ireland, for example, claims Northern Ireland, currently under the territorial jurisdiction of the United Kingdom.

A territory may also be an area under the legal jurisdiction of a nation-state but not integrated into it on an equal footing with other areas. Like an autonomous region or a colony, such a territory or possession is usually considered not sufficiently developed for political independence or assimilation into the main body of the nation-state. The Northern Territory of Australia and the island of Guam, a U.S. possession in the northern Pacific Ocean, are examples of this kind of territory. Under Article 4, Section 3, of the U.S. Constitution (1789), Congress is authorized to make rules respecting the territory of the United States.

Constitution of Russia (1993), Part One, Chapter 1, The Principles of the Constitutional System, Article 4: "1. The sovereignty of the Russian federation shall extend to its entire territory. 2. The constitution of the Russian federation and federal laws shall have priority throughout the territory of the Russian federation. 3. The Russian federation shall ensure the integrity and inviolability of its territory."

Constitution of the Philippines (1987), Article I, National Territory: "The national territory comprises the Philippine archipelago, with all the islands and waters embraced therein, and all other territories over which the Philippines has sovereignty or jurisdiction, consisting of its terrestrial, fluvial, and aerial domains, including its territorial sea, the seabed, the subsoil, the insular shelves, and other submarine areas. The waters around, between, and connecting the islands of the archipelago, regardless of their breadth and dimensions, form part of the internal waters of the Philippines."

Constitution of Ireland (1937), Article 2: "The national territory consists of the whole island of Ireland, its islands and the territorial seas."

Democracy in America, Alexis de Tocqueville's 1835 analysis of the workings of the new constitutional government of the United States, had a positive effect on the constitutional development of many European countries.

Tocqueville, Alexis-Charles-Henri Maurice Clérel de

As a result of his incisive commentary on the early performance of the American experiment in constitutional government, Alexis de Tocqueville (1805–59) played a role in both Europe and the United States in shaping the future of democratic governments.

The son of a landed proprietor, Alexis de Tocqueville was born in Paris on July 29, 1805. The young Alexis studied under his father's tutor, Abbé Lesueur, who had high ambitions for his pupil. After studying law, he was appointed an assistant magistrate of Versailles in 1827.

After the July 1830 revolution in France, Tocqueville, because of his family's aristocratic background, was demoted to a minor judge with no salary. His request to travel with another judge, Gustave de Beaumont, to study prison reform in America was granted, however. The result of that trip was *Democracy in America* (1835), which became a world-famous analysis of the new American government. This work, which he hoped would help France create a better government, revealed him to be an astute observer and an accurate prophet of the future of national democracies.

In America, Tocqueville found that although republican forms of government do not always run like clockwork, republics provide something more important than a perfect despotism: they impart to the community a sense of involvement in the outcome of government decisions, as well as an energy and force that can achieve great things. He also observed that a unitary central government, as opposed to the American federal system of government, no matter how well meaning, cannot enact legislation to suit all the diverse groups in a country; therefore, some groups may feel excluded from the political process in unitary nation-states and become disenchanted with the government. In one area, however, Tocqueville has been proven wrong by history. In *Democracy in America* he says about the American president: "All his important acts are directly or indirectly submitted to the legislature; and where he is independent of it he can do but little."

In 1839 Tocqueville was elected to the chamber of deputies of the French legislature and served again as a deputy after the revolution of 1848. Elected that same year to represent Tocqueville in the constituent assembly charged with drawing up a new French constitution, he was then selected by his peers to be a member of the eighteen-member committee to draft the constitution. Fear of a socialist movement led him to concentrate on the question of the people's right to work (the obligation of the state to provide work). In both the committee and the assembly he argued against the right to work, believing that it could lead to socialism and the abolition of personal property, which he, like the English political philosopher John Locke, viewed as a natural right and indispensable to a peaceful society. Tocqueville also advocated the establishment of a bicameral legislature with a second legislative chamber, which others regarded as an aristocratic body like the British House of Lords, and he argued for the election of the president of the republic by popular vote.

Although Tocqueville's bicameral proposal failed, the next president of France, Louis Napoleon Bonaparte, Napoleon Bonaparte's nephew, was elected president of the Second Republic in 1848 by an overwhelming margin. In 1852, however, when his term was to expire without the possibility of reelection, he seized the government, declaring himself Emperor Napoleon III. Tocqueville was arrested with fifty other deputies but soon released.

He died in Cannes on April 16, 1859, during the reign of Napoleon III. Not until 1875 would the French assembly finally abandon any notion of a monarchical government and agree to create a Third Republic.

Totalitarianism. *See* Absolutism

Tradition. *See* Convention; Custom

Traditional Leader

Many constitutional processes and institutions have evolved from tradition and custom. Particularly in Africa, leadership of indigenous populations at the community or tribal level originated before the period of European colonization. After European-style nation-states were created from territories traditionally ruled by tribal chiefs and other local leaders, the role of these chiefs and leaders did not disappear. In fact, many traditional leaders have been stabilizing and unifying forces in their countries. The Zulu and Inkatha Freedom Party leader Chief Mangosuthu Buthelezi, for example, helped in South Africa's transition in the 1990s to a democracy for all its citizens.

Specific provisions defining the role of traditional leaders in the nation-state and government are included in various constitutions, which may also address traditional leaders' continuing relationship to citizens who have historically been subject to their jurisdiction in local matters.

Constitution of South Africa (1994), Chapter 11, Traditional Authorities, Recognition of Traditional Authorities and Indigenous Law, Section 181: "(1) A traditional authority which observes a system of indigenous law and is recognized by law immediately before the commencement of this constitution, shall continue as such an authority and continue to exercise and perform the powers and functions vested in it in accordance with the applicable laws and customs, subject to any amendment or repeal of such laws and customs by a competent authority. (2) Indigenous law shall be subject to regulation by law."

Constitution of Uganda, Simplified Draft (1992), Chapter 18, General and Miscellaneous (Various Matters), Traditional Leaders: "1. Traditional leaders may exist according to the culture, traditions, and wishes of the people concerned. 2. The following conditions shall apply to traditional leaders: (a) The government shall not be responsible for maintaining them; (b) no person shall be forced to be loyal and contribute to their maintenance; (c) they shall not participate in politics unless they leave [their traditional leadership] office. . . . "

A chief of the West African Ashanti tribe is a traditional leader, whose role is addressed in some constitutions.

Treason

The most serious crime a person can commit against a nation is treason—overt acts aimed at overthrowing the government to which a person owes allegiance or betraying the state into the hands of a foreign power. In *The Laws*, Plato makes treason a capital offense, and in 410 B.C., just after the restoration of democracy in Athens, a law was passed stating that "anyone who subverts the democracy of Athens . . . shall be killed with impunity, and his property shall be confiscated. . . . " Punishment for high treason against the English sovereign included hanging by the neck, removal and burning of the person's entrails while he was still alive, and then beheading.

Article 3, Section 3, of the U.S. Constitution (1789) defines treason—from the Latin *tradere* (deliver up or betray)—as levying war against or adhering to the enemies of the United States or giving them aid and comfort. "No Person shall be convicted of Treason," it states, "unless on the Testimony of two Witnesses to the same overt Act, or on Confession in open Court." Constitutions such as the U.S. and French documents make treason or high treason an impeachable (indictable) offense if committed by high officials such as the president.

Constitution of Argentina (1853), Second Part, Authorities of the Nation, Title I, Federal Government, Third Section, The Judicial Power, Chapter II, Powers of the Judicial Branch, Article 103: "Treason against the nation shall consist only in taking up arms against it, or in adhering to its enemies, giving them aid and comfort. The congress shall fix by a special law the punishment for this crime; but it shall not go beyond the person of the offender nor shall infamy of the criminal be in any degree transmitted to his relatives of any degree."

Constitution of Pakistan (1973), Part I, Introductory, Article 6: "(1) Any person who abrogates or attempts or conspires to abrogate, subverts or attempts or conspires to subvert the constitution by use of force or show of force or by other unconstitutional means shall be guilty of high treason. (2) Any person aiding or abetting the acts mentioned in clause (1) shall likewise be guilty of high treason. (3) Majlis-e-Shoora (parliament) shall provide for the punishment of persons found guilty of high treason."

Treasurer. *See* Treasury

Treasury

A treasury—from the Latin *thesaurus* (treasure or treasure house)—was the name given to a room or building for keeping valuables or money as early as the thirteenth century in England. Today the treasury of each national government forms a vital link in the process of generating revenue from taxes and spending public funds for government operations. Along with the policies and activities of central banking institutions, how the treasury borrows and invests its funds has a major impact on domestic and foreign economic activity.

England's treasury department, which originated in the twelfth century, is now known as the exchequer. Its work is overseen by the first lord of the treasury, a position always held by the prime minister; the chancellor of the exchequer; and five commissioners who are junior lords of the treasury. The chancellor of the exchequer is the functional head of the treasury.

The United States has a Department of the Treasury, headed by a secretary of the treasury, a policy-making cabinet position similar to the chancellor of the exchequer; he or she is appointed by the president with the advice and consent of the Senate. The treasurer of the United States, similarly appointed by the president, is responsible for holding and disbursing the funds of the national government when directed by the secretary of the treasury in accordance with congressional appropriations.

Constitution of the United States of America (1789), Article I, Section 9: "No Money shall be drawn from the Treasury, but in Consequence of Appropriations made by Law. . . . "

Constitution of Taiwan (1947), Chapter X, Powers of the Central and Local Governments, Article 109: "When any province, in undertaking matters listed in any of the items of the first paragraph [matters over which provinces are given the power of legislation and administration], finds its funds insufficient, it may, by resolution of the legislative *yuan* [body], obtain subsidies from the national treasury."

Treaty

The ancient Athenians entered into bilateral treaties *(symbola)* with other states to ensure fair treatment in their dealings with each other and each other's laws; these treaties then became part of the laws of each state. From Latin came the most fundamental principle of international law: *pacta sunt servanda* ("treaties must be performed in good faith"). By the fifteenth century a treaty—in Latin, *tractatus* (treatment or handling), related to *foedus* (treaty) and *pactum* (agreement)—signified a contract or an agreement between two or more states relating

The official terms of international treaties are so important that the U.S. Department of State stores them in a vault in its offices in Washington, D.C.

to peace, a truce, an alliance, commerce, or other international relations.

In essay 64 of *The Federalist* (1788), John Jay argues that the power to make treaties is important, especially in the areas of war, peace, and commerce. Most constitutions expressly prescribe how treaties, international agreements, and conventions may be entered into and who holds the power to negotiate, ratify, and abrogate them. The U.S. Constitution (1789) gives the treaty-making power to the president, with the concurrence of a two-thirds majority of the Senate. However, it forbids the states from entering into treaties—a provision that is the general rule in constitutions of federal nation-states.

Because nation-states may give some treaties the status of law, the courts often play a role in interpreting them. The U.S. Constitution provides that in addition to the Constitution and laws "made in Pursuance thereof," all treaties negotiated under the authority of the United States "shall be the supreme Law of the Land." Even in countries such as the United Kingdom, in which Parliament—not a written constitution—is supreme, a treaty such as the European Communities Act (1972) to sanction the country's admission to the European Community may be given precedence over other laws passed by Parliament.

Constitution of the Netherlands (1814), Chapter 5, Legislation and Administration, Section 2, Miscellaneous Provisions, Article 91: "1. The kingdom shall not be bound by treaties, nor shall such treaties be denounced without the prior approval of the states general [national legislature]. . . . 3. Any provisions of a treaty that conflict with the constitution or which lead to conflicts with it may be approved by the chambers of the states general only if at least two-thirds of the votes cast are in favor."

Constitution of Israel, Basic Law: The President of the State (1964), Section 11: "(a) The president of the state—. . . (5) shall sign such conventions with foreign states as have been ratified by the Knesset [parliament]. . . . "

Tribunal. *See* Court

NOTICE

U

Unamendable Provision

Unamendable provisions are parts of or concepts in a constitution that a constitutional document itself prohibits from being changed or deleted. Similar to entrenched provisions, which require stringent procedures for amendment, unamendable provisions are considered by the constitution's framers so important to the democratic character of the constitutional system of government that they should be beyond any popular desire to change or do away with them.

Varying levels of procedural difficulty for amending different types of entrenched provisions are usually specified. Some unamendable provisions are absolutely unamendable. Others, such as the requirement in the U.S. Constitution (1789) that no state may be deprived of equal suffrage in the Senate without its consent, could be considered virtually unamendable, because a state would probably never agree to a diminution of its own power.

Unamendable provisions pose a self-amendment paradox, raising a challenging constitutional question: can a provision that makes another provision unamendable be amendable itself by the regular process for amending the constitution, thereby rendering the unamendable provision amendable? Fortunately, such questions are rarely, if ever, put to a practical test. Rather than give rise to an intellectual stalemate, a constitution is far more likely to be scrapped altogether.

Constitution of France (1958), Title XIV, On Amendment, Article 89: "The republican form of government shall not be subject to amendment."

Constitution of Romania (1991), Title VI, Revision of the Constitution, Article 148, Limits of Revision: "(1) The provisions of this constitution with regard to the national, independent, unitary, and indivisible character of the Romanian state, the republican form of government, territorial integrity, independence of the judiciary, political pluralism, and official language shall not be subject to revision. (2) Likewise, no revision shall be made if it results in the suppression of the citizens' fundamental rights and freedoms, or the safeguards thereof. (3) The constitution shall not be revised during a state of siege or emergency, or at wartime."

Unconstitutional

A law or an action by a government official that is contrary to a constitution is unconstitutional. Conversely, any law or action that is in accordance with or not prohibited by a constitution, whether written or unwritten, is constitutional. The question of just what is and what is not constitutional is not always clear.

Many changes have occurred in what the U.S. Supreme Court, for example, finds to be unconstitutional under

Beginning in 1954, the U.S. Supreme Court has ruled that state-sanctioned segregation of racial minorities is unconstitutional.

the U.S. Constitution (1789), a written constitution. Even in the case of an unwritten constitution, such as the United Kingdom's, the fact that the British Parliament is supreme and theoretically can change the constitution at will does not mean that the constitutionality of a law is moot. If, for instance, the majority party in Parliament were to enact a law banning all opposition parties, would such a law be constitutional or enforceable?

Under written constitutions specifying the traditional separation of powers, the constitutionality of laws and actions can be questioned by all three branches of government. Legislators may determine that a proposed law is unconstitutional and vote it down; the president may veto what he or she considers to be an unconstitutional law; and, of course, the courts may refuse to apply a law that they determine to be unconstitutional.

In countries with unwritten constitutions, the legal sophistry regarding the constitutionality of laws passed by a supreme parliament—one that has the power to change the constitution simply by a majority vote—is even more complex. Could the British Parliament pass a law today that would limit a future parliament? In 1911 and 1949 it did reduce the power of the House of Lords. Could the House of Commons also reduce its own power? Does being "all powerful" mean that a parliament can use that power to diminish its own power? If it cannot diminish its own power, is it in fact "all powerful?" The answers to such questions are determined by whether a future parliament chooses to be bound by the acts of a former one. If it chooses to be bound, then its power is limited, and the act limiting it is constitutional. If it chooses not to be bound, then its power is not limited, and the prior act is unconstitutional. Pragmatism, not legal theory, generally decides such questions.

Some constitutions define which government authorities have the power to declare laws or actions unconstitutional. In the United States and other countries with similar constitutions, this power is called judicial review, although it is not expressly stated in the U.S. Constitution. Other countries entrust the determination of the unconstitutionality of laws to special or extrajudicial bodies. In some constitutions the review to determine a law's unconstitutionality, whether by a special body or a committee of the legislature, takes place before enactment. The scope of review may also be indicated, along with the nature of the impact of unconstitutional laws, provisions, or actions.

Constitution of France (1958), Title VII, The Constitutional Council, Article 61 (amended in 1974): "Organic laws, before their promulgation, and regulations of the parliamentary assemblies, before they come into application, must be submitted to the constitutional council, which shall rule on their constitutionality. To the same end, laws may be submitted to the constitutional council, before their promulgation, by the president of the republic, the premier, the president of the national assembly, the president of the senate or by 60 deputies or 60 senators."

Constitution of Hungary (1949, significantly revised in 1989), Chapter II, National Assembly, Article 26(5): "If the constitutional court, proceeding out of the order of its schedule, declares [an] act unconstitutional, the president of the republic shall return it to the national assembly, otherwise the act shall be signed and promulgated within five days."

Constitution of Greece (1975), Part Three, Organization and Functions of the State, Section V, The Judicial Power, Chapter Two, Organization and Jurisdiction of the Courts, Article 100: "1. A special highest court shall be established the jurisdiction of which shall comprise: . . . e) Settlement of contestations on whether a law enacted by parliament is fundamentally unconstitutional, or on interpretation of provisions of such law when conflicting judgments have been pronounced by the council of state, the supreme court, or the court of auditors."

Unicameral Legislature. *See* Bicameral Legislature

Union. See Labor

Unitary State

A unitary state is one in which the national government has complete hierarchical authority over all other institutions and officers at all levels of the government, including geographically defined administrative units or departments, counties, municipalities, and towns. Sovereignty resides solely at the top of the pyramid of political power—at the national level—because no sovereignty is shared with any political subdivision, except that which is granted and can be taken away by the national government. The United Kingdom is an example of a unitary state.

The opposite of a unitary government is a federal nation, such as the United States. Most constitutions of unitary nations do not expressly identify the unitary nature of the government, but all constitutions of federal nation-states of necessity must indicate their federal nature by setting forth how sovereign power will be shared with constituent states or provinces or other semisovereign political subdivisions of the nation-state.

Constitution of Chile (1980), Chapter I, Bases of Institutionality, Article 3: "The state of Chile is unitary. Its territory is divided into regions. The law shall provide that administration thereof be functional and territorially decentralized."

Constitution of the Czech Republic (1993), Chapter One, Basic Provisions, Article 1: "The Czech Republic is a sovereign, unified, and democratic law-observing state, based on the respect for the rights and freedoms of the individual and citizen."

Unreasonable Search and Seizure

In criminal law search and seizure refers to an examination of a person or a person's premises by officers of the law to discover evidence, such as stolen property or a weapon, to prove that the person committed a crime.

The Fourth Amendment to the U.S. Constitution (1789), a part of the Bill of Rights (1791), prohibits unreasonable searches and seizures and requires that a legal warrant—one issued by a court of law—be granted by a judge only on probable cause and describe the place to

Throughout history the machinery of the state has been used to harass citizens and confiscate personal property. The U.S. Bill of Rights (1791) expressly prohibits the government from invading homes without written authorization by a court of law.

be searched and the persons or items to be seized. The U.S. courts have held that a judicial warrant is not necessary when the situation does not permit time to acquire it. However, the U.S. Supreme Court has ruled that evidence obtained without a warrant in situations when time permits the issuance of one must be excluded from use in a federal trial.

This right to be secure in one's person and home is similarly included in other constitutional guarantees of rights and freedoms. The phrase *search and seizure* is not often used, and the guarantees against seeking evidence on a person or in personal effects or the home are generally not as strict as the language of the U.S. Constitution.

In international law the right of search and seizure allows warships in wartime to stop, board, and search merchant vessels at sea to determine if their cargoes contain supplies en route to the enemy. Under the rules of war such supplies are liable to seizure.

Constitution of the United States of America (1789), Amendment IV (1791): "The right of the people to be secure in their persons, houses, papers, and effects against unreasonable searches and seizures shall not be violated, and no Warrants shall issue, but upon probable cause, supported by Oath or affirmation, and particularly describing the place to be searched, and the persons or things to be seized."

Of the seventy-six members of the Senate, the upper house of the Australian Parliament, twelve are elected from each state and two each are elected from the capital territory and the Northern Territory.

Constitution of Liberia (1986), Chapter III, Fundamental Rights, Article 21(b): "No person shall be subject to search and seizure of his person or property, whether on a criminal charge or for any other purpose, unless upon warrant lawfully issued upon probable cause supported by a solemn oath or affirmation, specifically identifying the person or place to be searched and stating the object of the search; provided, however, a search or seizure shall be permissible without a search warrant where the arresting authorities act in conjunction with the commission of the crime or in hot pursuit of a person. . . . "

Constitution of Ghana (1992), Chapter Five, Fundamental Human Rights and Freedoms, General, Article 18(2): "No person shall be subject to interference with the privacy of his home, property, correspondence or communication except in accordance with law and as may be necessary in a free and democratic society for public safety or the economic well-being of the country, for the protection of health or morals, for the prevention of disorder or crime or for the protection of rights and freedoms of others."

Upper Chamber. *See* Upper House

Upper House

The upper house or chamber of a bicameral legislature is generally the smaller, less representative, and more conservative of the two houses. The upper house of the British Parliament is called the House of Lords; the upper house of the legislatures of both France and the United States is called the Senate; and the upper house of the Netherlands is called the first chamber.

The qualifications, method of selection, and duties and powers of upper houses vary widely from country to country. Members of the House of Lords in the British Parliament include the archbishop and bishops of the Church of England and hereditary and life peers of the realm. Although acts of Parliament in 1911 and 1949 reduced its legislative role to only delaying bills, a portion of the House of Lords still functions as the United Kingdom's highest court of appeals. The membership of the U.S. Senate consists of two members called senators who are elected directly and at large in each state of the United States, one-third of the total membership being elected every two years for six-year terms. The U.S. Senate plays an equal part with the House of Representatives in the passage of legislation. Under the 1958 French constitution the fate of legislation in some cases may ultimately be decided by the lower house alone.

Constitution of Canada, Constitution Act (1867), IV, Legislative Power, Section 17: "There shall be one Parliament for Canada, consisting of the queen, an upper house styled the Senate, and the House of Representatives."

Constitution of Ireland (1937), National Parliament, Seanad Éireann, Article 18: "1. Seanad Éireann [the upper house] shall be composed of sixty members, of whom eleven shall be nominated members and forty-nine shall be elected members. 2. A person to be eligible for membership of Seanad Éireann must be eligible to become a member of Dáil Éireann [the lower house]."

Usage. *See* Custom

V

Vacancy

From the early seventeenth century in England the word *vacancy*—based on the Latin *vacans* (unoccupied)—has been used to mean an office or position that is not filled. An unoccupied official position is vacant immediately after the position has been created and before it is filled, as is a position after the departure of an incumbent and before it is refilled.

In constitutions a vacancy may refer either to an appointed position, such as that of judge, or to an elected position, such as that of president or member of the legislature. Many constitutions describe the manner in which vacancies may occur and prescribe procedures for filling vacancies for an interim period or the balance of a term of office. Technically, a vacancy in an elected position occurs when a term of office expires or otherwise terminates normally according to the provisions of a constitution.

Most constitutions also deal with unusual events that may result in untimely vacancies, including death, disability, and removal from office for cause.

Constitution of Algeria (1976), Title II, The Organization of the Powers, Chapter I, The Executive Power, Article 84: "In the case of coincidence *(conjonction)* of the death of the president of the republic and an adjournment *(vacance)* of the [legislature], the constitutional council meets by right and declares a definitive vacancy of the presidency of the republic."

Constitution of New Zealand, Electoral Act (1956), Section 32: "How vacancies created—The seat of any member of parliament shall become vacant—(a) If for one whole session of parliament he fails, without the permission of the House of Representatives, to give his attendance in the House; or (b) If he takes any oath or makes any declaration or acknowledgement of allegiance or adherence to any foreign prince or power . . . or (e) If he is convicted of a crime punishable by death or by imprisonment for a term of two years or upwards . . . or (f) If he becomes . . . a public servant; or (g) If he resigns his seat . . . or (i) If he dies; or (j) If he becomes mentally disordered. . . ."

Veto

In ancient Rome when the tribunes of the people were opposed to actions of the Senate or the magistrates, they would indicate their opposition by saying, "Veto" ("I forbid"). In feudal Poland a *liberum veto* rule in the Sejm (the parliament) meant that any member could say, "Nie pozwalam" ("I do not allow"), thus thwarting any legislative proposal.

The modern concept of the veto is a feature of presidential systems of government, such as that in the

A woman votes in Turkey's first secret-ballot election in the 1950s by placing her marked ballot in the ballot box.

United States. It is an element of the checks and balances principle that permits the president, as head of state and government, to reject legislation passed by the legislative branch. Veto power is not usually absolute, however. Under the U.S. Constitution (1789) Congress may override the president's veto by a two-thirds majority vote in both houses.

True parliamentary constitutional monarchies, such as the United Kingdom's, do not grant veto power to the head of the executive branch. In parliamentary systems the head of government is responsible for getting his or her legislative program passed by a majority of the legislators. Once passed, the bills are presented to the monarch for his or her assent, which is mandatory.

The constitutions of other countries incorporate variations of veto power. France, for example, has a presidential-style parliamentary system in which the president stands in for a constitutional monarch. He or she, nevertheless, is authorized by the 1958 constitution to ask the parliament to reconsider a law it has passed or a portion thereof, and the request for reconsideration may not be refused. Perhaps more important, the French president, unlike a true constitutional monarch, may dissolve the parliament on his or her own initiative, albeit after consultation with the prime minister and the heads of the two parliamentary chambers, the Sénat and the Assemblée Nationale.

Constitution of Mexico (1917), Title III, Chapter II, The Legislative Branch, Section II, Introduction and Enactment of Laws, Article 72(c): "A bill or proposed decree rejected in whole or in part by the executive [president] shall be returned, with his objections, to the chamber of origin. It must be discussed anew by the latter, and if it is confirmed by a vote of two-thirds of the total vote, it shall again be sent to the reviewing chamber. If it is sanctioned by the latter by the same majority, the bill shall become a law or decree and shall be returned to the executive for his promulgation."

Constitution of Ghana (1992), Chapter Ten, The Legislature, Procedures in Parliament, Article 106(8): "Where the president refuses to assent to a bill, he shall, within fourteen days after the refusal—(a) state in a memorandum to the speaker any specific provisions of the bill which in his opinion should be reconsidered by parliament, including his recommendations for amendment, if any. . . . "

Vice Chancellor. *See* Vice President

Vice President

Although not assigned any important duties under the U.S. Constitution (1789), the second highest ranking executive officer of the United States is the vice president. The word *vice*—from the Latin *vicis* (a change or instead of)—was used as early as the late sixteenth century in England to mean one who acts in the place of another.

The position of vice president was first associated with the presidential system of government. The title, like that of president, has since been established in various constitutions and invested with various powers and responsibilities in both presidential and parliamentary governments. Some constitutions authorize more than one vice presidential position. A true parliamentary system, such as the United Kingdom's, does not have a position analogous to the U.S. vice president.

Under the U.S. Constitution the vice president is elected together with the president; they are from the same political party and stand for election on the same party ticket. The duties of the vice president, except for the constitutional requirement of serving as the mostly ceremonial president of the Senate—casting a vote only in the event of a tie among the senators—are left to the discretion of the president. The vice president's main responsibility is to assume the president's duties in the event of his or her disability, death, resignation, or removal by impeachment.

The office of vice chancellor, a judicial office, was created in the United Kingdom in 1813 to assist the lord chancellor with cases of the first instance under this equity jurisdiction. In Austria the title of vice chancellor is given to the cabinet minister who is deputized to act for the federal chancellor (prime minister) in his or her entire sphere of competence. According to the 1949 German constitution, the federal chancellor appoints a federal minister as his or her deputy, also called the vice chancellor.

Constitution of China (People's Republic of China) (1982), Chapter Three, The Structure of the State, Section II, The President of the People's Republic of China, Article 84: "In case the office of the president of the People's Republic of China falls vacant, the vice president succeeds to the office of the president. In case the office of the vice president of the People's Republic of China falls vacant, the national people's congress shall elect a new vice president to fill the vacancy."

Constitution of Syria (1973), Part Two, Powers of the State, Chapter II, Executive Power, (1) President of the Republic, Article 95: "The president of the republic nominates one or more vice presidents and delegates to them some of his powers."

The vice president of the United States, who is constitutionally also the president of the Senate, has an ornate ceremonial office in the U.S. Capitol.

Voltaire (François-Marie Arouet)

Like Jean-Jacques Rousseau, his countryman and contemporary, Voltaire (1694–1778) cut a path that led to the French Revolution with a pen, not a sword. The words of his poem *The Natural Law* are enshrined in Articles I and III of the Declaration of the Rights of Man and of the Citizen (1789), which is incorporated into the current French constitution (1958).

François-Marie Arouet, born in Paris on or about November 21, 1694, was only seven years old when his mother died. A precocious child, he was educated by Jesuits from 1704 to 1711. His father, concerned about the boy's hedonistic bent and interest in writing, obtained employment for him as secretary to the French ambassador in The Hague.

Undeterred, the young Arouet, who took the pen name of Voltaire, continued to write. Some of his verses were so offensive to powerful people that he was imprisoned in the Bastille and later exiled. He left for England in 1726, where he was praised by Alexander Pope, William Congreve, and Horace Walpole, among others. His study of the works of John Locke and Isaac Newton developed his understanding of the relationship between wealth and freedom and between free government and creative speculation.

Voltaire returned to France after three years and in 1734 published his *Letters Concerning the English Nation*, which has been called "the first bomb dropped on the Old Regime"—the French monarchy. This witty work urged political, religious, and philosophical freedom, improved living conditions, and use of the intellect to forward social progress. In the wake of its publication, Voltaire was again temporarily forced to leave Paris.

A prolific writer on many subjects, Voltaire was also a brilliant playwright. His best known work is *Candide* (1759), a clever philosophical conte, a literary form he invented. In later life, as he continued to champion liberty and help victims of persecution, he became known as the "Conscience of Europe." Frederick II of Prussia invited him to live in Potsdam, Rousseau corresponded with him, and John Morley, the English secretary for Ireland, said that his name would one day stand in history beside the Reformation and the Renaissance.

Voltaire did not propose revolution and was unsympathetic with republican government, saying that he would rather obey a fine lion, much stronger than himself, than

Although not an overt revolutionary, Voltaire criticized the unequal treatment of citizens under the law in France and facilitated the downfall of the French monarchy in 1789 and the establishment of France's First Republic.

two hundred rats of his own species. But his attacks on the status quo and inequality before the law opened the way for drastic constitutional changes in many countries. He died on May 30, 1778, in Paris.

Vote

In *The Politics,* Aristotle comments on various methods of choosing officials in a democracy—by lot (random selection), by vote, and by a combination of these two methods. The word *vote* meant first to indicate an opinion or choice in a matter and later came to mean to choose a member of a deliberative body and to formally express approval or disapproval on a matter under discussion. Today voting—from the Latin *votum* (a promise or wish) and possibly also *vovere* (a vow or desire)—is synonymous with casting a ballot, going to the polls, and participating in an election and is also called the franchise or suffrage.

In general, voting refers to the whole process of casting ballots and tallying the results to determine if constitutionally mandated procedures are met and to decide, based on the count, who is and is not elected to an office in the government or whether a proposal has been approved or disapproved. "The vote" may refer to the entire electorate, as in "getting out the vote," by which eligible voters are urged to go to the polls and exercise their right to vote.

Constitutions generally address two types of voting: voting for elected officials in general or special elections, and voting for measures or proposals such as bills and resolutions or policy actions. Other types of voting sometimes addressed include selection of officials of an elected body, such as the speaker or president of a legislature; referendums, in which the people vote on issues; and recall elections, in which voters may remove an official from office.

Constitution of Norway (1814), C, Rights of Citizens and Legislative Power, Article 55: "The polls shall be conducted in the manner prescribed by law. Disputes regarding the right to vote shall be settled by the poll officials, whose decision may be appealed to the Storting [legislature]."

Constitution of Nigeria (1992), Chapter V, The Legislature, Part I, National Assembly, B, Procedure for Summoning and Dissolution of National Assembly, Article 55: "Any person who sits or votes in the senate [upper house] or the house of representatives [lower house] knowing or having reasonable grounds for knowing that he is not entitled to do so shall be guilty of an offense and shall upon conviction be liable to such punishment as shall be prescribed by an act of the national assembly."

Vote of Confidence.

See No-Confidence Vote

Walesa, Lech

The dramatic events in Poland during the 1980s and 1990s, in which Lech Walesa (b. 1943) played a leading role, opened the crack in the Soviet system of communist domination that has led to many new constitutional democracies in Eastern Europe.

Walesa was born on September 29, 1943, at Popowo, in the administrative district of Wroclaw. After completing vocational school he was an automobile mechanic from 1961 to 1965. Following a two-year stint in the army, he began working in the Gdansk shipyard as an electrician.

In 1976 Walesa was fired from the shipyard for criticizing the communist trade unions, and he, along with other activists, began organizing an independent labor union. In July and August 1980 the workers at the Gdansk shipyard, unhappy with a number of firings, including Walesa's, went on strike. Walesa was chosen to chair the Inter-enterprise Strike Committee, and even after an agreement was reached with the workers at Gdansk, the strike continued in a show of solidarity with workers on strike elsewhere in Poland. On September 18, 1980, representatives of newly legalized labor groups formed a National Committee of Solidarity, with Walesa as chairman. The committee, known as Solidarnosc, became the first legally registered

Lech Walesa, the tenacious leader of the Polish workers' Solidarity movement, which helped peacefully overthrow the communist regime by 1989, served as the democratically elected president of Poland from 1990 to 1995.

U.S. President Franklin D. Roosevelt, in accordance with the U.S. Constitution, requested from Congress a formal declaration of war against Japan after the surprise bombing of Pearl Harbor on December 7, 1941.

independent trade union in a country controlled by the Soviet Union through the Communist Party.

By December 1989 Poland had emerged from the Soviet Union's shadow to the extent that the Sejm (the parliament) voted to make significant changes in its 1952 "Stalin"-type constitution, including dropping the word "People's" from the country's official name, the Polish People's Republic. Walesa, who never compromised, continued to criticize the government. Still the head of Solidarnosc, he ran for president of Poland and, after winning seventy-five percent of the vote, was sworn in on December 21, 1990.

A constitutional commission had earlier been formed by the Sejm, but attempts to create a joint committee with the newly constituted and elected senate, the upper house of the parliament, failed. A draft constitutional proposal was prepared by the lower house's constitutional commission in 1991, but instead a "little" constitution containing new provisions was combined with the few salvageable provisions of the earlier constitution and adopted as the Constitutional Act of October 1992, with Constitutional Provisions Continued in Force.

Although Walesa's influence on the redesign of the Polish constitution was indirect, his uncompromising leadership was crucial to the process—from the early days of the Gdansk workers' strikes to his commanding presence as president of Poland during its transition from a single party dominated by the Soviet Union to an independent multiparty democracy. Ousted from the presidency in the 1996 election, Walesa, who was not entitled to a government pension at the time, returned to Gdansk to reapply for his old job as an electrician.

War

"Is the power of declaring war [in a constitution] necessary?" James Madison asks in essay 41 of *The Federalist* (1788). His response: "No man will answer this question in the negative." Practiced by the Romans, the custom of issuing a declaration of war to an enemy is ancient. The English word *war* is derived from Scandinavian and High German words meaning confusion, discord, and strife. War in French is *guerre*, in Spanish *guerra*, and in German *Krieg*.

Hugo Grotius, the early-seventeenth-century Dutch jurist, statesman, and author of *On the Law of War and Peace* (1625), defined war as simply an armed contest between nations. For Karl von Clausewitz, the nineteenth-century Prussian military strategist, Aristotle's political animal—man—was also a war-making animal; Clausewitz called war "the continuation of political intercourse intermixed with other means," a euphemism for mass murder and destruction.

From a historical point of view war seems inevitable and never more practiced than during the twentieth century. By describing how governments of nation-states will make war and peace, the framers of many constitutions have thus been merely prudent. As Aristotle warns in *The Politics,* the tyrant is fond of making war in order to give his subjects something to do and a reason to need a leader.

Almost all constitutions contain provisions regarding how war may be declared. A declaration of war is a public and formal proclamation by a nation, through the executive or legislative branch, that a state of war exists with another country or countries. It triggers a number of military, diplomatic, and legal consequences under domestic and international law—for example, making it a crime to give aid or assistance to the enemy.

The U.S. Constitution (1789) grants Congress the power to declare war, but the president directs the actual waging of war as the commander in chief of the armed forces. The framers of the Constitution, notes Alexander Hamilton in essay 22 of *The Federalist,* had firsthand experience in the Revolutionary War to inform their deliberations on how to organize a federal nation to fight wars. But even with its constitutional safeguards, the United States has been involved in military actions short of declared wars; consequently, the War Powers Act of 1973 declared the right of Congress to participate with the president in sending troops abroad.

In a bow to "international peace," Japan's constitution, as revised in 1947 following World War II, renounces war altogether as a sovereign right of the nation.

Constitution of the Netherlands (1814), Chapter V, Legislation and Administration, Section 2, Miscellaneous Provisions, Article 96: "1. A declaration that the kingdom is in a state of war shall not be made without the prior approval of the states general [parliament]. 2. Such approval shall not be required in cases where consultation with parliament proves to be impossible as a consequence of the actual existence of a state of war. 3. The two chambers of the states general shall consider and decide upon the matter in joint session. 4. The provisions of the first and third paragraphs shall apply by analogy to a declaration that the state of war has ceased."

Constitution of Switzerland (1874), Article 8: "The confederation alone has the right to declare war and to make peace, as well as to conclude alliances and treaties, especially customs and commercial treaties, with foreign states."

Constitution of Jordan (1952), Chapter 4, The Executive Power, Part 1, The King and His Prerogatives, Article 33(i): "The king declares war, concludes peace, and ratifies treaties and agreements."

Constitution of Austria, Federal Constitutional Law of 26 October 1955 on the Neutrality of Austria: "(1) For the purpose of the permanent maintenance of her external independence and for the purpose of the inviolability of her territory, Austria of her own free will declares herewith her permanent neutrality which she is resolved to maintain and defend with all the means at her disposal."

Constitution of Japan (1889, significantly revised in 1947), Chapter II, Renunciation of War, Article 9: "Aspiring sincerely to an international peace based on justice and order, the Japanese people forever renounce war as a sovereign right of the nation and the threat or use of force as a means of settling international disputes."

Warrant

A warrant is a written authority empowering a person to perform some action. A treasury warrant authorizes withdrawals from public funds, an arrest warrant provides for the detention of a person accused of a crime, a search warrant issued by a judicial official permits the search and seizure of possibly incriminating evidence, and a death warrant orders the legal execution of a criminal sentenced to capital punishment.

As used in constitutions, a warrant usually refers to a judicial warrant issued to a law officer or another official, authorizing some action and also guaranteeing or requiring some action or response. Derived probably from High German and High Dutch words, *warranty*—someone or something that protects or authorizes—was used in England as early as the thirteenth century.

WARRANT OF ARREST–MISDEMEANOR (STATE) VA. CODE §§ 19.2-71,-72

CITY OR COUNTY General District Court ☐ Criminal ☐ Traffic

☐ Juvenile and Domestic Relations District Court

TO ANY AUTHORIZED OFFICER:

You are hereby commanded in the name of the Commonwealth of Virginia forthwith to arrest and bring the Accused before this Court to answer the charge that the Accused, within this city or county, on or about .... DATE .... did unlawfully in violation of Section ...., Code of Virginia:

I, the undersigned, have found probable cause to believe that the Accused committed the offense charged, based on the sworn statements of ...., Complainant.

Execution by summons ☐ permitted at officer's discretion. ☐ not permitted.

DATE AND TIME ISSUED ☐ CLERK ☐ MAGISTRATE ☐ JUDGE

SUMMONS (If authorized above and by serving officer)

You are hereby commanded to appear before this court located at .... on .... at .... AM/PM

I promise to appear in accordance with this Summons and certify that my mailing address as shown at right is correct.

ACCUSED

WARNING TO ACCUSED: You may be tried and convicted in your absence if you fail to appear in response to this Summons. Willful failure to appear is a separate offense.

SIGNING THIS NOTICE DOES NOT CONSTITUTE AN ADMISSION OF GUILT.

CASE NO.

ACCUSED:

LAST NAME, FIRST NAME, MIDDLE NAME

ADDRESS/LOCATION

To be completed upon service as Summons

Mailing address ☐ Same as above

☐

COMPLETE DATA BELOW IF KNOWN

RACE	SEX	BORN MO.	BORN DAY	BORN YR.	HT FT	HT IN	WGT.	EYES	HAIR

SSN

Commonwealth of Virginia

WARRANT OF ARREST

CLASS ________ MISDEMEANOR

☐ EXECUTED by arresting the Accused named above on this day:

☐ EXECUTED by summoning the Accused named above on this day:

☐ For legal entities other than individuals, service pursuant to Va. Code § 19.2-76.

DATE AND TIME OF SERVICE

ARRESTING OFFICER

BADGE NO., AGENCY AND JURISDICTION

for SHERIFF

Attorney for the Accused:

HEARING DATE AND TIME

An arrest warrant issued by a court authorizes a law enforcement officer to take into custody a person or persons alleged to have committed a crime. A warrant is any legal authorization that allows an otherwise illegal act to be performed.

Sometimes called a writ, a warrant is also a document issued to candidates who have just been elected to government offices, certifying that they can fill their positions.

Constitution of Germany (1949), IX, The Administration of Justice, Article 104: "(3) Any person provisionally detained on suspicion of having committed an offense shall be brought before a judge not later than the day following the day of apprehension; the judge shall inform him of the reasons for the detention, examine him, and give him an opportunity to raise objections. The judge shall, without delay, either issue a warrant of arrest setting forth the reasons therefor or order his release from detention."

Constitution of Sweden, Riksdag Act (1974), Chapter 1, Sessions, Article 5: "The report of the election review committee of the Riksdag [parliament] on the examination of the warrants of election of members and alternate members shall be read at the first meeting of the chamber in the new session. A report on the examination of a warrant which has been received during a session shall be read as soon as possible."

Welfare. *See* General Welfare

Women

Since World War II women have made obvious strides toward political and social equality in many countries. Some women, such as Golda Meir, Indira Gandhi, Margaret Thatcher, and Benazir Bhutto, have risen to the ultimate positions of political leadership in traditionally male-dominated national governments.

In part to recognize the needs of women as distinct from those of men and in part to ensure the government's awareness that women have often not been fully protected by or represented in traditional government institutions, many modern constitutions contain provisions relating specifically to women. "Steps shall be taken to ensure participation of women in all spheres of national life," state 1977 amendments to Bangladesh's 1972 constitution. The 1957 Malaysian constitution singles out women, children, and young persons for social services protection in the states of Sabah and Sarawak on the island of Borneo. And Article 35 of the 1995 Ethiopian constitution contains nine clauses especially relating to women.

The mere fact that a country recognizes the need to give women better access to government power and decision making and therefore includes language to that effect in its constitution is no guarantee that such provisions will be effective. The Nongovernmental Organizations Forum on Women held in 1995 in the People's Republic of China occasioned an official Chinese attack on the treatment of women in the United States, with a specific reference to the fact that the U.S. Constitution (1789), unlike China's 1982 constitution, does not enshrine equal rights for women. In the context of a nation dominated by the Communist Party, however, neither women nor men have enforceable rights similar to those in constitutional democracies.

Constitution of Italy (1948), Part One, The Duties and Rights of the Citizens, Title III, Economic Relations, Article 37: "Female workers have the same rights of male workers, and equal pay for equal work. Labor conditions must allow women to carry out their essential family functions, and ensure a special and appropriate protection for mothers and children."

U.S. Supreme Court Justice Sandra Day O'Connor, nominated and confirmed in 1981, was the first woman elevated to the nation's highest tribunal. Since then, Ruth Bader Ginsburg has joined Justice O'Connor on the Court.

Constitution of Iran (1979), Chapter III, Rights of the People, Article 21: "The government must ensure the rights of women in all respects, in conformity with Islamic criteria, and accomplish the following goals: 1. create a favorable environment for the growth of woman's personality and the restoration of her rights, both material and intellectual. . . . "

Constitution of China (People's Republic of China) (1982), Chapter Two, Fundamental Rights and Duties of Citizens, Article 48: "Women in the [People's Republic of China] enjoy equal rights with men in all spheres of life, political, economic, cultural, and social, including family life."

Women's Suffrage. *See* Suffrage

Work. *See* Labor

Writ

As a legal term *writ* (something in writing), derived from Scandinavian and Old English words, has evolved to mean a written command or formal order, like a warrant, issued by a court in the name of the state or sovereign or some other legal authority and directing the addressee to do or refrain from doing something. By the thirteenth century three kinds of writs were generally recognized in England: charters, which often granted lands; letters patent, which granted commissions to royal officials; and letters closed, which conveyed orders or information.

In modern British legal practice a writ is an order in the sovereign's name that may be used for several purposes—for example, initiating an action in the High Court. A writ in the United States is similar and is generally a court order used for various purposes. Other types of modern writs include writs of inquiry and writs of execution.

In constitutions a writ generally refers to a judicial writ, such as a writ of habeas corpus—an order for a person being held in official custody to be brought before a court so that it can determine if the detention is legal.

Constitutions may also provide for a writ or warrant after an election to verify the right of a winning candidate to take office.

Constitution of the Philippines (1987), Article VII, Executive Department, Section 18: "In case of invasion or rebellion, when the public safety requires it, he [the president] may, for a period not exceeding sixty days, suspend the privilege of the writ of habeas corpus. . . . "

Constitution of New Zealand, New Zealand Constitution Act (1986), Part III, The Parliament, Section 17, Term of Parliament: "Term of Parliament—(1) The term of parliament shall, unless parliament is sooner dissolved, be 3 years from the day fixed for the return of the writs issued for the preceding general election of the members of the House of Representatives, and no longer."

Y

Yeas and Nays

Yeas and nays are voice votes of members of a deliberative body such as a legislature. Yea—a simple affirmative in answer to a question—comes from Teutonic languages and was in use as early as the eighth century; its current meaning of affirmative vote dates from the seventeenth century. Nay—a simple negative answer—is derived from Scandinavian languages and, like yea, appears in the King James Version of the Bible.

Parliamentary procedures allow several methods of voting: by voice *(viva voce)*, which may be by yeas and nays or ayes and nays; by silently raising hands, first by those for a measure or motion and then by those against; by roll call vote, which may be by yeas and nays or ayes and nays and in which each member's vote is recorded along with his or her name; by general consent or acclamation; and by secret ballot.

Some constitutions and all parliamentary or legislative procedures prescribe how votes on various questions are to be taken. In some circumstances the accountability of the members voting is important, in others secrecy is important, and in still others the method does not particularly matter.

Constitution of Argentina (1853), Second Part, Authorities of the Nation, Title I, Federal Government, First Section, The Legislative Power, Chapter V, Enactment and Approval of Laws, Article 72: "In all such cases [of an attempt to override a veto] the voting in both chambers shall be by roll call, by yeas and nays; and both the names and opinions of those voting as well as the objections of the executive shall be immediately published in the press."

Constitution of the United States of America (1789), Article I, Section 5: " . . . the Yeas and Nays of the Members of either House on any question shall, at the Desire of one fifth of those Present, be entered on the Journal [of the proceedings of that house]."

Yeltsin, Boris Nikolayevich

Personally involved in drafting and promoting the current constitution of Russia, Boris Yeltsin (b. 1931) in the 1990s became a leading player in establishing constitutional democracy one of the major countries of the world.

Born on February 1, 1931, in Sverdlovsk, Yeltsin was educated at the Urals Polytechnical Institute and worked as a construction worker from 1955 to 1968. A member of the Communist Party of the Soviet Union, he held a number of party posts, including head of the Moscow City Party Committee from 1985 to 1987, and in 1989 he was elected to the Congress of the People's Deputies of

Universally acceptable ways of registering a nonsecret vote in a meeting, both at the local level and in a national legislature, include saying yes or no, yea or nay, or aye or nay or raising one hand to indicate concurrence with a proposal.

the Union of Soviet Socialist Republics. From 1989 to 1991 he was a member of the supreme soviet (council) of that body.

In June 1990 the Russian congress adopted a declaration of sovereignty, and the next month Yeltsin resigned his membership in the Communist Party. The following year—1991—was a key year for him. He became a member of the supreme soviet of the Russian Soviet Federal Socialist Republic and then acting head of the Russian federal defense ministry, and in June he was elected president of Russia by a landslide. During an attempted coup in July to overthrow Mikhail Gorbachev, president of the Soviet Union, Yeltsin led the resistance against it. In October the Russian supreme soviet granted Yeltsin extraordinary powers to rule by decree, and on November 6 he banned the Communist Party. In December he and the leaders of Belarus and Ukraine participated in dissolving the Soviet Union.

In March 1993, with Russia beset by many economic and political problems, Yeltsin drafted a decree on emergency rule, but the constitutional court declared it unconstitutional. After surviving a vote of impeachment, he received enough support in a national referendum in April to remain in office but was forced to dissolve the parliament in September.

During the respite from fighting with the parliament, Yeltsin began revising a draft of a new Russian constitution, which had been prepared for him during the summer. He strengthened the powers of the president, making the position more powerful than that of either the United States or France, limited the sovereignty of the constituent republics, and added a transitional provision postponing presidential elections beyond the scheduled June 1994 date. Yeltsin then submitted the personally revised document to the people in a nationwide referendum, held at the same time as new parliamentary elections, and decreed that a majority vote of approval out of at least fifty percent of the eligible voters would be sufficient to ratify the new constitution. The constitution was barely approved.

Boris Yeltsin was the first democratically elected president of Russia after the fall of the Soviet Union. He played a key role in creating the 1993 Russian constitution, which grants the president a strong position in the government.

With obstacles such as a militant secessionist movement in the province of Chechnya and eroding support for his reform policies in the mid-1990s, Boris Yeltsin's path to a democratic Russia was made difficult in spite of his handcrafted constitution.

A Note on the Sources

A work such as *The Illustrated Dictionary of Constitutional Concepts* draws on many sources, the most pertinent of which is the author's research conducted for *Constitutions of the World* (Congressional Quarterly Books, 1995). The primary sources of concepts and terms in the present volume are the constitutions of the countries from which excerpts have been taken. These countries are Algeria, Argentina, Austria, Australia, Bangladesh, Belgium, Brazil, Bulgaria, Cambodia, Canada, Chile, China, Colombia, Cuba, Czech Republic, Denmark, Ecuador, Egypt, Ethiopia, Finland, France, Germany, Ghana, Greece, Haiti, Honduras, Hungary, Iceland, India, Indonesia, Iran, Iraq, Ireland, Israel, Italy, Japan, Jordan, Kenya, Kuwait, Lebanon, Liberia, Libya, Malaysia, Mexico, Monaco, Mozambique, Nepal, the Netherlands, New Zealand, Nicaragua, Nigeria, North Korea, Norway, Pakistan, Panama, Peru, the Philippines, Poland, Portugal, Romania, Russia, Singapore, Slovakia, South Africa, South Korea, Spain, Sweden, Switzerland, Syria, Taiwan, Thailand, Turkey, Uganda, United Kingdom, United States, Venezuela, Vietnam, Zambia, and Zimbabwe.

Secondary sources encompass both historic and contemporary works. Historic sources include *Plato—The Laws,* translated by Trevor J. Saunders (London: Penguin Books, 1975); *Great Dialogues of Plato,* translated by W.H.D. Rouse (New York: New American Library, 1956); *Aristotle—The Politics,* edited by Stephen Everson (Cambridge, England: Cambridge University Press, 1993); *Leage's Roman Private Law,* by A. M. Prichard, 3d ed. (London: Macmillan, 1961); *Commentaries on the Laws of England: Of Public Wrongs,* by William Blackstone (Boston: Beacon Press, 1962), and *The Federalist Papers,* by Alexander Hamilton, James Madison, and John Jay (New York: New American Library, 1961).

Contemporary sources include *The Oxford English Dictionary,* 2d ed. (Oxford, England: Oxford University Press, 1989); *Black's Law Dictionary,* 3d ed. (St. Paul, Minn.: West, 1933); *International Law: Cases and Materials,* by William W. Bishop Jr., 2d ed. (Boston: Little, Brown, 1962); *Stroud's Judicial Dictionary of Words and Phrases,* by John S. James, 4th ed. (London: Sweet and Maxwell, 1974); *The Oxford Companion to Law,* by David M. Walker (New York: Oxford University Press, 1980); and *Comparative Legal Traditions: Text, Materials, and Cases,* by Mary Ann Glendon, Michael Wallace Gordon, and Christopher Osakwe, 2d ed. (St. Paul, Minn.: West, 1994).

Credits

AP/Wide World Photos: 15, 58, 165, 231, 275

AP Photo/Alexander Zemlianichenko: 314

Archive Photos/ Archive France: 164

Australian Foreign Affairs and State Department: 179, 298

Australian News and Information Bureau: 125 both

Bibliothèque Nationale, France: 30 top

British Information Service: 129, 152, 166, 229

British Library: 69

Columbus Memorial Library, OAS: 10, 48, 51, 113, 120, 268, 285

Congress of the Federated States of Micronesia: 253

Corbis-Bettmann: 17 (Reuters), 93 (UPI), 102 (UPI), 103 (UPI), 117, 154 (UPI), 238 (Reuters), 254, 273, 281, 291, 294 (UPI), 297, 310 (Reuters), 312 (UPI)

Egyptian Press and Information Bureau: 259

Embassy of Austria: 162

Embassy of Greece: 161

Embassy of Iceland: 130

Embassy of Malaysia: 2

Embassy of Poland: 307

Embassy of South Africa: 187

Embassy of Spain: 60, 153

Fairfax County, Virginia, Magistrate's Court: 309

German Information Center: 26, 66, 118

Linea Press: 33 (Sarfoto)

Library of Congress: xvi, 3, 4, 5, 7, 8, 12, 14, 19, 21, 24, 27, 30 bottom, 31, 34, 36, 37, 38, 40, 41, 42, 43, 46, 49, 50, 52, 55, 56, 59 top, 62, 70, 72, 74, 76, 78, 79, 81, 82, 83, 86 both, 88, 89, 94, 97, 100, 101, 105, 107, 110, 115, 126, 128, 134, 136, 139, 141, 142, 144, 147, 148, 150, 157, 160, 168, 170, 172, 174, 176, 178, 180, 181, 182, 184, 188, 190, 191, 193, 194, 196, 198, 202, 203, 205, 206, 209, 214, 215, 217, 218, 223, 225, 227, 228, 230, 237, 242, 244, 247, 249, 251, 256, 258, 260, 261, 262, 269 (Embassy of France), 270, 271, 276, 279, 282, 283, 287, 289, 292, 300, 303, 304, 306

National Aeronautics and Space Administration: 286

National Archives: 57

National Archives of Canada: 91, 92

New York Public Library Picture Collection: 146, 211, 265

Reuters/George Ashi/ Archive Photos: 20

Royal Norwegian Ministry of Foreign Affairs/Teigen fotoatelier A.S.: jacket, 64, 111

United Nations Information Center: 87, 109, 121 (UN Photo 172543/ J. Isaac), 133, 192, 222, 255

U.S. Congress: 28, 212

U.S. Senate Historical Office: 232

World Health Organization: 44 (Jean-Pierre Laffont)

Index

Dictionary entries are listed in **bold type.** Page numbers in *italics* refer to illustrations.